D1612963

Towns & Villages of The Lake District and Cumbria

by

Alan Bryant

We gratefully acknowledge the support of the firms whose advertisements appear in these pages. As a reciprocal gesture we have pleasure in drawing the attention of our readers to their announcements.
It is necessary however for it to be made clear that whilst every care has been taken in compiling this publication and the statements it contains, the Publishers can accept no responsibility for any inaccuracies or for the products or services advertised.

Published and distributed by Village Publications,
29 Lowther Street, Kendal. Cumbria
Printed and bound in Great Britain by Blackpool Independent Printers
ISBN Number 0.9523287.0.4

Authors Introduction.

It is with considerable pleasure that I introduce you to the first edition of 'The Towns and Villages in the Lake District and Cumbria'.
This book, it is hoped ,is the all purpose guide for the Lake District and Cumbria,suited to all visitors,whether walkers,cyclists,or motorists. Its arrangement is such that it ensures visitors of the greatest coverage and ease in finding the information that is generally required.

Accurate detail on the lakes,towns,villages,poets,local sports,and other topics is included, as are innumerable photographs.The large pull-out map is meant to complement the book and assist visitors in their choice of direction.

As will be seen considerable research has gone into preparing the book...but nevertheless still only 'skims' the surface of the history, beauty,and wonder of this lovely county.To produce a book of this nature and complexity means that out of sheer necessity some items of information have had to be omitted,but I hope that the detail included will be sufficient to enable it to be your favourite companion on your travels throughout Cumbria and the Lakes.

I have endeavoured to incorporate the majority of information that will be required by the majority of visitors...i.e.map location,market days,half-day closing,bus and train services,tourist attractions,and Tourist Information Centres,not over-looking the all important data of the towns and villages festivals and gala days.Many of these festivals are steeped in history and often give a good indication of Cumbrian life,past and present.

Visitors to our beautiful County often head for the better known places such as Bowness,Keswick,Ambleside,Grasmere,etc.The purpose of this book however is to introduce all travellers to those hundreds of often lesser known spots each of which in its own way has so much to offer.

I should like to take this opportunity too of thanking the many individuals ,too numerous to mention,who have been so helpful in submitting data,and correcting my many errors.In particular the Cumbrian Tourist Board for its advice and assistance.

How my wife Muriel,put up with me over the past three years whilst researching and writing this book I will probably never know,but her help and support over this time I seriously could have not done without.

Alan Bryant..Kendal. 1993.

ABBEY TOWN.

Map Ref: C5.

Bus Service. Cumberland Bus Service Route 38/38A

Location B5307.
Nearest Town or Village "Silloth"

MILL GROVE

Centuries ago Abbey Town was one of the most important places in the North of England. It is a crossroads village and stands on the Solway Plain, almost midway between Wigton and Silloth, in the parish of Holm Cultram.

The village, formerly a market town, is a hotch-potch of homes with its main claim to fame being the church of St. Mary, known as Holm Cultram Abbey. The Abbey was built in the 12th century originally as a Cistercian monastery, and enjoyed great power for many centuries, even entertaining Edward 1. on two occasions, until the Dissolution in the reign of Henry VIII. It is actually one of the few monasteries to survive as a parish church, though only a small portion of the original building remains. The church itself is made from what was at one time the nave of the Abbey. Within a century of the dissolution Abbey Town had regretfully proved itself unworthy of the great church left in its care, and by the 17th century is was already a ruin. The 18th century saved what could be saved, the 19th century restored it, and the great Tudor porch is now a little museum of old things rescued. The museum itself has one of the finest pieces of Norman architecture in Cumbria, the magnificent west doorway, with its five moulded arches and its eight pillars with carved capitals. It is 16 feet high and stands in a wall eight feet thick.

To be seen also is a relatively modern inscription to the man who was the last Abbot, and then the first Rector, and another to Joseph Mann, who on his farm hereabouts did a great service to farmers when he invented the first crude reaping machine, one of the primitive fore-runners of the first reaper invented by Cyrus McCormick a year or two later.

In the graveyard will be found the tombstone of the father of Robert the Bruce who was buried here in 1294. (25 years in fact before Robert the Bruce himself sacked the Abbey.)

Many of the buildings associated with the monastery are still inhabited today...one of them being Mill Grove dating from 1664, which originally was the infirmary; cottages belonging to the Abbey were transformed into a library and offices.

At one time the village had no less than five public houses, but nowadays this is reduced to one, together with a post office, with two additional shops. The oldest business in the village is the blacksmiths which has been trading as the original smithy since 1925.

Amateur archaelogists will no doubt discover the moated mound (probably a burg) just north of the church. Also nearby is the Raby Cote Farm, the sixteenth century seat of the Chambers family.

HOLME CULTRAM ABBEY

AINSTABLE

Map Ref. G5.

Next nearest Town or Village "Armathwaite"

Location. 5 miles East of Armathwaite

Formerly known as Aynstapellith, Ainstable is the village where a nunnery was founded under the instructions of William Rufus,and which later was removed to Staffield.

The church of St Michael has been on its present site for over 900 years.

Ainstable's most famous resident was one John Leake, who was born here in 1729.He was known as the 'Man-midwife' and wrote many books on childbirth and woman's diseases,also founding the Westminster Lying-In hospital near Westminster Abbey.He died in 1792 and was buried in Westminster Abbey.

Nearby in the Broomrigg Plantation stands two stone circles and a cairn circle.There is another ancient stone circle known as 'Grey Youds', which following the Enclosure Act of 1770 was vandalized,when all but one stone was removed to provide foundations for the drystone walls near-by.The work of removing the stones was done by the local labouring families, men, women, and children, with most of the walls remaining to this day as a monument to their endeavours.

Between Broomrigg and Ainstable,the two west-facing fields above the village are deeply furrowed,and were the highest fields in England ploughed compulsorily to provide corn during the Irish potato famine of 1820.

In 1702, a Rowland and Mary Smith built a sandstone house.In 1982 this house became the home of the Eden Valley Woollen Mill,and from that point on the muted sound of the loom was added to the hum of tractors as a background to the normal village noises.

ALLITHWAITE.

Map ref.F.13.

Next Nearest Town or Village Grange-Over-Sands

Cumberland Bus Service

Route No. 530/531/535/730/735.

Train.Cark - Kents Bank - Grange - Cartmel - Ulverston - Kendal stations are nearest.

Location.B5277 2 miles north West of Grange-over- Sands

Allithwaite is a village two miles north-west of Grange-over -Sands and between Cark and Kents Bank stations.

Back in the 17th century, the village boasted a corn mill,and later on a brewery, which are now converted into very attractive cottages.Quarrying was the main industry.

Half a mile south of the village is Wraysholme Tower a ruined pele, which was forfeited by the Harrington's after the battle of Bosworth, and subsequently granted to the Staveley's,whose crest will be found on a small piece of stained glass window.John Carter,of Cart Lane, whose family for years had prospered as guides of the infamous sands of Morecambe Bay, bought Wraysholme Tower in the mid 1700's.For information the present Queen's Guide is Mr Cedric Robinson who lives at Guides Farm, and can be seen most weekends during the summer guiding parties who wish to cross the Sands from Arnside.His is a Royal Appointment.

The church of St Mary's, together with the school were built in 1851, together with a schoolhouse and vicarage with money bequeathed by a Miss Mary Lambert who lived at Boarbank.

Part of the old manor of Allithwaite, to the south, is 'Humphrey Head'.In the 18th and 19th centuries,visitors used to flock to the Holy Well, dedicated to St.Agnes, to sample its waters.In particular it was the miners of Yorkshire and Cumberland who thought that illnesses caused by their employment could be cured by the water. Another interesting story of these parts is the legendary fame that comes from the fact the last wolf in England was killed here.

Also nearby is a cave where prehistoric and Roman artefacts have been found, including spear heads, pottery, axe heads...even rings and coins.

Guide - Over - Sands
"Whitbread Pub"
The Square, Allithwaite
Nr. Grange-over-Sands
Cumbria LA11 7QE

Grange-over-Sands, which includes the hamlet of Allithwaite claims to be the loveliest spot on the Lakeland coast, and all visitors will certainly agree there is a certain elegance to this very Edwardian resort. Protected by hills and mountains on three sides the climate is second to none. Fog is virtually unknown and the little snow that does fall here quickly vanishes.

From this centrally situated Inn the view across Morecambe Bay and down the estuary is one of the most splendid in Britain.Of late the Pub is enjoying an upsurge in popularity due in part to the recent refurbishment, but more especially the special care and attention of the licencees Chris and Kate Pearson, who are continually improving their service.

Locals and visitors alike are very welcome - in fact they have a very active and popular darts and pool team here, which always ensures busy evenings.

Bar snacks - with a wide choice available including take-away Pizza.
FIVE REAL ALES AVAILABLE.

ALLONBY.
Map ref. B5

Location. B5300
Nearest Town or Village "West Newton"

It has the sea, and certainly fine sands to enjoy...a long line of Scottish hills to look at across the water...a certain quaintness of plain old houses, and one thing to see in the very plainest of early Victorian churches.It's a marble monument carved with the head of Joseph Huddart, who was born here in 1741 and lived to win a place for himself in the story of navigation.For two things he is remembered...his charting and surveying of the coasts and ports he visited in the East, and his invention, after seeing a mishap caused by a broken cable, of a new way of making cables so that the strain fell equally on the different strands of yarn.Going into business with his idea he grew rich and died in London.

Allonby has a long history as a 'sea-bathing' resort, going back to the 18th century, and still popular to this day.It was in the 18th century when the fashion for bathing and even drinking sea-water was considered as a health-cure, first emerged, and it will be noticed that the town keeps much of its Georgian and Victorian charm.Many low cottages, one time homes of fishermen. There are cobbled lanes and curious corners to explore,and certainly some interesting old houses.In what was once the main street stands an imposing colonnaded building which was once the indoor baths where delicate Victorians could have their sea-water comfortably warmed. Allonby was an important centre for herring fishing and some of the old kippering houses can still be seen.

The quiet lanes of Allonby it will soon be discovered take you into a veritable hinterland which itself has many interesting places to explore.Hayton for example is built around a long green and has good views across the Solway Firth.Hayton Castle just north of the village,and now a farmhouse, was beseiged by Cromwell during the Civil War.

ALSTON

Map ref. I.5
Nearest Town or Village "Nenthall"
Tourist Information Service. Based at The
South Tyne Railway
Location. A.689.Alston/Brampton road.
Early Closing. Tuesday.
Gala Days/Festivals.Alston Sheep & Goat
Show. 1st Sat.Sept.
Alston Gala Day. 2nd Sat.July.
Alston & District Flower Show. 2ndSat Sept.
Alston Moor Sheepdog Trials.3rd Sat June.
Steam Enthusiasts Weekend.Last weekend July.

MARKET CROSS

Derives its name from 'Aldenstone' meaning 'old stone'.
A one time mining district in the upper valley of the South Tyne,Alston is 17 miles by road northeast of Penrith, over a pass 1800'high.
Alston also claims to be the highest market settlement in England. It is also very remote being approximately 20 miles from the nearest town.Its relative remoteness has meant that 'progress'has passed it by and visitors will now find surroundings more reminiscent of a bygone age.
The streets are cobbled and steep.Many interesting 17th and 18th century buildings remain on the main street and in the stone flagged lanes of The Butts, whilst farm houses of the same era are comparatively common in the villages and hamlets of Alston Moor. Some of them even retain their external staircases surviving from the days when their families lived above the cattle byre.One dated 1681, near the church, has a gallery above the pavement.Below the little slanting market place are the much worn steps of the market cross of uncertain date. Alston, too, can be proud of its small Town Hall set up in 1857 with a clock tower, its canopied buttresses, and oak sprays carved in niches. The lead and silver mines were originally worked here in 1350 by a German named Tillman, who hailed from Cologne. Many years later the mines were in the hands of The London Lead Co, controlled by the Quakers, who worked the Garrigill and Nenthead mines with philanthropy and profit until 1882 when they were sold to the Nenthead and Tynedale Lead & Zinc Co. These days the mines are currently being researched and part restored by the North Pennines Heritage Trust.
Legend here states that 'Jack Ironteeth'haunts the lead mines.He has gleaming sharp teeth made from Fluorospar and protects the mines from intruders! The recreation ground known as Fairhill, was at one time the area that drovers from the east en route to Penrith would rest their animals.A metal ring, still to be seen, is set in a large stone,and to which the bulls were tethered.In the early part of the 20th century many circus's also came and camped on this spot .
The size of the three churches in Alston is witness to the fact that the population was once more than double its present size.St.Augustine's, St Pauls Methodist, and the former Congregational church are all large buildings.The Quakers too have always been a dominant force in this area and continue to be so today.
The trees by the river shade Randal Holme, a rambling farmhouse of 1746, built around a 14th century keep with walls six feet thick, and a stone stairway to the roof of which traces can still be seen.In the vaulted cellar is a tiny window of which one bar of the mediaeval grating still remains. The oak rafters in many of the old rooms still bear the mark of the adze. CONT.

Gossipgate Gallery

....AT ALSTON IN THE NORTH PENNINES

GOSSIPGATE GALLERY lies in a quiet blackland of Alston on the way to the Seven Sisters Waterfall and Packhorse Bridge at Gossipgate

The converted Congregational Church which houses the gallery, complete with original gaslights, was built in 1804. The Gallery specialises in displaying the work of contemporary artists and craftspeople from theNorth of England and the surrounding counties of Cumbria, Durham and Northumberland. The proprietor Sonia Kempsey opended the gallery with her husband Peter in 1983, and the emphasis each season is on showing quality and originality from within this region. A programme of exhibitions displaying the work of well established and aspiring young artists and craftspeople from the North of England is complimented by a permanent selection of northern work in the gallery shop. This includes painting, prints, sculpture, pottery, jewellery, glass, wood and textiles as well as books of local interest, cassettes of Northumbrian pipe music, local mustard, honey and preserves.

Ground coffee and home-made cakes are available in the Coffee Shop and Tea Garden...Outside is a collection of herbs and local gardenware.

The Gallery is open daily including Sundays from mid February until the end of Decemb er. Admission Free

Gossipgate Gallery, The Butts, Alston, Cumbria CA9 3JU Tel: 0434 381806

Brownside Coach House

Alston Cumbria CA9 3BP
Tel. Alston (0434) 381263
Proprietor: Mrs. M.J. Graham

2 Miles outside Alston on the A686 to Penrith

The Coach House, built in 1689, is situated in quiet surroundings where meals may be served outside on fine days and one can admire the beautiful views of the South Tyne Valley and Pennines.

The food is freshly prepared and cooked on the premises, a wide variety of scones, quiches, pies, salads, gateaux and sweets served all day.
MORNING COFFEE, LUNCHTIME REFRESHMENTS, SALADS, AFTERNOON TEAS,
Included in the Egon Ronay "Just a Bite" guide since 1979
Open: Easter to early October 10 am - 6 pm Closed: All day Tuesday
A selection of antique glass to purhase.

In 1983, a narrow gauge railway began operating out of the area under the auspices of a local voluntary group...the South Tyne Railway Preservation Society.

The one time Congregational church is now the Gossipgate Gallery where all forms of arts and crafts are exhibited and sold.

At one time there was a dam on Fairhill which fed the millrace.This flowed down through the village and powered machinery for two small grain mills.The wheel house of the High Mill is in the process of being restored and stands just off the Market Cross.

Near Alston is Nent Force, a delightful waterfall where 10 years before he built Eddystone Lighthouse, John Smeaton began an underground canal about five miles long called Nent Force Level.

AMBLESIDE.

Map ref.E.10.

Nearest Town or Village Rydal and Grasmere

Bus Service. Cumberland Bus Route 555/556/505/506/516/518/W1/W2

Trains Ambleside - Keswick - Cockermouth - Carlisle - Lancaster - Kendal

Tourist Information Service. The Old Courthouse. Church Street.Telephone.Ambleside.32582.

And National Trust Information Centre

Location. A.591.Windermere/Grasmere road.

Early Closing. Thursday. (Winter Only)

Market Day. Wednesday.

Gala Days/Festivals.

Ambleside Gala. Last Sat.July.

Spring Flower & daffodil Show. 3rd Sat/Sun in March.

Flower,produce and handicraft show. 2nd Fri/Sat in August.

Rushbearing ceremony.1st or 2nd Sat in July.

Lake District Summer Music Festival 1st and 2nd weeks in August

PEGGY HILL

On the main highway through the Lakes, Ambleside is Lakelands most central town.It stands at the foot of Wansfell Pike, where the Stock Gill and the Kirkstone Pass, enter the green valley of the Rothay, a mile above the head of Windermere. It's situation, as seen when we come to it up the lake, is very beautiful.Though the town nestles somewhat closely under the hills, views of great and varied beauty expand from any side.

Shut in by Wansfell on the east, it is faced on the north by ridges which lead up to the summits of the Fairfield range, and hold the upland valleys of Rydal and Scandale.Loughrigg Fell blocks the head of the lake with the Rothay, a river of many memories,passing its foot on its way from the vale of Grasmere, and the Brathay from the Langdales on the other side. A very short walk along the lower slope of Wansfell to Jenkin Crag opens out the western view of the Langdales,with the chief summits of the highest mountain mass in England in the distance.Loughrigg a small plateau with rocky points of view raising from it, just across the flat of the Rothay valley, has easy paths to where lake, valleys, woodlands, and hills compose a striking panorama.

There are so many short walks hereabouts.One of the most popular being to Stock Ghyll Waterfalls.These falls have a drop of 70' and are in woodland under fine trees which have a carpet of daffodils in the Spring.

Although Ambleside is often referred to as a village, in reality it has been a market town since it received a charter for a weekly market in 1650.It has a resident population of some 3,000 people,and at first glance seems quite a large place for so few people. However during the summer months the population increases substantially owing to the area's popularity as a holiday resort.

The Romans arrived here in AD79 on their way to establish a port at Ravenglass.They made their base, which they called Galava, on the flat land to the north of Windermere now called Borrans Field.Their first fort was built of wood and clay,though this was replaced some years later with a stone one. This later fort has been excavated on several occasions. Today what can be seen there is some piles of stones on a grassy platform,`150 yards by 100 yards. Two of the gates can still be traced, along with the stout walls of the praetorium, the commandant's headquarters, and the foundations of the granaries...an important department in any Roman camp, where the army expected wheat bread as its staple food. The sill of the south gate is still in a wonderful condition. It is a stone nearly 11 feet by 5 feet, about a foot thick, and in its ends are the holes the Romans cut to receive the pivots of the double gates. Once the hob-nailed sandals of Roman soldiers made a great clatter on the flagstones of the fort...today, of course, all is quiet.

Certainly, without fear of argument , one of Ambleside's most popular landmarks is the tiny 17th century Bridge house on the Rydal road. This was built originally as a summer house in the gardens of Ambleside Hall. During its long life it has had many uses, initially seeing service as a cobbler's workshop, with a pigeon loft in the upper storey, then an antiques shop...and in earlier days was the home to a man, his wife, and six children, the family earning their living by basketmaking (also on the premises). Finally the house was purchased by local people (in 1926) for the sum of £450 and handed over to the National Trust who opened their first information office in the house. Of Ambleside Hall itself only the barn and one wing remain. It is now a cottage, and has an old staircase and a delightful balustrade.

Also not to be missed is the old Stamp House at the top of Church Street, which stands on the site of the office used by William Wordsworth when he was collector of stamps for Westmorland (as the County was then known). He was apparently elected to the post soon after his family moved to Rydal Mount.

Salutation Hotel nearby is one of Ambleside's oldest Inns dating back to 1656, and was an important coaching stop.

In the area east of Rydal Road between Stock Ghyll and the Kirkstone Road lies the oldest inhabited part of Ambleside. On roads such as Smithy Brow, and Fairview Road there are many delightful cottages to be seen. They are in a good state of preservation and many date from the 17th century.

The 19th century church of St Marys should also not be missed. It has a Wordsworth memorial Chapel, and a window to Wordsworth subscribed for by English and American admirers, others to his sister and his wife. It also has a handsome Bible presented by Wordsworth's widow, well worth seeing for so often must the poet have sat in his armchair reading that actual book.

In town the old mill is worthy of a visit. A waterwheel is a feature of this ancient building. It stands beside Stock Beck and is two storey's high.

There is reference to a mill here in 1175, and at one time Stock Gill provided power for five mills.

Ambleside was not the home of any of the Lake poets. They lived at Grasmere, Rydal, and Keswick. But it became through them a centre of intellectual interest. Dr Arnold built himself a holiday home here after he became Master of Rugby School. Mr W.E. Forster, who introduced popular education into Parliament, married a daughter of Dr Arnold and lived at the foot of Loughrigg Fell. Harriet Martineau came in 1846 and built The Knoll, and here she lived for 30 years and wrote on the social topic of her day. Felicia Hemans...a noted poet of the early Victorian period lived in Ambleside for many years.

Today though she is almost solely remembered for just one poem 'The boy stood on the burning deck...' Wray Castle is just south of Ambleside. Though called a castle, it is in fact a Victorian folly. Beatrix Potter stayed here when she was sixteen, for a short holiday.

Many places throughout Cumbria have a particular sweetmeat associated with them, and Ambleside is no exception. It is not in production today but older residents may remember the 'tooth-pulling' confection 'Ambleside Clag-em, being made in one of the old cottages in Church Street. Mary Dugdale, known to the children as Mammy Dugdale was the maker and vendor of the toffee.

Visitors who are puzzled by the Norwegian log cabin erected beside Lake Road may be interested in knowing that it was erected in 1911 (after first being imported from Norway) by the father of Grasmere artist W. Heaton Cooper. He too was an artist and used the cabin as a studio.

BRIDGE HOUSE

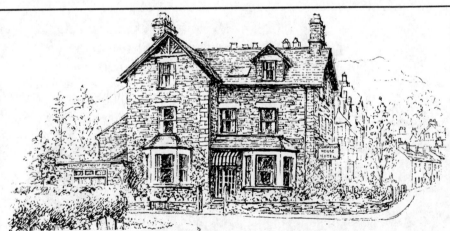

This book is one of a series of

'Towns and Villages'

in

Great Britain

published by

Village Publications

C U M B R I A
W I L D L I F E
T R U S T

Church Street, Ambleside,
Cumbria LA22 0BU
Tel: (05394) 32476
Fax ((05394) 32556

Cumbria Wildlife Trust protects and conserves both the wild life and wild places of Cumbria. Founded in 1962 the Trust, with over 3500 members has 40 Nature Reserves throughout Cumbria and plays a major role in conserving Cumbria's rich wildlife heritage. Cumbria Wildlife Trust is primarily a voluntary organisation. It is affiliated to RSNC - The Wildlife Trusts partnership, the parent body of all the County Wildlife Trusts in Britain. Many volunteers are working for wildlife throughout Cumbria. Some help directly on nature reserves, helping to manage the land both to protect and enhance its wildlife value, while others organise Local Groups that hold local walks, talks and fund raising events.

All members of the Wildlife Trust receive regular magazines detailing wildlife events throughout Cumbria and giving up to date information on conservation in Cumbria.

The Trust also works in partnership with industry, commerce, statutory and other bodies to help conserve Cumbria's wildlife. Recently BASS have sponsored "Nature Reserves in Cumbria" a free leaflet (available from Cumbria Wildlife Trust, Church Street, Ambleside, Cumbria LA22 0BU) that highlights 33 of Cumbria's premiere nature reserves. Not all of these belong to the Wildlife Trust, reserves that belong to the RSPB,the Woodland Trust and the Forestry Commission are also included.

Cumbria Wildlife Trust's nature reserves cover a wide range of habitats and help conserve a wide range of wildlife. South Walney, near Barrow in Furness is famous for its breeding birds, while the sand dune complex of North Walney is better known for its plant life. On the West Coast, Clints Quarry near Egremont, once an old quarry, is home to bee orchids, while Dubbs Moss near Cockermouth is an area of fen and woodland. In North Cumbria Trust nature reserves conserve some of the last fragments of peatland in England and in South Cumbria nature reserves support a rich limestone flora.

All these reserves are open to Cumbria Wildlife Trust members and the public.

The Trust's activities do though, extend far beyond protecting wildlife through nature reserves. Liaison with land owners, education, commenting and where necessary, opposing potentially damaging planning applications are but a few elements of the Trust work.

If you would like to help to secure a safe future for Cumbria's wildlife heritage why not join Cumbria Wildlife Trust or give a donation to Cumbria Wildlife Trust's 30th Anniversary Appeal.

For more information please contact:

CUMRIA WILDLIFE TRUST
Church Street, Ambleside,
Cumbria LA22 0BU
Telephone: (05394) 32476
Fax (05394) 32556

AMBLESIDE

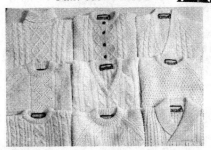

In the Heart of the Lake District

SUPERLATIVE APARTMENTS TO RENT

A prestigious development has been constructed to an exceptionally high standard. Its unique position overlooking Ambleside combines unspoilt views of the surrounding countryside whilst the apartment interiors are furnished with quality in mind.

The living room boasts an unobtrusive dining area. Whilst for private entertainment there's a colour

should never be a chore on holiday). As well as having ample space to work in. The Lakelands Leisure Centre provides an enjoyable range of activities, including a large swimming pool (with adjoining children's pool) jacuzzi, and patio area. The upper floor houses the sauna, steam room, and sunbed. The perfect environment for complete relaxation.

...and whilst you are staying at the Lakelands you enjoy privileged membership to the leisure centre free of charge, being exclusive to members only. The leisure complex opens at 7.00am daily and closes at 11.00pm. So whether you visit us for a few days or a few weeks you can be assured of a wonderful time at the Lakelands

TV, Video recorder and Hi-fi system. It is carpeted throughout, has full central heating and is also double glazed. There is plenty of storage space all adding to the comfort of your holiday whether you visit us in any of the four seasons.

The kitchen has been fitted with modern Hi-tech. appliances such as microwave, dishwasher, fridge, cooker etc., all labour saving devices (cooking

How to find us

Leaving the M6 motorway at Junc. 36 if you are travelling from the south/Junc. 37 from the north, and follow the signs to Windermere. Then carry on the A591 to Ambleside. Just before enetring Ambleside you will see Hayes Garden World on your left. At that point take the first right into Old Lake Road - travel along into Lower Gale and the Lankelands is on your left.

**The Lakelands, Lower Gale, Ambleside
Cumbria LA22 OBDTel. 05394 33777**

Langdale Chase Hotel

Windermere, Cumbria LA23 1LW, Tel. Ambleside (05394) 32201
★★★ RAC & AA Appointed   Fax: (05394) 32604

In 1890 Mr. Howarth, a businessman from Manchester, discovered and bought the site, so aptly described by Wordsworth, "A charming retreat for rest and recreation in 'The loveliest spot that man hath ever found'", with the intention of building a small retreat. Unfortunately he died before building had begun, and his widow, Mrs. Edna Howarth decided to erect the larger house as her permanent residence and to call it Langdale Chase. The foundation stone was laid by her only child, Lily, on the 8th April 1890. The house was built of Brathay Blue stone by Mr. Grissenthwaite of Penrith, and took five years to complete. It required ten men to dress the stone for three stonemasons and cost £32,000 to build. It had the proud distinction of being the first residence in Windermere to have electricity installed.

In the year that she died the property was bought by Mr. and Mrs. Willows from Scarborough, who left Yorkshire rightly judging that Scarborough would be shelled from the sea. Mr. Willows was a great collector and brought with him to Langdale Chase all his treasures including some of the fine old oak, the painting and china plates which are displayed in the Hall.

New kitchens were built and by 1937 the old kitchens and pantries had been converted into the Dining Room. This was extended in 1950 and the windows were, at the time of building, unique in the Lake District, providing panoramic views of Lake and Mountains. The original Butler's Pantry and Servant's Hall have now been replaced by the Cocktail Bar. The original flue still remains and has an open hearth fireplace of fossilised Ravenstonedale marble beneath it. The large bay window in the Reception Office, to the left of the Main Entrance, was bought from Grizedale Hall, which was built in similar freestone in 1900 and was demolished in 1955 when alterations to the Office at Langdale Chase were taking place.

The original Dining Room, now used as a lounge, has an overmantle deeply carved by the Grasmere Hermit bearing the date 1892 and the crest of the Howarth family. The Grasmere Hermit lived on the island in the middle of Grasmere and it is believed that he did his carving in Easedale, near Grasmere. The fine oak panelling is early Tudor and was bought in London by Mr. Willows where it was discovered under other panelling.

All the bedrooms here are individually furnished; the majority having lake view and private bathrooms, all equipped with colour TV., radio and telephones, tea/coffee making facilities. There is even a unique bedroom, with bathroom, over the Boathouse where you will drift to sleep to the sound of lapping water.

The oak staircase together with the carving round the Hall was the work of Arthur Jackson Smith of Sale, Cheshire. He came to Windermere especially to carry out this work and settled with his wife and family in Coniston. One of his grandsons still lives there and is the well-known maker of violins. Workmen came especially from Italy to lay the mosaic floors in the porch and ground floor corridors. The latter have in recent years been carpeted.

Here, we are sure, is an hotel set apart from all others you have ever visited. At "Langdale Chase" under the emblem of the Squirrel you will be treated, not as a transient visitor but as a personal guest in a well-run country home. For the energetic there is a choice of water skiing and bathing from the hotel jetty, tennis, croquet, putting or simply a rowing boat on the lake. The more leisurely inclined can choose a stroll through beautiful gardens, enjoy afternoon tea on the wide lawn fringed terraces overlooking one of the finest views in Europe. Here, in the welcoming crackle of a log-fire in autumn or spring, is born again that spirit of genuine hospitality that once graced ancient homes of England. Little wonder that "Langdale Chase" has become as "One of England's Most Gracious Hotels".

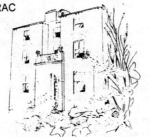

LOW WOOD

More than just an hotel

Surrounded by mature trees on the shores of Lake Windermere, Low Wood is committed to providing the very highest standards of service and care.

You can choose from any one of three bars with the option of an aperitif in the cocktail bar, real ale in our country pub Lady A's, or a more tropical taste in the Water Margin Bar, which is part of the impressive Low Wood club pool and leisure complex, which also serves full meals, grills, lunches and snacks.

With its splendid uninterrupted views across the lake to the magnificence of the Langdale Pikes, which can be enjoyed from many of our bedrooms, and its central setting at the heart of the Southern Lake District. Low Wood provides one of the very best bases to tour and explore the region.

Our prestigious Low Wood Club is an acclaimed development with probably the Lake District's finest indoor pool and leisure complexes. This superb centre has a spa bath, waterfalls, bubble bursts and a 50 foot length swimming pool if you wish to do some serious swimming.

The club's "Roman Baths" include sauna, steam room, plunge pool, and power showers. More strenous sport is provided by the two squash courts and fully equipped fitness centre.

As a guest at the Low Wood you will be given an English Lakes Hotel Privilege Card which entitles you to specially discounted prices on all activities at the watersport centre, lunches at any of our hotels, and entrance fees and tickets

to a number of attractions including historic houses, museums and lake cruises.

All bedrooms at Low Wood are ensuite with bath or shower and have remote control TV, direct dial telephones, trouser press and hair dryer, complimentary tea and coffee and a baby listening service.

We make families welcome by making children special. Every child staying at the Low Wood automatically becomes a member of Sam's Club and therefore qualifies to receive our special gift box - modelled in the shape of a kennel and stuffed full of all sorts of surprises.

The Low Wood Watersport Centre

The range of outdoor on-site watersports available at Low Wood is unparalleled in the Lake District. The combination of an ideal location, the latest equipment and the best tuition makes it the greatest possible place to learn to water-ski windsurf or sail.

The Low Wood, commended by the English Tourist Board and Winner of their 1990 England for Excellence Award, has a four Crown rating in addition to being AA ✯✯✯ RAC.

The complete resort Hotel

Low Wood Hotel
Windermere, Cumbria LA23 1LP
Telephone:(05394) 33338
Fax: (05394) 34072

ANTHORN.

Map Ref.C.4.
Bus Service. Cumberland Bus Service Route No. 71. 9. 3.
Nathorn - Silloth - Carlisle - Kirkbampton - Kirkbridge - Newton Arlosh
Nearest Town or Village " Cardurnock"
Location. Glasson to Cardurnock road.

Anthorn is listed as an area of natural beauty, situated on the shores of Morcambe Bay (an inlet of the Solway Firth).

The name means 'single thorn bush'. Visitors travelling along the coast road from the village shop will notice a bridge over a small stream. Just over the bridge on the left will be seen a very old thorn bush. Records of the area show that freemen of the shire used to gather around this thorn bush to hold important meetings.

The village is actualy in two parts; the older part, mostly in an agricultural setting, dates back to 1279 and houses a Congregational Chapel and manse dating back to 1869, and a public elementary school built in 1875.

The residential part was built as recently as the 1950's for Naval personnel use. A NATO radio station opened in 1964, the masts of which dominate the skyline.

At the west end of the village approximately half a mile along the coast, almost buried in a mound of soil, will be found an ancient cross which is thought to mark the limits of an early sanctuary. Opposite this cross stands what is known locally as 'Mary's Tower' which has windows on all sides. It is said that Mary Queen of Scots was held prisoner here for just one night in 1568 on her way to the south. Underground tunnels are believed to run from the village to the tower. The area is said to have been frequented by smugglers who at one time used the tunnels to hide themselves and their contraband of tobacco, spirits, and wine.

Often to be seen here is what is generally known as Haaf fishing, or fishing Norwegian style. Fishermen stand in the flood of the rising tide, holding large square nets on poles in which they catch the fish.

APPLEBY.

Map ref. I.8
Bus Service. Cumberland Bus Route No. 100 561
Trains. Appleby (Settle- Carlisle)
Tourist Information Centre.
Moot Hall. Boroughgate. Tel; Appleby 51177.

Location. A66. Brough/Penrith road.
Early Closing. Thursday.
Market Day. Saturday.
Gala Days/Festivals.
Appleby Agricultural Show. 2nd Thursday. August.
Appleby Town Carnival & Sports. 3rd Sat in July. Appleby New Fair (Horse Fair) 7 days prior to 2nd Wednesday in June.
Appleby & District Gardeners Society Show. 1st Sat. Sept.

APPLEBY CASTLE

Old Westmorland's most historic town lies in the fertile Vale of Eden with the Pennine fells rising in a magnificent escarpment to eastward. It claims,

with a population of just over 1800 to be England's smallest county town and smallest assize town with a history going back before the Norman

Conquest.The corporation is one of the oldest, and in 1201 William de Goldington was made the first mayor.

Appleby was originally the County town of Westmorland,with a Royal Charter dating back to 1174, following the Norman Conquest.

The Romans marched this way, along High Street on the outskirts of the town, to the Wall.Saxons and Normans built churches here, a Scottish king captured the castle, and centuries later Lady Anne Clifford defended it for a king.The attractive main street with the layout of a mediaeval market town slopes gently downhill from the castle which once gave it protection,to the church.At each end of this street is a tall black and white pillar with a sundial on the top known as Low Cross and High Cross, the latter has an inscription to the local people'Retain your loyalty,preserve your rights'.

From High Cross the buildings of the Grammar School can be seen across the town where there was a School House Lane as long ago as the mid 15th century. and Queen Elizabeth 1 granted a Royal Charter to the free Grammar School.One of its scholars was Dr Addison, Dean of Lichfield, father of the essayist,and two others have the immortal name of Washington:Lawrence and Augustine, brothers of the famous President. Lawrence,in fact, was at Appleby school the year George Washington was born.

Though not retaining such an air of importance these days it is nevertheless an attractive market town with a village atmosphere,and certainly retaining a great deal of interest and charm.

Appleby's main street Boroughgate,has been descibed as one of the nicest in England.The avenue of mature lime trees, flanked by well kept properties dating from the 17th to the early 20th century,certainly confirm this.In the lower market area will be found the Moot Hall and which is still used to this day for council meetings. An indication of the age of the building will be found by a plaque over the door which is dated 1596.

On a hill overlooking the town will be found Appleby castle,one time owned by Lady Anne Clifford.These days the castle is more known as a conservation centre. Of all her castles, Lady Anne preferred Appleby and spared no expense in repairing the property and making it more hospitable,heating it with coals from her own pits on Stainmore.She restored massive Caesar's Tower and built a small bee-house in a sheltered hollow above the river. The castle has seen stirring times as the valley here lies open to the north and from this direction came William the Lion to capture the stronghold over 800 years ago.During its long history successive owners have altered and extended the buildings.It was Thomas,8th Lord Clifford who rebuilt the main block in the 15th century.Two hundred years later Lady Anne Clifford defied Cromwell by restoring the castle to its medieval splendour.There was once a draw-bridge over the moat, and a gatehouse where the entrance today opens on to beautiful lawns.Although many changes have been made to the castle down the centuries much of the old stonework remains, including the 12th century Caesar's Tower, parts of the curtain wall, and the 13th century round tower in the north wall.

The keep is open to the public and is a particularly fine example of Norman architecture.The Great Hall is especially interesting and contains many paintings of the Clifford family...the most important being 'The Great Picture'.Look for display of chinese porcelain salvaged in 1985 from the wreck of the 'Nanking'...a ship that had been on the seabed for over 220 years.

Across the bridge over the Eden is a part of the town known as 'The Sands'.Above the Sands steep streets of sturdy 19th century terrace houses lead to the railway station of the famous Settle and Carlisle line. The 12th century church of St Lawrence is well worth visiting even if only to visit the tombs of Lady Anne and her mother Lady Margaret.Beside Lady Anne's well known work in restoring so many of her properties one which also should be mentioned is St

The Gate Hotel
Bondgate, Appleby

Anybody entering today's Gate Hotel here in Appleby should be forgiven for thinking they had stepped back to the beginning of the century, when they discover they are ostensibly in a relaxed and luxurious ships salon...where polished panelling, along with luxurious palm plants certainly give a unique atmosphere.

Its certainly no illusion however, for the actual interior comes from one of Cunard's famous 'floating hotels', which was salvaged by the previous owners and transported to Appleby back in 1946. Both the bar and dining room are panelled with Peruvian mahogany which at one time graced the salon of the German White Star liner RMS Berengaria, which, in her day was in fact the biggest liner in the world. She was actually launched by the Kaiser in 1912. The story goes that the liner was being broken up at Jarrow when an Appleby man recognising the historic importance of the salon furnishings set about the purchase of them.

Today you can enjoy these opulent surroundings. Although a comparatively small hotel with just five bedrooms, all offer en-suite facilities. Traditional Sunday lunches are amongst their popular meals, and other top dishes here include fishermans pastry, and the famed home-made 'Gate' pie, ingredients including beef and onions, bacon and real ale, topped with a suet pastry crust.

The Gate Hotel now caters for all manner of private functions in the sixty-cover dining room, as well as providing a wide range of excellent dishes for both local and visiting diners.

The hotel also offers vegetarian and vegan dishes, plus an extensive list of wines from many parts of the world.

Tel: 07638 51498

One of the most charming corners of Appleby lies hidden behind the old houses in Boroughgate. Enter the doorway beneath the sign of the Courtyard Gallery and walk along a passage, and you find yourself in a small and unexpected courtyard. Vines and shrubs soften the ancient stonework and overhang a table and benches in a corner, while through a wrought-iron gate and along another passageway a secluded garden can be glimpsed. The Gallery itself is housed on the upper floor of a centuries old granary, which in its time has served as a dame school and an artist's studio. This is approached from the outside by a flight of wooden stairs. The character of the building, with its beams and deepset windows, has been preserved and now affords an ideal setting for a distinguished collection of original paintings, pottery, glass, jewellery, turned wood and cards.

One end of the Gallery is furnished with tables and chairs where coffee or a choice of blends of tea and homemade cakes and biscuits can be enjoyed. Whether you buy or browse, for those who delight in quaint and tasteful surroundings a visit to Courtyard Gallery will remain among the happy memories of a good day out.

32 Boroughgate, Appleby-in-Westmorland, Cumbria Tel: 07683 51638

Annes Hospital.

The almhouses at Appleby, known as St Anne's Hospital were founded in the middle of the seventeenth century by the local landowner Lady Anne, Countess Dowager of Dorset, Pembroke, and Montgomery.

The present site in Boroughgate was bought on the last day of December 1650, having spent £36 on the land where the almhouses are built. Provision was made for the accommodation of twelve Sisters and a Mother (so called still to this day)..the latter to be responsible for general administration in accordance with a set of rules drawn up. The building itself consists of a quadrangle of small self-contained dwellings enclosing a cobbled courtyard with seats and fountain. Overhead in the gate-house, hangs the bell that was rung every three months to call the Mother and her Sisters to receive their small allowance of pocket-money...part of Lady Anne's forethought in view of her strict ordinance forbidding them to run up bills in the town.

Visitors are very welcome.

Last, but by no means least, should be mentioned the famous Appleby New Fair (or Horse Fair) renowned as the single biggest gathering of gypsy people in Britain. The fair itself is now well over three hundred years old and these travelling people arrive from all over the country every year on the second Wednesday in June to buy and sell horses and race them in the trotting races.

ARMATHWAITE.

Map Ref. G.5.
Nearest Town or Village "Ainstable"
Trains, Armathwaite (Settle - Carlisle)
Location:.1mile east of A6 Penrith/Carlisle road.

The beautiful village of Armathwaite nestles by the river Eden in a wooden hollow, renowned by many for its salmon fishing.

The name Armathwaite means 'the clearing of the hermit'believed to derive from a hermit who once lived in a clearing in Inglewood Forest, near,in fact to the site of the present castle.

The castle is a four storey high Pele tower, built originally to prevent Border raiders from penetrating further into what was then known as Cumberland.The castle was originally owned by the Skelton family.John Skelton was Poet Laureate to Henry VIII..Later he was to seek refuge from the anger of Cardinal Wolsey by taking sanctuary at Westminster where he eventually died. The delightful chapel of Christ and Mary was originally built in 1402.For many years it was in disrepair and by the 17th century was actually being used as a cattle shelter.Richard Skelton rebuilt it around 1600 and today it can be seen almost as it would have been over three hundred years ago.

Further along the Eden,near the weir, a mill was built for grinding corn at the beginning of the 19th century.In the early 1930's the mill was altered to operate electrically, and consequently the village cottages received electricity for the first time.

Arthurian legend runs deep in these parts and visitors to the area will soon learn of the 'Giant of Tarn Wadlyn'.He apparently lived at the same time as King Arthur and Queen Gwenever' resided in Carlisle.According to popular belief the giant Ewen Caesario by name, now lies buried in St Andrew's Churchyard,Penrith.

The impressive Nunnery Walks lead through a leafy avenue of trees to the Gorge, returning via a woodland walk which includes the enchanting view of Croglin Water. Just downstream is Sampsons Cave. Sampson was apparently a labourer who worked on the construction of the Carlisle to Settle railway line.He became involved in a brawl which culminated in murder.Sampson hid in the cave but was eventually discovered and taken to Carlisle where after a lengthy trial, was hanged.

The Eden Gorge between Lazonby and Armathwaite is one of Cumbria's best kept secrets and is well worth exploring,on water, or on foot.

High Hesket, Carlisle, Cumbria (old A6 Rd. Jct. 41 - 42)

Morning Coffes - Lunches - High Teas - Open 10am - 12 Midnight

Caravan Touring Halt

Tel: 06974 73345

ARNSIDE.

Map ref.F.12.
Nearest Town or Village "Milnthorpe"
Bus service. Cumberland Bus Service
No. 552   Arnside - Milnthorpe - Kendal
Trains. Arnside Station
Location. On coast, near to
Grange over Sands.
Early Closing. Thursday.

A seaside resort these days, at the mouth of the river Kent.Designated as an area of outstanding natural beauty it enjoys one of the loveliest sites on the north-west coast.

The estuary itself is a bird watchers paradise and has been described by Peter Scott as the second most beautiful estuary in the British Isles. For example, on low ground not far away which was once farmland is now an inundated area of open fresh water and large reed beds,Leighton Moss is a nature reserve where ornithologists may always find much of interest at any time of the year.

Arnside is a village of steep streets,many of them cul-de-sacs, with narrow inter-connecting passages for pedestrians.Until the 19th century it was part of the village of Beetham.

The oldest building here is Arnside Tower (a

ruined Pele) and testifies to the need for defence against the Scots.In the 17th century to both refresh weary travellers (and no doubt the occasional smuggler) their were several inns here, though now only one remains.The Fighting Cocks Hotel...which incidentally still has the cockpit in its cellars.

The church was built only a century ago, but round about are traces of six or seven towers, places of refuge and defence in the days of the Scottish invasion.One is Hazelslack Tower enshrined in trees, a lonely place a mile away. Roughly built about 500 years ago, it has walls three feet thick and traces of great fireplaces and a winding stair to a magnificent view from the top, where trees are growing in the crumbling stone.Saltcoates is the villages oldest house,and was the centre of a thriving salt industry.Other houses from the 17th and 18th century still survive. It wasn't until the 19th century that Arnside became known as a seaside resort. Pleasure boats would sail from Morecambe and Fleetwood with passengers coming ashore to enjoy

COTTAGES

their famous shrimp teas, or even to take rides by wagonnette up to the Knott. More importantly however was the arrival of the railway in 1857, together with the opening of the viaduct, which made Arnside far more accessible.Today the viaduct is one of the great tourist attractions, as in these days of nearly universal diesel or electric traction, this is one of the few lines over which British Rail allow steam trains to run. Nearby Steamtown Museum, at Carnforth, provides most of the historic

ARNSIDE PIER

locomotives of yesteryear to haul the specials and the now well known Cumbrian Coast Express.The viaduct is one of the most popular venues for the hordes of railway photographers who invade Arnside to capture on film a favourite or rare steam train. Behind the village rises the Knott (owned by the National Trust) a rounded hill with woodland walks...from the top can be seen the magnificent panorama of the Lakeland hills,and the Northern Pennines and a beehive momument to Queen Victoria.

ASBY.

Map ref. I.9
Next Nearest Town or Village "Hoff"
Location. 5 miles south of Appleby.

Asby is a scattered parish some five miles south of Appleby,and contains the villages of Great and Little Asby.

The older village is Little Asby, two miles south-east.It is a tiny hamlet which in ancient times had a chapel dedicated to St.Leonard, the patron saint of Lepers,and probably explains its isolation.Nearby is an ancient earthworks, one of several in the district.Also close by is Sunbiggin Tarn, which is well known locally as a nesting site for black headed gulls.

Situated on either side of Asby Gill is Great Asby, rising on the west side of the village, where the entrance to Pate Hole, a cave which extends to 1,000 yards will be found.

Just below the church is St Helen's Well, a strong spring of clear water which gushes all year.The water is believed by many to have medicinal purposes.

The church of St.Peter dominates the village.Theoriginal church built in 1160 was demolished in 1863, and subsequently rebuilt. Locals at the nearby Greyhound Pub will happily tell visitors that their studded door came from the old church,

The two most historically interesting buildings herabouts are the old rectory with its 14th century pele tower(now a private house) and Asby Hall....a tall black and white painted farmhouse, built in 1694..originally owned by the Musgrave family. In addition the village school, endowed in 1688,still survives.

This is a village which year by year is becoming better known ,mostly by walkers along the Westmorland Way.

ASPATRIA.

Map ref. C.6.
Next Nearest Town or Village "Hayton"
Bus Service. Cumberland Bus Service No.39
Aspatria - Carlisle - Wigton - Mealsgate -
Blennerhasset
Train. Aspatria
Location. A.596. Carlisle/Maryport road.
Early closing Tnursday

This former mining town straggles along the A596
for about a mile.Its name is supposed to mean
(St.Patrick) Ash,but other derivations have been
suggested.
In the market square is an ornate memorial fountain
to 'Watery Wilfred' as his political opponents called
Sir Wilfred Lawson, a local landowner who spent his
forty years as an M.P. crusading for the temperance
movement together with international peace. Me-
dallions on either side of the monument symbolise
these causes...a bronze relief portrait of Sir Wilfred
is on the front ,and above them stands a fine statue of

St.George slaying the dragon.The inscription says
Sir Wilfred believed in the brotherhood of man
and defended his somewhat unpopular ideas with
'gay wisdom and perseverance'.He was,of course
a great teetotaller, and no man in his day made
more people laugh at temperance meetings.He
lived in the big park of Brayton Hall, later burned
down..Here Sir Wilfred Lawson lived out his long
life, dying early in this century
The church here only dates from 1846, but incorporates two Norman arches of an earlier
building.There are also some tenth and eleventh
century carved stones, including a wheel-head
cross, a hog-back stone, and a grave cover with a
swastika on it.In the churchyard is a holy well
probably indicating that St.Kentigern ,to whom
the church is dedicated, baptised his converts
there. It is now known as the Bishops Well..Also
in the churchyard is a magnificent memorial carved
by the man who lies in the grave close by it. He was
the well known archaelogist W.S.Calverley, who
was vicar here, and the memorial they have set up
to him is a copy of the Gosforth Cross, one of the
best surviving anywhere.

AYSIDE.

Map ref. F.12.
Nearest Town or Village "Lindale / Field
Broughton"
Location.Close to A.590.Newby Bridge to
Lindale road.

Ayside is a tiny hamlet situated some three miles
from Newby Bridge at Lake Windermere's south-
ern-most tip.
It is a delightfully pretty spot with many colourful
gardens...twice in fact in recent years winning the

prettiest small village competition.
It takes its name from the tiny beck, which at one
time supplied the monks at Cartmel Priory with
their fish.
Not so very long ago clogs and shoes were made
and repaired in the village, and near to the main
road is the old house where carters and drivers
would stop for a change of horses.
Heading towards High Newton will be found a
quarry, and here it was that a man lived perfectly
happily for many years beneath an upturned
boat.The family butcher here has been in business
for over 100 years.

BACKBARROW.

Map ref. E.12.
Next nearest Town or Village Newby Bridge
Trains. Lakeside & Haverthwaite Railway
Location. A.592. Newby Bridge to Ulverston
road.

The village of Backbarrow is in the parish of
Haverthwaite,on the banks of the Leven, where at
one time the monks of Cartmel Priory had a flour
mill.
It has had a long history of industry, all of which has
been powered by water from the river. The mill has
changed many times from its beginnings in the

BIGLAND HALL ESTATE
BACKBARROW - NEWBY BRIDGE - CUMBRIA

Perhaps the finest way to enjoy scenery of outstanding natural beauty is to take part in an activity amongst it...

Bigland Hall offers opportunities for just this.

Bigland Hall, a magnificent country house, dates in part from 1125. The Hall stands in over 1,000 acres of private estate, overlooking the tranquil water of its own 13 acre tarn. This peaceful lake and its surrounding expanse of woodland and parkland offer a staggering variety of pursuits.

TROUT FISHING
☎ 05395 31361

OPEN ALL YEAR ROUND
Specifically designed to cater for the discerning trout fisherman, our trout fishing water, of sixteen acres, was man-made in 1977 by the Bigland Hall Estate. It is stocked regularly with Rainbow Trout only - the record being 12lbs 0oz. Fly fishing only with barbless hooks is permitted and the number of rods per days is strictly controlled. Early booking, especially for weekends, is necessary.

COARSE FISHING
☎ 05395 31361

Bigland Tarn is a paradise for the pleasure angler, in addition we cater for matchmen. A careful balance between the two is being maintained - a 40 peg contest will be allowed some weekends, leaving plenty of room for the pleasure angler; but early bookings for matches and groups are strongly recommended - especially for Saturdays and Sundays.

ARCHERY
☎ 05395 31361

Target Archery, under supervision, is held in the parkland, situated at the centre of the estate.
Booking essential

CLAY PIGEON SHOOTING
☎ 05395 31361

Clay shooting for both the beginner and the more experienced shot. Down the line or sporting. Tuition and gun hire. Bookings taken daily.

RIDING CENTRE

Bigland Hsall's own Riding Centre offers pony trekking for the beginner, hacking on the estate's own woodlands, parkland and fells for the rider, and has a splendid indoor riding school offering lessons for riders of all levels - there is even a cross country course. Livery facilities are also available for visitors.

DEER WATCHING

Deer watching, clay pigeon shooting, game shooting and target archery (under supervision), add to the list of pursuits avilable. The Estate also offers opportunities for glorious walks in splendid scenery, with an abundance of plant, animal and bird life.

early days, when very young orphans from Liverpool and London were the major work force.After the mill closed down it was eventually taken over by the Lancashire Ultramarine Company, and finally by Reckitt and Colman. Both of these companies made industrial blue for laundering purposes..the dust from their tall chimneys(now demolished) used to stain everything around blue.

Most famous and long lasting of the furnaces hereabouts was that built in 1711 and whose remains can still be seen...though now sadly dilapidated and requiring preservation.It was here that young John Wilkinson (1728-1808) began his amazing career which was to make him the greatest ironmaster of the eighteenth century and a seminal figure in the Industrial Revolution.He worked with his father at Backbarrow, where he invented the box iron,much esteemed by laundresses for ironing the fancy lace frills of the period, and where he experimented with iron boats on the River Leven an idea he was to develop later on the River Severn;the first practical iron boats the world had seen.

Today the mill building has been tastefully turned into the Whitewater Hotel and timeshare lodges collectively better known as The Lakeland Village.

Just up the hill near where the Victorian school was located, is the 'Headmasters House' still known locally as 'The School House'. Also nearby is Bigland Hall, home of the one-time squires.

BAMPTON.

Map ref. G.8.
Next nearest Town or Village "Shap"
Location. West of A6 ,two miles from Shap.

Bampton...which means the 'place of the beam' is a pleasant village set in the valley of the Lowther.

Once famous for its Grammar School founded in 1623, the village is situated four and a half miles west of Shap, at the point where the river Lowther is joined by the stream from the Haweswater Lake.

In Bampton Grange stands St Patrick's Church, and was erected in 1726...though there has been a church on this site for over 800 years.Bampton's church is one of the rare ones with timber arcades.A copy of the parish register, dated Thursday June 20th 1728 is on display in the building and records the consecration of the fabric after building.There is a pew dated 1684 from the old church, a table in the vestry and the pulpit are 18th century, and the altar rails and a chest are a century earlier. There are paintings on the wall one of which shows Mardale church as it stood before the level of Haweswater was raised.

Opposite is the vicarage which houses the famous Tinkler Library containing many books written in Latin.

Bampton Grange has had many commercial uses, though today these include a hat box maker, a breeder of Shetland Sheep, and the Crown and Mitre Hotel.

The local pub here is 'St Patrick's Well' the meeting point for the 'Shephers Meet' held annually in November...dating back to the time when stray sheep were reclaimed.The Mardale Hunt also meets here nowadays. The day is also a lively social event when the fell hounds meet and traditional songs are sung. On Bampton moor above Haweswater are the trees of prehistoric man, earthworks, cairns and stone circles, and a group of rocks known as the Giant's Grave. Hamlets within the parish are Knipe, Butterwick,and Beckfoot.

BARBON.

Map ref. H.12.
Next nearest town or village "Casterton"
Location. East of A.683 Casterton to Middleton road.
Barbon Sheepdog trials & local sheep show 2nd week in August

OLD SMITHY

Barbon which means 'the stream of the bear' is a pleasant village of about 100 homes, situated in the Lune Valley midway between Kirkby Lonsdale and Sedbergh ,Barbon is recorded in the Domesday Book as Brerebrun and was originally made up of a few small holdings and cottages.

St.Bartholomews church was built in 1892, replacing the previous one which dated back to the 12th century.Today only the porch and vestry of the earlier version remain, and they are currently being used as tool sheds.In the chancel is a chest dated 1659, a cupboard and a finely carved chair of 1662.

The village store celebrated its 100th birthday in 1990.The old school built in 1867 still survives but has been nicely converted into a private house, and though the village smithy himself hasn't survived, his home has, and now houses a clockmaker and repairer.

The Barbon Inn close by is a 17th century coaching inn.
Of interest to many.Just outside the village is a curious old cross, believed to be the gravestone of a Roman soldier slain here in a long gone battle.

Past the church ,the fell road winds through Barbondale.At the hamlet of High Beckfoot, close to the Lune, the old pack-horse bridge spans Barbon Beck.It is near to an old ford, and is exactly as high as it is wide...two feet six inches...and in direct contrast to its modern counterpart only a few yards away.The old road leading over the pack-horse bridge continues through the fields to Treasonfield.
Just outside the village is a new 18 hole golf course.

THE OLD SCHOOL HOUSE

The Barbon Inn

Barbon, Nr. Kirkby Lonsdale,
Cumbria. Tel. (05242) 76233

Seventeenth Century Coaching Inn.

Welcome to the Barbon Inn in the delightful village of Barbon, nestling deep between the Yorkshire Dales and the Lake District. Originally built in the 17th Century as a coaching inn, the Barbon Inn offers a lively, but relaxed atmosphere to while away a pleasant lunch time drink, evening meal or comfortable overnight stay.

Whatever you seek, you will always find a peaceful haven of friendly hospitality, fine food and soothing comfort - the ideal combination for the perfect holiday.

A leisurely house in our pretty and secluded beer garden creates a relaxing mood, followed by a meal from the table d'hote menu served in our exquisite restaurant: sample the Lunesdale Duck served with Elderberry Sauce, or a selection of other local specialities. A traditional Roast Lunch with all the trimmings is also served each Sunday.

Make yourself at home - choose from ten bedrooms, each individually furnished and all well supplied with colour televisions and tea trays. Spoil yourself for that special night away: choose our elegant mini-suite with solid oak four-poster bed and en-suite facilities.

Come morning, wake fully refreshed to a full English breakfast, with plentiful tea and coffee, ready for the day ahead. Whether you want a gentle or energetic holiday enjoying the magnificence of both the Yorkshire Dales or Lake District, we know you'll find the Barbon Inn to be the ideal choice for comfort, hospitality, good food and the warmest welcome.

"We do hope to see you soon"

BARDSEA.

Map ref. E.13.
Next nearest Town or Village "Ulverston"
Bus service. Cumberland Bus Service No.11 Ulverston - Coast Road - Roa Island - Barrow Location. A5087 Two and a half miles south west of Ulverston.

A picturesque village on the Furness Peninsula two and a half miles south-west of Ulverston.

Upon entering the village the houses in Main Street have been built on the one time site of Bardsea Hall.The Ship Inn was in 1750 a farm, with opposite the old school...now the church hall. Many of the older limestone cottages are in close proximity to the lychgate...one of which incorporates the village shop and post office.

In the 12th century there was a hospital here.'St John of Jerusalem'...later given to Conishead Priory. Conishead Priory was an Augustinian hospital which later received priory status. One of its early charges was to provide a guide to lead travellers over the treacherous sands of Morecambe Bay.

Following the Dissolution, and the disposal and dismantling of the Priory, the land went to William Stanley who built a house here.By the mid 17th century it passed to the Braddyll family, and in 1818 Colonel Thomas Braddyll found the house in such disrepair that it had to be completely rebuilt. Later the house became a hotel and in the 1930's a miners convalescent home, after which it stood empty for many years.

The present owners Manjushri Institute is an educational charity concerned with furthering understanding of Buddhism.They purchased the property in 1976 at which time they embarked on a mammoth task of restoration...which is still continuing to this day.The house is built in an elaborate late Gothic style.The entrance through a gatehouse flanked with high towers opens onto a large hall with a high ribbed-vaulted ceiling, ornate plaster ceilings are also a notable feature.A gallery at first floor level has a 16th century oak screen brought from Samlesbury Hall near Preston, and the Oak Room has some beautifully carved woodwork.

The house and grounds have recently been opened up to help raise revenue for restoration.The grounds extend to 70 acres, and a very pleasant nature trail has been laid out.

Opposite the Braddylls Arms the road sweeps down to the shore with many recently renovated cottages...one time homes for the local fishermen and labourers.Here too will be found the former water driven corn mill, which is now a licensed restaurant.

On any clear day from hereabouts the views can be quite overwhelming...Nearby the farmland rises to the extensive bracken covered land of Birkrigg which has an ancient stone circle and 17th century Friends burial ground.223 Quakers are buried here, including the renowned Margaret Fell.

Quite recently a strip of the shoreline has been designated a country park.Bardsea Country Park by name.175 acres of woodland and shingle foreshore, which in itself offers a peaceful vista of the bays shingle and sands.Fishing is still very much a way of life here.Tractors can often be seen at low tide bringing in fish and shrimps.

CONISHEAD PRIORY

Conishead Priory, now a Buddist Centre, is a 19th century gothic mansion under restoration, surrounded by Acres of woods and gardens, just south of the Lake District on the shores of Morecambe Bay.   Priory Road, Ulverston, Cumbria Tel: 0229 584029

Open 2.00 - 500pm Sat/Sun/Bank Holidays-Easter to the end of September

BARROW IN FURNESS.

Map ref. D.13.
Nearest Town or Village "Rampside"
Bus Service.Cumberland Buses
Routes 6, 6A & 6B, 7, 11, 12, 518
Trains. Barrow in Furness
T.IC. Town Hall,Duke Street.Tel; Barrow. 870156.
Location.At the tip of the Furness peninsular.
Furthest point of A.590.
Early Closing. Thursday.
Market Day. Friday/Sat.
Gala Days/Festivals
Barrow Horticultural society show early September.

Situated at the tip of the Furness peninsular,just twenty minutes from the Lake District, Barrow-in-Furness projects into the Irish Sea with Morecambe Bay to the south and the Duddon Estuary to the north.

Barrow is a bustling Victorian town with wide tree-lined streets and a wealth of fine vernacular buildings typified by the imposing Gothic style Town Hall.

The name'Furness'is of considerable antiquity and refer to 'Far-ness', namely distant headland. The earliest settler here was stone-age man. Archaelogical evidence points to small groups of people occupying the adjoining Walney Island.Material on display in the Furness Museum (currently closed) for example, clearly dates back in excess of 6,000 years.Furness was once settled by a tribe known as Angles, who originated in Northern Germany.

By the 9th century, Furness was part of the Kingdom of Strathclyde, with the King residing in Penrith, after which it was controlled by the Earls of Northumbria until the times of the Norman Conquest.

Amongst Barrow's many places of interest the first port of call for all visitors is undoubtedly Furness Abbey (or Abbey of St Mary of Furness) situated just outside the town. "in the valley of the deadly nightshade!' These days it is a magnificent ruin of a vast and imposing building constructed in the distinctive red sandstone,and set in the deep wooded valley of Bekansgill.

The Abbey was founded in 1127 on land granted by King Stephen to the Abbot of Savigny in Normandy. The governing monastic order was originally Benedictine, an order dedicated to learning and prayer, but by order of the Abbot of Savigny, the Abbey became Cistercian in 1148. Regretfully with the Dissolution of the Monasteries in 1537 the lead roof was removed and melted down, and the walls partly demolished.The building is, to everybody's eyes,still very impressive, being some 275'long.The whole cluster of buildings show a mixture of styles from several periods as the Abbey would have been built, extended and re-built many times throughout its long active life. Furness Abbey has survived through many troubled and turbulent times, and it is not without good cause that it is now known as the most haunted place in Furness.

The transepts,choir and western tower of the church stand almost to their original height but much of the nave has vanished.As originally designed the transepts were of two bays with apsidal eastern chapels, but they were later enlarged and given chapels with square ends. Much of the church dates from the second half of the twelth century, but the eastern end was rebuilt in the late fifteenth century and the western tower was built about 1500.

The east range contains a thirteenth-century chapter house, parlour and vaulted undercroft over which ran the dormitory, now destroyed.To the east is the reredorter or latrine block built over a stream. Little remains of the south range but further south is a fourteenth century infirmary with a chapel at the east end. East of this are foundations of an octagonal kitchen and beyond the stream is an earlier infirmary converted into the abbot's house.

The west range which had the kitchen and refectory of the lay brothers at the south end and a dormitory above, was probably one of the first buildings erected by the Cistercians.South-west of it was the lay brothers reredorter.

Barrow in Furness has long been synonymous with the building of ships.In fact Gladstone opened Barrow's first dock in 1867.The first ship to be built here was the steam ship 'Aries' originally constructed for Sir James Ramsden in 1870 by the Barrow Iron Shipbuilding Company.By 1882, 13 merchant ships were launched including an early submarine in 1886. By 1896 the shipbuilding yard was taken over by Vickers ,and it is the great covered building of Vickers Shipbuilding Engineering Ltd's (VSEL) Devonshire Dock Hall,that

today dominates the southern part of the town. Recently opened in Barrow is the Dock Museum, a spectacular steel structure building suspended over a Victorian graving dock.This permanent exhibition focused on the industrial history of Barrow with particular reference to its shipbuilding tradition. The exhibition draws on the extensive VSEL collection of glass photographic negatives, dating from the 1870's and on loan to the Museum Service since 1991.These images document the development of the shipyard and of a town dominated by shipbuilding,and are an extraordinary resource. The museum also has a fine collection of ship models...many of the world's greatest ships,built in Barrow.Collection vessels include the Emily Barratt, the last wooden trading schooner to be built in Britain and of particular importance to the West Cumbrian coast.

Many sites of interest are to be found in and around the town, including the isolated Piel Castle, and the peaceful expanse of Roanhead and Black Combe to the north. Within the Borough are a number of fascinating rural and urban nature trails which cover a wide range of interests all of which have been clearly marked for visitors.

Miles of unspoilt sandy beaches, bird sanctuaries, and nature reserves offer a haven for anybody searching for peace and tranquility. In all Walney Island adjacent has 11 miles of coast, including the picturesque hamlets of North Scale and Biggar Village.On Walney's eastern side is Walney Channel which is extensively used for yachting.

On the mainland Rampside is a small pleasant village that looks out on Morecambe Bay and a long stretch of sand. Rampside Hall is an old house with a range of 12 curious chimneys.

BASSENTHWAITE.

Map ref. D.7.
Next nearest town or village "Bothel"
Location.On A.591 Keswick to Bothel road.

A parish between Skiddaw,and the lake of Bassenthwaite in existence since the 8th century when marauding Vikings came to the valley....and stayed!!

The village is in a pefect setting,nestled as it is at the foot of Skiddaw,and just a mile from the four mile long lake,and six miles north of Keswick.

The village green is flanked by attractive terraced houses,and nearby is a stream (Halls beck) complete with ducks.

It was here in August of 1780 that the first Lake District regatta was held.In those days one of the main 'spectacles' involved several horses,which were towed out into the lake on rafts which were then sunk,forcing the poor animals to swim for the shore...wagers being placed on the first horse home.

At the Ireby/Robin Hood crossroads,lies Cobblers Hollow,where wood was collected for soling clogs.Here sheep stealers were hanged,and gives rise to the 'Ghost of Cobblers Hollow' which is said to haunt the area.

The village is served by two churches,the Norman St.Bega by the lakeshore is the better known of the two probably because it is considered the most romantically situated church in Cumbria.

Here will be seen a Norman chancel arch...a south aisle with broad arcading,and a handsome monument to Walter Vane,poignantly inscribed 'Mortally wounded at the Battle of Bayonne 14th April 1814.Died on the 19th of the same month in the 19th year of his age'

It is believed that in 1794 William and Dorothy Wordsworth visited the church of St.Bega,and which later featured in Wordsworth's 'A guide to the English lakes'

In 1835 Alfred Tennyson paid his first visit to the church which is probably the setting of the opening of Morte d'Arthur...Sir Bedivere carries King Arthur.

A story locals enjoy telling of St Bega church is the one about the arrival of the Irish Saint Bega who arrived here with her nuns looking for a place for her settlement.The then Lord of the Manor said that they might have as much ground as the snow covered on Midsummer's Day....and on Midsummer's Day...Lo and behold....Snow!!

Saint Bega was the daughter of a seventh century Irish Chieftain. At an early age,she resolved to devote herself to the service of God,and renouncing worldly pursuits,she 'wedded herself' to the cause of Jesus Christ.She fled from Ireland to avoid marriage to a Norse Prince,selected by her father.Having crossed the Irish Sea, she landed at St.Bees Head.She possessed a bracelet bearing an image of the Cross,which is recorded as having had a miraculous healing property.This bracelet was kept and held in veneration at St Bees Priory until the twelth century.

Close by is Bassenfell Manor built around 1842 by William Rathbone of shipbuilding fame,and which today is a Christian Holiday Centre.To the north stands Armathwaite Hall, former home of the Spedding and Vane families.Armathwaite Hall(now a luxury hotel) in itself has had a long and varied history over its (known) 450 years of life, having been owned by Sir Adam de Bassenthwaite originally,and then Sir Wilfred Lawson,together with three generations of the Spedding family and 150 years of the Fletcher - Vane family..

Situated close to St.Bega's is Mirehouse,built in 1666.It was a literary centre entertaining many writers including Carlyle, Tennyson,Wordsworth, and Southey.In fact it was here in 1835 that Tennyson wrote his Morte d'Arthur,which tells of the sword Excalibur being cast into the water.

The house even without its literary connections is well worth visiting.The central part of the house was built by the 8th Earl of Derby,originally as a lodge.The Spedding family,the current owners,have had the property in their family since 1802.The house is open to the public on Sundays and Wednesdays.The gardens too are a delight,especially 'Lovers Lane',Catstocks Woods and the Lakeside View.

The Calvert Trust Adventure Centre for Disabled People

in the English Lakes

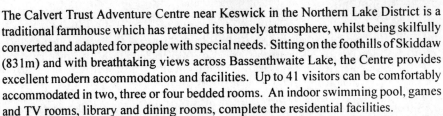

The Calvert Trust Adventure Centre near Keswick in the Northern Lake District is a traditional farmhouse which has retained its homely atmosphere, whilst being skilfully converted and adapted for people with special needs. Sitting on the foothills of Skiddaw (831m) and with breathtaking views across Bassenthwaite Lake, the Centre provides excellent modern accommodation and facilities. Up to 41 visitors can be comfortably accommodated in two, three or four bedded rooms. An indoor swimming pool, games and TV rooms, library and dining rooms, complete the residential facilities.

Many groups of people come to the Centre each year from all parts of the British Isles, with all natures and degrees of physical, mental and sensory disability. The emphasis during the multi activity courses is on ability, achievement and enjoyment arising from participation in adventure activities, and from sharing these experiences with friends. A wide range of activities is available under the care and guidance of experienced and suitably qualified staff. Bassenthwaite Lake provides splendid conditions for sailing, canoeing and other water activities in the Centre's own large fleet of craft. The surrounding hills, crags and forests are perfect for rock climbing, abseiling, mountain walking and orienteering. Further choices include archery, camping and fishing. The Centre has its own riding school (BHS approved) with modern stabling for eleven horses, an indoor school and outdoor riding areas and trails.

For further information please contact:
The Warden,
The Calvert Trust Adventure Centre for Disabled People
Little Crosthwaite, Keswick,
Cumbria, CA 12 4QD
Telephone: 07687 72254

PHEASANT INN

Bassenthwaite Lake
Nr. Cockermouth, Cumbria CA13 9YE
Telephone: (07687) 76234/ Fax (07687) 76002

Just off A66 Road *British Tourist Authority Commended Country Hotel*

Picture your ideal of a typical English Inn - and here it is. The Pheasant is long and low, with a rustic porch, whitewashed walls and mossy slate roof. Only a minor road separates it from the lakeside.

There is a snug bar serving real ale, which has tobacco-brown walls and ceiling, small windows and oak settles. Two quieter sitting-rooms are furnished with antiques and William Morris or floral fabrics; there is soft lighting and an open fire. But most people congregate in the largest sitting-room overlooking the gardens at the back (exceptionally good light lunches are served here). This is a long, airy room with a beamed ceiling that has developed from the kitchen of the 400-year old farm from which the inn originated. Blue cretonne chairs are grouped on oriental rugs over the parquet floor. At one end logs blaze under a copper hood. There are old hunting-prints and shotguns on the white walls and Mrs. Wilson's big flower arrangements stand everywhere.

In the beamed dining room, the tables are laid with damask and candles in brass candlesticks. A typical meal might comprise game broth, smoked haddock vol-au-vent, venison with orange sauce, bilberry tart and cream (there are several choices at each course).

The bedrooms are outstanding. Each differs but is predominantly - crisp, clean, delicate white - with occasional touches of colour in the curtains. The overall effect is light and refreshing. Modern rooms, also popular, are in a bungalow in the grounds.

Cumbrians both, Mr. and Mrs. Barrington Wilson have been running the Pheasant in this style for so many years that it has become well known to regulars who return every spring or autumn in particular - so it is wise to book well ahead.

Outside the inn a flower garden with iron seats slopes down towards beechwoods belonging (as does the inn) to Lord Inglewood's estate. These are open to walkers, who can wander uphill looking for the spring from the pure water of which the farmers used to brew the beer that eventually caused the farm to change to an inn. Across the road are the prehistoric earthworks of Castle How. Visitors often enjoy watching sheepdog trials, agricultural shows, hound trails and foxhunts on foot - as well as exploring other lakes and the Lakeland towns of Cockermouth and Keswick.

LAKESIDE
Bassenthwaite Lake,
Near Cockermouth
CA13 9YD
Telephone: 07687 76358

Lakeside Licensed Guest House

An elegant Country House offering friendly and relaxing hospitality, having oak floor and pannelled hall with superb views across Bassenthwaite Lake to Skiddaw and surrounding Fells. Keswick is only a short drive away and the peaceful western fells and Lakes of Buttermere and Crummock water. 8 tastefully furnished bedrooms with en-suite, T.V. and Tea and Coffee facilities. A pleasant lounge in which to relax and delicious home cooking with a 5 course evening meal and wine if required.

Open January to November. Full Central Heating. One of our rooms on the Ground floor. Private Car Park. Residents Licence.

Brochure on request from your hosts Joan and Eric Murray

BAYCLIFF.

Map ref. E13.
Next nearest Town or Village "Bardsea"
Bus Service. Cumberland Bus Service No.11
Ulverston - Coast Road - Roa Island - Barrow
Location. A.5087. Ulverston to Rampside road.

Over the many centuries that the village of Baycliff has existed, the villagers would have paid their tithes to the rector of Aldingham...in fact the barn to be seen in the rectory grounds is probably the tithe barn from that era.

History records that much poverty existed in the village. A workhouse was here which provided for the older parishioners and it was not uncommon for the orphan children to be put to work as parish apprentices...or sent to the mills at Backbarrow. Quarrying and mining of iron ore provided the work here. The carts of ore were brought down to the shore at Baycliff where the flat bottomed boats would take the iron ore to the furnaces at Backbarrow. Visitors will notice that the soil here is still red today from the ore.

Two inns at Baycliff, one of them the 'Farmers Arms' was run for almost 200 years by the Porter family.

There are many lovely walks in this region...with rights of way clearly marked. The area is a great feeding ground for seabirds.

BEAUMONT.

Map ref.E.4.
Location. One and a half miles east of Burgh.
Next nearest Town or Village "Burgh-by-Sands

Beaumont...which means 'beautiful hill' is a small village situated on the west bank of the river Eden, one and a half miles east of Burgh, and four miles north west of Carlisle.

The line of Hadrian's Wall runs through the village, and follows the bank of the Eden from Kirkandrews to the church. whence it turns west to Burgh by Sands.

The church here is situated on an early mediaeval burgh which was built out of a mile castle on the Roman wall.Here too was a ford often used by Scots raiders wishing to avoid hostile Carlisle.A great hoard of English,Scottish and foreign coins covering the period Henry 111 to Edward 111 were found here in 1884 which gives rise to much speculation as to whether there could still be more to find.

The village has seen some of the great figures of history passing by, for here came Edward 1 on his last journey, before he died at Burgh-by-Sands, and here a few years later came Robert Bruce to camp for five days.

Stones from the wall were often used to build the local houses.In a garden wall opposite the church is part of an ornamental inscription which was discovered in the river a 100 years ago.

It was in 1823 that the Carlisle canal was opened for the first time,which allowed the passage of shipping up to 100 tons into the canal basin.Ships would have been sailing through the fields below Beaumont.A lock was built at the west of the village, and the lock-keepers cottage still remains.

BECKERMET.

Map ref. B.9.
Next nearest Town or Village "Egremont"
Location. Two miles south of Egremont.

The parish of Beckermet occupied for 5,000 years according to pre-historic finds...is situated just two miles south of Egremonand is actualy two villages.St John's Beckermet,and St Bridget Beckermet, named somewhat naturally after its respective churches.

The church of St John has many interesting pre-Norman stones in the churchyard, which include the old font, a collection of corbels,coffin lids, together with fragments of eleven crosses.

The 13th century St Bridgets church stands between the sea and the village...has four services a year, though the churchyard is still occassionally used for burials.

These two churches are reputed to have been a nunnery(St Bridget) and a monastery (St John) in pre-Norm..n times,though unfortunately there is nothing to confirm this. Both however were servedby secular monks from the Cistercian abbey at Calder until the suppression of that Abbey in the 16th century.

In the churchyard of St Bridget's stand two interesting cross shafts;the heads vanished long ago. They are of a form not found anywhere else in the locality.One carries an inscription that has long baffled antiquarians..so far five translations have been produced.

The natural mounds located hereabouts actually mark the motte of Caernarvon Castle, the roman area itself offering views towards Scafell Pike and the Roman fort of Hard Knott.

Visitors should note ,on common land opposite the river, the old open truck, a relic of Beckermet's iron ore mining days.A railway engine is reputed to be buried in the bogland close by.

Village events here include fete,sports days,and Christmas fair and party.

BEETHAM

Map ref. G.12.
Next nearest Town or Village "Milnthorpe"
Bus service. Cumberland Bus Service No 555
Kendal - Lancaster
Location. On the A.6 Milnthorpe-Beetham road.
Gala days/festivals.Beetham Sports. Saturday
before Bank Holiday monday in August.

Beetham,which means flat area, is an attractive village lying in the vale of the river Bela.It was here on the banks of the river that King Arthur defeated the Saxons in AD650.

A 12th century church together with what was at one time Beetham Hall...the Great Hall nowadays is a barn! are part of a mid fourteenth century fortified manor house. Beetham Hall was a noble place in the 14th century.Fragments of an outer wall 70 yards long and about 15 feet high surround it and it has a barn with traceried windows, a huge kitchen, a tower with an ancient fireplace, and a chapel.Much of the Hall was built in the 15th century, but a simple wing with a quaint 17th century porch is Jacobean. Down the centuries the Beethams, the Stanleys and the Cliffords have at one time owned this fortified place, part of which was damaged during the Civil War.

The deBeetham family who were mentioned in the Domesday Book held the manor for eleven generations.A Baldwin deBeetham actually fought at the Battle of Hastings.Thomas deBeetham was a Knight of the Shire of Westmorland and was granted a charter for a market and fair in Beetham in the early fourteenth century.

The current church St Michael and All Saints was badly damaged in the Civil War when Parliamentary troops are said to have stabled their horses in it.Inevitably they are also blamed for the damage to the two 15th century effigies said to be of Sir Thomas Beecham and his lady.

Dame Clara Butt the opera singer was married here in 1900,with Ivor Novello as her page boy!

A fault in the limestone causes the river here to fall 16 feet, creating a spectacular waterfall.Nearby is 'The Fairy Steps' a natural staircase in the limestone crag which is massed with ferns throughout the summer months...it is said locally that if you can get down the steps without touching the sides,then all your wishes will come true.

The Heron Corn Mill was founded here by the Canons of Conishead in 1220, aptly named, for to this day herons still fish here.The only shop here is the post office located in a 18th century building.The building is unusual inasmuch that it still has a block and platform above the door for hoisting up sacks. Just out of the village upwards to Slackhead is a lovely little shrine.Inside the cell is the figure of St.Lioba,in the habit of a Benedictine nun, holding a bell.

HERON CORN MILL & MUSEUM OF PAPER MAKING
By Waterhouse Mill, Beetham, Nr. Milnthorpe
Tel: 05395 63363

HERON CORN MILL on the banks of the River Bela is one of the few working mills in the area. There is documentary evidence to show that a Mill existed on the site prior to 1096. In 1220 the Lord of the Manor of Haverbrack granted lands to the Canons of Coningshead for the erection of a corn mill. A little later the abundance of water falling over the weir was used to drive a falling mill, and later still to drive the paper mills which were predecessors of Henry Cooke's Waterhouse Mills on the opposite side of the weir. The Mill was referred to in archives several times during the Middle Ages. The name "Heron Mill" derives from the heronry which existed in the woods to the north of the mill until 1726. At that time the mill was already part of the land holdings attached to Dallam Tower.

HERON CORN MILL has been restored as a working waterwheel-driven corn mill. In 1975 the Mill was opened by Princess Alexandra and has continued up till the present time to show the mechanics of a water driven corn mill to the public who have come to see this unique piece of South Lakeland's industrial heritage.

In 1988, to commemorate the 500 years of paper making, the Barn on the site was refurbished to house the "MUSEUM OF PAPER MAKING' which now adds another dimension to the site. This museum shows the process of making paper, both modern and historical, by means of wall displays. It also attempts to show the sources of the raw material and the species of trees used in the production of pulp. Various 'tools of the trade' are on show including a number of moulds used in the making of paper by hand. Occasional demonstrations of the hand making of paper are mounted each season, and anyone can try their hand at the craft during these demonstrations.

Open Daily (Except Monday)Open Bank Holidays
Easter -End Sept. 11am - 5pm

BEWCASTLE.

Map ref. G.2.
Next nearest Town or Village "Roadhead"
Location. 20 miles north-east of Carlisle.

Sometimes known as 'Shopyord'...beware the sign posts show both!!.A gazetteer lists the village under this latter name...probably named originally after a blacksmith's shop.

Bewcastle lies 20 miles north-east of Carlisle, dangerously close to the England-Scottish border (as would have been the case many years ago) At Bewcastle the Romans used the natural six sided plateau above the Kirk beck on which to build their fort. It was directly linked with Hadrian's wall at Birdoswald, via Gillallee Beacon and the maiden Way. The plateau is nearly six acres.Excavations show that a fort was originally of timber with turf ramparts, and the gates probably of stone.The fort was given up in 142AD when the Army moved north to the Antonine Wall, but was re-occupied in 163AD following the withdrawal from the Clyde-Forth Line.During the second and third centuries there was upwards of one thousand men stationed at Bewcastle.

At the time of the Norman Conquest a castle was built in the north-eastern corner of the Roman fort and Beuth declared himself "Lord of Bewcastle Dale'.Roman ditches were used to form two sides of the castle and two more were dug to make a square emplacement. The earth from the ditches was thrown inwards and a timber fortification erected on top. This was adapted and eventually rebuilt as a stone castle during the reign of Edward 1. The remains of the castle can be seen to the north of the church.

A church was also built during the reign of Edward.1.using stones from the Roman fort. The world renowned Bewcastle Cross is in the churchyard and is in a good state of repair considering it is 1300 years old.Also known as Alcfrith Cross, the cross carries what is thought to be the earliest known carving of Christ in England. The head which once crowned its 14 foot shaft has gone unfortunately, but the carving of the shaft is exceptionally well preserved, enough to show at a glance that the sculptor who fashioned it was a master of his craft. The most interesting portion of it is undoubtedly the west face where three of the four panels are carved with human figures.One shows John the Baptist holding a Holy Lamb, another Christ standing on a lion and an adder, with his right hand raised in blessing,

BEWCASTLE / BLAWITH / BLENCOW

whilst the third shows a man holding a hawk on his wrist, his hair falling over what looks like a cape on his shoulders. The fourth panel is the key to it all, for its inscription tells us why the cross is here...it was set up as a victory column, long before the days of Alfred. There is incidentally an excellent replica of the cross in Tullie House Museum, Carlisle.

The names of farms and cottages here evoke memories of long gone days, Names like winter-shields, Pele-o-Hill (with its remains of a pele tower) and Askerton Castle...now a farmhouse.

"Raiding and reiving' raged throughout the borderlands in the sixteenth century and many farms in the area were fortified. Remains of pele towers survive either as isolated ruins or else are incorporated into farm buildings,

Up until the nineteenth century the people of Bewcastle were thought of as rough as dangerous. It used to be said that only women-folk were buried here...the men were all hanged sooner or later at Carlisle

Here and there old lime kilns remain, and the farm named Kilnstown, and a pub called Lime Kiln Inn is sufficient evidence of a now defunct industry.

BEWCASTLE CROSS

Visitor's shouldn't miss the small museum exhibiting items of Bewcastle history in the grounds of the church.

BLAWITH.

Map ref. E.11
Next nearest Town or Village "Lowick Bridge"
Bus service. Cumberland Bus Service No.512
Ulverston - Coniston
Location. Lowick Green to Torver road.

Blawith...nick-named 'Black Forest' is a parish situated at the head of the Crake valley, and extends to the south western shores of Coniston water. The village consists of little more than twelve houses situated alongside the road, together with several farmsteads in close proximity.

The church of St John the Baptist, built in 1883 to replace an earlier chapel which was in existence prior to 1577 is now closed. The ruins of the chapel can be found up the hill leading south out of the village, hidden behind trees, and with the tombstones overgrown with brambles.

The school now closed, and converted into a house was rebuilt in 1859 . Many mediaeval cairns and enclosures hereabouts.

BLENCOW.

Map ref. F.7.
Nearest Town or Village "Greystoke"
Location. 4 miles west of Penrith.

Situated in Dacre parish between the main road to Keswick and the main road to Wigton, approximately four miles west of Penrith.

Blencow is a pretty little village, with its village green and the river Petteril running through the centre under a hump-backed bridge. It is the river that divides the village. Little Blencow to the north is actually in Greystoke parish, whilst Great Blencow to the south is in Dacre.

The 16th century Blencow Hall...an imposing building is situated about 400 yards out of Blencow. The northern section is the oldest part...believed to have originated as a pele tower. Today it is a farmhouse.

Burbank House was a one-time important Grammar School. First built in 1577 and re-built in 1795, it continued as a school until 1913 when it merged with the Penrith Grammar School. The school bell-tower is still intact. Among its famous pupils were the great Quaker George Whitehead, who did much

to improve the status of the Friends, and the great lawyer Edward Law, who was leading counsel for Warren Hastings and became Lord Chief Justice, raised to the peerage as Lord Ellenborough.
The attractive country house...Ennim, located here is the current home of Viscount and Viscountess Whitelaw, one time local Member of Parliament and Deputy Prime Minister.
Many stone quarries, all now defunct, are to be found in and around Blencow.Many stones were used to build parts of Keswick.

BLINDCRAKE

Map ref.C.6.
Next nearest Town or Village "Bridekirk"
Location.Eastern side of the A595.

Blindcrake is a small village of around 100 inhabitants to the north east of Cockermouth, built on the site of a one time British settlement.
Sheltered by Moote Hill and Clints Crags, Blindcrake today is basically a farming village...there are seven farms nowadays with farming mainly mixed with dairy, suckler beef and sheep.
The eighteenth century houses and farms surround a neat little green in one of the most north-westerly villages in the National Park. Many of the houses have 'date-stones' showing the years 1719,1728,and 1729.

The most imposing house in the village is undoubtedly Blindcrake Hall with its elegant Georgian facade. To the rear of the Hall is the town well which was the villages only water supply until 1936.
The village green was at one time a pond known as Mortar Dub, and was used for watering stock and washing horse's legs after ploughing.It was drained in 1900 and replaced by four drinking troughs.At one time the village had the unusual custom of burying its dead horses in the village,most of them in the south-east corner. One such gravestone has been marked'Marmaduke' and belonged to the vicar of Isel.
The most famous character here would have been Adam Slee, who died as recently as 1988.He lived at Woodlands and his flair for painting was shown on the walls of his house. Coach parties would stop just to admire his handiwork.

BOLTON.

Map ref. H.8.
Next nearest Town or Village "Cliburn"
Location. 4 miles north-west of Appleby.

The village of Bolton lies on the banks of the river Eden four miles to the north-west of Appleby.
Evidence abounds that there was a settlement in Bolton over 1200 years ago, though the church of All Saints only goes back to the 12th century. It is relatively famous for its stone relief of two knights jousting...one of only two such reliefs in the country...and an indication of age is the fact that the other one is situated in Dorset and is dated 1110. One sculpture depicts a tournament and shows two mounted knights in chain mail with kite shields and lances.They are charging each other and the one of inferior rank, with a banner on his lance, appears to have broken the guard of his opponent. Another striking feature of the church is the oak screen in the chancel. It is of unusual design with open tracery,quatrefoils and geometrical patterns.Also in the chancel is a massive 16th century chest with three locks, and against the south wall by the main door is a padlocked poorbox dated 1634.Oak beams in the roof are said to have sailed the seas in the bottom of a ship.
The 14th century ruins of Bewly(or Builly) Castle is located just over a mile south west. Its name derives from the French 'beau lieu'...meaning beautiful place.One time home of the Bishops of Carlisle, then later the deBuille family...though they died out in 1213. It was here that the Bishops found convenient refuge during Scottish incursions. As long ago as the 13th century it was an episcopal residence with a chapel and Lord's Chamber restored by Bishop Strickland in 1402. Parts of these rooms still remain and there are broken arches with grandeur still left in them and barrel vaulted cellars still used to this day by the nearby farm, which itself was built from stone and have walls of five feet thick.

BOOT

Map ref C.10.

Next nearest Town or Village "Eskdale"

Location. Off the Eskdale to Hardknott road.

Boot is a beautiful little village just north of the Eskdale valley road. Parking here being next to impossible, most motorised vistors park in the car park at Dalegarth station a short distance away. Beyond a short range of cottages, and over a pack-horse bridge will be found Eskdale Mill, an ancient corn mill on the Whillan Beck which operated from the sixteenth century until the 1920's. Milling has been a feature of the Eskdale valley life since the 12th century. The first documented evidence of Eskdale Mill itself dates from 1578 when brothers Henry and Robert Vicars were the tenants paying an annual rent 8 shillings! (40p in todays currency).

The mill continued to grind cereals until the early 1920's when a dynamo was installed for the last miller Edward Bibby who died in 1924. The upper wheel of the mill continued to make electricity until 1955 when mains power came to the valley.

Inside the mill today will be found a quite informative exhibition with display stands and old photographs, and the atmosphere is well re-created even to the point of cobwebs and a moth-eaten bowler hat on a chair.

A delightful wooded area to the rear of the mill is well worth a visit. Impressive waterfalls provide a powerful head of water to feed ponds and sluices, necessary to power two huge water wheels. A wonderful setting for a picnic.

Boot is in fact a railway terminus, The Ravenglass and Eskdale Railway winds its way from Ravenglass on the coast to Dalegarth Station, close by a seven mile journey completed in 40 minutes by miniature train.

Two miles east of the village is Hardknott Pass.....site of the Roman fort of Medibogdum.....also known as Hardknott Castle.

ESKDALE MILL

A FASCINATING HISTORIC CORN MILL....

Eskdale Mill, dating back to 1578 is located near the head of one of the most picturesque and dramatic valleys of the Lake District.

Just a quarter of a mile away is Dalegarth Station, terminus of the famous Ravenglass and Eskdale steam railway. The Station car park is ideally situated for visitors and arriving by car (or train) to visit the mill just a short walk away.

Why not take the opportunity of visiting one of the very few remaining two wheel water corn mills and learn more about life in Cumbria, its industry and its people. Experience the charm of the tiny hamlet of Boot, surely one of the loveliest parts of Lakeland.

A delightfully wooded area to the rear of the mill is well worth a visit. Impressive waterfalls provide a powerful head of water to feed ponds and sluices, necessary to power the two huge water wheels. What a wonderful setting for a picnic.

Small shop, with a range of postcards and gifts, ice creams and light refreshments.

Opening hours: 11.00 a.m. to 5.00 p.m. Closed Mondays.

April to end of September.

Further information: The Manager, Eskdale Mill, Boot Village, Holmrook, Cumbria.

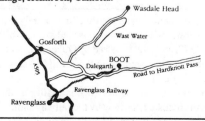

Character Country Cottages
Bridge End Farm, Boot, Eskdale,
Cumbria CA19 1TG Tel/Fax: 09467 23100

ENGLAND FOR EXCELLENCE
SELF-CATERING
HOLIDAY OF THE YEAR 1992
SILVER
sponsored by Rombersons

In pretty Eskdale - one of Lakeland's loveliest valleys - these fine Grade II listed barns, dating back to Elizabethan times, have been imaginatively converted and comprehensively equipped to the English Tourist Board's exacting "4 keys - Highly Commended" standard. Reached down a quaint cobbled lane, they are tucked away in the friendly and tiny hamlet of Boot, which nestles in a picturesque setting beneath the mighty Scafell Pike. "Silver Award Winners" in the E.T.B.'s 1992 'England for Excellence' awards, these are romantic cottages of tremendous character and quality, featuring ancient beams and local pink granite stonework, together with fine oak kitchens, period style bathrooms and sumptuous furnishings. They enjoy the benefit of a peaceful walled garden and a scenic riverside paddock with a picnic spot; all in the most glorious surroundings. Boot is a delightful village, with a restored corn mill, a packhorse bridge, church, shop/post office, art/craft gallery and traditional inns. For dining out, a choice of five inns in Boot and nearby Eskdale Green serve good food, from bar meals to a full restaurant service.

This is magnificent walking country - visitors may take a leisurely stroll across the lane to the waterfalls of the tumbling Whillan beck and

a little further (on level ground) to the stepping stones of the River Esk; swimming is possible in the various natural rock pools of these streams and in Boot's waterfall plunge pool. Eskdale descends from the highest and wildest mountains in the district to the sands of Ravenglass in a swift transition from grandeur to beauty. In Wainwrights words this "perfect Arcadia in the hills is the finest of all valleys for those whose special joy is to travel on foot and a paradise for artists".

Within walking distance are: Scafell Pike, England's highest mountain; its steepest mountain road, Hardknott Pass, and its deepest lake, the dramatic Wastwater. There is also the well preserved Hardknott Roman fort, and the 60ft Stanley Force Waterfall.

The all year round service provided by the Ravenglass and Eskdale narrow-gauge steam railway (which begins just a quarter of a mile away) is one of England's most beautiful train journeys and within a 10-mile radius are opportunities for numerous outdoor activities, including climbing, canoeing, abseiling and riding.

FOLD END GALLERY
BOOT, ESKDALE, CUMBRIA, CA19 1TG TEL: Eskdale 094-67 23213

Open Tuesday to Sunday 10.00 a.m. to 5.30 p.m.
Contemporary paintings, ceramics, glass, sculpture and Jewellery
Michael & Anne James

BOOTLE.
Map ref.C11.
Next nearest Town or Village "Corney"
Bus service. Cumberland Bus Service No.16
Trains. Railway Station
Location. Astride the A.59

Bootle, the name means 'the dwelling'..is a former market town with its charter issued by Edward 111 in 1347, and later renewed by Queen Elizabeth 1 in 1567. Once said to be the smallest market town in England.

Bootle, in fact, consists of two small villages, the old on the roadside, the new by the railway station. The town(s) are situated just one mile south-east of

St. Michael's church which is Norman in origin. The tall 15th century font here has shields around the bowl carved with initials and old lettering signifying the Trinity. A fine little brass portrait is shining on the chancel wall. It shows Sir Hugh Askew who was knighted by Edward VI at the Battle of Pinkie, when Protector Somerset marched against the Scots, slew thousands of them, and gained nothing by his victory. But Sir Hugh gained his knighthood, and here he stands in his armour with his hands in prayer.

About a mile to the north is the remains of Seaton (or Lekely) Nunnery....a Benedictine foundation dating back to before 1227, and dedicated to St Leonard.

Dominating the skyline is the mass of Black Combe at a height of 1970 feet. From here travellers will have the most extensive view from any point in Britain......14 counties in England and Scotland can be seen, together with Snowdon, Isle of Man, and the mountains of Mourne..Such a view may well expplain why William Wordsworth visited here on occasions.

BOTHEL.

Map ref. C.6.
Next nearest Town or Village "Plumbland"
Location. Where the Keswick road joins the A.595.

Bothel...from the name 'Bot-Hill',signifying the beacon on the hill...in fact in mediaeval times the inhabitants were required to perform a service called 'seawake'. or seawatch, such duty entailing lighting fires as warnings which could then be seen for many miles across the Solway. Todays visitors are not expected to perform such duties but they will nevertheless enjoy the fine views across the Solway to Criffel and southern Scotland.

These days Bothel is separated from its neighbour Torpenhow by the busy A595 Whitehaven-Carlisle road, but nevertheless is inextricably linked by the circa 1120 Norman church of St.Michael.which was built during the reign of William Rufus or in the reign of Henry 1.. Most of this early church remains, namely the western end of the chancel,the chancel arch and masonry adjoining, along with the walling above the nave arcades.

One of the most interesting features of the church is the nave ceiling, adorned with conventional flowers and gildings.. Of interest is the fact that a Priest-in-Charge of the parish between 1735-1757, while a former Dean of Carlisle was Vicar, was a Reverend Ralph Brocklebank, the father of the Founder of the Brocklebank (later Cunard) Steamship Line.

Up until some 60-70 years ago the village would have been very different to what the visitor will see today. Bothel Parks Farm for example had its own water wheel which allowed the farmer to grind his own grain.The grinding stones are now a feature of the farm's garden.

St Bathan's Lodge,Park View farm, and Greenfell Cottage have all been pubs at one time or another over the years.The only pub these days is the one known as the "Greyhound Inn'

BOUTH.

Map ref. E.12.
Next nearest Town or Village "Oxenpark"
Bus service. Cumberland Bus Service No.514 Bouth - Rusland - Ulverston
Location.2 miles west of Newby Bridge.

Bouth is a small village(of Norse origin) situated in the Furness Fells...once famous for its woodland industries.

Years ago,after farming,coppice products supplied wood for bobbins, barrel hoops, staves and ships fenders.In fact nearby at Sparkbridge the trade of bobbin making, together with the making of reels and wrought iron work is still continued at Spark Bridge Mill.

Oak bark was used for tanning leathers and Bouth still has its Bark House to this day. A few Kiln Cottages survive too.. Close to Bouth House, horses were kept to pull the coppice wood up the hill.The hill is still called Horses Hill.

Bouth was at one time called the capital of Colton. It has a very attractive village green and has for many years won the coveted 'Best Kept Village in South Lakeland'.Adjacent to the village green stands The White Hart with its unusual inn sign....white hart,couchant, wearing a golden crown round its neck, and tethered to the ground by a golden chain.In olden days the White Hart would have been an important coach stop.

Close by on the Broughton to Furness road is the 14th century 'Farmers Arms' originally a farmhouse with spinning gallery.

BOWNESS ON SOLWAY.

Map ref. D.3.
Next nearest Town or Village "Port Carlisle"
Bus service. Cumberland Bus Service No.93 Bowness on Solway/Anthorn - Carlisle
Location.On the Cardurnock to Port Carlisle road.

ST. MICHAEL'S CHURCH

Bowness on Solway has the distinct flavour of a border town.Its almost possible to lob a stone into Scotland across the Solway marshes.Years ago, in ancient times ,when it was England's turn to settle differences,the villagers would have been able to watch Annan burn!(as in 1547).

Just before the Cardurnock road begins to rise to Bowness, you will note on the left a great embankment crowned with gorse, and hawthorn jutting out into the firth.There is a similar one on the Scottish side, for this is where the Solway Viaduct, a huge iron bridge provided a rail link between the two countries from 1869 to 1921.It was intended for the transportation of West Cumbrian iron ore to the Lanarkshire steelworks, but it later carried passengers also.The engineer was Sir James Brunlees and at that time his achievement in constructing a bridge across the Solway's shifting sands was considered a mighty feat, notwithstanding the fact that he had also built the longest bridge in-Britain too.

At Bowness the firth is little more than a mile wide, and is the last westward place where it can be forded.The Romans were aware of this too and built one of the biggest forts here at the believed end of Hadrian's Wall.There are many humps to be seen in the fields relating back to those days for the wall was used as a quarry by builders.Some Roman masonry,in fact, was used to build St Michael's Church.These days the village occupies the fort site and there are Roman stones also in the walls of many of the houses hereabouts,one of them a tablet of the 3rd cohort of the 2nd Augustan Legion.In a roadside barn wall near the Kings Arms Inn is a small inscribed altar.The Roman guard-room was near the school.

In the days of the Border raids some stranger things than cattle were taken across the firth.In the year 1626 some Scotsmen saw fit to visit Bowness and take the Bowness church bells.Rather naturally this irritated the local men who launched out in chase of the Scots.To lighten their boat which was being overtaken, the Scots visitors threw the bells overboard into the Solway, at the place now called 'Bell Dub'or 'Bell Pool'.A short time later the Bowness men paid a visit to Dornock and Middlebie in order that St Michael's church could be fully equipped once more. They were fortunate and arrived home safely complete with the bells.

There are smuggling stories too.In the churchyard a headstone of Snaefell slate marks the grave of a Manx smuggler who was drowned on a free-trading run to this coast. It is said that his young widow had the stone brought over by boat and then carried it to the churchyard herself.

At Drumburgh, four miles from Bowness, is the site of the smallest Roman station on the great Wall, a few mounds being left to mark it.Here too amid the houses clustered on the hillside, rises a tall gaunt farmhouse that was once a castle, with a fine flight of steps leading outside to the second storey where an ancient doorway has kept its old studded door.Over the doorway is a coat of arms and on a small parapet of the roof are two stone eagles keeping watch above the hamlet.

BOWNESS-ON-WINDERMERE.

MAP ref.F10
Next nearest Town or Village "Windermere"
Bus Service: Cumberland Bus Service No W1/W2,
108 505 506 518 W1/W2
Location A592 Ambleside Road
Tourist Information Service: Bowness Bay
Gala Days /Festivals:
Lake Festival & Flower Show last Sat/Sun in June

BOWNESS BAY

Everybody at some time in their travels through the Lake District visits Bowness on Windermere. Unashamably given over to tourism it has a cheerful cosmopolitan character far different from the 11th century when the Vikings were the first to settle here.

Windermere is named after the Viking chief Vinand, who named the lake 'Vinand's Mere' and for centuries remained little more than a settlement. It wasn't until the arrival of the railway in the 19th century that it grew into a sizeable village to cater for the influx of visitors mostly from Lancashire and Yorkshire. Many wealthy industrialists settled here building large homes many of which today are luxury hotels.

For example, Henry William Schneider, an industrailist who made a vast fortune in iron-ore brought Belsfield in 1869, that impressive mansion now a hotel which overlooks the Bay. With a style which typified the elegance of those days, he would walk from his residence each morning to the jetty where his steam yacht Esperance was moored, preceeded by his butler carrying his breakfast on a silver salver. He ate a leisurely meal as he sailed down to Lakeside where his special train would be

awaiting to carry him to Furness Abbey, from whence he would take his brougham the rest of the way to his office in Barrow. Schneider's name has over the years become immortalised for his connection with the Schneider Trophy awarded to the forerunner of the Vickers Supermarine Spitfire, renowned of course from the Battle of Britain in the last war.

St Martin's Church was built in 1843 and replaced a previous church which had been destroyed by fire. Inside will be found local heraldry together with the arms along with the Stars and Stripes of one John Washington dated 1403, an ancestor of the first President of the U.S.A. Under the chancel too is the mass grave of 47 people who were drowned when a ferry in which they were travelling capsized on the way to a wedding in Hawkshead. Its an interesting 15th century building with its most remarkable feature being the considerable quantity of ancient window glass which it contains in greater part brought here from Cartmel Priory around 1623. The oldest part of Bowness is behind the church and is known as Lowside. Here will be found a number of narrow streets and cottages which are more in keeping with Old Bowness. The New Hall Inn, better known as Hole In't Wall due to the time when ale was served through a hole in the wall into the adjoining smithy. Back in 1857 Thomas Longmire was the landlord and was a famous Cumberland wrestler. Charles Dickens, a great admirer of Longmire often stayed at the Inn. The oldest building in Bowness is now better known as 'The Spinnery Restaurant'. Laurel Cottage was the first local school here. Today a delightful guest house establishment it was originally a fee paying Grammar school founded in 1637. Between 80-100 scholars, boys and girls were taught at 'LaurelCottage'. There were no scholarships unless they could write with the facility of two syllables. School hours were 8am to 12noon and 1pm to 4pm in the winter and 9am to 12noon and 1pm to 5pm in the summer. Schooling would of course have to coincide with daylight hours. The earliest name recorded of a school master was Thomas Hobson in 1705 who earned the princely sum of £10 per year. Children were educated here until 1836 when a retired business man from Bolton built a new Grammer School on a hill above Laurel Cottage.

BOWNESS-ON-WINDERMERE

"THE TERN" WATERHEAD PIER HEAD

Bowness Bay together with the Lake feature in many books about the life of the village. One such tale is told about local boatmen who would go out at night looking for a creature known as Twizzie-Whizie. Said to be a cross between a hedgehog and a bird with a squirrels tale. No doubt the boatmen encouraged the story as a means of promoting boat hire.

This is the boating centre for England's busiest lake for at the height of the season it has over 1500 craft upon its waters.

There has in fact been ferries across Windermere for at least 500 years. The earliest recorded craft were in fact rowing boats in the days when passengers would be expected to help with the rowing!.

Bowness is a regular intermediate stop for the passenger vehicles which run throughout the season from Lakeside at the southern end of Windermere to Waterhead at the head of the ten and half mile long lake.

Opposite Bowness Bay are the pretty islands which appear almost to cut the lake in two. On Belle Isle is the unusually designed Round House built in 1774 for a Mr English, but later acquired by the Curwen family. J.C. Curwen was responsible for much of the tree planting which now beautifies the island and the east slopes of Claife Heights above the lakes west shore.

Whilst here a visit is suggested to the fascinating Windermere Steamboat Museum, half a mile to the north of Bowness, on the lake shore. It has Victorian and Edwardian steamboats and other vintage craft including the earlier mentioned 'Esperance' made famous by Arthur Ransome in his book 'Swallows and Amazons'.

The area is of course renowned for its hotels of which there are hundreds. Some have stories of their own to tell. One private house on the lakeside was the scene of a particularly gruesome murder, the owner being butchered in a rather unpleasant way. The reasons for the crime are unknown, but lurid stories always spread like wildfire and one of these is the Old England Hotel was haunted by the murdered man. Fortunately today, the hotel is free of that uninvited guest!

The White Lion (later to become the Royal) was honoured by a visit from Queen Adelaide in 1840 and the Crown was patronised by the Rothschilds along with many American Presidents. The Old England had the Kaiser for lunch...he was a guest of Lord Lonsdale at the time...Apparently whilst out shooting that morning he had shot 67 rabbits in less than half an hour. Local gossip has it that the Earl's gamekeepers had released hundreds of the unfortunate creatures under the guns so that the guest was not disappointed in his 'sport'.

So many tourist attractions, almost too many to mention. Of particular importance however is the 'The Old Laundry' Visitor Centre the home of the 'World of Beatrix Potter' with Peter Rabbit and Mrs Tiggy Winkle very much in attendance. Beatrix Potter enthusiasts should additionally look out for the shops 'Peter Rabbit and Friends' who have an enormous display of souvenirs relative to her work. Going north from Windermere will be found the National Park Visitor Centre, Brockhole. There are displays and lectures, and a lovely garden by the lake shore with superb views.

LAKE WINDERMERE

HIGH ADVENTURE
R.M. TRAVEL
RAYRIGG ROAD
BOWNESS-ON-WIND-
ERMERE,
CUMBRIA
TEL: (05394) 46588

SPECTACULAR BALLOON FLIGHTS OVER LAKELAND

"Let HIGH ADVENTURE give you the experience of a lifetime with a balloon flight over the stunning English Lake District. Flights take place all year round, mornings and evenings, weather permitting. Each flight lasts approximately 1 hour and afterwards you can celebrate with a glass of champagne and a commemorative flight certificate.

Within a few miles of HIGH ADVERTURE's carefully selected take-off sites lie the homes, fells and lakes which are at the heart of much of Britian's most creative genius. Our flights include an inflight commentary on points of interest whilst providing almost effortless access to the natural wonders of the Lake District.

Ballooning, man's oldest form of flight, relies on drifting weith gentle winds (5-15mph) at a height of between 500 and 2000 feet above the ground.
Looking down on a miniature landscape, from a wholly new perspective...everything looks different...glinting mirrored reflections on the water and the map-like layout of streets and houses. With a birds-eye-view, wild life, unaware of your presence, go about their daily routine below.

Majestic cloud formations or silver mist add to the visual delights as you take in views which perhaps no other human being has seen before. Certainly part of the thrill of a balloon adventure is the unknown destination. The pilot cannot predict exactly where the winds will take him, but uses his skill to guide the balloon to a gentle landing in a sheltered field or on a heather slope.

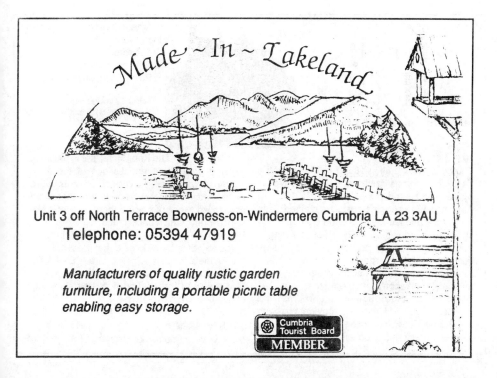

WHITE LODGE HOTEL
Bowness-on-Windermere
Telephone: (05394) 43624

WHITE LODGE HOTEL was originally a Victorian country house....situated on the road to the Lake, and only a short walk from Bowness Bay....

The spacious rooms are centrally heated, some have commanding Lake views, four posters, and all have en-suite bathrooms. All have colour televisions and complimentary tea-making facilities.

We are a small, friendly, family-owned hotel with high standards and good home cooked cuisine. We serve a traditional full English Breakfast.

In addition to our licensed residents dining room, PLANTS is our coffee house. The residents lounge has a colour television.

We can arrange walking, cycling and golfing holidays, and welcome your enquiries.

Near to the White Lodge Hotel we are able to offer our guests membership of the Lake District's premier leisure club, where free use of the indoor swimming pool, spa-pool and gymnasium is offered, along with access to the squash courts, sunbeds and beauty therapy.

English Tourist Board ♥♥♥ Commended Award
Member of English Lakes Hotel & Caterers Association   Cumbria Tourist Board Member

---

Knoll Hotel

Lake Road, Bowness-on-Windermere
Cumbria LA23 2JF
Tel: (05394) 43756

☆Ample free parking within the grounds
☆ 12 bedrooms
☆ Centrally heated.
☆ Rooms with bath or shower en-suite
☆ Colour TV in all rooms.
☆ Telephone, clock and radio in all rooms
☆ Bed & Breakfast from £26,00
☆ Dinner Bed & Breakfast from £40.00

The house was built in 1882 for Admiral of the Fleet...Sir Thomas Pasley, and was later lived in by the High Sheriff of the County....

All of the house's original features: stained glass windows, panelled hall, galleried staircase and shuttered windows...remain intact, creating a homely comfortable atmosphere. This is continued into the garden which contains many rare specimens of trees and shrubs where peace and quiet relaxation can be enjoyed.

Without fear of argument, the rooms and facilities of the KNOLL can provide you with every comfort for the holiday you need, or the weekend break that is so essential these days.

The Knoll Hotel, set in pleasant wooded grounds, overlooks one of the most superb views in the Lake District. From its public rooms and from most of the bedrooms there is an unparalled vista of the northern half of Lake Windermere, with a backcloth of high fells, from Bowfell in the West, through the climbers paradise of the LangDales to the great mass of the Fairfield-Heluelyyn group in the East. Yet within a few short strides lie the shops of Bowness and the beauty of its bay alive with pleasure craft of every type.

AA ★★ RAC ★★

ETB ☺☺☺   Les Routiers
Guests enjoy free use of Parklands Leisure Club

The POSTILION Restaurant

The name derives from the association of the stables and coaching quarters of the White Lion Hotel (now the Royal Hotel) in the centre of Bowness. The Postilion Coach was the preserve of the nobles, the rider sits on the nearside horse to navigate the smoothest course of travel. Packs of Dalmation's were imported and trained to run alongside the coaches snapping at the riff-raff and keeping them from boarding the coach or relieving the coach of its luggage
Whilst the days of coaches and horses have passed it is our aim to provide a welcoming atmosphere and good English Fayre to satisfy the travellers healthy appetite.

The Postilion Restaurant is a relatively new addition to the restaurants in Bowness, and as diners will soon discover it is located on the recently cobbled thoroughfare of Ash Street.
The Chef/Proprietor is David Farraday, who has served his apprenticeship at a variety of high class restaurants. The four course speciality menu is a diners delight. You can choose from the chef's homemade pate or mushrooms cooked with port, mature English Stilton, Dijon mustard and cream. Main courses include Drunken Chicken cooked in a rum whisky, lemon and orange sauce and Steak Diane with its sauce of mushrooms, red wine, French mustard, brandy and cream. An extensive a'la carte menu is also available, featuring Fish, Vegetarian and Steak dishes along with a wide choice of desserts which change daily.
A modest but varied wine list compliments any meal here.

Ash Street,
Bowness-on-
Winderemere
Cumbria
LA23 3EB
Telephone
(05394) 45852

'GILLERCOMB' Bed and Breakfast.

97, Craig Walk, Bowness on Windermere Cumbria, LA23 2JS

A Victorian Terraced House, in a quiet location but near to shops, Pubs and Restaurants. All our pretty bedrooms have shower cubicles, CTV, Kettle, Razor point. After your hearty English Breakfast your fell walking hosts will be pleased to help you plan your day. Sorry...no smoking bedrooms.

Telephone: Mrs. Jones 05394 45928

LAUREL COTTAGE Bed & Breakfast....*and just a little bit more!*

Sympathetically converted from an early 17th century grammar school, Laurel Cottage retains traditional calm and charm whilst offering our guests every modern convenience. Choose family, twin, double orsingle accommodation from our Victorian or Cottage bedrooms. Whilst most of our rooms offeren-suite facilities, all the bedrooms are charmingly decorated and provided with complimentary tea and coffee and colour T.V. A delicious full English breakfast is served in our oak beamed dining room.

St. Martin's Square, Bowness on Windermere, Cumbria LA23 3ET. Tel: (05394) 45594

Sandown, Lake Road, Windermere, Cumbria. LA23 2JF

Superb Bed & Breakfast accommodation, with own colour TV Tea/coffee making facilities.
Situated two minutes from Lake Windermere.
Shops and cafes nearby...many lovely walks. Plenty of parking space.
SAE of telephone for further details.

Prop: Irene & George Eastwood TELE (05394) 45275

BRAITHWAITE.

Map ref. D.8.
Next nearest Town or Village "Portinscale"
Bus Service:
Cumberland Bus Service No.43/555
Braithwaite - Thornthwaite - Keswick

Location. A.66 Keswick/Cockermouth road.

Braithwaite, with a name meaning 'the broad clearing' is a small village nestling at the foot of the Whinlatter Pass, one time seat of the woollen industry.It has a beautiful backdrop of the mountains of Grisdale,Causey Pike, High Stile and Barrow, all of which form the well known Coledaw Horseshoe.

From here the Coledale beck winds its way down through the valley where it enters a narrow gorge before tumbling through the village where it is crossed by two hump-backed bridges..High Bridge and Low Bridge. Low Bridge is effectively the hub of the village.Village streets have the evocative names of Duck Street,The Puddle and The Island. In days of old there were woollen and pencil mills here, together with a flour mill on the common.

The church here is dedicated to St.Herbert (a close friend of St.Cuthbert). St Herbert lived in a simple cell on an island which bears his name in the middle of Derwentwater.

The Blencathra Hunt appears in the village from time to time.The red coated Master of the Hunt is on foot.

BRAITHWAITE

Tel: 05394 33434

With over 200 years of horticultural experience, Hayes Garden World in Ambleside is a major attraction to visitors and residents alike and is a thriving internationally known garden centre. All year round the nursery gardens will hold your interest with its huge choice of gardening delights of plants, shrubs, trees, heathers, roses and many more varieties.

With over 40,000 square feet of displays under cover, which includes the magnificent Crystal Palace, a wide selection of houseplants are displayed from all over the world throughout the

year. You will be able to browse at your leisure through the garden aids department with gifts of every type and description. Very popular with the children is the adventure playgound where the imaginative facilities will keep them happy and busy. As it is situated next to the gardens, this will allow you to continue your own exploring. A visit to Hayes Garden World would not be complete without a visit to the Patio Coffee Lounge to enjoy real homestyle food, light meals and tempting delicacies, none of which should be missed. In addition to flowers, plants, trees, shrubs and gifts, of every description there is also Aqualife. The Tropical Section has Saltwater Fish both tropical and cold and a magnificent selection of Koi Carp, coral and accessories:-everything from the beginner to the professional. Our highly trained staff are always available to provide information and advice on all our products. In essence, at Hayes Garden World, sheer inspiration is the key to our ambition and with us, this is a by-word which grows in abundance.

CHALET,
CAMPING & CARAVAN
HOLIDAY PARK

COME AND ENJOY SCOTGATE...

... an outstanding holiday centre on the threshold of the Lake District's most spectacular scenery Superbly placed between Derwentwater and Bassenthwaite Lake, with dramatic views towards Skiddaw, and the northern fells, it makes the perfect base for exploring Lakeland.

Careful thought and years of experience have gone into the planning of Scotgate. The result, as you will see, is a spacious and comfortable holiday park on a well-screened five acre site. Our range of holiday accommodation has been tailored to suit all needs. The latest additions are seven luxury chalets, built with families in mind. Each has ample room for up to six people with two bedrooms, a lounge, well equipped kitchen, shower and colour T.V. Equally comfortable are our permanent caravans catering for up to six people and providing everything you need for a trouble-free stay. All caravans are on mains water and electricity, with free Calor gas for cooking.

There is a parking space next to each caravan and a large games area at the centre of the site adds to the feeling of spaciousness. We are always happy to welcome touring caravans and all types of tents at Scotgate. Scotgate has all the facilities you would expect from a modern well-run site. A shop adjoining our office sells essentials such as groceries, newspapers and snacks, and at the centre of the site is a laundry room with washing machines, tumble driers and ironing facilities. Showers, shaver points and hair dryers are also provided in the

toilet blocks. The site has its own games room with pool tables and video machines. Scotgate is a family run site. All our chalets and caravans are maintained to the same high standard and we try to ensure that your visit to Lakeland is pleasant and enjoyable.

**BRAITHWAITE, KESWICK
CUMBRIA CA12 5TF
TELEPHONE (07687) 78343**

BRAMPTON.

Map ref. G.3.
Next nearest Town or Village "Irthington"
Bus service. Cumberland Bus Service No.95, 94, 97,
95a, 605
Trains. Brampton Railway Station.
Tourist Information Centre. Moot Hall,Market Place.
Location. A69 Brampton/Newcastle road.
Early Closing. Thursday.
Market day Wednesday.
Gala days/festivals.
Brampton Sheepdog Trials 3rd week September

NAWORTH CASTLE

Brampton is a market town just over one mile from Brampton station, and three miles south of Hadrian's Wall.It is situated in a hollow formed by glacial action which took place during the Ice Age.Gravel ridges form part of the surrounding countryside which ensures the town is hidden from sight until it is approached more closely.

In the market place (Charter since 1250) stands the octagonal Moot Hall, built originally in 1648,,,though the present building dates from 1817.Unusually it has an external staircase.Below the steps are the stocks and a bull-ring...reminiscences of the days of bull-baiting.

It is interesting to note that in the 19th century Brampton, although always a small town, had over 40 public houses and drinking rooms.This number was greatly reduced through the action of Rosalind, the 9th Earls wife who was a staunch supporter of total abstinence.

For centuries Brampton and the surrounding countryside suffered at the hands of the Scots who swept over the border regions killing and burning all in their path.Peace was brought to the borders around 1601 through the efforts of Lord William Howard, forbear of the present Earl of Carlisle, who today lives at Naworth Castle.

In High Cross Street is a building which was the headquarters of Bonnie Prince Charlie in 1745. Following his defeat at Culloden, six of his supporters were hanged from the Capon Tree.The tree itself is no longer there, but a monument erected on the site gives their names.

The great local family since the 16th century has been that of the Howard's, Earls of Carlisle, and owners of Naworth Castle. This historic border fortress, built in

the early 14th century by the Lords Dacre, was the residence for almost 300 years of the Wardens of the March, responsible for law and order in the strife-torn North.Renovated by the Howard family in the early 17th Century, it has been the home of the Earls of Carlisle since 1660 when the first Earl was created by Charles 11.In the 18th century, the fifth Earl was one of England's greatest collectors of works of art, antiquities and furniture.In the late 19th century the castle was a centre of activity for the pre-Raphaelites, for whom George Howard, the 9th Earl was both a great friend and patron.

Brampton is a leisure, walker's paradise surrounded as it is by many attractive footpaths.Fine views from the top of the wooded Mote and along the ridge.Mote-hill was the one time seat of an early Lord, and nearby is a bronze statue of the seventh Earl of Carlisle which was erected in 1870. Nearby too is Gelts Woods . About 50 feet above, if you look carefully you will find a rock with an inscription carved by a Roman soldier in the 3rd century.Today it is known as 'The Written Rock'

Brampton old parish church, built on the site of an old hospital chapel, is known to date back to 1169, and was built by the Normans with stone from Hadrian's Wall. It has a splendid west tower and a tiny lead spire,and has much beautifully carved oak in the sanctuary and the stalls.However it is for the magnificent Burne-Jones windows that travellers come to Brampton from afar.They have a wealth of colour and a noble series of portraits.The great east window glows with red and purple, blue and gold, in the

BRAMPTON

finest Burne-Jones style, with 14 dazzling figures against a rich background of flowers and leaves.

There used to be a famous oak tree near to the parish church around which newly married couples would dance immediately after leaving the church...in order to secure fertility and future wealth.Apparently irate clergy had it chopped down in the 19th century!.

The story still survives here of one Lizzie Baty...'a canny auld body' a kind of witch, willing to use her magic to help rather than hurt.She was also capable of using her powers to discipline those who needed a lesson in manners.On the day that she was buried, so it is said, at the age of 88, one of the worst storms in living memory burst over Brampton.

Just outside of Brampton is the ruins of Lanercost Priory founded in 1166 by Augustinian monks.The church survives.There are remains of the priors house and the cellarium with its

TALKIN TARN

fine vaulted roof. It contains Roman cellars brought from the wall.

South-east of Brampton, just two miles distant is Talkin Tarn, in an area preserved by the County Council as a country park. The tarn has a lovely setting amongst woodland.There are boating facilities, and a golf course nearby.

BRIDEKIRK.

Map ref, C.6.
Next nearest Town or Village "Papcastle"
Bus service.Cumberland Bus Service No.58
Maryport - Dearham - Dovenby - Cockermouth
Location. 2 miles north of Cockermouth off the
A66.

Bridekirk means'Church of St.Bride' (or
St.Bridget) and relates to the 6th century Irish
St.Bride, and the Norman church of the same
name is a dominant feature of the village.
The church is known as St Bridget's and amongst
its many interesting features is the 12th century
font reputed to be one of the finest pieces of
Norman sculpture in the country.
This famous font would almost certainly have
been used at the baptism of two particular men
on Bridekirk roll of fame, both sons of vicars
and both born at the vicarage in the 17th century.

BRIDEKIRK / BRIGSTEER & HELSINGTON

One was Sir Joseph Williamson, who became Secretary of State in 1674 and four years later,in the scare
of a Popeish plot was shut up in the Tower of London
by Parliament, only to be let out again by the King a
few hours later.He gave Bibles and prayer books and
plate to his fathers church and £500 for the poor of
Bridekirk.The other vicar's son was Thomas Tickell,
friend of Addison, whose works he edited.He is
particularly remembered for his lines on the death of
Addison.
Bridekirk keeps alive the name and fame of St Bridget
(or St Bride).Legend is told that when Bride was a girl
she went to Palestine and became a serving-maid in
the Inn at Bethlehem.She would have been there
when Joseph and Mary arrived, and would have seen
the shepherds and the wise men ,together of course
with the donkey in the stable..
On the outskirts of the village one time stood Wood
Hall. Today only the acres of beautiful parkland
originally surrounding it,remain.
Thoroughbred race-horses are a familiar sight here.

BRIGSTEER & HELSINGTON.

Map ref. G.11.
Next nearest Town or Village "Underbarrow"
Location. 3 miles from Kendal in the Lyth Valley.

The village of Brigsteer is situated between the
parishes of Helsington and Levens some three miles
from Kendal.
The earliest permanent houses date from the 16th
and 17th centuries,and include a mill.The Wheatsheaf
Hotel, originally the Wheatsheaf Inn...was a smithy
until the beginning of the 20th century.
St.John's Church which serves both Brigsteer and
Helsington is actually in the parish of Helsington,and
will be found sited at the top of the steep hill out of
Brigsteer. Founded originally in 1726 and rebuilt in
1845, when at the same time the school was built.
The manor house of the parish was Helsington
Laithes, and in 1341 belonged to one William of
Thweng. It is thought that part of the present house
could be 15th century.
The oldest house here is Sizergh Castle....a very

popular tourist attraction..
In the Pele tower(the oldest part of the castle) is
the Queens room...named after Catherine Parr,
who as a youngster used to visit her Aunt Agnes
and Uncle Thomas Strickland here...and the
room above it is said to be haunted by the ghost
of a widow and one of the early Strickland's.
Apparently he was madly in love with his wife
and very jealous, so when he was called upon to
lead his men off to war (against the Scots) he was
determined no other male eyes would light upon
her.To ensure this he locked her in her room and
threatened death to any of his staff who released
her.The mistresses's hammerings and pleadings
were subsequently ignored so frightened were
they of their master.Days, then weeks and months
went past and it was clear that the poor woman
had gone mad...then silence.. Now today ,some
600 years later, the wails are still heard at
times...pleading for release..
It is interesting to note that in 1300 a Strickland
family married a de Wessington...so connecting
them with the family from which George Washington sprang.

BRISCO.

Map ref.F.4.
Nearest Town or Village "Carleton"
Location. 3 miles south of Carlisle

The village of Brisco. lies just three miles to the south of Carlisle, ostensibly in the parish of St.Cuthbert Without.
An early name for the village was Birkscleugh...

meaning birchwood.
St Mungo's Well is of particular historical interest.It is reported that many Christians were baptized here by St.Ninian in or around AD400.
The property known as The Cottage still has a front door, which is studded and heavy, and dates back to the time of the Border Wars when it offered a great deal of protection in times of siege...a similar one can be seen at Brisco Hall.

BROMFIELD.

Map ref. C.5.
Next nearest Town or Village "Blencogo"
Location.Between Allonby & Wigton Near A.595

Bromfield,meaning 'broom covered land' is a scattered parish between Aspatria and Holme Cultram, and within easy travelling distance of Wigton. Bromfield parish comprises the villages of Blencogo and Langrigg, together with the hamlets of Crookdale and Scales.
The parish church is dedicated to St.Mungo (St Kentigern) and the nave and chancel still remain after 800 years.There have in fact been four churches altogether on this site...The first one was erected in the 2nd Century, and was British; this was followed in AD 449 with one built by the Romans, and subsequently administered by St.Kentigern, then a Norman, followed by the current one. The oldest relic here is an ancient British cross carved in white sandstone, believed to date from AD400. and there is

also the tomb of the warrior Adam Crookdale dated 1304.
Cockfighting was apparently a popular pastime at this church at one time, being held in the churchyard...for the vicar at the time was an ardent supporter.
Nearby is St Mungo's Well where most villagers would have got their water until 1929 when mains water was laid on for the first time.
The Gill, near High Scales, is said to have been given by William the Lion, of Scotland in the 12th century to ancestors of the Reay (or Ray) family. It should be noted that The Gill is the oldest entailed property in England...now over 800 years old...and as to be expected...haunted.
The Old Smithy at Langrigg still survives and one can still see horses being shod here.
The only pub 'The Greyhound Inn dates back to 1720 and has the sign of a greyhound over the door lintel, and the old school building of 1612 is still surviving..though is currently a paint store.

BROUGH.

Map ref. J.8.
Next nearest Town or Village "Warcop"
Bus service. Cumberland Bus Service No 561
Tourist Information Centre. Post Office and General Stores
Location.A.66 Penrith road.
Early closing. Thursday
Gala days/festivals. Brough Hill Fair End of September

Eight miles from Appleby and four miles from Kirkby Stephen ,Brough lies at the head of the beautiful Eden Valley, well known to thousands of travellers over the past centuries as a place of shelter and refuge before the pass of Stainmore.Now it is a quiet and friendly village and a haven by-passed by the noise and disturbance of todays traffic.
The Pennines here rise to 2,000 feet and from the roads climbing over the moors to Middleton-

BROUGH

in-Teesdale and to Tan Hill (at 1,732 feet the highest Inn in England) magnificent views of the Eden Valley and surrounding mountains are obtained.

The name 'Brough" means 'fortified place' for the site of the town controls the ancient track over Stainmore.

Because of its strategic position guarding the passes of Stainmore and Mallerstang, the Romans built an important camp here. The remains of fortifications date back almost 2000 years and are still plainly visible, though these probably superceded earlier ones which have long been lost. The earliest defences are now the ditches and mounds of the two and a half acre Roman fort of Verterae which probably held about 500 infantrymen, traces have been found under the present keep of stone buildings which were probably their barracks.

Outside the gate of the fort remains of the timber clay-floored dwellings of the civilian settlement dating back to the early second century, have been traced in recent excavations.

Norman conquerors reached this area about 1090 and under William Rufus strengthened the defences and built his castle within the northern part of the Roman fort.

The ruins of the Norman Brough Castle today dominate the village of Brough, and date from the 11th century. The Scots took it in the English incursions of 1174, but it was strengthened by Robert de Vipont, and although the village was burned in further Scots raids the castle remained unbreached. In the War of the Roses it was held by Lord Clifford, a Lancastrian, but he was killed and the castle was taken by Warwick the Kingmaker. It was restored to the Cliffords by the Tudors. The castle suffered an accidental fire in the 16th century and was restored by Lady Anne Clifford, though it was further engulfed in fire in 1666.

The church, dating from Norman times has a 'leper squint'. Most of the building is 14th century to 16th century. The porch contains a stone inscribed in tribute to a Roman commander of the fort and records its re-building in AD 197. There is also a copy of a memorial found nearby to a Syrian youth, probably in the Roman Army who died at the age of 16.

'Market' Brough received its charter from Edward 111 in 1330. Markets were held once weekly on the Thursday, and a four day fair was held each September. The last market was held here in 1867, the only ancient fair remaining now is Brough Hill Fair, which is believed to go back to Roman times, and which is now a popular gypsy gathering held every year at the end of September.

This area, as previously mentioned was frequently harried by the Scots, and it was not until the Union with Scotland that the first stone-built houses and cottages appeared. In the following more peaceful times, up to 10,000 cattle were regularly driven from Scotland to be sold with local stock at the important market here, and thousands of geese, sheep and cattle changed hands before being driven over the many wide drove roads which radiated to the developing counties of Yorkshire, Lancashire and further south.

At one time there were the remains of three ancient stone crosses...one had on it the initials B.M.C. and the date 1331. This market cross was the site where one of the ancient local traditions took place on the eve of Epiphany. From early primitive times it had been a tradition to hold a midwinter fire festival in the village..to encourage the re-birth of the waning sun apparently.

This used to take the form of a burning holly brush, which was carried high through the streets at the head of a procession led by a band of musicians..

Castle Hotel

Brough, Cumbria
(07683) 41252

The discreet elegance of the Castle Hotel provides the most up-to-date facilities and amenities in warm and comfortable surroundings. The interior still retains the welcoming atmosphere of the original 19th century coaching inn whilst the stained glass screen and the pageantry of the painted walls evoke the ideals of chivalry. There are fourteen bedrooms all with private bath, hand basin and toilet, colour television, telephone, radio/alarm and tea/coffee making facilities. In most bedrooms, the businessman will find ample writing space.

Close to the main A66 for the convenience of the businessman and midway between Scotch Corner (A1(M)) and Penrith (M6) the hotel enjoys the quiet seclusion and charm of a traditional Westmorland village with magnificent views of the Norman Castle and the Surrounding Pennines. The friendly and obliging staff complement an unforgettable stay.

FALSTAFFS RESTAURANT

The Restaurant offers and excellent choice of traditional English and regional food.

BROUGHAM.

Map ref. G.7.
Next nearest Town or Village "Eamont Bridge"
Location. A.6. South of Eamont bridge.

Brougham stands by the crossroads of the M6/A6 going north and south and the A66 going west to east across the Pennines

Brougham,pronounced 'Broom' today is little more than an area of a scattered homes..the original ancient village having been demolished by Lord Brougham to make way for Brougham Hall.

Nearby is the Roman fort of Brocavum..meaning 'the hill of the badgers', and is of course where the name of Brougham originates. The fort is on private land and to date has not been fully excavated.At one time it accommodated up to a thousand infantry and cavalry.Now only the foundations can be seen , as the stone was 'quarried' to build the Norman castle on the banks of the River Eamont.

The ruins of Brougham Castle are located in the north-west corner of the Roman fort, they are in an irregular moated enceinte, and form a small court,

with a late Norman keep. James 1 and Charles 1 are said to have sprent three days here in 1617.Later it was the 16th century home of Lady Anne Clifford, daughter of the Earl of Cumberland.

Annually on the 2nd April, visitors will see the local vicar with his parishioners standing beside the "Countess's Pillar'on the A66 taking part in the dole ceremony.This was inaugurated by Lady Anne to distribute £4 annually to the poor of the parish in memory of her last parting from her mother before re-joining her husband, the Earl of Pembroke, in London.

Close too is Brougham Hall...or what is left of it. In spite of the fact that the hall was at one time the home of the fourth Lord Brougham (the fellow who twice broke the bank at Monte Carlo) it still ended up in ruins.Fortunately a charitable trust has begun an ambitious restoration of the Hall.The Hall reached its zenith in Victorian times when it became known as the 'Windsor of the North' and home to the Lord Chancellor of England.At the turn of the century it played host to King Edward V11 on a number of his private visits.

Across the road from the Hall, and connected to it by

a narrow stone bridge, is a churchyard and delightful sandstone chapel. St Wilfred's. Its most famous possession ....a magnificent Flemish triptych..is on virtual permanent loan to Carlisle Cathedral. Mason's marks suggest that the chapel was built substantially on the site of an earlier chapel by the 14th century castle builders. In 1840 more restoration was done...the interesting profusion of woodwork now to be seen was brought from France by Lord William Brougham, and cut to fit by local workmen.

Further east, in a secluded spot stands the old church of St. Ninian which has barely changed since being rebuilt by Lady Anne. Though now redundant, its doors are still open to visitors. Beautiful in its simplicity...stone flagged floors, white-washed walls and old pew boxes.

Not so long ago early 19th century skeletons of early day warriors were found here, including, it is believed, the Crusader Udard de Brougham alongside which was his sword.

At Eamont bridge nearby there are two pre-historic earthworks dating from the late neolithic times....known as Mayburgh, and King Arthur's Table.

BROUGHTON-IN-FURNESS.

Map ref. D.11
Next nearest Town or Village "Torver".
Bus service. Cumberland Buses Route 7, 9, 513, 507
Trains. Foxfield Station
Tourist Information Centre. Old Town Hall
Location. Between Barrow-in -Furness and Millom just off the A.595.
Early closing. Thursday.
Market day. Tuesday.

Until Ulverston stole its thunder by linking itself by canal to the sea in 1847, Broughton-in-Furness was an important market town serving a wide area of Furness. It still has its cattle market but now it's just a friendly little unspoilt village.

Broughton nestles in a hollow, between wooded hills midway between Barrow in Furness and Millom. Many of the houses are Georgian including those in the elegant square, set out by the Lord of the Manor to resemble a London square. In the middle of this 'market square' stands an obelisk erected in 1810 to commemorate the Jubilee of George 111, together with the ancient fish-slabs, once used for the sale of fish caught in the nearby River Duddon.

Also adjacent is the village stocks, no doubt well used in times gone by, but nowadays very much a sense of amusement to the villages' many visitors.

Opposite is the "Town Hall' dating from 1766, one time market hall with lock-up shops, but these days housing the Tourist Information Centre.

Broughton was at one time the centre of the wool trade. together with the manufacture of oak baskets (known locally as swills) and a livestock market is still held here on alternate weeks. There are several yards leading between the old buildings with unusual restrictions placed upon them, still in force today...because of the rights of way necessary to reach the wells.

The village is ancient in origin having been mentioned in the Domesday Book, and the two important buildings, the church and the castle are Norman in foundation. The church of St. Mary's Magdalene was consecrated in 1547. It has been rebuilt during Victorian times and has a ring of ten bells...most unusual for such a small place.

Broughton Tower, a 18th-19th century mansion built around a 14th century defensive tower is set in parkland a little to the north of the village..the ruins are complete with dungeons. Broughton Tower unfortunately is not open to the public.

Just three miles from Broughton in Furness is Broughton Mills so called because of the woollen mill that was at one time located here. There are remains of old kilns where lime was made for the land and buildings.

A row of cottages is still called 'Shuttle Street' which at one time was occupied solely by weavers. The old Inn, the Blacksmith's Arms, dates from the 18th century and still has old beams and fireplaces. There is no bar...just a shelf. Visitors sit on benches around a big table before an open fire.

In the 18th century a busy forge stood by the River Duddon one and a half miles to the west. The ruin of Duddon Gorge is open to the public on application to the National Park Authority.

BURGH-BY-SANDS

Map ref. E.4
Next nearest Town or Village "Beaumont"

Tourist Information Centre
Location. 5 miles north west of Carlisle.

Leaving Drumbrugh the road runs straight alongside the marshside with the track of the old Carlisle-Silloth railway on the right, till it reaches Burgh by Sands. This is a long village of fine houses, some of them seventeenth and eighteenth century, set well back from the road. The village, famous for its mushrooms, is five miles north-west of Carlisle, where the River Eden runs into the Solway Firth, on the site of Hadrian's Wall.

About a mile from the village ,on Burgh Marsh is where Edward 1 died whilst preparing for war against the Scots, on the 7th July 1307. A monument marking the spot where he died can be seen here. Edward 1's Monument.. It stands by the marshes, isolated and atmospheric. The pillar was erected in 1685 and re-built and restored twice in the 19th century.

The Romans came to Burgh long before Hadrian's Wall was built across the marsh. Their first fort was discovered south of the village in 1978. It was dated as 95AD and had inside it a circular watch-tower which was earlier still. The later fort was a bigger, much more important one, housing 500 cavalry who were ready to dash off to any place where an invasion seemed to be pending. In the thirteenth century there was a castle at Burgh for the same purpose. It has long been demolished but two fields still named Spillblood and Hangman-tree tell their own story.

The parish church of St Michael was built in the main from stones from the Roman fort, on the site of which the church stands ,in the 12th century, though the tower was not added until the 14th century. The entrance from the nave of the church to the ground chamber is guarded by a cross-barred door, made of hammered iron. A stone staircase leads to an upper chamber and there are arrow slits for defence and light. One can assume the tower would have been used as a place for refuge during the Border wars, into this the villagers could flee on receiving warning, closing the heavy iron gate behind them. The gate is still intact to this day. Look at the foot of the tower, for here will be seen the marks on the stone-work where the village men used to sharpen their spears before a raid.

BURNESIDE.

Map ref. G.11.
Next nearest Town or Village "Staveley"
Bus service. Cumberland Bus Service No.45
Trains. Railway Station

Location. 1 mile east A.591. Kendal to Windermere road.

The entrance to the Kent valley and under the shelter of Potter Fell, lies the village of Burnside.There has been settlements here since the Stone Age, and is reflected by the remains of a stone circle on Potter Fell...in a part of Cumbria once known as Strathclyde.

In the 15th century a large variety of mills sprung up here alongside the River Sprint, to handle corn, wool, cotton,bobbin, and the original rag paper mill at Cowan Head.

James Cropper Co.Ltd the paper manufacturer, is the main employer in the area.In 1814 James Bateman of Tolson Hall erected Elba monument on a mound close to the Kendal to Windermere road. Mr Bateman intended to inscribe these words on the monument, but owing to the escape of Napoleon from Elba, the inscription was not engraved. The tablet should have read' In honour of William Pitt the Pilot that weathered the storm'. In 1914 a plaque was installed by Charles Cropper of Ellergreen, but is now missing.

There are a number of listed buildings in the parish, they include Burneside Hall, built in the 14th century as a defence dwelling with a gate-house and walled enclosure.The tower is now in ruins but the house with later additions was once the home ofthe deBurneshead family from which the village takes its name.

Tolson Hall was built in 1638 for Thomas Tolson (or Towson) a tobacco merchant. A small room was discovered inside one of the six foot thick walls, which was used in olden days for hiding a priest. The gateway on the south side of the house is a copy of the Castle gate at Lancaster.

Godman Hall takes its name from a family that used to live there, in a square Pele Tower probably of medieval date.The house was added late in the 17th century.

The present church was built in 1881 for the increasing inhabitants of the parish, a smaller church stood on this same site and was built in 1823..before this the church stood at the foot of the present church yard.Attached to the old church was the village school which dates from the 17th century.

The Manor of Burnside was divided up in 1750 by Thomas Shepherd who had inherited it from his father. The Hall and most of the farm land was sold to Christopher Wilson of Barbon. Cowanhead was sold to Lady Fleming of Rydal Hall, who subsequently re-sold it immediately toThomas Ashburner who built upon it a paper mill.Burneside Hall and land was sold to Mr Roger Wakefield, who built upon'the falls a cotton mill. When this trade declined it was used as a woollen mill and lastly as a paper mill.In 1845 these two mills were purchased by the James Cropper, who as a young man had recently graduated from the University of Edinburgh, and had decided whilst there not to go into the family business in Liverpool, but to take up the manufacture of paper. Over the years the generations of Croppers have helped Burneside to prosper, they were always concerned in the day to day activities of the people. Houses were built for the workers or land was released for them to build their own.John Bryce, a Director in the company, in 1897 built the Bryce Institute and was the village focal point of social activities.The present James Cropper is the fifth generation of the family.

JAMES CROPPER PLC

Creative Papermaking

Burneside Mills, Kendal
Cumbria LA9 6PZ England

Telephone 0539 722002
Telex 65226
Fax 0539 728088

The village of Burneside is the home since
1845 of James Cropper PLC, papermakers.

ENVIRONMENT
Matters

The history of the land on which the mill stands can be traced back to 1290 when Gilbert de Burneshead, Under-Sheriff of Westmorland, resided at Burneside Hall. A manorial corn mill was built on the River Kent to take advantage of the water power from the natural rock falls above Burneside.

In 1752 the Wakefield family of Kendal bought the mill and added a small cotton mill. At Cowan Head 1 mile up-stream from Burneside there was originally a fulling mill, which was turned into a handmade paper mill in 1746 by Thomas Ashburner, a Kendal stationer. In 1833 three young men, Hudson, Nicholson and Foster, leased the Burneside and Cowan Head Mills and installed one second hand Fourdrinier Paper Machine in each mill to produce printing and wrapping papers.

In 1845 James Cropper, a young man of 22, who had learned papermaking with Alex Cowan in Edinburgh, took on the mills. He was newly married to a Wakefield and was encouraged by that family to take over the rather derelict paper mills. The output when he took over was only 300 tonnes per annum and it needed only one horse at each mill to carry the goods and coal to and from the Kendal Canal.

From 1879 to 1965 there was a private railway connecting Burneside with Cowan Head Mill and a mill at Bowston preparing raw materials for the other two mills.

James Cropper and his descendants have now taken an active part in the management and development of the Company for five generations. His great great grandson James Cropper is presently Chairman.

The business moved from being a partnership to a private company in 1889 and a public company in 1951. It presently employs 436 people producing over 45,000 tonnes of coloured and other speciality paper and paper related products for a world-wide market. Indeed, it has the reputation of being one of the most modern mills in the world in its product areas with most of the plant having been renewed in the past ten years at a cost of over £40 million.

BURTON-IN-KENDAL.

Map ref.G.13
Next nearest Town or Village "Beetham".
Bus service. Cumberland Bus Service No.555
Kendal - Lancaster
Location. 4 miles south east of Milnthorpe.
Gala days/festivals. Burton/Milnthorpe/Carnforth.
Agricultural Show. Last Thurs.August.

An old market town four miles south-east of Milnthorpe. The early history of Burton goes back to William the Conqueror.In the Domesday Book the area was initially owned by one Torsin.
Later as a reward for helping Edward 1V capture his arch enemy Henry V1, an extensive grant of land was made to Sir James Harrington...Later in 1759, Burton ,together with Dalton,and Holme, were purchased by Colonel Charteris of Hornby Castle. Burton became a market town by a charter procured from Charles 11 by Sir George Middleton of Leighton in 1661, and by 1750 was the most extensive corn market in the county.It is on record that besides corn dealing, as many as eighty beasts were slaughtered in a day at Martinmas, such meat selling at 1d-2d(old pence) per pound.

The Lancaster-Kendal canal was opened in 1819, and the wharf and weigh-bridge where coal was brought to the area are to be seen a half mile to the west.
In the market place stands an 18th century cross once used as stocks...four recesses can still be seen in the steps for leg irons. The village was a one time important changing place for horses.In the days of pack-horses and stage coaches.The first stage-coach in fact passed through at six miles per hour, arrived twice weekly, and was given the name 'The Flying Machine'.The most important stops were at the Royal Oak (now the Royal Hotel) and the Kings Arms.
The parish church of St James has a Norman tower built in the 12th century, but added to in the 14th and 16th century.It contains a private chapel for the Hornby family of Dalton Hall,Its oldest possession are three fine fragments of a stone cross carved before the Conqueror's Domesday Book was made, one showing two figures under an arch, and a larger figure holding a cross below. Tradition says that one of Cromwell's horsemen was found dead here, the village folk burying him where they found him, and planted hawthorn over him.

BUTTERMERE.

Map ref. C.8.
Location.8 miles south-west of Keswick.
Gala days/festivals.Buttermere Shepherds Meet.3rd Sat Sept. Buttermere Show 2nd Week October

Buttermere is a small village surrounded by some of the higher mountains of the Lake District. Two particularly significant waterfalls here.Scale Force, with its spectacular single leap 200' waterfall (Lakeland's highest) whilst from Bleaberry tarn, Sour-Milk Gill cascades into Buttermere Lake.The waterfalls are approached by a roughtrack walk from Buttermere village.

Buttermere Lake is a little under one and a half miles long and a third of a mile broad. The village is accessible from the south east by the Newlands Pass, or the more austere Honister.

The church of St James used to be known as one of the smallest and poorest in the diocese,The current church dates from 1846. A wrough iron gate depicts a shepherd and sheep and is hung at the entrance to the porch.The church itself is worth investigating even if its only for the antique organ dated 1820.

The old Fish Inn (now the Fish Hotel) stands by Mill beck, and was the home of Mary Robinson'The Beauty of Buttermere' immortalised in a novel written by Melvyn Bragg.

The general views over Buttermere are extensive. They include the Buttermere Fells,Honister Crag and the descent from the pass.Southward over the lake the bold summits of Red Pike, High Style and High Crag.Down the Red Pike comes the white,tumbling, vociferous waters of Sour Milk Gill seen from afar. Red Pike, after a rugged climb, has the best view from these Buttermere hills, and over that way, under High crag, goes the walking path to the central cone of English mountains; Scafell Pike, and its peers.

CALDBECK & HESKET-NEWMARKET.

Map ref. E.6.
Next nearest Town or Village "Skelton"

Location. 8 miles south-east of Wigton.

Market day. Gala days/festivals. Caldbeck & Hesket-Newmarket Sheepdog Trials. Last Thurs August.
Hesket Newmarket Show. 1st Saturday in September.
Vintage Motor Bike Trials. Hesket-Newmarket. Whit Bank Holiday weekend.

JOHN PEEL'S GRAVE

Caldbeck..Cumbria's second best known village. A typical stone-built Cumbrian village situated at the most northerly point of the Lake District National Park. There are extensive views to the south over the Caldbeck fells at the 'back o' Skiddaw. In earlier times Caldbeck was a largely self-sufficient village and supported a considerable amount of industry. It boasted a brewery that supplied 16 inns and ale-houses, and had 13 mills which were powered by the Cald beck (i.e. cold stream), from which the village takes its name. many of these buildings survive as handsome relics of a bygone era...for example The Brewery...the handsome old building near the bridge.

The village is a parish on the northern slope of the Skiddaw group of mountains. The two villages are some eight miles south-east of Wigton and is said to have grown up around a hospital (or hospice) built originally by Cartmel Priory, for travellers through Inglewood. Caldbeck village marks the northern boundary of the National Park.

In the past bobbin, cloth, clog making, brewing farming and mining have given Caldbeck an air of prosperity. Today only the clog making and farming survive...the clogs being available from one of Britains few remaining cloggers. Still very busy even in this day and age, Stongs of Caldbeck find their clogs are still very popular with Cumbrian farmers, postmen County Council workmen, motor wagon drivers, and of course Clog dancers.

The dedication of Caldbeck's parish church to St Kentigern (or Mungo), together with the nearby Mungo's Well suggest a missionary visit by the saint who was the Bishop of Glasgow in the 6th century. Tradition has it that he baptised the first Christians of the village here in the 6th century. Nowadays children are still brought to be accepted into the Christian family at St Mungo's Well beside the little arched bridge which crosses from the church to Friar Row.

The churchyard is the resting place of Mary Harrison (the beauty of Buttermere) and of John Peel, the famous huntsman. As related by the well known novelist Melvyn Bragg, Mary, wife of farmer Richard Harrison had been the innocent victim of a scandal of the early 19th century through her 'marriage' to John Hatfield, the bigamist...he was later hanged in Carlisle...not for bigamy however.: for forgery!. John Peel (1776-1854) was, as most people will know, made famous by the song written by mill-manager John Woodcock Graves at whose Caldbeck mill the 'hodden grey' of Peel's coat was woven.

The church, in itself, is somewhat of a celebrity, having been written about by William and Dorothy Wordsworth, Coleridge, the Lambs, and Thomas deQuincey.

At least ten major mines have been worked in the nearby fells. Tunnels and shafts penetrate for a great way beneath the hillside. Visitors should call at the Caldbeck mining museum, which additionally specializes in guided walks to the mine sites.

CONT.

PRIESTS MILL, CALDBECK

T H E

Watermill
RE S T AURANT

Priests Mill is an old watermill built by a Rector of Caldbeck on the riverbank just below the church. From 1702 to 1933 it was used as a stone grinding cornmill. After that it was mainly used as a sawmill and joiner's workshop until 1965 when floods caused the mill dam to be destroyed.

The award winning restoration of the mill was completed in 1986. The only machinery left is the 14ft diameter waterwheel which is now restored to working order. The inside wheel pit area also displays a local collection of old rural implements.

Most of the early 18th century stone building is used to house an attractive cafe overlooking the river, interesting shops including a countryside gift and card shop, and a unique museum of Lakeland mineral mines.

Priests Mill is well worth a visit to browse at leisure in shops and perhaps buy unusual and beautiful gifts, to feel the history and atmosphere of the buildings, or simply to enjoy the quiet surroundings.

The shops & Museums are open from mid March until October 31st
Every Tuesday to Sunday 11.00 - 5.00
In November & December they open
Saturdays & Sundays only
Office Tel: (06974) 78369

The upper floor of this early 18th century stone building is used to house the Watermill Restaurant, which overlooks the river. This unique restaurant with its polished wooden floor, low oak beamed ceilings, woodstove (for those cold winter months) has a cosy welcoming atmosphere, where you can enjoy light refreshments or full meals at any time of the day. All the food is made on the premises from the best quality produce available. Some tables actually overlook the river, or you can sit outside on the grassy terrace next to the village cricket pitch. Evening parties and an outside catering service are available by arrangement. For all catering enquiries please ring (06974) 78267.

OPENING HOURS -
The Watermill Restaurant is open
Everyday from mid February - 30th September
including Bank Holidays 10.00 - 5.00.

During June, July and August There is later opening
from Tues - Sat 10.00 - 7.00
with Sunday and Mondays still 10.00 - 5.00

Winter opening hours
1st October to 24th December
Every Tuesday - Sunday 10.00 - 5.00

CALDBECK MINING MUSEUM

The Caldbeck Mining Museum, complete with its own shop specialises in mineral mining and quarrying in the Caldbeck Fells and the Lake District. The museum is unique in Cumbria & houses a large collection of original artifacts, plans, photographs & memorabilia of this ancient & important industry. Guided walks to surface remains are a speciality as are slide shows and lectures. To book these please ring Ian or Jean Tyler on (0228) 41255 or 561883. The shop offers for sale local & world minerals, fossils & crystals, the largest selection of mining & geology books in the N.W. and a range of locally made gemstone jewellery.

AND ALSO: Mill Gifts ● Greenleaves Recycled Bookshop
The Jewellers Workshop ● The Wheelpit Museum
ALL AT PRIESTS MILL, CALDBECK

CALDBECK & HESKET-NEWMARKET

Early in the 12th century the area around Caldbeck had such a reputation for being a wild place, frequented by rogues and vagabonds, that a licence was granted to the Prior of Carlisle, by the Chief Forester of Inglewood, to build a hospice for the relief of distressed travellers, probably on the site now occupied by the Rectory, next to the church. The monks who ran the hospice probably lived in the vicinity of Friar Row. Caldbeck seems now to be a quiet place , but in Elizabethan times there was a saying;

'Caldbeck and Caldbeck Fells
Are worth all England else'

This was when the silver, lead and copper mines up on the fells were producing wealth for the country. At Hesket-Newmarket one and a half miles to the east, has a fine wide street with many 18th century houses and a central market cross on the well kept village green. It still has its market cross and bull-ring though the market established in 1751 was discontinued in the mid-19th century. Foods peculiar to this area is 'Tatie Pot'...rum butter and herb pudding, plus Caldbeck rolled gingerbread. Caldbeck is the home of Chris Bonington, the well known mountaineer.

CALDERBRIDGE & PONSONBY.

Map ref. B.9.
Next nearest Town or Village "Gosforth"
Location.On A.595 close to Seascale.

Calderbridge is an inland village situated on the A.595, close to Seascale and Sellafield, the river Calder runs through the village, from whence it gets its name.

Calderbridge's most famous building is undoubtedly the Abbey. Calder Abbey is a small picturesque ruin about one mile east of the village. Founded in 1134 by Ranulf Meschines, Lord of Copeland, for a colony of monks from Furness Abbey, originally as a Benedictine monastery, which some fourteen years later adopted the reformed order of Cistercians...The Abbey has been described as being one of the most enchanting of any of the monastic ruins in the British Isles.

During its long life the Abbey made great contributions to the lives of the community...alms to the poor, animal husbandry, crop production, and bee-keeping...Even 'Abbey Mead'.Not too surprisingly, for a property of this great age, the Abbey is reputed to be haunted.

Calder Abbey lies just within the National Park but it is not open to the public at any time.The ruins stand in the grounds of a private residence and can only be glimpsed from a public footpath which passes a few hundred yards away. This path, known as the Monk's Road, begins close to the church at Calder Bridge and goes through an area of pasture-land adjoining the river.Behind a group of converted buildings it meets the drive of the private house and from here the Abbey ruins are just visible, a few graceful arches in the Early English style in a sylvan setting. Calder incidentally, was amongst the first of the monastic foundations to be dissolved and in 1538 its lands were acquired by the chief agent of the dissolution Dr Thomas Legh.It has remained in private hands ever since.The highest detail of the Abbey is the remaining portion of the church tower, supported by four arches.Other parts of the church, including the north arcade of the nave,and the chapter house, remain.A late Georgian private house occupies part of the site on what was the monks frater and dormitory.   CONT

PONSONBY FARM PARK

CATHY MILLER & DAVID STANLEY would like to welcome you to Ponsonby Farm Park and give you the opportunity to see aspects of a modern day farm together with a glimpse of the past, ranging from farm animals to buildings and machinery.

There has been a farm on this site for several hundred years, being originally the home farm of Ponsonby Hall, built in the 17th century for the Stanley family. The family, in fact, still own the farm though the old Hall has been demolished. It is now the centre of a large mixed farm with modern breeds of farm animals together with an extensive collection of rare breeds of cattle, sheep, pigs, goats, horses and poultry...not forgetting Oberon and Miranda the Llamas, most of whom will allow you to stroke and feed them...Not only does the FARM PARK offer the experience of seeing a variety of different breeds of animals, there is also a Pets Corner with baby animals and donkeys. Children's Play area & Tearoom/ Gift shop cater for all ages and tastes.

As well as seasonal activities such as silage making, harvesting, etc, there is the opportunity to see milking in progress from approximately 4.15pm daily.

Visitors are also welcome to take one of the farm walks and follow the feet signs to explore the wider aspects of farming and conservation areas, including 'wetlands' and the remains of an Iron Age Settlement.

OPEN DAILY.
(except Mondays)
All Bank Holidays in the Summer
10.30a.m-5.00p.m.
from Good Friday to October 1st.
PONSONBY FARM PARK
Ponsonby,
Nr. Calderbridge,
Cumbria CA20 1BX.
Tel: 0946 841426

Nearby is Pelham House on the site of the manor house of the Stanley's, who settled in Ponsonby in 1388. Along by the stream is Sella Park with interesting old houses with pele-like walls and an old oak recalling the country life of 300 years ago. The church of St.Bridget's, built in 1842 by Thomas Irwin of Calder Abbey, is located in the centre of the town. Ponsonby parish has been a united benefice with Calderbridge since 1957, and today is served by the vicar of Beckermet.Ponsonby church stands in the park of Pelham House which at one time was Ponsonby Hall. The tower and spire were built by the Stanley family in 1840. Ponsonby Old Hall is today farmed by the Stanley family.In recent years the farm has diversified and it is now a Farm park.

CALTHWAITE

MAP REF. F.6.
Next nearest Town or Village "Hutton in the Forest"
Location. 1 mile west of A.6 between Penrith and Carlisle.

The name means'the meadow where calves were kept' and lives up to its name, for it possesses one of the largest Jersey herds in the country.

This area was at one time the Royal Forest of Inglewood, as many local names will confirm...Aikbank Farm, Low Wool Oaks,High Oaks, Inglewood House...all have their origins in the forest.Calthwaite's parish is Hesket in the Forest, and nearby is Hutton in the Forest...the home of Lord Inglewood.Roe deer can still be seen in the woods here.

Thiefside, east of Calthwaite was the site of the gallows where the unfortunate poachers and sheep stealers were hanged. Many of the buildings here are made of local sandstone, with much of the building done around the years 1880-1900. The 'Globe Inn' here is an old coaching Inn where adjacent is the old village smithy.The area in front would have been the village green and duckpond. The old school, complete with its bell-tower and bell was re-built in 1875.

A traditional Calthwaite event, now over 100 years old is the annual Christmas party held three days after Christmas.

FOUR SEASONS FARM EXPERIENCE
SOMETHING FOR EVERYONE AT THE

FOUR SEASONS FARM EXPERIENCE

A warm Cumbrian welcome from the Pattinson family awaits all those calling in at the Four Seasons Farm Experience two and a half miles north of Calthwaite on the old road to Carlisle. Based in and around the old Sceugh Mire Farm, Four Seasons offers a range of sights and activities to entertain everyone in the family. The attractions include a wide varitey of rare and unusual farm animals, many descended from the wild or semi-domesticated breeds present centuries ago in Inglewood Forest, an ancient royal hunting reserve in which the farm lies. These range from shaggy Highland cattle, rare British white cattle and

red and fallow deer to bagot goats, donkeys, pigs and poultry. Many of the animals can be fed and handled.

Energetic visitors, both young and old,will also enjoy the woodland nature walk and children's playground. Those with a creative streak can try their hands at making fresh farmhouse bread or hand-churned butter with help from a local expert.

Having worked up a healthy appetite, visitors can refresh themselves with snacks and drinks which can be enjoyed in the pleasantly situated picnic area. A selection of gifts, souvenirs and fine local produce is also available in the shop.

The Four Seasons Farm Experience is open seven days a week from 10.30am to 5.00pm between Easter and the end of September. Please call **06974 73753** *for further information and opening times out of season.*

FOUR SEASONS, FARM EXPERIENCE
SOUTHWAITE, CARLISLE
CUMBRIA CA4 0LS

CAMERTON.

Map ref. B.7.
Next nearest Town or Village " Broughton"
Location.5 miles west of Cockermouth.

Camerton is a parish on the Derwent, in a hollow, with three mains roads leading into it...each consisting of a steep hill;some four miles north of Workington, and five miles from Cockermouth.Originally a mining village.
Camerton's best known building is without doubt its ancient parish church of St.Peter's, which dates back to the 11th century, though in fact there was a church here for many years before that. There is no road to St.Peters...just a path across the fields.
Inside there is a sandstone effigy of a warrior which has been painted black, and is known locally as 'Black Tom of the North'.He was a direct descendant of the Curwen family of Curwen Hall at Workington.He was a smuggler leading very much a Robin Hood type of existence, stealing from the rich and giving it to the poor.he died in about 1500

and today is still very much a source of discussion, particularly at the 'Black Tom Inn 'The statue of him came to the church around 1500 though he himself is reputed to be buried in Shap Abbey.He makes a bold figure in his black armour,with his long hair resting on a crested helmet, and holding a mighty double-handed sword.
Near to St Peter's is a grassy field with a bridge at one end connecting Camerton to the village burial ground.The bridge is known as 'Miser's Bridge' after a Joseph Parkin who died in 1800 and was the first person to be buried there. He was nicknamed thus due to his reputation for hoarding money.
On the outskirts of the village is Seat House Farm where the well-known strain of Clydesdale horses are bred.
CamertonHall is a very large house on the outskirts of the village and has been designated as a building of historic and architectural value. It is said to have been designed by Indigo Jones, and is built on the site of a Pele tower of the 14th century.

CARK IN CARTMEL.

Map ref. E.13.
Next nearest Town or Village "Flookburgh"
Trains.Railway Station.
Location. two miles south of Cartmel .

Cark in Cartmel is a village two miles south of Cartmel on the sharp bend of the Grange to Haverthwaite road, a little way inland from the sea(the B.5278 Haverthwaite to Flookburgh road) This village had a burst of prosperity in the 18th and 19th century, when several mills were established in the locality.The first was a paper mill erected in 1782 and later cotton mills.One of these used a steam engine to pump water back to the mill dam, and it is from this that the Engine Inn located here takes its name...though there are many locals hereabouts who will disagree and say that the name relates to the fact that the horse-drawn fire engine

used to be kept there!
The mill was one of the first cotton mills erected in England.Cotton was brought in by ship, as Cark was a busy port in the 1700's.Ships were built by the river near Crook Wheel, and trade was carried out with the Baltic, America and the West Indies.

Cark Hall nearby was built by Thomas Pickering.The Hall has mullioned windows and a magnificent entrance.George Fox was once held prisoner here.
The most famous landmark in the vicinity is Holker Hall, home of Lord Cavendish, famous for its annual hot air balloon extravangaza, the gardens, its countryside festival motor museum, and deer park.
The railway here was opened in 1857, and Cark station is on the line between Ulverston and Carnforth.

The Engine Inn

Cark in Cartmel
Grange-over-sands

Tel. 05395 58341

Cark in Cartmel is a village just two miles south of Cartmel, on the sharp bend of the Grange to Haverthwaite road...a little way inland from the sea.

This country inn built so it is believed around 1689 is full of charm and character. It was originally called the Fire Engine Inn, but as there is no fire station nearby no one really knows the reason for this old name. The inn stands besides a fast flowing stream in the village, and is only a short way from the famous 12th century Cartmel Priory and the stately home of Lord Cavendish...Holker Hall/Cartmel was the site of Lancashire's first cotton mill. Grange over Sands is four miles away with, as to be expected, many facilities for golfing and fishing. The Cartmel peninsula is flavoured with a mild climate and makes for an ideal walking area.

The Engine Inn and Restaurant (its correct name incidentally) is extremely popular with locals and visitors alike for Clifford and Hazel Birt have in a relatively short time built up a reputation for their excellent food. The beautiful dining room with its atmosphere of original oak beams, and open wood fire has an excellent display of painting by local artists John Gale. Here you will be offered an excellent range of fare including the locally caught Flookburgh shrimps cooked in hot butter, together with their, now, famous steak, ale and mushroom pie. Locally caught game including venison, pheasant and salmon from the estate of

Holker Hall is regularly shown on their blackboards.

For visitors wishing to stay overnight, five en-suite rooms are available at economical rates, with weekend breaks being arranged at anytime.

CARLISLE.

Map ref. F.4.
Bus service.
Trains. Railway Station. Town Centre.
Tourist Information Centre. Old Town Hall.
Location. Junction.A.595/A.6. Junction 43. M.6.
Early closing. Thursday.
Market day. Mon to Sat.
Gala days/festivals...
Cumberland Agricultural Show. 3rd Thursday July.
Border D.T.C. Obedience Dog Show. 1st Sat.June.
Carlisle & District C.S. Obedience Show.3rd Sat July.
Wigton D.T.C. Obedience Show.Last Sunday August.
Carlisle Great Fair.Nearest Sat to 26th August
(for eight days).
Carlisle & Borders Spring Show. 1st Sat/Sun
August.
Solway & Hadrian Fuchsia Group. 1st Sunday
August.
Penton Sheepdog Trials. Last Saturday May.

Carlisle is Cumbria's cathedral city,and a major market and industrial centre,It has enjoyed an extremely important status since the Roman occupation when it was set up as an adminstrative centre...back in AD78. It those days it was known as Luguvalium with the town being laid out in grid squares, and was considered by all as a 'handsome'city The city is the classic border settlement...constantly fought over by quarrelsome neighbours to north and south.Its history of turmoil survives today in the great castle ,the city walls and other relics which provoke the visitor to contemplate how uncertain life must have been amid such years of turmoil.

Carlisle has the distinction of being the only English city not listed in the Domesday Book (it was in Scottish hands when the Normans carried out their survey).But even before Hadrian marked the northern extent of the Roman colony by building his wall from Solway to Tyne, the Celts had their own settlement at Carlisle, the name of which ...Caerluel... seems scarcely to have changed through subsequent occupations.

Besides the dramatic stretches of Hadrian's Wall, where it rides the rugged outcrops of the Great Whin Sill just a short trip to the east of Carlisle, some sections of Wall survived centuries of plunder in the city itself and can be seen in the grounds of Cumbria College of Art and Design.

Towards the end of the 9th century, it was the Danes who sacked Carlisle, destroying it completely by burning it, knocking down the walls and killing every man,woman, and child.The few records that do still exist of those days show that it was impossible to distinguish Carlisle from its surrounding area, so completely had the town lost its identity.

More recently, firmly Royalist Carlisle stood out against General Lesley's 4,000 strong army during the Civil War.For nine months then the city was besieged until the citizens, reduced to eating dogs and rats,were starved into submission and the gallant 700 man garrison surrendered.

In 1745 it was the Jacobites turn to beseige the city.Bonnie Prince Charlie rode in on a white charger,preceded by 100 pipers,and proclaimed his father James 111 of England.

The cathedral bells were rung in celebration...but by the following month the prince was in retreat. The Scots.. those, of course,who weren't hanged..returned to Scotland,and Carlisle returned to England. The King apparently was not amused by the Prince's reception in Carlisle and the cathedral bells were removed by royal decree and not returned until 1926.

Carlisle Castle, which incidentally is open to the public, has over the years been shattered, restored and improved many times in its long history. The castle was originally founded by William Rufus in 1092, and few English castles can claim such a long history of military occupation as Carlisle. The grim and forbidding appearance as it watches over England's frontier with Scotland lays perfect testimony to many hundred's of years of warfare,struggles and feuds.Visitors should look especially at the prison rooms in the keep, where graffiti,names and figures have been carved in the stone walls by some of the many captives the castle has held over the centuries.In the walls will be seen the holes for the iron staples which held the prisoners in chains...on one occasion 96 in one night!...Most prisoners were left to die here, though a few were transported.As to be expected many famous names are associated with the castle most notably being Mary,Queen of Scots who was locked in the tower at the corner of the inner yard.Note the patch of grass below the southern wall ...known as Lady's Walk, and is where the unfortunate Queen would exercise before eventually being imprisoned in Bolton Castle.

The Castle today contains an exhibition which tells the castles own fascinating and extraordinary history and is undoubtedly a 'must' on every visitors itinerary. In addition one of the buildings houses the King's Own Royal Border Regiment museum.

Within walking distance will be discovered Carlisle's other gem, its Cathedral. As Cathedral's go it could be said to be relatively small, but in all fairness it did lose six bays of its nave when Parliamentary forces took the stone away to repair the city's defences back in 1644. The first building was actually started by Augustinian Canon's in the early 12th century,and in 1133 it became a cathedral under the orders of Henry.1. As a matter of interest Sir Walter Scott was married here (in the nave section) on Christmas Eve 1797.

The Cathedral's masterpiece is undoubtedly the great east window,which attracts vast numbers of visitors. However,also not to be missed is the 15th century paintings on the back of the choir stalls...a sort of strip cartoon of the lives of the Saint Cuthbert, together with Augustine and Anthony,and the 12 Apostles.

The coming of the railway in the latter part of the last century became tremendously important to Carlisle's economy.At one time seven railway companies had lines terminating here with trains arriving and leaving all around the clock,making the Citadel Station a place of perpetual bustle.

Today besides being an important stop on the West Coast route to Scotland the station is also the terminus of the famous Settle-Carlisle railway, without fear of argument the greatest scenic line in England, as well as the Tyne Valley and Cumbrian Coast scenic lines.

During the last decade Carlisle has undergone what amounts to a rebirth and is now presenting a bright new face to the world.In 1991 it earned second place (highly commended) in the English Tourist Board's 'Destination of the Year's' award for which there were around 250 entries.

In the pedestrianised centre of the city, where the old Carel Cross can still be seen, is where the great fair, first held in 1352 brings history to life each year ,with many of the stallholders in colourful period costume.Make sure you are here for the 26th August...

Close to the cathedral is the 17th century Tullie House, which has recently received a £5 million refurbishment programme. Tullie House today is one of Britain's most innovative historic attractions,and portrays Carlisle's fascinating place in Border history.The galleries captivate and enthrall visitors of all ages with the power of their images,objects,stories and hands-on displays.

Visitors,or more probably the children...can crawl through a tunnel,emulating the Roman miners,or get in some target practice with a stone-thrower or a Roman crossbow in a turret on Hadrian's Wall.The highlight of the museum however is the history of the Reivers, the name given to the many border families who looted,kidnapped and even killed each other in an orgy of violence that continued for over 300 years,Their horrific deeds led to the establishment of a whole new language and in fact many of the words that were born out of this terrible period of history remain in the English vocabulary today.Words like *bereave* and *blackmail* have their roots in the Reivers.

Many modern surname also derive from those families.Names such as Dacre,Heron,Laidlaw and

CARLISLE

Yarrow all stem from this period, as do more common names such as Hall,Scott,Taylor and Watson.An ancestral research leaflet is available for those who wish to discover if they are related to the lawless Reivers.

Visitors to Carlisle may also find St Cuthbert's church of interest too. This quaint little 18th century building has a most surprising pulpit, a massive thing which slowly slides on rails from its place by the wall and takes up its stand for the sermon in the middle of the church.The sermon over,the preacher back in his seat,the pulpit moves off again, drawn by ropes attached under the floor to a handle turned in the vestry.

Sightseeing over..visitors will subsequently discover that shopping here is a pleasure, rather than a chore.The city centre is compact and easily reached from its many car parks.The major shops are located along English Street, and where English Street and Scotch Street meet, visitors will find The Lanes...Carlisle's award winning shopping centre, where will be found major stores and a variety of well known and local names blended into the Carlisle street scene.Between Scotch Street and Castle Street is the Fisher Street walks area where traders have joined together to promote a city centre area of specialist shops and local stores.In this area you will find crafts and antique shops, bookshops,gifts and local foods.

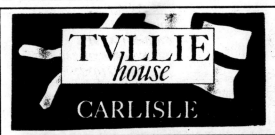

WILL OUR PAST COME BACK TO HAUNT YOU?

Opened on 6th January 1991 after a £5m refurbishment. Tullie House is one of Britain's most innovative historic attractions.

Portraying Carlisle's fascinating and turbulent place in Border history, the galleries captivate and enthral visitors of all ages with the power of their images, objects, stories and hands-on displays.

Focusing on the Romans, the historic Railways and the notorious Reivers of Border history, the experience is of walking back in time, while the environmental dome speeds the visitor through the sky-scape of the borders in just 8 minutes. Children especially love those exhibits in which they can play an active part - be it querning grain, exploring the mine tunnel, using the micrarium scope or writing on Roman wax tablets. Rubbings of the Bewcastle Cross are a souvenir of the visit, while they can climb on to Hadrian's wall and try their skill with the Roman crossbow. There are many other exhibits which appeal to all ages and interests and which make Tullie House a treasure house of discovery.

Tullie House

★ is open all year except Christmas Day

★ opens at 10 am from Monday to Saturday

★ From January 1994 admission will be half-price between 10am and 11.00am

★ opens at 12 noon on Sunday

★ has many admission charge discounts

★ recommends you allow at least 2 hours for a full visit

★ validates tickets for up to a week, on request

★ has comprehensive facilities for the disabled

★ welcomes groups and school visits

**Tullie House,
Castle St. Carlisle
CA3 8TP
Tel: 0228 34781**

CARLISLE

In Omnibus Caritas

Austin Friars School
Carlisle CA3 9PB
Telephone: 0228 28042
Fax: 0228 810327

AUSTIN FRIARS SCHOOL was founded by members of the Augustinian Order in 1951. The school provides secondary education for over three hundred boys and girls from the ages of eleven to eighteen. Austin Friars stands in its own twenty-five acres of grounds on the northern outskirts of Carlisle. It is an independent, Catholic School which welcomes pupils from all faiths.

Austin Friars has high expectations of its pupils and enourages them to develop their potential in a happy and productive atmosphere. The talents of each pupil are appreciated and are developed within the school community for the wider community in which they will eventually take their place. Academic and spiritual progress are nurtured with equal care. Close attention by tutor and by subject or form teacher provides a framework for a positive attitude to study. Visitors to the School will see current examination results available.

Music and drama are strongly supported. Team and individual interests, both cultural and sporting, are a vital part of the School's life. Qualified staff coach and lead our day pupils and boarders in a wide variety of non-academic activities.

Parent-teacher meetings, mid-term grades, end - of - term reports help to give a picture of a pupil's progress. Parents are invited to contact the School at any time to discuss any aspect of their son's or daughter's life at school. We know that the partnership of parents with the school brings constant benefit to the children.

Each year the School holds an Open Morning, usually in October, for parents and children who would like to know more about Austin Friars, and we would like to invite interested parents to telephone or to write at any time to arrange a visit.If you would like to know more, please phone us on **0228 - 28042 or write to The Secretary, Austin Friars School, Carlisle, Cumbria CA3 9PB.**

CARLISLE
THE GREAT
BORDER CITY

great heritage •

great attractions •

great accommodation •

great shopping •

great activities •

great holidays •

CARLISLE, Britain's largest city, (397sq. miles in fact), offers everything you could want from that perfect short break or even longer holiday.

For centuries Carlisle was the coveted prize in the bloody struggles between England and Scotland, whilst the tranquillity and unspoilt beauty of the surrounding country side make Carlisle an ideal base to enjoy Hadrian's Wall, the Lake District and the Borderlands of England and Scotland.

Our border history is graphically brought to life in TULLIE HOUSE, one of Britain's newest and most innovative museums as well as the 900 year old CASTLE and majestic CATHEDRAL.

Stay awhile — accommodation in Carlisle is as varied as the city itself, from high class international hotels to friendly guest houses to cosy inns and farmhouses or if you prefer self–catering, we have a wide choice of holiday cottages. Wherever you choose to stay you will be assured of the warmest of welcomes.

Shopping is a pleasure in the compact pedestrianised city centre offering large department stores, all weather shopping malls, speciality shops and the covered market.

There is so much to do if you feel active. Walking in the beautiful countryside, cycling, golfing, sailing, fishing, going to the races, in fact you can almost do anything.

Our VISITOR CENTRE will introduce you to Carlisle and offers a comprehensive range of guided walks and tours by qualified Carlisle Heritage Guides. If you need further information about our great city write to:

Carlisle Tourism & Marketing (VP), Civic Centre, Rickergate, Carlisle, Cumbria, CA3 8QG
or telephone **0228 34339** *or* fax **0228 511370.**

CARLISLE

The Great Border City

BACT
British
Association of
Conference
Towns
MEMBER

CARTMEL

Map ref. F.12.
Nearest Town or Village "Grange Over Sands"
Bus service. Cumberland Buses 530, 531, 535 730,
735, 536
Location. 2 miles from Cark,
Cartmel Agricultural Show.1st Wed.in August.
Cartmel Steeplechases. Spring Bank Holiday.
Cartmel Races August Bank Holiday Sat/Sun.

Everyone loves Cartmel...a parish and old market town two miles from Cark and just over two miles from Grange-over-Sands.The name alone is very ancient...the land was originally given to St.Cuthbert (by King Ecgfrith of Northumbria) in AD 678.
The village is centered around the market square (referrred to by the locals as "The market cross and fish slabs') Around the square is a delightful assortment of genuine 'olde worlde' buildings, serving as they have for centuries, as friendly inns, well stocked shops, together with private dwellings.
Cartmel is one of South Lakeland's oldest villages and grew up around its famous 12th century priory.Cartmel Priory was founded in 1189 by William Marshall, the Regent of England, to be a Priory for regular Canons of the Order of St.Augustine. Not now completely intact, but nevertheless very well preserved, and a constant attraction to its many thousands of annual visitors.Note in its cemetery the graves of several people who tried to make the hazardous journey across the estuary, between tides...and failed!
An unusual, but endearing feature is the tower which is set at a 45 degree angle to its base.
Having recently celebrated its 800th anniversary, the Priory to this day still serves as the centre of the community offering not only a place of worship, but a place to give concerts and other special events. The Priory, additionally, contains many treasures.These include small fragments of manuscripts, a very famous umbrella(claimed to be one of the first..over 200 years old) a Vinegar Bible of 1716, and the first edition of Spenser's Faerie Queen, printed in 1596.(In 1929 it was stolen, but recoved later in America...today for safe-keeping it is kept at Lancaster University)
Also note the loaf of bread set out daily in the north aisle for the poor.
Legend has it that the monks started the very popular Cartmel Races as their Whitsunside recreation. Originally the wooden grandstand was taken down

PRIORY GATE HOUSE

every year and put away in the tithe barn in Barn Garth.Nowadays it is a permanent course,with various races throughout the year.
From the square, ancient streets wend their way out of the village.Here you'll find flower filled corners, stream-side walks, and hump-backed bridges..
The old Gothic style village school is still the most popular primary school for miles around, and the modern Priory School is a worthy successor to the original school held in the 14th century priory gate-house, between 1624 to 1790,It was, in fact, on the 7th July 1624 that 'The Tower of Cartmel' as the gate-house was then called, was purchased by the inhabitants of the district from George Preston, of Holker, for £30.00 in order to convert it into a public schoolhouse. With such a long history, it seems only a relatively short time ago that the school-children were expected to pay annually what was known as the 'cockpenny' to the schoolmaster to pay for the very popular cock-fighting organised under his supervision.
Edmund Law who became Master of Peterhouse, Cambridge,and subsequently Bishop of Carlisle was educated at the gatehouse school early in the 18th century.
Finally..Cartmel has lots to offer the visitor with some four pubs, together with cafe's, shops and hotels, not overlooking the many places to walk.You can sit and watch cricket and football in the park in season.Cartmel Cricket Club is one of the oldest in the District.

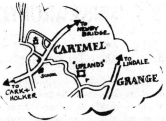

CARTMEL / CARTMEL FELL

CARTMEL FELL

Map ref.F.11.Bus Service.
Nearest Town or Village "Bowland Bridge"
Location. 6 miles west of Kendal.

BOWLAND BRIDGE

Cartmel Fell....the name means 'sandbank by rocky ground' is a chapelry in the northern(and hilly) part of the district of Cartmel between Windermere and the Winster.It enjoys expansive views of Whitbarrow Scar on the one side and the Coniston range on the other...and has remained relatively unspoilt throughout the centuries.

Raven's Barrow, the highest point on the fell.looks down on land which has belonged in turn to the early Scandinavian settlers, to Stephen of Boulogne (later King of England) to the Augustinian Priors, to the Duchy of Lancaster, and to the yeoman farmers who built their manor houses and halls along the valley Hodge Hill, Thorphinsty, Cowmire.Witherslack and Burblethwaite.The two or three hundred folk who lived in the parish made a living from sheep-farming,charcoal-burning. basket-weaving, leather-work,woollen manufacture.as well of course from the corn mills. fulling mills and bobbin mills.

St Anthony's chapel here was founded in 1504 in accordance with the will of Anthony Knipe who lived in the parish of Burblethwaite...and is the only church in the north-west of England dedicated to St.Anthony the patron saint of charcoal burners and basket weavers.The church escaped the ravages of zealous Puritans and well meaning Victorian restoration and is still very much as it was 400 years ago. even including its unusual 17th century three decker pulpit.

Visitors should make a point of going into the vestry and see the chapels most interesting relic. It is a figure of Christ which used to belong to the Crucifix which all churches would have had erected over the chancel screen.Its now the only one of its kind surviving in the country.Originally it would have been gilded, but it has been badly treated, and within living memory was being used as a poker! Near the entrance to the porch should be noticed the marks in the stone where men used to sharpen their arrows.In the churchyard will be found a horse mounting block.

Below the hill will be found Hodge Hill a 16th century statesmen's house of great charm, with outside gallery and interior kept in its old style.Nowadays the building is a hotel.

Cowmire Hall is an elegant 17th century house of three stories built on a pele tower of the 14th century.Thorpinsty Hall is the oldest property around, for earliest reference is shown in 1275.

CASTERTON.

Map ref. H.12.
Next Nearest Town or Village "Kirkby Lonsdale"
Location. 1 mile north of Kirkby Lonsdale.
Gala days/festivals. Casterton Folk Dance Weekend. 2-4th April.

A parish east of Lune, close to the A.683.Two hamlets actually...High Casterton and Low Casterton.

The name 'Casterton' comes into one of the most famous books in the world, and beautiful as it is, it was remembered with bitterness by Charlotte Bronte, who spent twelve unhappy months at Cowan Bridge close by, where her school can still be seen.She was only nine years old when she left, but she never forgot how wretched she had been,as she tells us all in Jane Eyre.

The name 'Casterton' means 'the farmstead near the fortification' and has been a community long before its entry in the Domesday Book. For example at Overburrow two miles south of Kirkby Lonsdale a Roman fort can be clearly seen in the narrow,deep valley. At one time it housed an infantry battalion of 500 men within its three acres.It was first explored in 1883 when gateways and remains of a Roman bridge were discovered.

Early evidence of man here is the Druids Circle on Casterton Fell, which is thought to date from the Neolithic Period about 1400 BC.The next arrivals were the Celts in 600-400 BC who called the river 'Al-iam' or 'White Water'.The Romans arrived in about 78AD and built a road through the area along the bottom of the fell,which remains to this day.The Romans left in 410AD and were eventually followed in about 890AD by Norsemen.After 1066,Casterton became Crown Property and was granted at times to various noblemen until comparatively recently, when it was sold to the Earl of Lonsdale.In the wake of the Battle of Bannockburn in 1314 the Scots devastated the area, but Casterton recovered well for in 1492 a fulling mill was in use and a corn mill erected.Coal mining was carried out on the

Casterton Fell from 1620 to 1850.Communications improved in the 18th century and in 1777 a pack-horse track up the valley was made into a road, followed by the railway in 1847. The railway,incidentally, only opened after strong opposition to the original route would have taken it through the garden of the Clergy Daughter's school.

The name Carus-Wilson figures frequently in Casterton history.The Carus family acquired the manor of Kirkby Lonsdale in 1558, and later a descendant of the family married Elizabeth Wilson and adopted the name Carus-Wilson..In 1823 his eldest son founded the Clergy Daughters School at Cowan Bridge and later moved it to Casterton...where today it is a boarding school for 360 girls. The schools register of 1824 incidentally contains the names of the four Bronte sisters,Charlotte,Emily, Elizabeth, and Maria.The junior department of the school is known as Bronte House which is a building also founded by Carus-Wilson originally as a school for servant girls.

HOLY TRINITY CHURCH

This nine hole golf course is situated one mile north of Kirkby Lonsdale. Set in beautiful countryside overlooking the market town, it is well worth a visit.

The course is within easy reach of the Lake District, Yorkshire Dales and North Lancashire. It provides a challenge for all players, and visitors are very welcome.

There is a clubhouse serving light refreshments and clubs are available for hire.

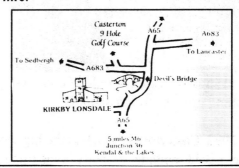

For further information contact:-
**John & Elizabeth Makinson
(05242)) 71592**

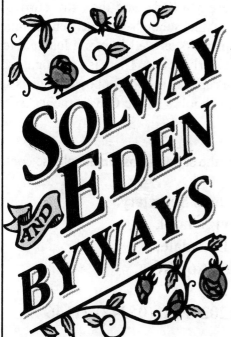

Far from the madding crowd! Quality holiday cottages in undiscovered North Cumbria - from the Northern Lake to the Scottish Border.

Nursery provision, Romantic Evenings at Home, and Something Special - Intrigued??

For our brochure and further information, please contact:
Jane Simmons,
Solway and Eden Byways, (Ref: C 94)
FREEPOST (CE665)
Bowness-on-Solway, Carlisle
Cumbria CA5 5BR
Tel/Fax: 06973 51745

CASTLE CARROCK.

Map ref. G.4.
Next nearest Town or Village "Cumwhitton"
Bus service. Cumberland Buses 96
Location. 4 miles south of Brampton.

Castle Carrock is a parish four miles south of Brampton, and means 'the fortified castle'...though frankly one has never been found here.
The village nestles with its back to the foot of the north-western tip of the Pennines... designated an area of outstanding natural beauty. Panoramic views of the Eden Valley to the south, the Solway Firth to the west and Scottish hills to the north.

There is considerable evidence of early habitation in the area, which includes pit dwellings on the Castle Carrock fells, together with the discovery of an ancient stone coffin containing artefacts dating back to the Stone Age. A large stone cairn, six metres high is prominent on the skyline and is known as Cardunneth Pike. It has been identified as a meeting place and burial site for people of the Bronze Age 1800BC-500BC,

Though no castle exists here..it is believed that a fortified manor house existed here in the past, complete with moat.
Among a small group of stone houses is the simple little church, with an outside stone staircase leading up its tower to the belfry.It is of no great age, but it stands on the site of a church said to have been built from stones of the vanished castle, and on the sanctuary floor, cut with a flowered cross and a chalice, is the gravestone of a Rector who preached his first sermon the year Crecy was fought, six centuries ago.Another Rector here, was Richard Dickenson, who preached his last sermon at the age of 94.

CAUSEWAYHEAD.

Map ref.C4
Next nearest Town or Village "Silloth
Location. South East of Silloth

Causewayhead lies just over a mile south-east of Silloth and is dominated by the church of St.Paul...erected in 1845.

Of note is the fact that the Earl of Lonsdale donated a piece of land for burial purposes in 1893.Today this graveyard has graves of some of the airmen killed during the Second World War.

CLAPPERSGATE & BRATHAY.

Map ref. E.10.
Next nearest Town or Village "Ambleside"
Location. One mile from Ambleside.

A picturesque hamlet on the Brathay...one mile from Ambleside on the Coniston road...beneath Loughrigg Fell.
Back in the 16th century Clappersgate would have been classified as a port.The port today is a boat house and harbour of 'The Croft' a large house built around 1850 for a Liverpool merchant, accompanied by many picturesque houses and cottages. At the entrance to the stables there was once a vagrant's whipping post.

Just over Brathay Bridge the house called 'Old Brathay' has many literary associations.In the Middle Ages it was a farm named 'Low Brathay'.In 1880 the property was owned by Charles Lloyd a friend of Wordsworth...Lloyd often entertained Wordsworth, along with Coleridge,Southey,even Constable, the artist.

Cleator & Cleator Moor.

Map ref. B.9.
Next nearest Town or Village "Gosforth"
Bus Service: Cumberland Buses No. 17, 22.

Location. 4 miles from Whitehaven.
Early closing.Wednesday.
Market Day.Friday.
Gala days/festivals.
Cleator Moor Sports. 3rd Sat in July.

ST. MARYS GROTTO

Cleator and Cleator Moor are situated some four miles from Whitehaven, and three miles from Ennerdale, lying in beautiful countryside.The villages lie on the edge of the great hills of Lakeland in a countryside once rich in iron but now dotted with the desolation of red waste heaps of the hematite mines. Great industrial depression has passed this way and many left, but new industries in the area are bringing people back again.

Just outside the town, close to St Mary's Roman Catholic Church is a small grotto similar to the one at Lourdes in France.

Under the capable supervision of Father Clayton...in 1926 utilising local people during the height of the depression years, he built a grotto which he wanted as near as possible to be an exact replica of the one at Lourdes. It took the workers a little over a year to build. It was opened and blessed on the 30th October 1927 by the Abbot of Douai.Dom.Edmund Kelly O.S.B. President of the English Congregation of the Benedictine Order.

Each year many thousands of pilgrims and visitors come to the grotto...though in September there is a pilgrimage which attracts many thousands from all over the country.There has been many stories of pilgrims being restored to full health after visiting the grotto.The most famous visitor here was his Eminence Cardinal Basil Hume, who came on the 27th July 1980 and re-dedicated the Grotto.

Besides Cleator's most popular attraction, other interesting features are in the market square.One is the memorial to the iron ore and coal miners, produced by the well known local artist Conrad Atkinson, and the Victorian awning around the Co-Op store.

A popular beauty spot on the River Ehen is Wath Bridge,known locally as 'Hen beck' This is an

CLIBURN.

Map ref. H.7.
Next nearest Town or Village "Temple Sowerby"
Location. 5 miles south-east of Penrith.

A small village situated in the Eden Valley some

5 miles south-east of Penrith. The name means 'Stream by the Bank'...the stream being the river Leith.

The main street runs downhill and is lined with attractive sandstone buildings, much of the stone coming from quarries in the Whinfell Forest nearby.Many of the buildings date from the 18th

and 19th century, and it is thought that there has been a settlement here since Saxon times.
Cliburn Hall was built in the 14th century, as a pele tower ,by Robert de Cliburn, the then Lord of the Manor,Today it is a farmhouse.
Nearby is St.Cuthbert's Church.Originally Norman, with Roman stones in the porch, it is approached by a short avenue of lime trees.On the English altar is something very beautiful...a gift from an Admiral of the American Navy.He was Admiral Cleburne , and he found this beautiful thing in Italy and brought it back home to Cliburn. For 700 years it was treasured in the Abbey of Vallombrosa and,being homeless when the monastery was closed last century, the admiral brought it back with him.

CLIFTON.

Map ref. G.7.
Next nearest Town or Village "Eamont Bridge"
Location.1 mile south of Penrith on A6.

Clifton is a village south of Penrith and Eamont Bridge, and is named after the two cliffs above which it stands.
It was here on the 18th December 1745 that this little village was the site of the last battle to be fought on English soil.It was between rebel Highlanders and the Duke of Cumberland's dragoons, on Clifton Moor.The dead of both sides are buried in the village...the Scots under an oak tree (The Rebel tree) opposite Townend Farmhouse, and where there is a plaque commemorating the fact...and the English are laid in the churchyard. The following entry in the church burial register at Clifton states...'The 19th December 1745, 10 Dragoons...to wit six of Blands, three of Cobhams, and one of Mark Kerrs Regiment buried, who was killed ye evening before by ye rebels in ye skirmish between ye Duke of Cumberlands army and then at ye end of Clifton Moor next ye town..' in addition seven Highlanders were killed and buried at Town End.Town End Farm where the Duke of Cumberland spent the night is still a farmhouse and opposite is the large oak.. The aforementioned Rebel Tree. under which a stone says "men of the army of Prince Charles lie here'
Nearby is the 13th century church of St.Cuthbert.It is said that it is one of the places where the monks from Lindisfarne rested with St.Cuthberts body when they fled from the Danes in the late 19th century.This small church was built over Saxon foundations by Norman craftsmen and some of their work can be seen in the south doorway.Two stained glass windows here are very old and were originally in the Lady Chapel.One shows a figure of St.John, the other a picture of Eleanor Engayne,

CLIFTON HALL

a mistress of Clifton Hall in the 14th century.She is in a blue gown with a cloak of white and gold.During the 17th century for some obscure reason the windows were removed and taken to Mardale, from whence they were returned after Mardale village was transferred into a reservoir.
Clifton Hall, like many old manor houses in one-time Westmorland was the home of one family for generations. The Wyberghs became Lords of the manor some time in the 14th century and the same family probably built the three storeyed tower some hundred years later.It was built on to a mediaeval house which has long since been destroyed.The large windows in the ruined tower suggest that it is only semi-fortified but there is still a small watch tower on its embattled top looking across to Penrith beacon.In a wall of the modern farmhouse nearby is a Roman stone with two carved figures and an inscription.
The first school here came about in 1764 when a Mary Scott left £40 in her will towards payment for a schoolmaster.
Just outside of the village will be found Wetheriggs Pottery which first started in business in 1760 making bricks and tiles. In those days it was part of Lord Brougham's estate.The pottery today still makes slipware in their distinctive brown, green or blue, and the same patterns of old using white clay poured through a cow horn with a goose quill in the end. The pottery nowadays is an industrial museum and open to the public.

The White House. Clifton

"As sweet a little snug spot as man could wish for."
William Hogarths' description of the White House in 1829 is as apt today as it was then. Anne and

Christine Broadbent make it their concern to provide for their guests a relaxing and happy atmosphere where they can be comfortable and spoilt throughout their stay.

The White House built in 1765 by a member of the Hogarth family, is a converted farm house full of character, with an interesting history at present being researched by its owners. It has had connections with farming, the church, the law, horse racing and has housed a dolls' museum.

The White House has converted most successfully into a guest house becoming well established over the last six years for non-smokers. It is fully licensed providing excellent meals. The home is set in attractive gardens and is convenient for visiting the Lake District and the Eden Valley, or as a break on the way to Scotland.

"No amount of compliments can show our appreciation to two charming sisters who certainly know how to spoil their guests in so many ways." A recent quote from the Visitors' Book.

For further details contact A & C Broadbent
The White House, Clifton, Penrith, Cumbria, CA10 2EL Tel 0768 65115

COCKERMOUTH

Map ref.C.7.
Next nearest Town or Village "Papcastle"
Bus service. Cumberland Buses 35, 36 54, 56 55, 58, 101, 102, 103, 104, 105, 555, 556, 600
Tourist Information Centre. Riverside car park.
Location. A.66 10 miles east of Workington.
Early closing. Thursday.
Market Day. Monday.
Gala days/festivals Cockermouth & District Agricultural Show.Sat prior to 1st Mon August.
Cockermouth Children's Carnival. 3rd Sat June.
Broughton Children's Carnival (nr Cockermouth) 3rd Sat June.
Cockermouth Festival. Whole of month of July.
Cockermouth Sheepdog Trials. 3rd Sat May.

The ancient market town of Cockermouth, as its name implies,is located at the mouth of the river Cocker, where it joins the river Derwent.
The town is probably most famous for being the birthplace of the Lakeland poet,William Wordsworth. On Main Street will be found the 18th century house in which he was born in 1770 and lived until his mother died.The house is open to the public ...seven rooms are open to view all furnished in 18th century style,along with several of the poet's personal effects;even his childhood garden with its terraced walk.
Beside the house is a little lane leading down to the riverside with views of the castle and brewery.Wordsworth's father John Wordsworth is buried in the churchyard of All Saints Church.He was Steward to Sir James Lowther...who owned

WORDSWORTH HOUSE

the King to beseige and destroy the castle. The lower part of the western tower shows traces of this siege.

The castle was again beseiged some 400 years later during the Civil War, and subsequently relieved on the 29th September 1648 by Parliamentary troops, sent out by Cromwell from Lancashire. Regretfully thereafter the building was partly dismantled and allowed to fall into decay..in fact much as it stands today...with the exception of one wing re-built during the last century. Mary Queen of Scots was one of the famous visitors who stayed there in 1658 with 16 followers from her defeat near Glasgow, and here she was received by the wealthy merchant Henry Fletcher, who gave her 16 ells of rich crimson velvet to replace the poor clothes in which she stood. With Darnley murdered, Bothwell taking refuge far away, her throne gone, and her cause lost, her visit here would have been amongst her last days of freedom before the long years of imprisonment ahead.

The castle nowadays is rarely open to the public (being lived in by the Egremont family) and even then only to groups or parties by appointment.

The oldest part of the town is at the bottom of Castlegate. Percy House was built in 1598 by Henry Percy, Ninth Earl of Northumberland. Originally the home of the Earls bailiff, though now converted to three shops. One of the upstairs room's, even today, bears the coat of arms of the 'Percys;.

The churchyard is a place of many memories. It has the grave of Wordsworths father. John, along with Fearon Fallows. As a boy friends sent him to develop his genius at Cambridge, and by 1820 he became the first Astronomer Royal at the Cape of Good Hope. He planned the first observatory there and saw it built...he made a catalogue of southern stars; and he died far from home at the early age of 43.

The town has several links with famous people...apart from the Wordsworth's. John Dalton the mathematician and chemical philospher was born nearby in 1766. He was the inventor of atomic theory. A little known fact is that he was a child prodigy, even teaching at Pardshaw Hall school at the early age of 13 years!!

Turner stayed here in 1809, and his painting of the castle now hangs in the Turner Room at Petworth.

Robert Louis Stevenson was another visitor staying in the town in 1871.

(CONT)

most of the nearby Cumberland coalfields.

Cockermouth has been a market town since 1226, and today cattle auctions are held here each Monday and alternate Wednesdays...with additional sheep sales on Fridays in the autumn. Mondays is for the stalled market held (logically enough) in Market Place,,, which in the summer months is announced by the traditional ringing of the 'Butter Bell'.

The first historical mention of Cockermouth is made in the year 1069, when the then County of Cumberland then formed part of Scotland. It was gifted to Ranulph des Meschines, and subsequently added to England. Later it came into the possession of Waltheof, First Baron of Allerdale, who,....it is said, built the Norman castle, with most of the stone coming from the Roman fort at Papcastle.

Most of what we see was built in the 13th and 14th centuries, and the structure is divided into two wards by a group of buildings in the middle. The lower ward has the flag tower and the great gatehouse, with its barbican walls seven feet thick, and its arms of famous families. The ruined walls of the upper yard are shaped like the bows of a mighty ship, with three storeys of windows at the tip looking out over the Derwent far below. The central buildings include an inner gatehouse and a roofless tower with two storeys. The upper storey was the kitchen and still has two wide fireplaces. The lower seems to have escaped damage and is the best complete room in the ruins, with a finely vaulted ceiling supported by a single column in the middle. There are also two little vaulted dungeons.

In 1221, the Sheriff of Westmorland was bidden by

ESTD. 1828

JENNINGS BREWERY TOUR

C O C K E R M O U T H

It's our round!

Since 1828 Jennings have been brewing a range of real ales to suit every palate.

Today you can enjoy our Dark Mild, original mellow Bitter, Light hoppy Cumberland Ale or the strong dark Sneck Lifter bitter in over 90 warm-hearted Jennings pubs throughout Cumbria.

And if you've a thirst for knowledge too we'll show you around our Castle Brewery in Cockermouth, let you into a few of our secrets and explain the workings of the Hop Back and the Mash Tun.

Our Brewery Tours last one hour. An admission fee is payable. Regretfully we cannot admit children under 12 years of age.

Tours may be booked at the Brewery Shop or by calling - **0900 823214 Ext. 133**

JENNINGS
BROTHERS PLC

Castle Brewery, Cockermouth, Cumbria CA13 9NE

The Riverside

RESTAURANT

'The Bridge', 2 Main Street, Cockermouth,
Cumbria, CA13 9LQ
Tel: (0900) 823871

Formerly the Old Court House of Cockermouth, this delightfully warm and friendly restaurant is situated in the Town centre, yet in a quiet spot adjacent to the River Cocker.

The cosy bar area offers an open log fire, along the with equally cosy Dining room with its exposed beams and secluded alcoves...just perfect for those intimate dinner evenings whilst on holiday. Three menu's are on offer. The A La Carte offering a wide range of dishes to suit all tastes. The very popular Table d'hote menu, and more recently we have added a vegetarian menu...which already is proving very popular with our regular clients. All meals are cooked to order from fresh local produce.

The food and service is at all times prepared under the supervision of the Proprietors, thus ensuring an evening to remember.

Open all year..6.30pm - 10pm
7.00pm - 9.30 Sundays. Closed Tuesdays

Table reservations 0900 823871

Main Street, Cockermouth,
Cumbria CA13 9LE
Tel.Cockermouth (0900) 822126

The GLOBE HOTEL

A friendly, family run hotel dating back to the early 17th century. Centrally placed in picturesque market town, birth place of the great poet William Wordsworth.

Most of the 30 bedrooms have en-suite facilities equipped with direct dial telephones, colour TV, radio/intercom, tea/coffee making facilities.

Adding to the relaxing atmosphere is a restful lounge, residents bar, public bar, ballroom (accommodating upwards of 100 guests), and a spacious dining room.

Guests are assured a comfortable stay at the recognised northern gateway to the English lakes.

GARDEN CENTRE

Lamplugh Road, Cockermouth, Cumbria. CA13 0QT
Tel: Cockermouth (0900) 822180

Stockists of: Environmentally Friendly Products, Teracotta Pots, Reconstituted Stone Containers, Garden Ornaments, Sundials, Bird Tables, Garden Sheds, Wheelbarrows, Tools, Johnsons seeds, Dried Flowers, Basketware, House Plants, Fison's P.B.I. Products, Arthur Bowers Composts, 300 Litre Bales of Peat, Calor Gas Stockists, Bags of Logs and Bags of Dog Food at Discounted Prices.

Oakhurst is a picturesque Centre just of the A66. As the name suggests it is set amidst oak trees and woodland. With ample car parking space it makes the ideal centre for those in the locality. It has developed over the years and now offers a wide range of garden related items.

The outside area is occupied by tree, conifers, shrubs and fruit trees, and there are over 100 varieties of roses. In the walled garden you will find locally grown quality bedding plants, alpines, herbaceous and perennial plants.

May sees dozens of hanging baskets full of colour and you are invited to bring in your basket for replanting by the experienced staff.

Inside the shop you will find everything for the gardening enthusiast, with stocks varying from season to season. For example, in early spring there are over 20 varieties of seed potato, whilst in Autumn dozens of types of bulbs will have taken their place.

The conservatory holds a wide selection of house plants which again changes from week to week according to availability. For the specialist a good selection of bonsai dishes is on display alongside teracotta pots and planters.

A new feature widely acclaimed is the impressive display of dried flowers, basketware & florists sundries in the upstairs showroom.

Hundith Hill

HOTEL

LORTON VALE, COCKERMOUTH
CUMBRIA, CA13 9TH
TEL: 0900 822092 VISITORS: 0900 822050

Hundith Hill offers peace and quiet in all of its 16 bedrooms. With views across to Redpike, Grassmoor, Melbreak and down the beautiful Lorton Valley to Buttermere and Loweswater, the hotel is ideally situated for a tranquil break.
14 of the rooms offer the luxury of en-suite bathrooms and facilities for the disabled are also available.
For that special occasion a four poster bridal suite is available/
Chiildren are welcome and there is a price reduction for a family room.
Central heating is installed throughout the hotel and a warm, comfortable welcome is guaranteed all year round.
Hundith Hill has a reputation for fine food. The dining room seats 30 in comfort and style. This family run Hotel offers its guests and visitors alike a vast choice of home cooked food.
Fresh seasonal produce is the basis for the traditional recipes prepared, both for the Dining Room and Bar where superb Bar suppers can be enjoyed

Fletcher Christian, the leader of the 'Mutiny on the Bounty' was born at Moorland Close in 1764. He was educated at the old Grammar School...now the site of the church rooms. Many people think that he is buried in the churchyard here...where an elaborate tombstone records members of his clan. If he had returned to England then he could easily have been the inspiration for S.T Coleridge's 'The Ancient Mariner' More accurately, however is the fact that he is buried on the Pitcairn Islands, and where today his descendants populate the islands.

Of recent years a common visitor to Cockermouth was the singer Bing Crosby on one of his regular fishing visits.

Other attractions in Cockermouth is the Cumberland Toy and Model Museum, situated in Market Place, and Jennings Brewery close to the castle. It is of interest to know that the well, which originally served the castle with water, is now used to produce beer and those people who tour the brewery can sample the Sneck Lifter, together with other Jennings fine ales.

COLBY.

Map ref.I.8
Next nearest Town or Village "Appleby"
Location. 1 mile from Appleby.north,

Colby means 'the coal' (or charcoal) a village just over one mile from Appleby.A very old village known to go back as far as 1086 when a family named Colby owned the entire village.

Many of the houses here are built of sandstone and date back to the early 1700's.Look carefully and you will notice some houses with windows blocked up reminding us of the time when the number of windows in a house related to the amount of tax you had to pay.

COLTON & OXEN PARK.

Map ref. E.12.
Next nearest Town or Village "Lowick Bridge"
Bus service. Post Bus
Location. 2 miles from Greenodd near the B5084 road.

Colton is a parish with church some two miles from Greenodd, whilst Oxen Park is a village.The name Colton is thought to be derived from Coleton or Charcoal Town....Between the two they cover an area of land spreading from Windermere to the east and Coniston Water to the west.

Holy Trinity Church stands on the top of the hill at Colton, with the old village school alongside.At this point a panorama of the fells and mountains is worth seeing.

One mile south of Colton is an old Baptist church at Tottlebank which was founded in 1669 under the Act of Uniformity.Historians will know that Charles 11 decreed that non-conformists could not worship within five miles of a corporate town.This Tottlebank is just five miles from the market town of Ulverston.

Colton Old Hall was the home of the Sandys family in the 17th century, and is just a half mile south-east of town.

Oxen Park village consists of little more than a farm and a few dwellings.The old blacksmith's shop still survives,and many of the properties date back to the 18th century and before. Investigation here will uncover a cockpit dating from cock-fighting days.

On the edge of the village is new House which was originally the poor house housing vagrants and tramps, together with homeless individuals.

CONISTON.

Map ref. E.10.
Next nearest Town or Village "Hawkshead"
Bus service. Cumberland Bus Route 7, 9, 513, 512, 505, 506, 507
Tourist Information Centre. 16.Yewdale Road.
Location. A.593 Ambleside road.
Early Closing. Thursday
Gala days/Festivals. Coniston Country Fair.
1st Sunday in August.
Coniston Water Festival Late May

Coniston is a beautiful and romantic valley.Its charms have lured some remarkable people since the first Viking settlers came in, and the valley had an interesting and varied history.

Coniston has earned its living from mining and quarrying for centuries.The quarrying survives for the slate a 'tuff' formed from fine volcanic material which is decorative and very hard.It can be highly polished, and in this state is used for facing buildings all over the world.But Coniston has also long been a popular holiday centre, increasingly so after the coming of the railway in 1859.The line has now gone, and with it one of the most picturesque journeys in the country.

Tennyson spent his honeymoon here..at Tent Lodge in 1848...a house incidentally that Turner had painted many years before. W.G.Collinwood moved here, as did Arthur Ransome.More recently in 1967 to be precise, Donald Campbell died tragically whilst seeking to break his own

world water speed record at Coniston. On the village green will be found a memorial to him.

Before the copper mines, dating back to Jacobean times, Coniston was a scattered rural community mainly settled around Coniston Hall...itself built in 1270 by the Fleming family.Nearby at Bowmanstead (near the Ship Inn) is where the bowman lived, producing bows and arrows, together with the men to defend the Hall.

Coniston Hall is the oldest building hereabout,which was originally a pele tower.In 1962 the property was purchased by the National Trust, with the grounds now being used as a camp site. Also owned by the National Trust is Yewdale Farm, two miles north, and which is interesting for offering a good example of a typical Cumbrian spinning gallery.

The village situated at the head of Coniston Lake was originally most likely a Saxon settlement.The present church was completed in 1891, though the village has had a chapel since early days...certainly before 1500. John Ruskin is buried in the churchyard.Not to be missed too is the Ruskin Museum which contains many items relating to him, amongst which is his fine collection of mineral specimens.

On everybody's itinerary has to be a visit to Brantwood, the home of John Ruskin from 1872 until his death in 1900.John Ruskin,writer, and philosopher, had a powerful influence on Victorian attitudes to art and politics.His eloquence, his critical faculty and his appeal to the best in human nature were irresistible. He was a giant of his time.He made Brantwood, on the east side of Coniston Water his home .He bought it as a 'small place' (his words) from one William Linton, a wood engraver and magazine editor, and added to it over the years. Ruskin loved the across-lake views from the house, and from the grounds where he laid

OLD MAN

out paths, he had a seat made for himself near a waterfall.

Brantwood is undoubtedly one of the most beautifully situated houses in the Lake District.The house,literally, became an 'intellectual powerhouse' and one of the greatest literary and artistic centres in Europe.

In 1196 Coniston Water was known as Thorstanes Watter, the name originating from its owner Thorstein, one of the district's Viking settlers. It is the third largest lake in the Lake District, and like its larger sisters has always been a highway. Once, ore from the mines and slate from the quarries were barged down the lake,and at other periods between the 11th and 17th century iron ore was brought up the lake to be smelted at lakeshire 'bloomeries' where wood for charcoal-making was in good supply. When the railway came to Coniston, the railway company set up a steamer service on the lake.Two boats were in operation, and one of them the 'Gondola' an iron steamship of elegant design, still survives,having been beautifully restored by the National Trust.It is now in service again.

From the summit of the mountain known as 'Old Man', on a clear day there are breathtaking views as far distant as the Scottish mountains, the Isle of man, even Snowdon on ocassions, and certainly around Coniston is lakeland scenery at its very best.

At Coniston will be seen three very old inns. The 'Crown', the 'Sun', and the 'Black Bull'. The "Black Bull' is the coaching inn where Turner stayed in 1797.Another inn visited by him in the neighbourhood was the old 'Halfpenny Alehouse' (on the spot a house called 'Lanehead' now stands) The 'Black Bull' was then kept by Tom Robinson and his wife, the daughter of a 'Wonderful Walker'.

TOWNSON GROUND

East of Lake CONISTON
Cumbria LA21 8AA
(05394) 41272
Proprietors: Ken & Barbara Nelson

TOWNSON GROUND is a 400 year old Lakeland country house located on the quiet eastern side of Coniston water (approximately one mile from the village).

It is tastefully converted into a quality, family run Guest House with a friendly atmosphere. It also includes three self catering units.

The spacious grounds provide a relaxed picturesque setting. The area is of outstanding natural beauty and there are numerous local walks as well as access to a private jetty on Coniston Water. It is an ideal location for touring and walking in the Lake District National Park. Some of the local attractions within walking distance are:

Tarn Hows. Hawkeshead...the pretty village which also includes the Beatrix Potter Exhibition, along with Wordsworth's Grammar School.

Brantwood, (the former home of John Ruskin) with views which are without equal in the Lake District, and offers woodland walks, craft gallery, painting exhibitions, cafe etc.

Coniston Old Man, Wetherlam etc., which are a challenge to the enthusiast.

Our accommodation offers a large comfy lounge with coal and log fires along with television and reading area. Olde worlde dining room where a good English breakfast is served....or if you prefer, a breakfast of your choice. Well appointed bedrooms, mostly en-suite facilities, catering for doubles, twins, families and singles. All have tea/coffee making facilities. Children over three years are welcome. Fire certificate held. Ample private parking. Pay phone. One dog by prior arrangement. Washing & drying facilites.

The three self catering units are:-

Ruskin apartment..level access..suitable for disabled (not wheelchairs) sleeps 4/5. 1 double, 1 twin and one sofa bed in lounge. Extras..video, dishwasher and microwave.

Garden House Sleeps 2/3...1 double and one sofabed in loung. Extras microwave and video

Cottage. Sleeps 4. 1 double & one bunk bed (full size). Extras coal and log fire.

All units are nicely furnished and beds are made up ready for use. Electric blankets are available if required.

HOW HEAD COTTAGE

East side of Lake
Coniston, Cumbria LA21 8AA
Tel: (05394) 41594

How Head Cottage is situated 1¾ miles from Coniston village on the east of Lake Road. Bed & Breakfast for non-smokers. We have two well appointed guest-bedrooms with vanity units, central heating and en-suite facilities. One twin overlooks the lake and one small double.

Our DEN, 80 yards from the main house has a double bedroom, en-suite shower room, a small TV area and tea making facilities. In the main house there is a TV lounge with a selection of books to read. Free tea dining area. Home made bread is our speciality.

In addition to our Bed and Breakfast arrangements we can further offer SELWYN COTTAGE and HOWHEAD

HOLIDAY FLAT...Self catering units... The cottage has a spacious loung, a small double bedroom, dining/kitchen shower room with wash basin and toilet. The Flat which is on groung level has one double bedroom, lounge dining room kitchen and bathroom. Both have fitted aarpets, colour TV, electric cooker and fridge, and both enjoy outstanding lake views...some people say the best views of anywhere in Cumbria.

OPEN ALL YEAR
WEEKEND BREAKS AVAILABLE
NOV - APRIL.

SUN HOTEL

AA ** and Coaching Inn **RAC** **

Standing proudly at he foot of Coniston' spectacular 'Old Man', the Sun is a fine country house hotel built at the turn of the century alongside its sixteenth century coaching Inn. A traditional meeting place for Lakeland organisations and long-standing headquarters for the Coniston Mountain Search and Rescue Team, the hotel and Inn have genuine charm.

Donald Campbell insisted on staying at the Sun Hotel whilst attempting the World Water Speed Record in 1967 and the hotel was subsequently used as a location for the BBC television drama 'Across the Lake', based on Campbell's famous exploits.The Sun is set above the village in its own superbly maintained and glorious gardens, and provides the perfect Lakeland retreat. The views of fells and forestry are inspiring and the hotel itself is furnished and decorated to provide the most relaxing surroundings. A log fire burns in the cosy lounge where a wide selection of books and games help while away those unstrained evenings.The Sun's four hundred year old adjoining bar is an unspoilt example of a traditional ancient coaching inn, where the burning logs in the

open grate warm the atmosphere and a selection of keg and hand-pulled real ales add to the conviviality.Delicious home-made bar food is served daily whilst the hotel menu offers a broad range of interesting dishes in plush and tasteful surroundings. Special diets can be catered for too.Most of the bedrooms come with en-suite bathrooms and are mostly complete with colour television, tea and coffee making facilities and telephone. There are two bedrooms with four poster beds, and all rooms are centrally heated and charmingly decorated.Homely splendour is the theme throughout the Sun Hotel and the staff are always on hand to make sure of your constant comfort.

Coniston, Cumbria LA21 8HQ Tel: Coniston (05394) 41248

BRANTWOOD
Winner - National Art Collections Award 1989

The Home of John Ruskin 1872 - 1900

Brantwood is the most beautifully situated house in the Lake District. It enjoys the finest lake and mountain views in England, and there is no other house in the district with such diversity of cultural associations

The home of John Ruskin from 1872 until his death in 1900, Brantwood became an intellectual powerhouse and one of the greatest literary and artistic centres in Europe. Tolstoy, the Mahatma Gandhi, Marcel Proust and Frank Lloyd Wright can all be numbered amongst Ruskin's disciples
.   Today, Brantwood still retains that special feeling which has given inspiration to so many, and Ruskin's thinking still has the keenest relevance.

Brantwood was originally built as a simple roughcast cottage (the present entrance) in about 1797, and was occupied by Gerald Massey, errand boy son of a bargee, who became something of a poet and philosopher. From him it went to W.J. Linton, who enlarged it considerably and set up a printing press there to publish *The English Republic*, a radical journal.

Linton married Eliza Lynn, a writer, and together they produced a book about the Lake District, but their marriage was less than harmonious, and when they parted, Linton sold Brantwood to Ruskin. Ruskin found the place damp, decayed and with revolutionary mottoes scrawled on the outside walls. During the next twenty-nine years, he spent thousands of pounds adding to the buildings and extending the estate until it encompassed some five hundred acres.

● *Splendid collection of Ruskin watercolours always on show.*

● *Woodland Walks with glorious displays of daffodils, rhododendrons, azaleas and bluebells. Glorious Autumn colours*

● *Ruskin Lace demonstrations Easter to October*

● *Jumping Jenny's Restaurant and Tea Rooms for delicious home cooked food besides a roaring log fire. Licensed. Panoramic lake views from the terrace.*

**BRANTWOOD, CONISTON,
CUMBRIA LA21 8AD**

Tel: Coniston (05394) 41396

★ **OPEN ALL YEAR** ★

Daily mid-March to mid-November
11.00 a.m. - 5.30 p.m.
Winter Season:
Wednesday to Sunday 11.00 a.m. - 4.00 p.m.

Arrowfield

Little Arrow,
Coniston, Cumbria LA21 8AU

ARROWFIELD is an elegant Victorian house with extensive and beautiful views of the surrounding countryside. It is set in a quiet and peaceful location 1 3/4 miles from Coniston, and is an ideal place in which to relax and unwind. There is immediate access to the fells, and horse-riding, sailing, and windsurfing are all available nearby.

One of the major features of the house is the decor, which combines elegance and style with a feeling of comfort and homeliness. There is a spacious sitting room with an open fire where one can recover after a hard day on the fells.

The accommodation consists of 5 bedrooms, 2 of which are en-suite. Colour TV, tea and coffee making facilities and vanity units are available in all rooms.

We attach much importance to good food at Arrowfield, and everything is home-cooked from fresh ingredients and local produce. Breakfast can be either of the large and hearty British variety or Continental with hot French rolls, croissants and patisseries. Dinner is optional, and consists of four courses plus coffee, featuring a mixture of British and Continental cuisine. We have a full residential licence, so you can enjoy an aperitif and a glass of wine or two with your meal.

ARROWFIELD is English Tourist Board. Two Crowns. Highly Commended.
Enquiries/Details, Tel. 05394 41741

Lakeland House

Coniston, Cumbria LA21 8ED
Telephone 05394 41303

Lakeland House is situated next to the village green and just a short walk from Coniston Water. It is owned and run by a husband and wife team

Accommodation is on a bed and breakfast basis at competitive rates. A full traditional English breakfast is provided but can be varied to cater for any special diet. Weekly terms are available and group bookings welcome.

All rooms are centrally heated, have colour television and tea and coffee making facilities. Family rooms, private shower and toilet, easy parking and superb mountain views from most bedrooms are some of the other attractions.

The guest house is open all year and is an excellent centre for the many and varied activities catered for in the area. It is popular with walkers, climbers, water enthusiasts and many others out to enjoy the delights of the Lake District.

A warm welcome is assured for guests and customers in the tea rooms where a lovely atmosphere, varied menu, and delicious home made food all combine to make a visit well worth while.

Lakeland Land Rover
J.F. & E. HADWIN LTD.
Torver, Nr. Coniston, Cumbria LA21 BBJ P
Telephone: 05394 41317 Fax: 05394 41719

Situated on the A5084 just east of Torver is J.F & E Hadwin Ltd.

We have over 30 years experience with 4 wheel drive vehicles and can offer extensive stocks of genuine parts as well as new and used Land Rover vehicles.

Our dedicated service team can tackle any Land Rover vehicle from the earliest Series 1 to a modern LSE.   We also carry out servicing on other vehicles, and recovery operations when required.

To cater better for our customers in the East of the County we have a recently opened facility in Kendal.

We are a wholly family owned and run business offering competitive rates and a friendly relaxed atmosphere...Come in and see for yourself..

Torver. Sales/Service/Parts. Tel: 05394 41317.
Open Mon-Sat. 8.30a.m. - 5.00p.m.

Kendal Service. Tel: 0539 734351
Open Mon-Fri 8.30 a.m. - 5.00p.m.

Coniston Launch

Castle Buildings Near Sawrey,
Ambleside, LA22 0LF
Tel & Fax (05394) 36216

History and Style

What more enjoyable way to experience the pleasures of Coniston Water than by taking a cruise aboard a traditional timber craft offering all the timelessness and quality of craftsmanship in wood. You can enjoy comfortable seats in a saloon offering full weather protection - or there is ample room on the forward deck for those hardy travellers - who just wish to relax in the sun!

The launch 'Ruskin' is the oldest passenger boat plying on Coniston Water, and as you journey on her you will hear about her 'war record', and about the other boats that have sailed on this lake. The commentary on this splendid sightseeing adventure follows in the footsteps of John Ruskin, Arthur Ransome, Beatrix Potter and Donald Cambell.

Personal Service

This is a small independent company dedicated to providing a friendly, personal service - happy to carry you, your dog, and pushchair - with the helpful crew on hand to answer your questions about this magical area.

Evening Cruises are a popular regular feature and private charter hire is available for that special occasion.

Hourly Sailings . . . and Savings

Boats from Coniston Boatlandings sail every half of the hour starting at 10.30 (11.30 in winter) calling at jetties around the lake including Brantwood the one-time home of John Ruskin. Brantwood House tickets can be bought on board at a 50p discount - this is to encourage visitors not to take their cars along the narrow, congested road on the east shore of the lake. There is a special rate for those travelling to Coniston by bus (the Coniston Rambler) - just ask your bus driver for full details.

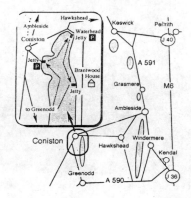

CORNEY.

Map ref. C.11
Next nearest Town or Village "Bootle"
Location A.595. Ravenglass to Silecroft road.

Corney is a parish on the south coast, between Bootle and Waberthwaite. It is a small community made up mainly of farming families spread over an area rich in ancient settlements.

Coming to its little church on a lonely hilltop we are rewarded with a splendid view of this fascinating countryside.Far in the valley below a mountain stream chatters under a tiny bridge,and here and there among the hills the farms are dotted. Over the lowlands we look to the sea, and inland rise Black Combe and Buck Barrow.

The church here is dedicated to St John the Baptist and at its height of 600 feet looks protectively over the parish.This church is a little over 100 years old, though there has been one here since the 12th century. In the churchyard is a sundial dated 1882, the gift of one Edward Troughton, Corney's most famous son. Despite being blind and deaf he became famous for his work on scientific instruments, and was awarded the Copley medal by the Royal Society.

The Brown Cow Inn built around 1800, and in its early days provided bed and board for huntsmen and hounds. It wasn't until the late 1950's that electricity first came to Corney...lighting until then had been by oil lamps and candles.

Corney folk have a reputation for longevity. A gravestone here shows one John Noble lived here 1658-1772 (114 years)..his life stretching from the end of Cromwell's to the beginning of Napoleon's.

CROOK.

Map ref. F.11.
Next nearest Town or Village "Underbarrow"
Location. Midway between Kendal and Bowness.

A pleasant Lakeland village situated midway between Kendal and Bowness on Windermere.
Thwatterden..Now Crook Hall, stands on high ground to the south of the church, and the present building dates from the 18th century. It stands on the site of the memorial hall and demesne farm of

Crook which dates back to mediaeval days.The original Thwatterden Hall was built by the Philipson family in about 1450.They also built the still surviving pele tower at Hollins Hall.

A prominent landmark on the hill to the north is "The Monument' which at one time was the lookout point for Scottish raiders.

The old church of St Catherine is in a field to the west of Crook Hall...though today only the tower remains...in a very unstable condition!.Originally it was the manor chapel in use from 1506-1880. A bell from the old church now hangs in the present

St.Catherine's.,and is believed to be one of the earliest church bells in the north-west.

Village functions prior to the erection of the Memorial Hall used to take place on premises known as Mill Slack..in Mill Yard. Across Dobby Lane...which inci-dentally is supposed to be haunted, is the site of Crook Mill. Most of the remaining cottages in Mill Yard were one time workers cottages. as it is thought a fulling mill was operated here in the 1500's

CROSBY GARRETT.

Map ref. I.9.
Next nearest Town or Village "Soulby"
Location. 7 miles from Appleby, 3 miles from Kirkby Stephen.

Crosby Garrett is a small, but attractive village situated between Warcop and Kirkby Stephen, and seven miles from Appleby .

Many archaeological finds and several prehistoric burial cairns prove that the area has been inhabited since at least stone age days. Evidence exists of ancient dwellings at 'Several', and burial grounds at Bents and Raiset Pike.

The village probably had its origins in Saxon times and in fact the oldest part of the parish church of St Andrew shows remnants of a Saxon arch.The chancel too has a 13th century piscina and a doorway carved a century earlier, the nave roof is over 300 years old, and a carved chair is 17th century. One of two old bells here may be 13th century. The church incidentally· is built on the highest part of the ridge, once used, it is believed as the site of pre-Christian sacrifices. and known as Arklow.

Close by is the Crosby Garrett Viaduct,54 feet high, and used by the Settle-Carlisle railway.The Crosby Garrett Fell is a regulated common of 2,000 acres, rising to 1254 feet at Nettle Hill.

CROSSCANONBY

Map ref. B.6.
Next nearest Town or Village "Maryport"
Location. 3 miles north-east of Maryport,

Crosscanonby is a village three miles north east of Maryport.

Crosby, Birkby, Ellengrove, Allerby Hall, Kirkby, together with part of Bulgill combine as a township...first recorded in the 11th century.

Crosby and Kirkby are villages in the parish,which was given by Alan, second Lord of Allerdale, to Carlisle Priory...and served by the Canons...hence the name Cross Canonby.

Many of the buildings are built of sandstone, probably from large slabs hewn from Crosscanonby quarry, and man-handled to site. Sandstone in fact from a much earlier church was used to build St.Johns, an 11th century church, which can be seen with its Roman chancel arch along with two stone statue alcoves. Recent excavations here have brought to light relics over 1,700 years old including a 2nd century fortlet.

Many historical features in the church, all well displayed.In the graveyard is a Viking Hog-back gravestone..shaped to imitate a little house.. Another stone is a tall cross with a very crude human figure, thought to be St Lawrence.

The area is one where the Solway views and sunsets combine with the panorama of the Cumbria mountains.

CROSBY RAVENSWORTH & MAULDS MEABURN.

Map ref. H.9.
Next nearest Town or Village "Shap"
Location. 4 miles east of Shap.

The sister villages of Crosby Ravensworth and Maulds Meaburn are situated four miles east of Shap, and five miles south-west of Appleby.It is an area with delightful and curious place names...Silver Street, Liquorice Hill and Harberwain to name but a few.

Approaching from Shap, one cannot fail to see the circle of standing stones at Oddenndale and descending from Crosby Fell, the ancient iron-age settlement (Romano-British) called Ewe Close, and reputed to be one of the finest in the North of England. It takes the form of a complicated series of enclosure walls and hut circles...the largest being more than 50 feet in diameter.

King Charles 11, halted with his army at Black Dub in August 1651...a spring on the moors lying south-west, whilst being pursued by Oliver Cromwell. A monument here marks the event. Many great houses in Crosby Ravensworth.Crosby Hall once fortified with a pele tower was acquired from the Lowthers by the Todd family (who are still there today)The house has been re-built within the last 200 years, and when the tower was demolished the ghost of a white bull apparently also disappeared!

Crake Trees, a ruined mediaeval fortified house lies between the village and its twin Maulds Meaburn...itself a spacious and beautiful village with old cottages. The houses here are linked by stepping stones and small bridges over the clear Lyvennet.There are wide sweeps of green and charming houses. Meaburn Hall here..nowadays a farm, was the home of the Lowthers until 200 years ago when the main block was rebuilt, but it still retains 16th century woodwork.In front of the house are traces of the extensive gardens and a bowling green, and two stone summerhouses still stand in a field close to the hall.

The church of St.Lawrence, often described as a cathedral in miniature, contains the tomb of Sir Lancelot Threlkeld who died in 1512. He saved the young Cliffords during the War of the Roses.The church was built to replace a wooden structure early in the 12th century, and it came into the care of Whitby Abbey.Like other buildings in the area it was destroyed by Scottish raiders. The village belonged to Scotland at the end of the 12th century and the beginning of the 13th century, and the church was then rebuilt...work of the latter period can be seen in the six piers of the nave..

The old school (1784) and the old forge are close by. The one time home of one Thomas Bland too may be seen hereabouts. He sculptured statues of many famous people and placed them in his extensive garden.He added his own oil paintings and hung them in alcoves and he put up a building for his musicians. He called the garden his 'Pleasure Grounds' and people at one time flocked in their hundreds to see all his creations. The paintings were removed in 1907 and today the statues stand, some bold, some forlorn, overlooking the sheep grazing contentedly on the grass below.

CROSTHWAITE & LYTH.

Map ref. F.11.
Next nearest Town or Village "Underbarrow"
Bus service. Cumberland Bus route No.540
Location. 4 miles south-east of Bowness.
Gala days/festivals.
Crosthwaite Sheepdog Trials. 3rd Sat. Sept.

The name Crosthwaite means 'a cross in a clearing'. The village is situated some four miles from Bowness on Windermere, and represents the start of the National Park.

It is a sprawling village with farms and cottages in small hamlets, well known for its damsons...brought originally from Damascus for their dye, when the area was involved with the woollen trade.

The village is like fairyland in spring, when its orchards are wonderful with the damson blossom.Not far from Windermere and in the charming Lyth Valley, it is a lovely place with trees and old houses along with glorious views.Close by is Gilpin Dale,and sheltered by

Whitbarrow Scar is Cowmire Hall, a 17th century farmhouse with a 16th century pele-tower. It has a quaint canopied doorway, round chimneys of a kind hardly seen in any other county, and little windows looking across the valley to Cartmel Fell. Within half a mile away at Pool Bank, South House has something of interest to show, for here the roof extends over a railed spinning gallery above a doorway.

The current church is St Mary's, built in 1878, but there has apparently been a chapel or church here for centuries.A strange bequest was made here...it was the gift of a man who died some 200 years ago and left two shillings and sixpence (12 new pence) a year to be paid to a villager for whipping dogs out of the church. He left to two friends his best and second-best coats!.

An old(but beautifully restored) corn mill stands by the River Gilpin...though the mill is not in use today, It dates from 1829. Currently the building acts as a management study centre.There is evidence of several other mills and lime kilns hereabouts, but the only trade left today in the village is the blacksmith's shop at the end of the village and the very attractive post office and general stores.

Damson Dene

A HOTEL
FOR ALL SEASONS
A Methodist Holiday Hotel

Welcome *to Damson Dene our newest hotel in the heart of the Lyth Valley in the beautiful Lake District National Park. The hotel is furnished to 5 crown standard offering luxury and super luxury bedrooms. All rooms have colour televisions, direct dial telephones, en-suite toilet, bath or shower and tea and coffee making facilities.*

At any time of the day there is a spacious lounge in which to relax with a roaring log fire in the colder months.

In summer months there are patios and the three acres of landscaped gardens in which to enjoy the sun and surrounding beauty.

Our restaurant serves a hearty Lakeland breakfast and delicious five course dinners, freshly prepared by our chef, using local quality produce. A very popular Sunday Lunch is served and at all other times Bar Snacks are available. Both our restaurant and comfortable bar enjoy views across the fields to the fells beyond.

For the energetic we have a full size squash court, a fitness room, sauna, jacuzzi, sun beds for a tan, indoor heated swimming pool. For the less energetic there are pool and full size snooker tables.

The hotel has an entertainment suite with dance floor area for functions and wedding parties.

Special weekends and conferences catered for. A video of the hotel is available for your consideration.

Damson Dene Hotel
Crosthwaite,
Nr. Bowness-on-Windermere,
South Lakeland LA8 8JE
Tel: 05395 68676. Fax: 05395 68227

where everyone
is welcome

CULGATH

Map ref H.7
Next nearest Town or Village "Edenhall"
Location.7 miles East of Penrith.

Situated just of the Penrith-Scotch Corner road, approximately seven miles from Penrith and Appleby.

Culgaith is sited on a promontory above the fertile Eden Valley, overlooking the Pennines on one side and the Lakeland Fells on the other.
The small Wesleyan chapel was erected in 1830.
Interesting walks can be taken around Culgaith Millrigg marked the boundry between the counties of Cumberland and Westmorland in one direction whilst in the opposite direction, the rivers Eden and Eamont meet.

CUMDIVOCK.

Map ref E.5.
Next nearest Town or Village "Dalston"
Location 3 Miles South West of Dalston.

Cumdivock is a small rural community 3 miles south-west of Dalston. Until the 19th Century the township comprised the Hamlets of Cardew, Cardewleas, The Gill, and Shawkfoot. In the centre stands the church of St John, consecrated in 1872.

Down the hill from the church lies Shawk quarries which have been worked here continously since Roman times. Of note is the fact that it is thought that stone from here was used to build Hadrian's Wall, west of Carlisle, and later on for the building of Rose Castle and Carlisle Cathedral, and the Citadel.

CUMWHINTON.

Map ref F.4.
Next nearest Town or Village "Wetheral"
Location B6263 Off A 6.

Known in ancient times as Quintins Combe or Combe Quinton, the village nestles in a valley near the Pow Maughan beck around three miles south-east of Wethral and four miles from Carlisle.

Many of the houses here are built of local red sandstone quarried locally in the 19th century. The quarry these days is a nature reserve.

There is no church here, but it is known as a caring village with prayer meetings weekly taking place in different people's homes.

The famous Settle-Carlisle railway line passes through the village.

CUMWHITTON.
Map ref.G.4.
Next nearest Town or Village "Wetheral"
Location 9 Miles from Carlisle.

Cumwhitton is a small picturesque village situated some nine miles from Carlisle, 16 miles from Penrith and seven from Brampton.

The church is dedicated to St Mary, and records here show that there has been a church here since the 13th century...possibly a lot earlier.
Nearby is a 'bleak, hilly, trackless waste', where HenryVI encamped after the battle of Hexham..thus giving the area the name 'King Harry'. Close is the remains of a druidical circle know as Grey Yauds.
Water from springs on 'King Harry' has a reputation for bring some of the purest in the country.

DACRE,
Map ref. F.7.
Next nearest Town or Village "Pooley Bridge"
Location. 5 miles from Penrith.

A village in the valley of the Eamont some 5 miles from Penrith. A small and very pretty spot tucked as it is between the hills.Though small, the village nevertheless has a long history, being mentioned by theVenerable Bede in AD698.The name Dacre was probably taken from the sizeable beck which runs through the village.
Dacre is thought to be the site of the Anglo-Monastery mentioned by the Bede.Excavations in the churchyard have confirmed the existence of pre-Norman drains and walls.
The castle here used to belong to the Dacre family, and some of the Lords of Dacre led raids against the Scottish Borderers.Built about the middle of the 14th century,Dacre Castle was for years relegated to the status of a farmhouse, but in the last 30 years has been restored to its former glory...and more.
The pride of the castle is the first floor which was previously unoccupied.It is a single enormous room with a trussed roof with fireplaces on opposite walls...one is Elizabethan and the other of the ingle-nook variety.
The room has a direct link with early history and has always been known as 'The Room of the Three Kings' as it is believed that the Kings Athelstan of Scotland, Constantine of Scotland, and Eugenius of Cumberland met here to sign a peace treaty.
It was in the reign of Edward 11 that the Dacre family started work on this fortress which was to be midway between a fortified pele and a castle

SHEEP DOG TRIALS

proper.The Dacres originally took their name from the village, but through two famous elopements gained the Baronies of Gilsland and Greystoke and became one of the noblest and most important families in the North of England.
In the nearby church of St Andrew is the 'Dacre Stone' with carvings of two men walking hand in hand.Athelstan and Constantine after their Treaty of Peace was signed...Legend has it that the ghosts of these two Kings still haunt the grounds of the castle.
In the churchyard stands the famous ancient stone effigies known as the Dacre Bears...which are believed to have come from the castle originally.Inside the church is a pre-Norman cross shaft with figures of Adam and Eve. It is carved with quaint animals and two scenes, with the tree and the serpent.The other stone here is a smaller fragment of a cross and its detail is very fine.The chief on it is the Anglian Beast, a remarkable creature with an almost human face, beautifully chiselled about 1100 years ago...One of the tomb-

stones here covers the family grave of the Troutbecks, and on it, every Easter Day, the money one of them left 170 years ago is distributed to the poor.

There is no school here, but the cottages just below the inn bears a sign-board 'Dacre School,,builded 1749'

A nearby mansion was the ancestral home of the Hassall family since 1665. It is now the Cumberland and Westmorland Yeomanry Museum.

The deep pool by High Bridge is known locally as 'The Wash Dub', and it is where the farmers would wash their sheep prior to shearing. It was (and probably still is) a popular spot for local children to learn to swim.

DALSTON.

Map ref. E.5.
Next nearest Town or Village "Cumdivock"
Bus service. Cumberland Bus Route No. 91
Trains. Railway Station
Location. South west of Carlisle.
Gala days/festivals. Dalston Agricultural Show.
2nd Sat August.

Dalston is a small village located just south-west of Carlisle, and lies on the banks of the river Caldew.

Most of the buildings here date from the late 18th century when the 'Industrial Revolution' was brought to this quiet little village, by the emergence of four cotton mills and a flax mill...not overlooking a forge and two corn mills.

Rose Castle hereabouts is reached by passing through an arch crowned with a sculptured rose...the archway in fact is one of the oldest portions of the castle which itself dates back to the 13th century. The building is built of friendly red sandstone, and it seems that there was probably a stronghold of sorts on the site as early as 1230. There is certainly evidence that a Bishop was in residence as early as 1255. An ecclesiastical fortress was constructed in 1304 during the wars between England and Scotland.

Edward Bruce arrived at Rose in 1314 after invading England by way of Carlisle. The castle itself was badly burned three times in the next thirty years by marauding Scots. At the beginning of the fifteenth century Bishop William Strickland made extensive additions which included the tower named after him.

The legendary Lady Anne Clifford visited the castle in 1673 and presented her portrait to Bishop Rainbow. She also gave him one of her famous locks inscribed with her initials A.P. standing for Anne of Pembroke and the date. Today it is still used to secure the main door.

Today, though farming and textiles are still prevalent, Dalston in comparison is somewhat relaxed in atmosphere. The sandstone building of the church of St. Michael...with its Norman origins dominates the eastern end of the square, and is approached by entering through a lychgate.

The story of the church begins with the Normans and ends with much restoring and re-building in the last two centuries. At the bottom of some of the walls is 12th century masonry, and among the 13th century remains in the chancel are lancet windows, the priests doorway, and a low window near it. An old stone seat runs along the south aisle wall and in the wall of the modern porch is part of an ancient coffin stone with shears and four circles as well as a cross. Here too is a richly carved Norman capital.

Its not too surprising to find in this churchyard the graves of two Bishops of Carlisle, for we are but three miles from Rose Castle, their chief seat for seven centuries. Here lies Edward Rainbow bishop for 20 years after the Restoration and famous as a preacher, his grave marked by an upright stone on the south wall. Bishop Hugh Percy of the last century has a fine cross.

Dalston Hall in its park lies a mile down the valley..the buildings of its main front, irregular and delightful, were chiefly built in the 16th and 17th centuries. The house still has its defensive tower of the 15th century, with coats of arms and an inscription in reversed lettering telling how it was put up by John Dalston and his wife Elizabeth.

Close by is an ancient rampart and ditch known as the Bishops Dyke.

Amongst the village's better known personalities was John Denton, who from Cardew Hall wrote a history of Cumberland in the 16th century. Dalston was also the birthplace of Susanna Blamire (1747-1794) the 'Muse of Cumberland' who wrote songs in Scottish dialect and lovely poems about Cumbrian country life.

DALTON in FURNESS

Map ref. D.13.
Next nearest Town or Village " Barrow in Furness"
Bus service. Cumberland Buses Routes
6, 6A, 6B, 9
Trains. Railway station.
Location. A.590 Barrow road.
Early closing. Wednesday.
Market day.Tuesday.

Dalton or 'Dale Town' so called for it lies at the centre of the amphitheatre formed by the high land around.The town's early history is inextricably interwoven with that of Furness Abbey, for it formed a part of the great estates of the powerful pre-Reformation Abbots.

Situated on the A590 north of Barrow, it was at one time the main town of the Furness area until it was eclipsed by Ulverston and Barrow,partly it is thought due to the plague that hit the area in 1631. This was one of the important parishes of mediaeval Cumbria, covering the area which is now Barrow in Furness, as well as part of Lakeland to the north.The old parish church, with its nearby castle (really a pele tower, and now housing a museum) sits on top of the hill in the old quarter, along with a number of 18th and 19th century houses, including the parsonage.

Dalton Castle also known as 'The Tower' commanded the main square from the 13th century, and was built by the Abbot of Furness to protect the Abbey from marauding Scottish Borderers.The only part of the castle which remains today is the tower which was for many years used as a local prison and is believed to have been built in the reign of Edward 111. It was in 1257 that reference is first made to a prison at Dalton...and in 1292 the Abbot of Furness claimed the right to erect gallows at Dalton, and was allowed a pillory and ducking stool. Beneath where the toilets now stand is the dungeon, the present entrance can be seen in the floor of the ladies toilet.It is thought that the original entrance would have been a grill in the floor and this would have been used as a holding area for prisoners waiting to be taken to court above.

The Dissolution of the Abbey in1537 marked the end of the great monastic period, and in a smaller way, the end of the town of Dalton as the premier settlement in Furness. A thriving market and influx of visitors had enabled Dalton to prosper.The plague of 1631 helped reduce that prosperity.360 of the towns total of 612 population were killed and the market was moved to Ulverston.

The nearness of the influence of Holker Hall, favourite home of the Dukes of Devonshire in the Victorian years affected life in the parish.The Duke was the major land-owner involved in Barrow's meteoric rise, and took enormous interest in Furness affairs from the 1850's until the 1880's.

George Romney the celebrated portrait painter (1734-1802) was born in Dalton and is buried in the churchyard.

The present church of St Mary at Dalton was dedicated by the Rev Harvey Goodwin, Bishop of Carlisle on the 1st June 1885.It is built on exactly the same site as the earliest church which may well have been consecrated before Furness Abbey was founded.

The site of Dalton parish church is one of the finest in Britain and was probably chosen..some say by Agricola for a Roman camp...for defence.It has nevertheless been the scene of Christian worship for an unbroken period of more than 800 years, a period which included the dissolution of the Monasteries, the Civil War...and the Great Plague, which had its burial pit close by the churchyard, in what is now part of the Vicarage garden.

Until the middle of the last century,Dalton was noted for its observance of the ancient custom of Arval at certain funerals.This strange tradition which, amongst other things, permitted only male mourners to attend the ceremony, is believed to be Scandinavian in origin, and was quite possibly a direct link with the 9th century Norse invasion of Furness.

The Dalton Book Club is believed to be the oldest in the country, with a continous record of membership.Its members have met every month since it was established in 1764, and it is flourishing to this day.

DALTON CASTLE

DEAN.

Map ref.B.7.
Next nearest Town or Village "Pardshaw"
Location.5 miles east of Workington.

A parish one mile east of the river Marron, at Branthwaite, and consists of five small villages which lie between the western lakes and the sea. At Branthwaite, steep hills descend to what can loosely be described as the centre of town.Branthwaite Hall with its well preserved 14th century pele tower is on the edge of the village, in a very picturesque setting.

There is a legend hereabouts that in the early 17th century a headless female corpse was found in the old barn attached to Neuk Cottage. The ghost is reputed to appear in white wandering about and wailing...looking for her head!.Watch out for the 'Branthwaite Boggle'

The little church of St Oswald's is in a picturesque setting at the edge of the village and is partly 12th century, although the preaching cross is believed to be much older.Many gargoyles and several ancient gravestones are in the churchyard.

One of the villages here is Pardshaw, and is where in the 17th century George Fox, the founder of the Quaker movement held his first meeting on Pardshaw Craggs.'Fox's Pulpit' as it is locally known is actually two blocks of limestone.

Another village Ullock is set back from a stream.This is spanned by a pack-horse bridge, and eventually joins the river Marron.

DENT.

Map Ref:. I.11
Next nearest Town or Village "Sedbergh"
Trains. Railway Station
Location.4 miles south east of Sedbergh.

Dent is a village near Sedbergh (often known as Dent-Town)..originally in Yorkshire until 1974...but still within the boundaries of the Yorkshire Dales National Park.

Its major claim to fame is its best known son Adam Sedgwick...the 19th century father of modern geology in whose memory a great block of Shap granite is sited on the main street.

Adam Sedgwick was for 55 years the Woodwardian Professor of Geology at Cambridge University...and was one of the greatest field geologists of his time.He was also a gifted teacher and lecturer..Charles Darwin was in fact one of his pupils (though Sedgwick was later to be a stern critic of Darwinism) and a personal friend of both Queen Victoria and Prince Albert.

There is much archaelogical evidence around to indicate that there was a Roman presence here at one time.

The mediaeval church of St Andrew which dominates the village is over 900 years old, and within the churchyard the Jacobean Grammar School still stands.This tiny two-storey building in Dent churchyard, just to the right and rear of the church is the 17th century grammar school of those days, founded originally to teach local boys to read and write and to master church Latin and some mathematics.Adam Sedgwick was a pupil here as a child being taught by his father Richard, Vicar of Dent, whose duties included teaching at the school. Adam continued his education at nearby Sedbergh School before going on to Trinity College,Cambridge.

In the 18th and 19th century the town had a flourishing industry.'hand knitting'.Bringing considerable repute to the village 'The Terrible Knitters of Dent' produced vast quantities of hose and gloves.Both men and women knitted.In good weather the narrow cobbled streets and wooden galleries of the houses would be full of people talking and knitting.An indication of their output is shown in Kendal records,for during the period 1795-1801, 2,400 pairs of stockings were sent weekly to Kendal market. Regretfully the knitting trade died out when knee-breeches were no longer worn.

The parking space opposite to the Sun Inn was originally the site of a lodge for the drivers of pony trains. Next to it was the White Hart Inn.The mounting stone beside it served as a stand for any orator wishing to address the crowd.Here Adam Sedgwick stood to announce the victory at Waterloo.

Dentdale's other historic monument is the Settle-Carlisle railway with its magnificent viaducts at Artengill and Dent Head.They represent the great and heroic efforts which brought steam transport to Dent back in 1875.

Dentdale had ancient mining and quarrying industries.Bell pits on the hillsides reveal the sites of small open cast coal mines and the road from Dent Station over to Garsdale is known as the Coal road.There are still the remains of a primitive copper mine in the dale.The main mineral industry however was 'black marble' quarried and processed at Stonehouse in upper Dentdale,where the remains of the workings can still be seen.This marble was much prized in Victorian England for its unusual colour and the wealth of fossils. Whernside Manor hereabouts (now run by the Yorkshire Dales National Park) is reputedly not only home to three ghosts, but its 18th century slave-owning occupants...the Sill family...are suggested as having inspired Charlotte Bronte in creating the central characters in Jane Eyre, whilst Emily Bronte's Heathcliff in 'Wuthering Heights' was based on a no-good orphan boy.

At Hall Lane is a narrow lane that has changed little since the days of pack-horses and wheeled carts,and is lined with traditional tall hedgerows rich in wildflowers, typical of this part of Dentdale. High Hall Farm nearby has Tudor chimneys which are visible from the lane, is now in use as a rare breeds farm. The existence of limestone here is responsible for another important feature of Dentdale...Its underground caves. As is well known limestone is soluble in rainwater and over millions of years a complex system of caverns and underground passages has evolved.There are many skilled and experienced cavers in the dale, many of whom enjoy international reputation. The best known cave here is Ibbeth Peril Cave, the entrance being behind a small cliff overlooking a plunge pool about 100 yards downstream from Tommy Bridge. 400 feet of crawling on hands and knees leads eventually to an enormous chamber complete with stalactites and waterfall.

HIGH HALL
RARE BREEDS
FARM

THE FARM HOUSE

High Hall is without a doubt, the oldest building in Dent. The farm was first mentioned in the Domesday book and hence has a history of almost a thousand years.

A dove hole set in the gable end of one of the farm buildings bore a date of 1339 or 1389

The house bears a plaque which relates to a period during the seventeenth century. In 1625, Oliver Cromwell gave the freehold of the farm to a certain Richard Trotter. Apparently, Trotter rased part of the house in order to modernise it, However, he was taken to court and, after much legal wrangling, was ordered to quit in 1665.

In more recent times, there has been speculation regarding the siting of the famous Bronte novel Wuthering Heights. There are strong pointers to the fact that Whernside Manor was the place from which Heathcliffe came and that High Hall was the home of Kathy. An old slave trail goes through the farmyard and across to the field where the High Hall horses are now kept. Apparently, the slaves would be brought out in the mornings, deposited en route to various farmers and then collected again at night and taken back down to Westhouse, which is now Whernside Manor..

At High Hall we are now building up a number of cattle, goats, pigs and sheep whose future is threatened by extinction. As the years pass by we shall obviously add other stock and so play a fuller part in preserving our farming heritage

We have built up also an interest corner in which we have several rare breeds of farm dogs, donkeys, ponies.
Shire horse Drawn Drives Daily

OPEN DAILY
CONDUCTED TOURS STARTING 3pm to 6pm
EXCEPT TUESDAYS AND SATURDAYS
OR
BY APPOINTMENT
TELEPHONE DENT 05396/25331

DENTON.

Map ref. H.3.
Next nearest Town or Village "Gilsland"
Location. 1 mile from Gilsland.
Early closing.

Denton or Over Denton as it is sometimes called is just one mile from Gilsland.

The ancient church built of stone from the Roman Wall, has a 12th century chancel arch.In the churchyard will be found the tomb of Margaret Teasdale of Mumps Hall who died in 1777 aged 98 years.

Mumps Hall, now an Inn received notoriety when a secret door was found behind a great fireplace, which led to a staircase in the chimney...Here was found the skeleton of a child together with many other bones.To date, nobody has ever been able to give a sensible reason for them being there.

The mote-hills, at Denton Hall were the abodes at one time of the first Norman settlers and were used long before stone castles came into general use.Apparently a wooden house would have been built on the top to which one climbed by steps from the palisade at the base of the mound, having first crossed the ditch by a drawbridge.

DOVENBY

Map ref. B.6.
Next nearest Town or Village "Cockermouth"
Location. Half way between Maryport and Cockermouth.

Dovenby village straddles the A.594 Maryport to Cockermouth road and is situated about half way between the two,

Dovenby Hall was the seat of the Lamplughs...from Henry 1V through to Elizabeth 1.The pele tower has been built of stone taken from the nearby Roman road, and is probably Norman in origin.

In 1890 the Hall was owned and lived in by the Ballantyne Dykes family.By all accounts there is a ghost known as 'The Grey Lady'.Apparently the story is that a young girl living at the Hall committed suicide after being refused permission to marry some-one the family did not approve of.She was buried in Hall Park.

Dovenby School nearby, was originally built in 1628 and rebuilt in 1845, and still survives to this day.

DRIGG

Map ref.B.10.
Next nearest Town or Village "Ravenglass"
Trains. Drigg Railway Station.
Location. On west coast between Ravenglass and Seascale.

Drigg is a long village of scattered houses near the coast, it has fine views of the mountains towering up to the east.A long straight beach terminates in an extensive area of sand dunes and salt marsh between the River Irt and the sea, and has a bird sanctuary which may be visited, with a permit, during nesting time.

Here on a little hilltop the Normans built a church which was added to by 13th century builders, but what we see is a plain little structure refashioned in the last century, in which ancient masonry was used again. It has an arcade in 13th century style, and attractive woodwork in the door and reredos.

At one time Drigg had an annual fair which would have been held on Drigg Sands.A contemporary writer of the time described it as a fine sight that lasted for three days, and included such activities as horse racing.The description explains how officials from Egremont the Sergeant and bailiffs would all meet the tenants of 'His Lordship' on the outskirts of Ravenglass and went in procession to open the fair.This eventually started a 'great trade' in cattle and produce,between the local people and those who came from as far afield as Ireland and Scotland, with the majority of them coming by sea.

Visitors to Cumbria are sure to hear the story of how Herdwick sheep first came to the County.

Legend has it that there was a shipwreck on the coast at Drigg many centuries ago and about forty sheep which were being carried in the Spanish vessel managed to make their way to land, upon which they were subsequently taken possession of by the Lord of the Manor. The animals evinced a propensity for high ground and noting that they were capable of taking care of themselves the practice was started of letting them out in small herds to farms...and this apparently is the origin of the name Herdwick.

DUFTON.
Map ref. I.7.
Next nearest Town or Village "Long Marton"

Location. 3 miles from Appleby.

Gala days/festivals. Dufton Agricultural Show
& Sheepdog trials 4th Weekend in August

A very attractive village, three miles from Appleby
and two miles east of Long Marton, in an area
designated as one of outstanding natural beauty.
Many old houses border the village green, a few
with date stones showing origins in the 17th, 18th
and 19th centuries, with quite a few being built of
locally quarried red sandstone.
Dufton is at the centre of the Helm Wind area. It is
the only local wind in the country to have a
particular name. Dufton Hall at the east of the
green dates in part from the 16th century

The church here, dedicated to St Cuthbert, is about
half a mile out of the village and was erected at one
of the places where Lindisfarne monks rested when
they carried St Cuthbert's body as they escaped
from the Vikings in AD875. Church records go
back to 1292. In the outside south wall of the chancel
there is a small figure of possibly Roman origin, and
in the west wall of the nave there is a grave slab
thought to depict a Norman forester.
Back in 1858 the Quaker company installed a new
drinking water supply. Four taps are still in evidence,
together with the sandstone trough. The Stag Inn by
the village green is worth a visit dating as it does
back to 1702. The landlord will be happy to tell you
about the time during the 1939-45 war when a
Canadian aeroplane crashed nearby and all five
survivors walked into the village.
Unfortunately on their next flight over Berlin their
plane crashed, and all were killed.

EAMONT BRIDGE.

Map ref. G.7.
Next nearest Town or Village "Penrith"
Location, 1 mile south of Penrith.

Eamont Bridge is a village one mile south of Penrith at the confluence of the rivers Eamont and Lowther.

The area around Eamont Bridge has been inhabited since very early days, and the remains of two ancient fortifications can still be seen.'Mayburgh' dating back to around 250 BC is a huge circular embankment of stones 385 feet from crest to crest with a standing stone nine feet two inches high in the centre.It is believed to have been a Roman amphitheatre with the standing stone used for criminals to hide behind when wild beasts were pursuing them.

King Arthur's Table dating from about 1800 BC is to the south.The 'Round Table' is like a big cockpit and was formerly used for games which went on in the middle on the raised platform, whilst spectators sat on the banks around.

The village is typical of many northern villages, with many of the houses being joined together regardless of style or size.The practice apparently dates back to the time of the Border raids when their animals could be driven into the main street and the street blocked off and defended at each end.Many of the houses were built following the demolition of their homes in the village of Brougham (see Brougham editorial)

Less than a mile away stands Yanwath Hall which is a gracious place with the charm of 300 years in its walls and rooms. It has a fine courtyard, two huge buttresses, lovely windows,and a handsome doorway. The battlemented 14th century tower, with its turrets is a noble structure over 50 feet high with foundations six feet thick and a base with a vaulted roof.In what is now a farmhouse are magnificent oak beams.One of the rooms known as the Lord's Chamber has the arms of Queen Elizabeth 1 in plaster over the fireplace, and a delightful oriel, and a smaller room said to have sheltered Mary Queen of Scots, has a stone fireplace with a low oak kerb at which the Queen may have warmed her feet.

In the middle of the village is a large building once the local mansion house,but later the workhouse.Today it is business premises. Its the large pink building on the right just before the bridge on the A6.This 16th century bridge over the river Eamont once marked the old county boundary between Cumberland and Westmorland.

EDENHALL.

Map ref. G.7.
Next nearest Town or Village "Langwathby"
Location 4 miles north-east of Penrith.

Edenhall is a village some four miles north-east of Penrith, in a tranquil fertile valley. It is believed that there has been a settlement here from long before Roman times, if the finding of hatchets made of metal and polished stones are any indication.

The church of St Cuthbert's has been built on the site of one of the Saints many resting places during the 9th century, and lies about half a mile from the centre of town. Near the church is an old stone cross sited on top of a plague stone on which money would have been left for goods supplied during the time of the Black Death, between 1347-1361. Its history is obscure, but it may have had some connection with the vanished settlement which once stood to the south of the church.

The Musgrave family lived here from 1500-1900 in a large mansion. Sadly the house was auctioned off in 1934 and removed piece by piece.The present owner of the house now lives in the coach house, all that remains of that once great house.

One of the village legends is the story of the medieval glass chalice in a 15th century leather case that is said to have been a fairy gift.Known as 'The Luck of Edenhall' the fairies left the message "If the cup should break or fall farewell to luck of Edenhall" The priceless goblet was later purchased by the Victoria and Albert Museum in London in 1957 and is displayed (safely) in a glass case.

EGREMONT.

Map ref. B.9.

Next nearest Town or Village " St Bee's"

Bus service. Cumberland Bus Service Routes No. 22, 06, 12

Tourist Information Centre. Lowes Court Gallery 12,Main Street.

Location. Gosforth-Whitehaven road.

Early closing.Wednesday.

Market Day. Friday.

Gala days/festivals. Crab Fair. 3rd Sat in September. Egremont Fur & Feather Annual Show. 2nd Sat Nov. West Cumbria Rose Society Show 3rd week in July Egremont is a small market town (charter from 1267) inland from St Bees.

Here William de Meschines built his castle in 1135.The gatehouse and the surviving curtain wall survive today from the original building, and the herring bone pattern of the stone-work is very typical of the Norman period. It was one time home of the deLucy family.Between the inner and outer courts is the stern ruined front of the great hall which has stood since about 1270 and has still a row of open windows and a doorway, the most effective part of the castle seen from the town, silhouetted against the sky.From this meagre fragment of a great stronghold is a fine view of the town and the distant mountains.By one of the paths bringing us down from it is a piece of a cross believed to be some 700 years old.

The legend here of the horn which could be blown only by the true Lord of Egremont was told by Wordsworth.Hubert de Lucy,brother of the true Lord Sir Eustace,villainously assumed possession of the castle when he thought that he had successfully organised the murder of his brother who was away on the Crusades.Sir Eustace returned when his brother was feasting, and blew the horn. Exit Hubert in haste by a side door!

A bugle horn, stringed, is carved on the tomb of Sir John Hudleston who died in 1493 at Millom, representing his de Boyvill ancestry. The de Boyvills were kinsfolk of the powerful William le Meschin and were lords of Millom.The town has typically wide Cumbrian streets built originally to accommodate market stalls.

Egremont was once a busy haematite iron mining area, and this would have supplied the industries around Workington and Whitehaven. Records here show that mining was popular here in Norman days.The only ore mine still working is Florence Mine nearby.Specimens of ore are on sale here and underground visits can be made by prior arrangement.

The church dating from about 1220 has been restored and contains early sculptures. Wordsworth enthusiasts will remember his ode 'The Boy of Egremont'...meaning in effect... young William de Romilly, nearest in succession to the throne of Scotland.

The 16th century Lowes Court is now a gallery on the main street combining an interesting gallery, with regularly changing exhibitions, a local crafts shop, and the Towns Tourist Information Centre.

In late autumn the town celebrates the very popular 'Crab Fair' which goes back seven centuries, when the Lord of Egremont started a tradition of giving away crab apples.The applecarts still make this 'generous' gesture, these days showering the spectators with crab apples from lorries and trailers.Another famous amusement held at the same time, for which Egremont is renowned is the celebrated 'gurning' competition, where contestants try to pull the ugliest face framed in a horse collar. There is also a pipe smoking event, a greasy pole competition when youngsters try to scale a 30 feet high vertical slippery pole, along with the singing of hunting songs.

Elterwater & Chapel Stile.

Map ref. E.9.
Next nearest Town or Village "Grasmere"
Location. 1 mile south of Grasmere.
Gala days/festivals. Langdale Gala 1st Sat June.

Elterwater and Chapel Stile are two villages of Great Langdale with half a mile between them...sharing the same school and church,

Chapel Stile has grown around a simple stone chapel, itself perched on a rocky ledge under the steep fell. Prior to 1821 local folk would be carried over the fell to Grasmere to be buried, it wasn't until 1851 that the two Squires of High Close and Elterwater Hall had the present church built. In the churchyard will be found the grave of G.M.Trevelyan, historian of England.

The oldest of the 17th century houses will be found by the church, but later quarryman's cottages were built at the bottom of the hill.Both villages grew in the heyday of 19th century quarrying, together with the gunpowder works.

Elterwater is situated near the lake of the same name...half a mile long and a quarter of a mile wide.Elterwater was named originally by the Norsemen 'Swan Lake' and swans still frequent the tarn, including the Whooper Swans from Scandi-navia, often seen in winter.,

Of several 17th century houses by the high stone bridge,one was the home of the linen industry, set up originally by John Ruskin, and another has been a youth hostel since 1955. On either side of the maple tree, is the Britannia Inn, a busy pub for locals and tourists, together with the village shop and bowling green.

The gunpowder works eventually became the beautifully designed and equipped Time-Share complex with handsome timber lodges set amongst the trees.

HOLY TRINITY CHURCH

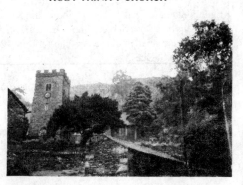

THE BRITANNIA INN ELTERWATER

English Tourist Board three crowns,AA listed three Q's
Egon Ronay Recommended Pub, Recommended in the Good Pub Guide & Good Beer Guide

The Inn on the Village Green

THE BRITANNIA, A GENUINE 400 YEAR OLD BUILDING, is the very picture of a traditional British Inn. Painted black and White, with colourful overflowing window boxes. It lies next to the village green on which stands a magnificent Maple Tree, in the unspoilt village of Elterwater. A mass of garden chairs and slate-topped tables on its terraced forecourt invite you to sit down, enjoy a drink or a bar meal, relax and take in the scenery.

Guests staying at the Inn are accommodated in nine attractively furnished double or twin bedded rooms, of which six have en-suite showers and toilets. All have individually controlled central heating, colour TV, telephone, a hair dryer and tea and coffee making facilities.

Alternatively accommodation is available at Maple Tree Corner, Elterwater's village shop immediately across the road from the Britannia. One single, one twin and two double bedded rooms, each prettily furnished with oak-beamed ceilings, vanity units, colour TV and tea and coffee making facilities, offer good value bed and breakfast accommodation. A traditional English breakfast is served in the Britannia Inn Dining Room, An en-suite shower and toilet is provided in one of the double rooms.

Should your preference be for a free and easy self-catering holiday, the Britannia Inn Holiday Cottages could fit the bill. Two traditional Lakeland slate cottages are available for weekly hire from March to October and for weekend or mid-week breaks in winter. Each is cosily furnished, fully equipped with all conveniences and has Calor Gas Central Heating. Please telephone for separate details .

THE BRITANNIA INN
ELTERWATER
AMBLESIDE,
CUMBRIA,
LA22 9HP
Tel: Langdale
(05394) 37210 - 3 lines
FAX: Langdale
(05394) 37311

The Eltermere Country Hotel

Elterwater
Nr. Ambleside
Cumbria LA22 9HY

The Eltermere is the perfect country Hotel set in 3 acres of beautiful landscaped gardens with a truly idyllic view across Eltermere Tarn. Situated on the edge of Elterwater village it is very convenient for walkers who can experience many delightful scenic walks from the doorstep. The hotel was acquired by he Stephenson family 4 years ago and since then has been tastefully refurbished without harming the character of this lovely 250 year old building.

The hotel has 15 double/twin rooms all en-suite and 4 single rooms, most rooms have views across to nearby Loughrigg Fell and the lake. Hotel facilities include a comfortable lounge with open fire, a cocktail bar and restaurant accommodating up to 40 people. An excellent varied menu with fine wines is on offer each evening this, coupled with a discreet yet friendly service, for which the hotel has become renowned, creates that special ambience in this the very best of country hotels.

Fellside & Lane Ends Cottages
Elterwater, Ambleside, Cumbria,
LA22 9HN
Telephone: Langdale (05394) 37678
Prop. Mrs. M.E. Rice

LANE ENDS COTTAGES

Land Ends Cottages are situated next to 'Fellside' Guest House, adjoining Elterwater Common. The property forms a L-shaped block around a forecourt parking area. One of the cottages was the Dame School and contains original features such as beams, bacon hooks, and wooden coat pegs. A picture of the interior of the Dame School was painted by John Harden in 1806. This cottage is furnished in keeping with its character, has been awarded a 3-Key grading and been Commended by Cumbria Tourist Board. The other two cottages were built at the same time as Langdale Church. They too are comfortably furnished, also have a 3-Key grading and are 'approved' by the Tourist Board.

The cottages cater for groups of 4-6 people and provide an ideal base for walking, climbing or touring holidays. Each cottage is well equipped with electric and solid fuel heating, electric cooker, fridge etc. The accommodation varies slightly in each cottage, but contains a lounge with open fire, separate kitchen, 2 or 3 bedrooms, and bathroom. A parking space is provided for each cottage with further parking opposite. Bed linen (sheets and pillowcases) is provided, towels can be provided on request (small charge)

FELLSIDE GUEST HOUSE

Fellside guest house is situated near the centre of the village of Elterwater. Bed and breakfast can be provided...Dinner is a five course meal ...and home cooking is very much our speciality. (Free range eggs, home made preserves, etc.) We regret, that for the benefit of our guests, pets are not allowed.

English Tourist Board
COMMENDED

Langdale, in the heart of the Lake District National Park, is one of the most beautiful and unspoilt valleys in the country. Here on 35 acres of woodland, tarn and beck is the Langdale Hotel & Country Club, which holds a Civic Trust Award for its contribution "to enhancing the quality of the environment".

The Hotel has 65 comfortable bedrooms, each finished to a high standard, with luxury en-suite bathrooms, direct dial telephone and satellite TV. Most of these rooms are situated slightly away from the main buildings, in order to obtain full benefit from the peace and seclusion of the Estate.

The Hotel has a spacious and attractive lounge and cocktail bar and the main restaurant, Purdeys, is noted for its excellent table d'hote menu of both continental and local dishes.

The Langdale Country Club is the centre of all social activity on the estate and has a lounge/cocktail bar, adjoining the Tamarind Restaurant on the terrace overlooking the pool. Every guest at Langdale receives membership of the club, during their stay, which includes free use of the indoor heated pool, saunas, steam room and exercise room. There are also two first-class squash courts in the club.

Langdale is in legendary fell walking country and is the ideal base for outdoor activities including abseiling,

climbing, pony trekking, mountain biking, sailing, canoeing, water skiing and so on.

**LANGDALE HOTEL & COUNTRY CLUB,
GREAT LANGDALE, Near AMBLESIDE,
CUMBRIA LA22 9JD
TEL: 05394 37302 FAX: 05394 37694**

EMBLETON.

Map ref. C.7.
Next nearest Town or Village "Thornthwaite"
Location. East of Cockermouth

Embleton is a scattered parish east of Cockermouth in one of the Lakeland's most attractive hamlets. The name is derived from Eanbald's Tun...meaning farmstead or land belonging to Eanbald. It was a Norman manor, but a community existed here in Brigantian times. There is no centre to the village as such,

The church of St Cuthbert is built on the spot of a further site where the saint's body rested. It was in Embleton that an iron sword was discovered in the 19th century, thought to have belonged to a Brigantian of the first century AD. In the churchyard a tombstone will be found that reads 'Sacred to the memory of Ann Sewell whose life was terminated by the hand of an assassin whilst in the discharge of her humble duties on the 26th March 1860 aged 26 years.' She had worked at Beckhouse Farm and had been stabbed to death by a farmworker named Cass, for Ann's purse. Cass was hanged at Carlisle.

Embleton is closely linked with the small hamlet of Wythop. It has its one church. St Margaret's. Branching off the Embleton valley is the lovely Wythop valley...or the secret valley as referred to in one of Wainwright's guide books.

In this valley lies the ruins of an early church dating back to the 16th century. Also here is the ancient Wythop Hall and beyond that the ruins of the silica works.

Wythop Mill here was originally owned by the Wythop Estate. It was used to provide timber for the repair of estate property. It has been fully renovated, and today is back in full working order.

ENNERDALE BRIDGE

Map ref. B.8.
Next nearest Town or Village "Cleator Moor"
Gala days/Festivals: Ennerdale & Kinniside Agricultural Show Last Wednesday August
Location. 1 mile east of Cleator Moor.
Gala days/festivalsEnnerdale & Kinniside Agricultural Show Last Wednesday August.

Ennerdale Bridge is a hamlet standing at the mouth of what must be the loveliest of great valleys of Lakeland.
It is the least frequented of all the Cumbrian lakes.Its beautiful setting however is all the village has to offer, for it lies where the Ehen and the Crossdale Beck meet near their bridges, as they come from lake and fell.The mountains and peaks which tower at its head ...Great Gable, Kirk Fell,Pillar, Steeple, and Haycock, are typical of the Borrowdale Volcanic series.
In prehistoric times iron was smelted beside Smithy beck at the head of the lake, whilst a hundred years ago haematite ore was mined both sides of the valley...the workings at Kelton Fell actually sup-

LOOKING OVER FROM ENNERDALE
TOWARDS BUTTERMERE AND BEYOND.

porting a railway system.
The village is divided by the river Ehen from which it derives its name.One part is clustered around the church, the other half around the school. St Mary's Church, founded in 1534 originally as a chapel of the Abbey of St Bees. Wordsworth visited the village in 1799, and wrote in his poem 'The Brothers' ,of the homely priest of Ennerdale, as he and his wife sat spinning upon the long seat beneath the eaves of the old cottage.

ESKDALE.

Map ref. C,10,
Next nearest Town or Village "Boot "

Location. 3 miles east of Ravenglass.
Eskdale 'Tup' Show Last Fri Sept.
Gala days/festivals. Eskdale Show. Last Sat.Sept.
Eskdale & Ennerdale Foxhounds Puppy Show.
2nd Sat.Sept.

Eskdale is one of Cumbria's most delightful valleys, full of interest and beauty, with little hamlets dotting along it, and with great rocky crags crowning lovely wooded slopes. The valley has a network of old routed roads, some of which are tarmac,but most are unspoilt, together with pony tracks.One of these leads over the bridge at Boot,up and over Burnmoor, and down to Wasdale.

Bordering on Eskdale is Birker Force, a fine waterfall to see after heavy rains, along with Dalegarth Force, one of the country's gems, a waterfall leaping over sixty feet into a wooded ravine.Not far away is Devoke Water, the small lake a mile long and half as wide, high up in the fells nearly 800 feet above the sea.It is famous for its trout.

The churchyard here was not consecrated for burials until 1901. Over this (aptly named) Corpse road, the coffins from Wasdale were carried to St Catherine's...Locals here still talk of the day that a pack-horse took fright and disappeared into the mist with the body of one Thomas Porter strapped to its back.St Catherine's Church is down by the river in an idyllic setting.It is typical of a small dale church, built like a barn and largely 17th century.The monks from Furness Abbey, which owned much of Eskdale, built the original chapel here long before this church was built.

.Note the Holy Well in a small plateau above the path, along with the tombstones of Tommy Dobson and Willy Porter, huntsmen of the Eskdale and Ennerdale pack, and of great local renown.

The village of Eskdale was changed considerably around a hundred years ago, when the Rea family bought Gate House Farm,and developed the Gate House Estate.These days the centre of the village is the post office cum shop, the owner of which is a cousin to the maker of Woodalls Cumberland Sausage.

The pub here 'The King George'..was at one time named the 'King of Prussia', but had its name changed at the outbreak of World War.1.

'La'al Ratty', the steam train from the Ravenglass and Eskdale Railway, makes a loop around the village, but has stations on either side.

Above Eskdale Green is 'Miterdale' where a ruined farmhouse is haunted by the ghost of a gypsy,known as 'Beckside Boggle' gurglings can still be heard on moonlight nights!

Beyond the village of Boot nearby, is a winding road up to Hard Knott pass four miles ahead.This is the entry into the valley from Central Lakeland, and zig-zags down past the Roman fort.The pass is where the Romans made a remarkable road connecting their settlements at Ravenglass and Ambleside.Halfway between the two they built their fort known as Hardknott Castle, guarding one end of the pass from a commanding position on a crag some 800 feet high, and glorying in some of the finest mountain scenery in the country, with a magnificent view of Scafell Pikes less than four miles away,The Roman fort has been excavated,and the remains show it to be roughly a square of 125 yards, enclosing just three acres, with the base of a tower at each corner, and a gateway at each side.The north tower on the highest point was perhaps a signal station,and the walls or rampart of the fort are five feet thick.

A mile down the river is Penny Hill which is one of the farms which Beatrix Potter bought for the National Trust...and two miles further on is Stanley Ghyll with Dalegarth Force.The Stanleys of Austhwaite have farmed the valley for 600 years, and are still doing so to this day.

Eskdale 'Tup' Show held at Woolpack on the last Friday in September.'Tup'Fair origins...when rams are hired out or sold for breeding purposes...later turning itself into a social gathering, and now currently, the Eskdale Show.

The low turf and stone dyke which crosses the green boggy wastes of Lincove in Upper Eskdale was built by the Cistercian monks of Furness Abbey sometime between 1284-1290.

FIELD BROUGHTON.

Map ref. F.12.
Next nearest Town or Village "Cartmel"
Location. 2 miles north of Cartmel.

The village of Field Broughton lies two miles to the north of Cartmel and about four miles to the south of Lake Windermere.

There will be found a lime kiln by Field Broughton church which was used until 1920 producing quick lime.. Additionally there is an old line kiln at Beckside.

Until 1796 all the land here was common land until it was divided and sold to a few wealthy people, thereby leaving many people very prosperous and others very poor. The one piece of common land remaining is the village pound, used for holding stray animals.

Back in 1731 a certain Miles Burn left £50 in his will towards building a chapel/schoolroom here.Today re-built, it can still be seen.

FINSTHWAITE & STAVELEY.

Map ref. E.11.
Next nearest Town or Village "Rusland"
Location. 1 mile north of Newby Bridge.

Is a village west of the foot of Windermere, and includes part of the area known as Newby Bridge...and was once a place of industry...a mill, limestone quarry, and a bloomery.The bloomery in fact was started by the monks of Cartmel Priory in or around 1230 for the smelting and forging of iron ore.

The beautiful little church of St,Mary's dates from 1608. It was restored in 1793 when the south aisle and tower were added.The church contains a cross made from a plank cut from a pontoon bridge over the river Piave in Italy. Buried in the churchyard, so villagers say, is a princess with wonderful fair hair, believed to be the illegitimate daughter of Charles Edward Stuart (The Young Pretender)...better known as Bonnie Prince Charlie.

The village of Finsthwaite was originally a settlement dating back to Viking times, and lies in the hills above Lakeside.It is reached by a narrow winding lane past the quaint Newby Bridge complete with its five arches of unequal size and sharply pointed buttrresses.

Woodcutting was very much part of their industrious life in the old days, the oak, birch, and hazel so freely available here, converted into furniture, and in later years..bobbins.

Finsthwaite Hall with a tower on top, is a monument of naval victories of Nelson's Day.In late Victorian times it was the home of General Thomas Sneyd (pronounced Sneed), of the Queen's Dragoon Guards.

Along the lane leading towards Hawkshead, lies Graythwaite, yet another area originally settled by the Vikings.Red Deer can still be seen here roaming through the woods.

FLIMBY.

Map ref. B.6.
Next nearest Town or Village "Maryport"
Trains,Flimby Railway Station.
Location. 2 miles south of Maryport.
Gala days/festivals. Flimby Carnival. 1st Sat.July.

A 12th century village on the coast two miles south of Maryport.

In 1279 land here was given to monks of Holm Cultram Abbey (see section Abbey Town) After the Reformation, Henry V111 granted Flimby to Thomas Dalston of Carlisle, who in 1546 sold the land to John Blennerhasset.This family resided at Flimby Hall until 1772 when William Blennerhasset sold the property to Sir James Lowther...these days Flimby Hall is now a farm.

Flimby as a parish was separated from Camerton in 1546.The present parish church of St Nicholas was re-built in 1794 (on the site of a previous church)

FLOOKBURGH.

Map ref. E.13.
Next nearest Town or Village "Cartmel"
Location. 1 mile south of Cartmel.
Gala days/festivals. Great Garden & Countryside
Festival.Holker Hall June-July.
Cumbria Steam Gathering. Last Sat'Sun July.
Various Car rallies.

A village,once a market town of some importance,
with charters by Edward 1 (later confirmed by
Henry 1V) and then again by Charles 11 in 1665.
Flookburgh has what certainly looks like a large
market square, but it is actually the site of the old
chapel and graveyard.In fact a chapel stood on this
site from the 13th century, served by the Canons of
Cartmel. There is a second 'Market Square' where
the market cross stands. Near is the Manor House
built in 1686, and few hundred yards up the road
is the parish church of St.John.

Up until the First World War ships used to come up
to Sandgate to fish the mussel beds off the Furness
Peninsula.Today shrimping is far more
popular...with shrimps from Flookburgh being
delivered far and wide across the country.Tractors
are driven onto the sands at low tide to catch the
cockles, shrimps, and flukes ...Flukes in fact is
from where the village derives its name.

Flookburgh has suffered two major disasters.In
1669 the plague raged through the village, the
bodies being buried in Ecclestan meadow, and
again in 1686 when a large section of the village
was destroyed by fire.

An area known as Ravenstown has many streets
named after First World War battles,as many of the
houses were built for the staff of a naval aerodrome
close by.

GAMBLESBY & UNTHANK
Map ref: H6
Next nearest Town or village "
Location 10 miles east of Penrith

The village of Gamblesby and the hamlet of Unthank are situated some ten miles east of Penrith in Eden Valley under, Fiends, Fins, or Finch Fell, a summit of the Pennines...an area which is generally known as East fellside.

Today Unthank is not located where its first squatters settled...for in 1597/98 the inhabitants succumbed to the Black Death, and a new hamlet was built some short distance away.

It was not uncommon for the area to fall victim to Scottish raiders, consequently Gamblesby developed its area by keeping farm buildings within the perimeter of its village, and the stock would have been kept on the village green.

In 1772 John Wesley, the Methodist preacher first arrived in Gamblesby from Newcastle. In 1784 he erected a chapel on the green and today this area is still much revered by all Methodists.

The stocks to be seen prominently on the village green were made by one William Toppon towards the end of the 18th century. Apparently they were last used to punish someone who had stolen a turnip.

GILSLAND
Map ref. H.3.
Next nearest Town or Village ' Denton'
Location.8 miles north-east of Brampton.
Gala days/festivals. Gilsland Agricultural Show.
2nd Sat. Sept.

Gilsland village is unique in that it is actually in two counties, three parishes...even two parliamentary divisions. Running through the centre is Poltross Burn which marks the boundary between Cumbria and Northumberland.The parishes of Denton Upper and Waterhead are in Cumbria, whilst Thirlwall is in Northumberland.

The Spa Hotel is one of the first buildings that attracts visitors attention.From its site there are some quite magnificent views of the Alston fells and the Lake District mountains.The Spa Hotel was formerly a convalescent home where miners and others came for the sulphur, iron water, and bracing air.

Gilsland is associated with Sir Walter Scott who stayed at the Spa in 1797. He actually met, and later married, a local lass Charlotte Carpenter, though the marriage was in Carlisle Cathedral(on Christmas Eve 1797).Here too is what is commonly referred to as 'The Popping Stone;' and is the local

name for the spot where he 'popped'the question.Regretfully many visitors have chipped away half the stone for souvenirs.Near too is 'The Kissing Bush'.

Birdoswald nearby is a unique section of Hadrians Wall, along with an informative Visitors Centre. It is located in one of the most picturesque settings along the whole of Hadrian's Wall, overlooking the Irthing Gorge.It is unique, because at no other point along the Roman Wall can all the components of the Roman frontier system be found together in such a small area.

The history of the fort begins in AD 122 with the construction of Hadrians turf wall.Evidence for one of the stone turrets on this wall has been found, together with a tented camp to the south of the site. Recent excavations have revealed the west gate of the fort, two granaries, a workshop, and smithy, together with a basilica for indoor military training.By 1200-1215 Birdoswald is mentioned by name in a series of charters as the home of one Radulph de Birdoswald. A building, a hollow-way and pottery of this period found near the west gate show that the Roman gate was still in use some 1,200 years after it had been built.

By 1600 the gate was no longer in use and the defensible castle house had been erected.

BIRDOSWALD ROMAN FORT

Birdoswald is located in one of the most picturesque settings along the whole of Hadrian's Wall, overlooking the Irthing Gorge. It is unique, because at no other point along Hadrian's Wall can all the components of the Roman frontier system be found together in such a small area.

Birdoswald helps us to understand the story of the Roman conquest of Britain. Here it is possible to see the early turf wall, built in AD 122, over which the original fort was built.

The fort underwent substantial alterations on a number of occasions during its three hundred year occupation. The turf wall, stone wall, Harrow's Scar Milecastle and the fort itself are all visible reminders of the period of Roman occupation.

The story of Birdoswald doesn't stop with the Romans, life carried on, and throughout the following centuries the wall and fort were frequently plundered for building stone. In fact stone from Birdoswald was used to build Lanercost Priory near Brampton.

In medieval time the border between England and Scotland was disputed and border raids were common. Houses, and barns were built within the fort for protection, and excavations here revealed two such houses were at Birdoswald.

In the 1850's the farm was owned by Henry Norman, a true Victorian romantic and an enthusiastic archaeologist. He in fact created the Birdoswald you see today. He extended the farmhouse and built the tower, and carried out much excavation work to the fort walls and gate. Over the next 100 years a number of further excavations have revealed much of the external wall including the well preserved east gate...although, frankly, much still remains to be discovered.

In 1984 Cumbria County Council acquired Birdoswald, and a four year excavation programme began in 1987. The results have been impressive.

In 1988 new facilities opened. A VISITOR CENTRE brings to life the fascinating history of Birdoswald and a new shop and picnic area add much enjoyment to your visit.

OPENING TIMES

Daily from 1st April to 31st October 10.00 - 17.30. Outside these hours and winter by prior arrangement only.

FURTHER INFORMATION

Birdoswald Roman Fort is owned and managed by Cumbria County Council in association with English Heritage and with financial assistance from the Countryside Commission and the Rural Development Commission.

For further information and bookings please contact.

**The Manager
Birdoswald Roman Fort
Gilsland, Brampton,
Cumbria CA6 7DD**

**Telephone
Gilsland (06977) 47602**

GILSLAND
SPA HOTEL

Gilsland Spa Hotel sits 700 feet above sea level, and commands spectacular views across the Cumbrian countryside.

Situated just over one mile from the pretty village of Gilsland, visitors can enjoy the magnificient Irthing Gorge, where the River Irthing seperates the counties of Cumbria and Northumberland.

An added bonus to a Gilsland stay are the many scenic walks to be found in the hotel's 140 acres of park and woodland.

For the more adventurous, Hadrian's Wall can be found nearby, and further afield, but easily reached by public transport, are the historic towns of Hexham and Carlisle. Even Gretna Green and the Solway Firth

are only a short car journey away.

Other local points of interest include a crystal factory at Allendale, and a trout farm at Brampton.

Walkers can venture beyond the hotel into Northumberland National Park, while for sports enthusiasts there are local golf courses close at hand, as well as an open air swimming pool at Haltwhistle.

At Gilsland Spa itself, bedrooms are on offer with en-suite facilities and superb views, while these and many more have televisions and tea and coffee making facilities.

Throughout the day Hadrian's coffee shop serves snacks and drinks; and those not counting calories can enjoy a special cream tea.

The hotel has a large screen television lounge, a secluded library for quieter moments, and a comfortable resident's lounge. Alternatively guests can explore the hotel's gift and souvenir shop.

Renowned for its entertainment programme, Gilsland Spa can call upon resident artistes and guest entertainers for dances, cabarets, afternoon tea dances and sing-a-longs.

Some of the competitions and fun events guests can enter

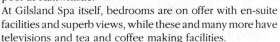

include indoor bowls, bingo, pool, deck quoits, putting challenges and the Spa Donkey Derby.

Prizes and trophies are awarded each Friday evening, before a farewell party for guests.

Enquiries and Reception only

Tel: (06977) 47203   Fax: (06977) 47051
Visitors' calls (Call boxes): (06977) 47233 and 47444
THE GILSLAND SPA HOTEL, GILSLAND, CUMBRIA CA6 7AR

GLASSONBY

Map ref. H.6.
Next nearest Town or Village ' Gamblesby"
Location. Two miles south east of Kirkoswald.

Gala days/festivals. Glassonby Sheepdog trials.
3rd Weds August.

The small rural village of Glassonby is situated in the Eden valley about nine miles from its nearest town..Penrith, and two miles south-east of Kirkoswald.
It is basically just a handful of small houses and barns, though it does have a lovely church by a plantation of pines.It is known as Addingham Church, but there is no Addingham for the village was washed away in 1350 when the River Eden changed its course and much of its church lies in the river bed.
The old church stood near Little Salkeld, and the 14th century church seen today contains some of the original stones from it, and is a simple structure of a nave, chancel and porch. In the nave will be found the base of an old stone cross. The most notable possessions of the church are the old relics from its predecessor found in the river bed, and brought here for safety.In the gable of the porch is a fragment of a Norman stone, and in the porch itself are several pieces of carved red-sandstone, including parts of 11th century cross-shafts with excellent knotwork.Here too are two old gravestones known as hogbacks, long and very massive and shaped like the roof of a house for the dead Saxon.
The churchyard also has its relic from the river bed, a curious ancient cross with an immense head on a small shaft. It has a spiral ornament, and the head has four holes and a raised central boss. It is thought probable that it came originally from a monastic house which stood in the village in the 7th century. Two stone circles will be found close by.Long Meg and her daughters, and Little Meg, together with a Bronze Age burial circle. One mile south of the parish church of Addingham
The White House farm is a late pele (or bastille) with the date 1598 over the door.

GLEASTON.

Map ref. D.13.
Next nearest Town or Village "Scales '
Location 2 miles south-east of Ulverston.

A village in Furness, with ruins of the castle of the Harrington's, built in the 14th century.Now in considerable ruins, ivy grown, but nevertheless very picturesque.
St Michael's Well close by, is believed to be named after St Michael le Fleming.

GLEASTON CASTLE

GLENRIDDING.

Map ref. F.8.
Nearest Town or Village "Patterdale"
Tourist Information Centre:At The National Park Information Centre
Location.A.592. Patterdale to Penrith road.

The A592 runs alongside the lake towards Glenridding, a one time mining village, but these days totally geared to tourism.The village has a National Park Information Centre within the car-park, and which inside has been re-created a mine shaft of the Glenridding mines.
.As a matter of interest the village's darkest hour was in 1929 when the nearby reservoir of Kepple Cove burst and some quarter of a million gallons of water swept down, battering and flooding the village. The damage,as to be expected, was great, but fortunately there were no casualties.
Visitors to the area may be interested in learning that the lakeshore walk from Howtown to Glenridding somehow has the edge over just about all other waterside walks in the Lake District.Its quality, one

GLENRIDDING

imagines has something to do with the constantly changing vistas, the alternations of the mixed woodlands, and open pasture, and possibly the slight rises and falls in the path itself, all of which give the walk a third dimension all of its own.

Many guided walks start from the car park in Glenridding, with one of the most popular being to Helvellyn at 3116 feet. Helvellyn is undoubtedly one of the Lakeland giants...the highest peak incidentally after Scafell Pike and Scafell.The summit, once reached, is grassy, remarkably flat, and friendly.Walkers should look for the Gough memorial, which commemorates the spot where in 1805 a dog guarded his master's body for three months after a fatal accident...an event that inspired both Wordsworth and Scott.

Helvellyn is certainly one of the most popular walks for fell walkers...in sunny weather there can be hundreds of people on its slopes at one time.

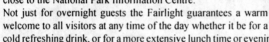

GOSFORTH.

Map ref. B.10.
Next nearest Town or Village "Calder Bridge"
Location. 3 miles south-east of Seascale.
Gala days/festivals. Gosforth Show. 3rd Weds in August.
Cumbria Riding Club. Dressage Day. 1st Sun April.
Cumbria Riding Club.One day event. 3rd Sun April.
Cumbria Riding Club.Gymkhana. 2nd Sun.June.
Cumbria Riding Club Combined Training. 3rd ßun July.
Cumbria Riding Club Hunter Trials. 1st Sunday October.

Gosforth is a village three miles south-east of Seascale.Once a Viking settlement as one can see from the famous Gosforth crosses, and hogback tombstone.Worn, but very fine, it is a remarkable sandstone monolith nearly 15 feet high..the tallest ancient cross in the country..it is thought to be a relic from the Scandinavian settlement here in the generations just before the Norman Conquest.The slender tapering shaft is partly round and partly

square, and is crowned by a fine four-holed head carved on the arms with the triquetra, the emblem of the Trinity. The cross head is said to be unique in the north of England for being carved with a crucifix.
The Viking influence is also to be seen in the name of the river ...the Bleng, together with the names of the surrounding fells and farms.
As to be expected in a country parish,many events centre around the church.Gosforth has the largest church in the united benefice with Nether Wasdale and Wasdale Head.The Norman church dating from the 12th century also contains the Viking 'fishing stone'..representing the Edda story of Thor, together with many monolith's of Norse mythology. The church's other claim to fame is reputed to be the country's most northerly cork tree.
The church itself has two old chairs, and a new oak lectern.There is a neat modern font with traceried panels, and there are some curious old collecting boxes in the vestry. A most unusual relic on one of the windowsills is a Chinese iron bell, perhaps the only one of its kind ever to ring in an English church.Though cracked, it is finely ornamented in Eastern fashion.It was given to Gosforth by Lady

CONT.

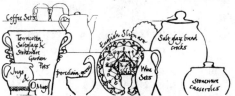

GOSFORTH HALL HOTEL
and
WESTO'S THAI RESTAURANT

A 17th Century manor, next door to a church which has long had Viking warriors buried in its grounds, is not really the sort of place where one would expect to find a restaurant serving authentic Thai food.

Lovers of good food however will be pleased to discover that this Grade 11. listed Gosforth Hall Hotel, situated on the road to Wastwater, now houses "Westo's Thai Restaurant.

Gosforth Hall has come a long way since one Robert Copley, a lawyer who was Chief Bailiff of Copeland Forest under the Earl of Northumberland, and his wife Isabel, obtained a piece of land in 1658. It then took them 15 years to build what many history books describe as a 'handsome house

windows.

Thai food, as many will know is a blend of Chinese and Indian cuisine, with the use of certain spices playing a big part in the creation of its own special tastes.

Rice is the centrepiece of any Thai meal and can be eaten with several side dishes, which may include soup, a salad with a spicy sauce, curries and fried steamed or grilled meat, fish or poultry. You can, ofcourse, choose as many dishes as you want (or can eat), and if you are in a group then there's no reason why you cannot sample each others choices.

Gosforth Hall offers a full bed and breakfast facility

with orchards and gardens"...and now today, some 330 years later many of the original features still remain, including the fireplace and inglenook, along with a newel stair built out as a turret, with several

OPEN 7 DAYS A WEEK...
52 WEEKS OF THE YEAR
GOSFORTH VILLAGE.
Nr. SEASCALE, CUMBRIA
Tel: 09467 25322

Senhouse after her husband Sir Humphrey Senhouse brought it from a fort he captured on the Canton River in 1841, and a tablet tells of his death on board HMS Blenheim after Canton was taken.By the bell are two old stone cannon balls from forts in the Dardanelles. Part of the village hall incorporates one of the oldest buildings in Gosforth.This was built by John and Margaret Shearwen in 1628 and now houses the library and the Supper Room. In 1658 Gosforth Hall was built using local sandstone.Here still are some fine stone pillars of the gate, along with an old fireplace, a newel stair, and some splendid old beams in the roof. In a corner of the field above the Hall is the site of an ancient chapel built over the Holy Well . The Hall was the seat originally of the Copley's, and is in fact the house where Bishop Nicholson used to go courting Barbara Copley when he was a young archdeacon.Today the Hall is a very popular hotel and Thai restaurant. Just outside the village in a long narrow field are the remains of an early Viking homestead known locally as Danes Camp.

GRANGE-OVER-SANDS.

Map ref F.13
Next nearest Town or Village ' Cartmel".
Bus Service.Cumberland Buses Route-530, 531, 535, 730, 735
Trains.Railway Station.
Tourist Information Centre.Victoria Hall, Main Street.
Location.South east of Cartmel.
Early Closing.Thursday.
Gala Days/Festivals.Summer festival of Music.
4th Thursday in July (for 3 days)
Lakeland Rose Show. 2nd Weekend in July.

Grange over Sands is at the end of a road which once crossed the tidal sands of Morecambe Bay to Hest Bank and Lancaster. ...In fact the route is still a public right of way, with a guide appointed by the Duchy of Lancaster, to take travellers through the changing river channels and the treacherous quicksands...Certainly under no circumstances should travellers attempt the crossing on their own.The Guide lives at Guides Farm on Cart Lane, which has been the official residence of the guide since the 16th century. It is vital when walking across the bay between tides to be a member of one of the organised

GRANGE-OVER-SANDS

parties. Those people who take to the sands without local advice could well be in serious difficulties

Grange with Kentsbank appears in the registers of Cartmel Priory as far back as 1536. The actual name Grange, could well derive from 'graunge' the old french word for barn, which seems fair enough as it was here the monks of Cartmel stored much of their grain...just as the monks of Furness Abbey stored their corn at that other Grange in Borrowdale. Sunny and sheltered, Grange over Sands is largely Victorian, and was originally developed by a railway company as a seaside resort at the coming of the trains in 1857, and today, with the nickname 'Torquay of the North' due to its amiable climate and high average temperatures, a pleasing blend of coastal and inland scenery, an unusually large number of narrow lanes and paths...not overlooking a heritage that is rich in ancient buildings...it is undoubtedly still a very popular 'select' resort.

The parish church of St Paul had its foundation stone laid in 1852...close by is the distinctive clock tower built in 1913 using native limestone and St Bee's stone facing. The oldest house hereabouts is Hardcragg (adjoining the library) and which offers magnificent views over Furness as far as Black Combe.

Until 1905 not one single plant was grown in Grange. These days however things are totally different with some 1000 alpines and around 6,000 bedding plants being introduced into the gardens adjoining the promenade each year. This interest in floral art makes Grange an ideal venue for the Lakeland Rose Show, founded in 1962...and which has quickly achieved national status. It is a two day event held in early July on playing fields overlooking the bay. Of all the viewpoints around Grange there is nothing to equal Hampsfell Hospice. A pilgrimage to the top is almost a pre-requisite for all visitors. At a point 727 feet above sea level, this four square tower was built in 1834 by the Rev Thomas Remington (a former vicar of Cartmel) for the benefit of wanderers over the fells. From the roof on a clear day, one can easily see, Black Combe, the mountains of Esk and Duddon, the Coniston range, Scafell and Bowfell the Langdale Pikes, and the Kentmere mountains...not overlooking many of the Yorkshire fells. Under certain conditions even Snowdon and the Isle of Man can be sighted.

Tradition states that a tumulus near the hospice contains the bones of many soldiers who fell during the battle between Dunmail, King of Cumbria, and Edmund, King of the invading Saxons in AD 946. A further incident took place here on the 25th November 1745 when Cartmel men gathered here to repel Jacobite rebels who were invading the district.

NETHERWOOD HOTEL

GRANGE - OVER - SANDS

A warm welcome awaits you at the Netherwood. With a long and renowned tradition for friendly personal service our attention to detail applies throughout all aspects of the hotel.

The hotel is set in extensive grounds, overlooking the Morecombe Bay estuary. Landscaped terraced gardens with unique topiary complete the setting.

Original oak pannelled rooms include the library, lounge bar and a ballroom. Each one has its own unique log fire.

All bedrooms are en-suite and beautifully appointed to the highest standards. Each room has a sea or woodland wiew, or overlooks the gardens. Room service is always available.

We are also very proud of our air-conditioned, elevated restaurant which again offers splendid views over the gardens and bay.

The Netherwood spa facilities include a heated pool, spa bath, steam room and beauty area. Lift access is provided for our disabled visitors.

NETHERWOOD HOTEL
GRANGE-OVER-SANDS
CUMBRIA   LA11   6ET
TELEPHONE: (05395) 32552

Hazelmere Cafe and Bakery
1&2 Yewbarrow Terrace, Grange Over Sands
05395 32972

The Hazelmere Cafe and Bakery is a family run business. Situated opposite the beautiful ornamental gardens and close to the famous promenade The cafe and bakery can be found at one end of a Victorian terrace under a superb full length glazed verandah modelled on Lord Street in Southport. During Summer tables are placed outside under the verandah overlooking the gardens .
The emphasis throughout the cafe and bakery is on high quality food made with the best of ingredients. All the bread, confectionery and savouries are prepared and baked on the premises. All the soups and paties are home made, the hams and beef are home cooked and nothing other than free range eggs and vegetarian standard cheese is used. All the chutnies, jellies and salads are made at the Hazelmere and as well as being served in the cafe, these can be purchased in the shop to take away. There is a wide choice on the cafe menu from snacks to full meals, and from the traditional to the exotic. Besides the extensive main menu there is always a daily specials board with usually a choice of two soups, two pates and at least three main courses.

Vegetarians are always well catered for with a choice of at least 4 dishes on the menu, and all home made.
The Hazelmere bakery won the Bakers of the Year for the North West region in 1993.
A large choice of speciality breads are for sale in the bakery such as foccacia, Hazelmere tea bread and rosemary and basil bread.
New recipes are being constantly devised and perfected. Even ready made meals are available, specially prepared to bake off in your own oven.
The Hazelmere also has a seperate upstairs room which was built as a Victorian gentlemans smoking room. It is used as an extra room when the cafe is busy or it can be booked for private parties.

The Birchleigh Guest House

Kents Bank Road,
Grange-over-sands,
Cumbria. LA11 7EY
Tel: 05395 32592

Proprietor: Mrs. Margaret Smith

Birchleigh is a non-smoking establishment, centrally heated, has two double bedrooms, two family rooms and one twin room on the ground floor all with en-suite facilities, shaving points, Teas-maids, TV and comfortable chairs. Pets are welcome. Good home cooking with a choice of menu served from 5pm to 7pm daily

AA Listed

GRASMERE.

Map ref. E.9.
Next nearest Town or Village " Rydal"
Tourist Information Centre. Town Centre.(Red Bank Rd)
Location. Ambleside to Keswick road.
Early closing.Thursday.
Gala days/festivals / Wordsworth Summer Conference 1st 2 Week Aug.
Lakeside Artists Exhibition. August.
.Grasmere Gala, 3rd Saturday in June.
Rushbearing Ceremony. 1st Saturday in August.
Grasmere Sports. 3rd Thursday after 1st Monday in August.

Grasmere is a village four miles north-west of Ambleside, past a lake one mile long and 3/8th of a mile wide, complete with its own small island. Living in a great natural bowl between the green craggy mountains, few villages in England enjoy a more dramatic setting than Grasmere.Rough slate cottages, an ancient church and the nearby lake have the intense beauty of a romantic painting, and many artists and poets have been inspired by this spectacular landscape.
The name Grasmere probably originated from the name Grisemere meaning Lake of the Swine...so called because one of the early uses of the (then) forest was for herding pigs.
The church of St Oswald dedicated to the Northumbrian King of the same name, who was killed at the battle of Massenfield in AD 42...stands upon the bank of the Rotha river. Its foundation date is uncertain, but a church is believed to have stood on the site since Saxon times.St.Oswalds

Well nearby, is today covered over, but at one time the church used its water for christening. The tower walls are some three to four feet thick and beneath is an ancient font, which is thought to have come from Furness Abbey.

Some of the yew trees in the churchyard were planted by Wordsworth. Near one is his grave with the simple inscription 'William Wordsworth 1850' Mary Wordsworth 1859' Other graves of this famous family are their daughter Dora and the poets sister Dorothy.

Obviously Wiiliam Wordsworth was Grasmere's most famous inhabitant. He arrived here on the 20th December 1799 where he took up residence at Town End...The Dove and Olive Bough Inn as it was then known...today better known as Dove Cottage. In 1802 Wordsworth married Mary Hutchinson and they lived at Dove Cottage until 1808. Today the rooms are furnished almost exactly as when the poet lived there. The parlour has a stone floor and much old woodwork, and on the same floor is Dorothy's bedroom. The staircase which brings visitors to the parlour with its three chairs covered by Dora Wordsworth, Edith Southey, and Sara Coleridge.

It was here that he wrote "Michael, Resolution and Independence, Ode, Intimations of Immortality, together with completing 'The Prelude'(in 1805). When the cottage became too small for his growing family, he moved to Rydal where he lived until his death in 1850. Visitors to the cottage are offered guided tours.

Amongst Grasmere's many festivals and events, the longest surviving one is the Annual Rushbearing Ceremony, which takes place on the Sunday nearest to St Oswald Day (5th August). It is a relic of the days when the church floors were strewn with rushes for warmth and cleanliness. During the period 1819 to 1849 (when the church was paved, and therefore became unnecessary to strew rushes), the rush bearers(mostly children) were given gifts of rush-bearers cakes..in other words the famous Grasmere Gingerbread. The Gingerbread shop itself still survives, still selling gingerbread, and is housed in the tiny schoolroom built in 1687...the place where Wordsworth taught during his time in Grasmere.

Grasmere Sports are held on the 3rd Thursday in August and remains as one of the most important fixtures in the Lakeland sporting calendar. Included is wrestling, pole vaulting, sprinting, hound trailing, and the event of the day...the race to the summit of Butter Crag and back.

Not to be overlooked by visitors is the fact that Samuel Taylor Coleridge, Poet and Philospher, lived at Grasmere from 1809.

THE LAKES
Crafts and
Antiques
GALLERY
GRASMERE

**3 Oak Bank, Broadgate,
Grasmere, Cumbria LA22 9TA
Tel: (05394) 35037**

Enter The Lake District and you enter more than a land of outstanding natural beauty. For many, one of the delights is the abundance of crafts and antiques, a fascinating world that adds an extra dimension to your time in Lakeland. A part of this journey for those with an eye for beauty and craftsmanship is a visit to The Lakes Craft and Antiques Gallery at Grasmere. More than just another shop, the Gallery is a rewarding gathering of collectors, dealers, and Crafts people, assembled together in a Victorian style indoor street market

Browsers and collectors alike will find their time here well rewarded. Apart from the products for sale, the specialists and dealers exhibiting their wares enjoy nothing more than sharing their knowledge and experience with others.

Whether you are sheltering from one of Lakeland's occasional showers, searching for that exclusive something different, that special gift, or trying to fill a corner of your home, you will find the Gallery a fascinating blend of past craftsmanship and present day Lakeland creativity.

We look forward to welcoming you to the Lakes Crafts and Antiques Gallery, we're sure your visit will be a pleasurable experience.

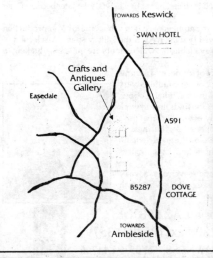

Dove Cottage

The Grasmere & Wordsworth Museum

In 1799 Wordsworth undertook a tour of the Lake District with his close friend Samuel Taylor Coleridge. It was on this tour that he first saw Dove Cottage, formerly an inn, *The Dove and Olive*. By late December 1799 he and sister Dorothy were in residence. Dove Cottage was Wordsworth's home until 1808. Eight years of "...plain living and high thinking" during which Wordsworth produced what are now regarded as his finest works. Among others *The Prelude* of 1805, *Ode: Intimations of Immortality, Resolution and Independence, Michael* and *I wandered lonely as a cloud*. It is through Dorothy's diaries kept at Dove Cottage that the daily life of the poet is illustrated so clearly. In the preface to the second edition of *Lyrical Ballads* (1800) Wordsworth explains the importance of the peaceful lifestyle at Dove Cottage for Creativity: "Poetry is the spontaneous overflow of powerful feelings: It takes its origins from emotion recollected in tranquillity"

The Wordworths were succeeded at Dove Cottage by their young friend Thomas De Quincey, later famous for *The Confessions of an English Opium Eater*. The tenancy of Dove Cottage was held by De Quincey until 1836. From 1836 there was a varied succession of tenants until 1890 when a Trust formed by the Reverend Stopford Brooke (1832-1916) bought the Cottage and opened it to the public a year later. All visitors are offered a guided tour of the Cottage. Guide books are available in French, German, Japanese and Dutch. Almost 90,000 visitors were welcomed in 1990. Wordsworth's furniture, family possessions, portraits, and typical nineteenth century household items are carefully displayed to retain the homely atmosphere.

The garden, Wordsworth's 'domestic slip of mountain', has been restored to the half wild state which William and Dorothy lovingly created.

The Grasmere and Wordsworth Museum was founded in 1934 and recreated in 1981 within the walls of an 1850's coach-house. There are on display, a unique collection of original manuscripts, eighteenth and nineteenth century landscapes, portraits of Wordsworth and his contemporaries and family possessions. Wordsworth's life and revolutionary times are mapped out using his autobiographical poem *The Prelude*. Treasures include manuscripts of the 1805 *Prelude*, Dorothy Wordsworth's *Grasmere Journals*, Coleridge's *Ode: Dejection* and Thomas De Quincey *Confessions of an English Opium Eater*. Works by Constable, Gainsborough, Joseph Wright of Derby and Joseph Farington contribute to a fine collection of 18 and 19c Lake District art. A special 'life' room' is a re-creation of the kitchen-parlour of a Lake District farmhouse in the early nineteenth century. Each year the museum presents a Special Exhibition covering subjects connected with the Romantic Period: Byron, De Quincey and Coleridge among others.

Along with Dove cottage, the quality of the museum has led to a number of awards, including the Museum of the Year Special Award in 1982, the Lady Inglewood Training Award in 1987 for '...excellent interpretation by guides, consistently high quality displays, evident attention to visitor handling techniques, all adding up to good value for money" and the Alfred H Barr Jr. Award for *William Wordsworth and the Age of English Romanticism*"... an especially distinguished catalogue on the history of art, published in any language", presented in San Francisco in 1989. In 1990 the Trust's Education Programme received a Sandford Award for Heritage Education. The citation describes Dove Cottage and the Wordsworth Museum as "A place to make the spirits soar"

Open Daily 9.30am - 5.30pm. Last admissions 5.00pm.
Closed January 10th-Feb 6th and December 24th, 25th, 26th.

For further information telephone Grasmere (05394) 35544/35547

WHITE MOSS HOUSE

WHITE MOSS HOUSE

RYDAL WATER, GRASMERE, ENGLISH LAKES, LA 22 9SE
TELEPHONE: GRASMERE (05394) 35295

This area, between Rydal and Grasmere, is very popular with walkers. White Moss Common and viewpoint were mentioned by Dorothy Wordsworth in her journal for 1st June 1802. "We went to look at Rydale. There was an alpine fire-look red upon the tops of the mountains... we saw the Lake in a new and most beautiful point of view between two little rocks. This White Moss; a place made for all kinds of beautiful works of art and nature, woods and valleys, fairy valleys and fairy tarns, miniature mountains, alps above alps".

White Moss House, built in 1730, was bought by William Wordsworth for his son Willie, and the poet often rested and composed poetry in the porch on his wanderings. He had moved to Rydal Mount at this time, but buying White Moss House gave William voting rights in Grasmere, which he used to help prevent the extension of the railway line from Windermere to Grasmere. The Wordsworths owned the house until the 1930s. In recent years it has been restored by Susan and Peter Dixon, and it is now an internationally renowned small hotel and restaurant.

White Moss House was bought by William Wordsworth for his son, and the poet often rested and wrote poetry in the porch on his wanderings. Built in 1730, it overlooks Rydal Water in the heart of the Lakes, and many famous walks and rivers, by Lakes and over hills begin from the front door.

Proprietors Sue and Peter Dixon have created an intimate family atmosphere. Personal care for the guests, and attention to detail are hallmarks of this charming hotel. There are five rooms in the main house, and two situated in Brockstone Cottage Suite, whose isolated beauty makes it a truly romantic spot. All are individually furnished with many thoughtful touches, including a large selection of books and antiques.

"Peter Dixon is a maestro of British cooking" said the Sunday Times. The wine list of over 300 bins offers distinguished bottles from around the world, and is exceptional value for money. Bon Appetit magazine said "Chef Peter Dixon is an intuitive cook, with a deep understanding of ingredients and flavours. He uses wonderful local produce for his five course dinners"

Peter's reputation has spread; in the past year White Moss has featured in magazine articles in Japan, The USA, Italy and Germany, where "Feinschmeker" magazine called White Moss "the smallest most splendid hotel in the world". It has been said that "Nature and man combine Harmoniously at White Moss House" (Richard Binns Best of Britain). Lovers of the best in food and wines, who appreciate the beautiful scenery immortalised by the Romantic Poets, will love White Moss House. White Moss House is highly recommended in all the leading guide books.

The Hotel is an AA Red Star Hotel
The Restaurant has 2 AA Rosettes
ETB 3 Crown Highly Commended

Visiting Grasmere Gardens is a must for anyone. Our idyllic position at the centre of Grasmere village, spacious Cafe and quality Gift Shop make us more than a Garden Centre. From extensive parking to our Main Studio, built using Westmorland Greenslate and our truly interesting Nursery. Grasmere guarantees a friendly welcome, making visiting and shopping a pleasure. You will enjoy our extensive range of outdoor and indoor plants. Gift Shop with its fine crystal, china and floral displays - and finally relaxing in our Cafe.

Opening Times Mon-Sun 9.00am - 5.30pm (Winter 9.30 am - 4.30 pm)
Large on-site car park. Easy access for disabled visitors. Coach parties
welcome by prior arrangment.

THE TRAVELLERS REST
G R A S M E R E

A FORMER 16TH CENTURY COACHING INN, THE TRAVELLERS REST EPITOMISES THE TRADITIONAL LAKE DISTRICT INN. Full of old world charm and character with oack beams and inglenooks. Roaring log fires in winter and beer gardens enjoying panoramic views in summer. Comfortable bedrooms, real ales, fine wines, renowned home cokking and genuine hospitality provided by resident proprietors the Sweeny family.

Seven letting bedrooms comprising of four double, two twin, and one single. All bedrooms are individually furnished with colour television, tea and coffee making facilities. Most bedrooms have superb views of the surrounging hills.

Located on the A591, just outside of Grasmere Village in the heart of the Lake District The Travellers Rest enoys an idyllic settting whilst being accessible from all areas of the country by road (M6 exit 36) and rail (Windermere 11 miles)

The Travellers Rest is open throughout the year, and offers Christmas, new Year and Easter packages please ask us for further details.

We present an extensive menu of home cooked dishes utilising the best of local produce and featuring , many local and provincial dishes We feature local Real Ales (we are listed in CAMRA's good Beer Guide and The good Pub guide). An extensive cellar of fine wines at affordable prices and a wide range of malt whiskies.

Grasmere, Cumbria LA22 9RR.
Telephone: 05394 35604

Red Lion Hotel
Grasmere, Cumbria LA22 9SS
Telephone: (05394) 35456
AA ★★★ RAC

Take a step across the threshold and into the warmth of a Westmorland welcome. The Red Lion Hotel began life over two hundred years ago as a coaching inn here in Cumbria, and has been receiving visitors ever since. Today you are greeted by an attractive and fresh series of refurbishments, which combine the merits of tradition, the benefits of modernity and outstanding value for money. The thirty-five bedrooms all have en-suite facilities. Whether for fell-walking, climbing touring or simply staying put, The Red Lion provides an excellent setting and ideal base for a Lake District holiday. It is, after all, set in the very heart of Wordsworth country.

As the sun sets low over Red Bank, the culinary benefits begin! An invigorating choice of wholesome, fresh English cuisine is available every night either a la carte or table d'hote. You can also brighten your day with a light meal in the cheerful Easedale Bar looking out over the hotel garden and up the fells to Helm Crag, locally known as the Lion and the Lamb.

A more easily attainable lamb is our own old-style Lakeland pub, the Lamb Inn - an ideal place for a pint of real ale and a bar meal after a day of effort on the fells.

Additional facilities at the Red Lion include an attractive residents' lounge and conference facilities looking over Easedale. This has built up a popular following as a venue for seminars and conferences accommodating up to 50 delegates. Whatever the purpose of your visit, we pride ourselves in providing a friendly and relaxed atmosphere at the Red Lion which we trust you will come and enjoy at your earliest opportunity.

Enjoy the peace & hospitality of the
Red Lion Hotel

GRAYRIGG.

Map ref. H.10.
Next nearest Town or Village "Kendal"
Location.On A685 Midway Kendal and Tebay.
Gala days/festivals. Selside,Grayrigg and
Mountain District of Westmorland Agricultural
Show.1st Thursday in September.

A scattered township situated on the A,685 road halfway between Kendal and Tebay, and includes the hamlets of Docker,Lambrigg,Dillicar, Whinfell,and Patton.Has fine views of the Howgill Fells to the east and Whinfell Beacon to the north. Here was born Frances Howgill (1610-69) who introduced George Fox to the Westmorland 'Seekers'..a group of radical Christians, which led eventually to the formation of the Quaker church."The Society of Friends'

The church here was built in 1837, although like so many other villages throughout Cumbria, has had a place of worship on the site for many centuries.The Quakers were a one time important part of Grayriggs community.They started meetings at Sunny Bank, but in 1696 built their own meeting house at Beckhouses, and continued to meet here for the next 200 years.

Grayrigg Hall, just down the lane, was built to replace an original Hall further out of the village where the Duckett family lived for generations. Mount Pleasant House stands across the lane from the church.It was a vicarage at one time. as well as being a public house.(The Brown Cow), during the time of the railway. Anvil Cottage (typically) used to be the old Smithy.

GREAT CORBY.

Map ref. F.4.
Next nearest Town or Village "Wetheral"
Location. 1 mile south of the A.69 Carlisle to Newcastle road.

High above the Eden, stands Corby Castle, its oldest walls, originally a pele tower, rising sheer from the steep cliff.In the heart of the superb house which the Howard's owners for the last 300 years have made of this mediaeval fortress, is still a spiral staircase trodden by many 12th century feet. Lord William Howard...the famous 'Belted Will', whose portrait painted over 300 years ago still hangs in the castle gallery, lived here.Two of the Howard lions will be seen standing on the imposing modern parapets.
In the village is a square exedra built in 1833, originally as a blacksmith's shop.It has a covered open space in front which is supported by thick sandstone piers...these days the building is a car repair workshop.
Another feature of interest is the railway bridge built by Francis Giles in 1834.It is 600 feet long and 100 feet high, and connects Great Corby to the station at Wetheral...a village on the west side of the river. The sandstone bridge additionally supports a cast iron footbridge which at one time had a toll of 1/2d

One of the best known legendary stories of Cumbria is the 'Radiant Boy' of Corby Castle.
No one knows who he is or why he haunts a room in the oldest part of the castle...but it is said he is a kindly appealing ghost.All those who have seen him report that he is a beautiful boy, always dressed in white, and always with a radiant light surrounding him. The story goes that whoever sees him is destined to rise to considerable power and wealth.. But before anybody rushes off to try and see him it should be added that there is 'a sting in the tail' It is also said that that same person will also suffer a violent death at the height of that power!
Apparently one such person to see 'The Boy' was Lord Castlereagh.His sleep was disturbed one night and he awoke to see the vision...which then disappeared in the direction of the chimney. As history tells us Lord Castlereagh did in fact rise to fame serving as Foreign Minister during the Napoleonic Wars...until in 1822 he had a mental breakdown and committed suicide.

GREAT SALKELD.

Map ref. G.6.
Next nearest Town or Village " Lazonby"
Location. Just over 5 miles from Penrith .north.

The small village of Great Salkeld will be found nestling on the western bank of the Eden valley, just over five miles from Penrith. Traces of Roman occupation hereabouts.
The oldest building here is the church of St Cuthbert's...itself standing on the site of what is thought to be an old wooden church.In 1380 a tower was added with walls 6 feet thick, and a narrow oak door which is reinforced by an iron grating and massive bolts...very much an indication that it was used as a look-out and a safe refuge from marauding Scots in times gone by.
Beneath the ground floor is a vault or dungeon.

According to legend Dick Whittington loved this old church and despatched four bells to Great Salkeld.When however they reached Kirkby Stephen some misunderstanding arose.Whittington had expected the Salkeld people to go and collect them,but they failed to do this, and so the bells remained at Kirkby Stephen...and eventually appropriated by the Vicar of Kirkby Stephen.
According to many (but argued against by just as many) is the story that Dick Whittington was actually born in the village in 1358. He was three times Lord Mayor of London 1398,1406,1419,. He was also Member of Parliament(in 1416) and upon his death in 1423 left his fortune for the rebuilding of Newgate Gaol (amongst others).
The first school here was actually in the church tower as early as 1515, though the school house proper was built in 1686.
Nunwick Hall, once a large estate, is now part of a holiday cottage complex.

GREYSTOKE.

Map ref. F.7.
Next nearest Town or Village "Gt. Blencow"
Bus service/Cumberland Bus Route 105, XS
Location 5 miles west of Penrith.
Gala days/festivals. Sports Day at Stone Carr.
May Bank Holiday Monday.

A pleasant little village lying just outside the perimeter of the Lake District National Park. Two miles north of the A66, and five miles west of Penrith.
It still retains its central small village green and ancient market cross,many of the houses here have been built of stone, complete with slate roofs.Quite a few are listed buildings.
Greystoke Castle...the seat of the Howard's of Greystoke stands in about 6000 acres, and its park is said to be the biggest enclosure in England

ENTRANCE TO GREYSTOKE CASTLE

without a road or a right of way running through. Its wall runs for miles, but of the castle itself little more than the flag can be seen. It is reached by a main drive directly from the village, and through a rather grand archway.Its 19th century facade hides a mediaeval pele tower. It is not old as castles go, having been burned down intentionally in the Civil War and by accident since, but it is certainly old in family history and in comparatively recent years built up again as a noble structure. Here lived the proud nobility of Cumbria, the Greystokes, the Dacres, and the Howards who still live there to this day .and can claim an unbroken line of descent going back over 900 years..to 1066 in fact.

The castle is not open to the public at any time of the year.

Greystoke Castle was at one time a stronghold of King Charles 11 until it was successfully besieged by part of Cromwells army during their encampment in the district.The castle now boasts of a resident ghost, with a disused room in the old tower being the supposed venue of its annual appearance.

Tradition has it that this is the ghost of a guest who once spent a Sunday hunting with Charles Howard, Duke of Norfolk.After an evening of merriment and feasting, he retired to his room at a late hour.Servants knocking on his door the following morning failed to wake him, and finally an entrance was made to his room.His bed had certainly been slept in, his clothes were lying about, but no trace was ever found of him...Since then a ghost has appeared in this room annually and it was said that anyone sleeping in the same room was greatly disturbed during the night...even by people unaware of the tragedy.

In the old chapel in the grounds, so legend has us to believe.a monk was once bricked up in an underground passage leading from the chapel to the haunted bedroom mentioned in the previous story.In past years, residents in the castle have regularly heard knockings on the wall which is believed to be the one covering up the entrance to the passage.

The interest of visitors is often aroused when passing down the main Keswick-Penrith road.close to Greystoke village when they catch sight of what appear to be the castellated walls of two forts or castles.Both are farms however.They were built by Charles Howard 11th Duke of Norfolk (sometimes known as the Drunken Duke) in 1783. At that time he was Whig M.P. for Carlisle. The farm having the appearance of a castle, was named Bunkers Hill after

Boot & Shoe Inn

Greystoke, Cumbria.
Tel: 07684 83343

GREYSTOKE on the B6288 road, and just five miles from Penrith is particularly noted for its collegiate church dating from the 13th Century...once the home of canons and literally as big as a small cathedral. Close by is the 17th century Boot & Shoe Inn a typical Cumbrian coaching halt which has been dispensing fine ales, wines and spirits since long before the first stagecoach dispensed its first load of thirsty hungry and tired travellers. The architecture and atmosphere may have stayed the same for the past 300 odd years, but fortunately home comforts as we know them are very much available in this delightfully run Inn.

The Boot & Shoe Inn today is an attractive and popular local 'pub' along with being a most comfortable overnight stop for those tourists requiring bed and breakfast accommodation. Mine host Beverley & Graham Kelso prides themseves on providing an ever changing menu of fresh food in her dining room along with a most impressive choice of bar snacks. Its not long since the Inn was completely decorated, but fortunately retaining its old oak beams and welcoming open fire. Single, twin, double, family rooms available..Licensed bar/ lounge.

Private car park. Large selection of beers, wines and spirits.
All rooms have H & C tea and coffee making facilities, Radio T.V.

𝔚𝔥𝔦𝔱𝔟𝔞𝔯𝔯𝔬𝔴 𝔙𝔦𝔩𝔩𝔞𝔤𝔢

LAKELAND'S
PREMIER HOLIDAY DESTINATION
Whitbarrow Hall, Berrier,
Penrith, Cumbria CA11 0XB
Tel: Greystoke (07684) 83797 / 83841
Fax: (07684) 83843

The street is designed around the converted farm buildings it is cobbled and flagged, with paths leading through archways to its courtyards which are lawned and surrounded by shrubs and flowers.

The Eamont cottages are the focal point of the street. The large sandstone clock tower overlooks the craft workshops and their rear balconies have views stretching to the Pennines.

Everyone can easily relax and enjoy the luxurious atmosphere which we provide in Eamonts. The kitchens are fully equipped with a dishwasher and microwave and the en-suite bathroom has a spa bath.

The Leisure Club is the social centre of the Village where you can meet your friends, enjoy the varied sports or book other activities such as horse riding, golf, or a quiet trip on the lake. Out staff are here from 8.30 am - 10.00 pm to help or advise you about where to eat or what is on in the locality. The leisure club was completed in 1989 at a cost of more than £1 million and has the following facilities:-

SPEED POOL   SOLARIUM
CARPET BOWLS SQUASH
TURKISH BATH   SAUNA
AEROBICS   CRECHE
MASSAGE   TABLE TENNIS
HEATED POOL   SNOOKER

In addition to the facilities in the Club there is also an all-weather tennis court, putting green, croquet lawn, boule pitch, draughts board and children's play area in Whitbarrow Village grounds. We are open all year and offer short breaks, weekly rentals or alternatively you can purchase one of our timeshare weeks.

The Derwent Cottages are designed as a typical country cottage with a stable-door. , tudor ceiling and a copper canopy in the lounge. By contrast the Bowscale Cottages were converted from the old Dutch barn, they have a gallery bedroom and the picture window gives an excellent view of the meadows and fells.

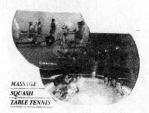

Leisure for life in Lakeland

the first Battle in the American War of Independence, and the other is named after the American General Israel 'Puffin' Putnam, the farm now being known as Fort Putnam. Charles Howard was a great friend of Charles James Fox and together they planned the efforts of the Whig Party to obtain justice for the American Colonies and also at the same time to upset the policies of Lord North of the Tory Party. When the Colonies put up such a fine performance at Bunkers Hill, the two farms were erected as memorials and, one assumes, as a perpetual irritant to the local Tories!.

Close by is another farm, which with its diminutive spire looks like a church. It is known as Spire House and was also built by Charles Howard and tenanted in the late 18th century by a member of a religious sect which maintained that worship in a church was unnecessary .This man apparently became such a bore that when he went off to a religious meeting some distance away Charles Howard had his workmen alter the farm to the way in which you see it today.

Close by on Church road will be seen the blue Whinstone 'Sanctuary Stone'. It has hatchet marks on it pointing towards the church.The right of sanctuary is said to have been granted in early times to all churches..Once behind (or beyond) the stone, individuals, or more likely, fugitives from the law could claim sanctuary within the church's precincts. Another stone hereabouts is the 'Spillers'.This has been hollowed out on top and is thought was once used as a plague stone where coins could be left to avoid possible contagion.

The lovely church here has been dedicated to St.Andrew, and records show it dates back to 1255. Visitors will immediately notice that it is larger than most Cumbrian churches, and this is because it was a Collegiate (or Mother Church) in

the Middle Ages.The copper and brass ornaments were made at the Old Smithy at Blencow, a village just to the north of Greystoke.

One person who perhaps knew this church as a child has no memorial in it. She was Isabel Foster, who was born at Greystoke.She married a Fleet Street, London cutler, and was burned for her faith with six others at Smithfield in the reign of Mary. The ancient village school here was erected by the Howard family in 1838.

The famous jockey Gordon Richards owns a very successful racing stable here training some 700 winners in the last few years, including two Grand national winners.

The Boot and Shoe Pub, origins unknown, is a regular haunt for locals and visitors and was until very recently run by three generations of the same family.

Located just outside Greystoke in the little hamlet of Berrier will be found the beautiful designed Whitbarrow Village, a privately owned resort consisting of time share lodges, leisure club, tennis courts, putting green, bar etc.

BECKSTONES

GRINSDALE.

Map ref. E.4.
Next nearest Town or Village "Beaumont"
Location. 2 miles north west of Carlisle.

Grinsdale is a village on the Eden just over two miles north west of Carlisle.The Roman Wall and Vallum runs directly through the village.

Back in 1747 there used to be a tannery here at Grinsdale Bridge, together with a blacksmith's

shop.In fact the original bellows and blacksmith's tools are still intact inside the building.

The church is dedicated to St Kentigern and is not easily accessible as the villagers have to walk over two fields to worship there. The church has been restored twice, once in 1740 and again in 1895...though it is believed to date back to the 12th century.

In the 18th and 19th century the village was well known for its linen industry, with many of the locals becoming weavers.

GRIZEDALE.

Map ref. E.11..
Next nearest Town or Village "Rosland"
Bus service. Post Bus + Cumberland Buses Route 504,510
Location. 3 miles south of Hawkshead.

FOREST SCULPTURE

South of Hawkshead is Grizedale, the largest area of Forestry Commission plantation in the Lake District.After the Forestry Commission acquired the estate back in 1936, it actually increased the size of the forest...then comprising ancient oaks and conifers...from 400 hectares to 1700 hectares. Red and roe deer frequent Grizedale...In fact there are public hides for watching wildlife in the forest...but what distinguishes a forest walk here for most visitors is the presence of forest 'sculptures'...made by artists who have used local materials,mostly wood and rock...along with the forest setting to create a sort of naturalistic modern art gallery...which adds a touch of enchantment to the forest.The sculpture trails, established in 1963 were the first of their kind in Britain,and today are the largest in Britain.There are more than 80 sculptures in the Forest,all made from natural materials by artists staying in Grizedale for varying lengths of time.

Along with outdoor sculptures, outdoor recreation plays a great role at Grizedale with activities such as walking, orienteering, deer stalking, photography and wildlife observation which is on offer all year.

Opposite the Visitor Centre ,which stocks a wide variety of products, giftware...and of course Forest maps, is The Theatre in the Forest, which began operating as a professional theatre in 1969.Today it seats over 200 people, and is a venue for regular concerts,plays, films and lectures.Adjacent is a playground with a gigantic wooden bird concealing a slide and a roundabout involving a perpetual

hare and hound race.The other building on site is a craft workshop and display room which has changing exhibitions on a regular basis.

Older generations may be interested in learning that the current site of the car park and picnic site was once the home of Grizedale Hall, which during the last war was used as a POW camp for high ranking German officers...one of whom successfully escaped.You may recall the film 'The One that got away', which was based on that escape.

FOREST SCULPTURE

The Grizedale Society

Theatre in the Forest - Sculpture in the Landscape
Crafts Workshop - Painting Studio - Exhibition Gallery
Grizedale, Hawkshead, Ambleside, Cumbria LA22 0QZ
Telephone and Fax: Satterthwaite (0229) 860291
Regd. Charity No. 500253

GRIZEDALE SCULPTURE & THEATRE IN THE FOREST

Grizedale Forest lies between Coniston and Windermere, in an area of great natural beaut·. It is a mixed forest and contains 1200 acres of oak woodlan I. Within this remarkable setting stands the Theatre-in-the-Forest, which is administered by the Grizedale Society, and began operating in 1969, seating over 200 people. Today it is a multi-media venue, hosting Classical music concerts, Jazz, Folk Music, Natural History, Drama and Dance etc. It has well-earned it's title "the theatre with a touch of magic".

Along with the theatre, the Grizedale Society administers the unique Grizedale Sculpture Project. In 1977, at the suggestion of Northern Arts, the Society began its move into the second arts activity - Sculpture-in-the-Landscape. The project is based on residencies, offered each year, which can last from a few weeks to a few months,.and the scheme works so successfully because the individual sculptors creative response to the environment keeps the work fresh and vital.

The sculptors work mainly in natural materials, often those found on the forest floor itself. This also decrees that the site-specific works produced will often be of a temporary nature. At present there are more than 80 sculptures sited on and around the Silurian Way, a nine mile trail, and also The Ridding Wood Trail, providing access for the elderly and disadvantaged, allowing them the same freedom to enjoy the arts experience fused with nature. Grizedale has the largest collection of site-related sculpture in the U.K., and possibly Europe.

In addition to this renowned project, the Society now has encompassed a craft workshop and painting studio, also working on residencies, both of great benefit to the many painters and sculptors who work there. An exibition gallery houses a fine collection of working drawings, paintings, maquettes and craftwork, predominantly serving as an appetiser for the many excellent works sited outside of doors.

The Centre at Grizedale can boast an average of 250,000 day visitors per year, and Sculpture Guide Maps are readily available both from the Visitors Centre and the Theatre office.

GRIZEDALE LODGE HOTEL

Discover the peace and tranquility of this comfortable and elegant shooting lodge tucked away in the heart of magnificient

Grizedale Forest Park midway between Coniston Water and Windermere. Here the aim of Jack and Margaret Lamb and their staff is to offer a small number of guests first-class accommodation in a relazed and friendly atmosphere.

The Hotel is well known throughout Cumbria and, together with its restaurant, is featured in all the leading guides. All the food is freshly prepared on the premises, using local produce as far as possible, under the close supervision of Margaret Lamb, who is a leading authority on traditional Cumbrian fare. In fact she has had her own series on border television, and contributed to various cookery books.

Meals are served in the pretty restautrant overlooking the valley and the forest beyond. The lounge bar is the ideal place to relax after dinner - a delightful comfortable room, where an open fire burns on cooler spring and autumn days. French doors lead on to the balcony where guests can relax in the sun with a drink whilst enjoying the peace and beauty of the forest. Each evening guests can look forward to a memorable five course dinner offering a blend of the best of British and French cuisine together with Cumbrian specialities such as Lake Esthwaite Trout, Grizedale Venison and Penrith Peppered Lamb. Any special dietary requirements or vegetarian meals can be catered for with appropriate notice.

All nine bedrooms are individually furnished and decorated. Each room has en-suite facilities, colour TV, tea and coffee making equipment and full central heating. Three of the bedrooms are located on the ground floor, and for that "Special Occasion" two luxury bedrooms with four-poster beds are available.

A unique advantage of making this delightful family run hotel your base, is its proximity to the famous "Theatre in the Forest". Just 500 yards away the Theatre offers a variety of high quality entertainment from classical to jazz from dramas to mime.

For those guests wishing to attend the Theatre, early dinner is available on request.

For further information contact:

**GRIZEDALE LODGE HOTEL,
NR HAWKSHEAD, CUMBRIA, LA22 0QL
TEL: 05394 36532**

RAC & AA ✿✿ Egon Ronay Recommended.

PEPPER HOUSE

Country Farmhouse

Satterthwaite, Cumbria LA12 8LS, England
Tel: Satterthwaite (0229) 860206

Welcome to Pepper House, a friendly Elizabethan farmhouse which was probably built circa 1570 for a yeoman farmer. It has oak cruck beams and thick stone walls and overlooks a wide 'summer clearing' in the beautiful Grizedale Forest Park. Pepper House with Blackberry Cottage annexe, has grown steadily over the years, to offer visitors more 'home comforts',but a still peaceful holiday. There are two lounges, a separate T.V. room and bar, log fire and central heating.

The bedrooms vary in size and character but all are well-fitted with comfortable beds and warm duvets (would guests who are allergic to feathers please mention it at the time of booking). All rooms are en-suite, with private toilet and shower, and are fitted with tea/coffee making facilities, hair-dryers, clock radios etc. Ironing facilities are available on request. One ground-floor bedroom is adaped for guests in wheelchairs. We DO accept guide dogs.

Food at Pepper House is still a major feature. Dining is 'farmhouse style' on polished pine tables, and the cooking is unashamedly British...home-made soups, succulent roasts, crisp vegetables and feather-light puddings and pastries. Some of the recipes are traditional, many are from my own imagination. Special diets are catered for with pleasure, as are our growing number of vegetarian guests. We now hold a full restaurant and residential licence, with wines and spirits at reasonable prices.

Pepper House is the guest house in Satterthwaite and definitely the place to come for holidays and for cream teas and refreshments after exploring some of the forest walks. Dinner is available for non-residents but pre-booking is essential.

Contact: M/s. Yvonne M. Menary Smith

HALLBANKGATE.
Map ref. H.4.
Next nearest Town or Village "Talkin"
Location. Midway between Carlisle and Alston.

Hallbankgate is a village midway between Carlisle and Alston at the northern end of the Pennines.
Just outside the village is 'The Kirkhouse' once a considerable industrial centre with its gas works, coke ovens, foundries, blacksmith's, waggon shops.equipment for the local quarries was also made here.
The local pub 'The Belted Will' was at one time closed down by Rosalind, the Countess of Carlisle, after which it became the 'Temperance Hotel' reverting back to its original state in the 1970's.
The village church situated just outside the village stands on ground which has had a church since 1169.

OLD SCHOOL HOUSE

At one time a railway ran through the village, and locals will proudly tell you that George Stephenson's famous 'Rocket' ended its working life here and was later presented to Kensington Museum by the

HAWKSHEAD.
Map ref. E.10.
Next nearest Town or Village "Near & Far Sawrey"
Bus service Cumberland Buses route 505, 506
Tourist Information Centre. Near Car Park.
PLUS. National Trust Information Centre.The Square.
Location. 5 miles east of Coniston.
Early closing.Thursday (winter only)
Gala days/festivals.Hawkshead Agricultural Show. 3rd Tuesday in August.

Hawkshead is a small town with a market charter dating from 1608,and is situated near the head of Esthwaite Water...lying roughly halfway between the lakes of Coniston Water and Windermere.
Hawkshead, at one time was almost certainly a Norse or Viking settlement, its name being derived from one Hawk who built what was originally a stockaded settlement in Grisedale Forest.
Hawkshead is certainly picturesque and its quaint houses,many now colour-washed, grey roofs of local slate, squares, arches, pillars and flights of stone steps make it unique in Lakeland.A stream, which flows down Vicarage Lane, on the north side, disappears under the village and joins the Poole Beck and enters the lake.At one time this stream, at the Flag Street end was uncovered and

local people drew water from it.The village today still appears to be the same as it did hundreds of years ago.
One of the oldest buildings hereabouts is The Red Lion Inn...an original 15th century coaching house.Look for the two figures on the outside wall, below the eaves...one showing a farmer taking a pig to market, the other a man with a whistle.
Ann Street, or Wordsworth Street leads from the main road to Vicarage Lane and Grandy Nook, and is yet another cobbled street.At one time it was (and sometimes still is) called 'Rag,Putty,and Leather Street'for two tailors, two cobblers, and two painters, had their business premises there.

MINSTRELL GALLERY

HAWKSHEAD

Hawkshead's most famous 'monument' has to be the original Hawkshead Grammar School...attended by one William Wordsworth during the period 1778-1783.The school founded in'1585 and closed in 1909..is now a museum containing an important antiquarian library..Wordsworth's name cut into a desk by the great man himself...can still be seen.For most of his schooldays he lived with Ann Tyson,at Green End Cottage, another building which still exists and can be seen. Today it is a very pleasant guest house,known as Ann Tyson's cottage.

By all acounts his schooldays at Hawkshead were as gay and lively as those of any boy of today. He climbed, skated, fished, snared woodcock, went nutting, and joined with his companions in wild gallops along the Leven Sands.He rowed on the lakes and rambled over the countryside with the keen eye of a country lad for everything worth observing.Wordsworth was not the schools only famous pupil, another pupil was William Pearson, the 18 th century astronomer.

OLD GRAMMAR SCHOOL

Also not to be missed in town is the Beatrix Potter Gallery, an exhibition telling the story of her life,with displays of original drawings and watercolours.The exhibition is housed in the former solicitor's office of her husband.

From 1608 until the 19th century, Hawkshead was a centre of the rural woollen industry. Today though its old woodland industries have all but disappeared, and the thousands of acres of deer forest are maintained by modern forestry methods.

The Parish Church too should not be missed. Built of local stone in a traditional style, Hawkshead's church dates from the late 15th century...the oldest part probably being the tower. The nave was rebuilt in the late 16th century thanks to the munificence of Edwin Sandys who dedicated a small chapel to his parents. There are some fascinating 17th and 18th century wall paintings, whilst a showcase includes measures used at Hawkshead's weekly market and annual fairs. In the north-west of the church a 'Burial in Wool' certificate is displayed, a requirement following a 1666 Parliamentary decree that corpses should be shrouded in wool to help the wool trade.

Hawkshead Courthouse dates back to the 15th century too. This little courthouse is the only surviving part of the large Manor House owned by the monks of Furness Abbey. The monks were industrious and wealthy. As well as having large herds of sheep, they made charcoal from the forest and smelted iron in little 'bloomeries' or outdoor furnaces, traces of which still survive today. A single room of the Manor House...the pre-Reformation Courthouse...survives.

An unusual local story is the one that relates to sufferers of toothache. As late as the 19th century sufferers would seek out the remains of an ancient gibbet or gallows and make a stopping from the wood, so it is said, all who did so became cured. Today, though the village is full of these charming centuries old white painted cottages it still benefits from the most modern of urban benefits... pedestrianisation. It is a great joy to wander around the streets and cobbled byways without the fear of traffic. Hawkshead has a wide range of cafes, pubs, and restaurants, and shops to suit all tastes.

GRAYTHWAITE HALL
GRAYTHWAITE, Nr. ULVERSTON, CUMBRIA
The home of the Sandys family for nearly 500 years..

Graythwaite Hall was begun, it is believed, in the latter part of the 15th century, or early part of the 16th century. The oldest part of the house is the two storey wing in the small courtyard by the front door. The south wing probably dates from the latter part of the 16th century. It is built in the local mannor of flat stones laid without mortared joints, rough cast outside. The east wing, once the (once the footman's wing) is now separetly occupied, as is the North wing which is on the site of the old brew house.

Visitors should kindly note that the house is private and NOT open to the public.
GARDENS

In 1889 one Thomas Mawson of Windermere, was commissioned to redesign the gardens. He was instructed to landscape about 6 acres around the hpuse using existing trees and introducing shrubs. Consequently its main attraction is the lie of the land, and Mawson's treatment of it. Inevitably it is a spring garden, with rhododendrons, azaleas, and spring flowering shrubs. Over the years there have been minor changes in layout and species, but the Mawson conception, as visitors will see today, is as he finnished it in 1895. The large wrough iron gate at the North end of the house, the sundial in the Dutch garden, and the sundial in the rose garden are all by Dan Gibson. The Dutch gardens with its commemorative wrough iron gates (golden wedding and silver wedding) are on the site of the old stables. The new stable yardwas built in 1890. The Dod's cemetary known as the "Happy Hunting Ground" is at the top of the steep flight of stone steps, on the far side of the stream. West of the pond is the Arboretum with specie trees planted to commemorate family births and marrieages.

THE GARDENS ARE OPEN..
1st April to 30th June.
For further information please telephone
(05395) 31248.

A Room with a View   Natural Food Cafe
Hawkshead Square . The Lake District

A new jewel for high class vegetarian cuisine is the Room with a View Cafe. Upstairs overlooking the picturesque village square at Hawkshead, open all year round for lunch and coffee 11am - 4.30pm and for dinner 6.30 - 9pm.

Serving freshly prepared imaginative cuisine, home baked breads, cakes and pastries.

Bookings taken for dinner

The Square, Hawkshead Village

Telephone 05394 36751

The Minstrel's Gallery. Hawkshead.

Up until the beginning of this century there used to be seven public houses in this small attractive villlage. Though some still remain to this day, others have now became private houses. One of them...a delightful 15th Century building was originally known as the Crown and Mitre....but nowadays is better known as the Minstrels Gallery".

Named after a genuine minstrels gallery....a diminutive enclosure that would have originally supported two to three musicians...though the uninterrupted view from the ground floor has long since gone unforunately. These days visitors will be pleased to learn that a tea room and gift shop has been established here, by the owner William Russell. the shop offers a wide selection of cards, pottery, books scented candles, framed and unframed pitcures, slate-are, toys, natural cosmetics, plus an extensive range of craft items too numerous to mention here.

As Willaim himself takes care of the baking, so if the range of goods doesn't entice you into the shop then the smell of fresh baking certainly will. Amongst his wide range of culinary skills will be found; Hawkshead gingerbread, scones and blackberry pie, chocolate fudge cake and stickly toffee pudding. The lunch time menu incidentally offers soups, baked potatoes with a wide selection of fillings, tasties along with a huge choice of sandwiches.

And for those visitors who can't bear to leave Hawkshead, (or Williams baking) then a holiday flat is available upstairs. bookings are available for all year through "Heart of the Lakes"

Minstrels Gallery Opening times: 10.30 - 17.30 every day except Friday. From Mid February to Mid Decemb er. **Tel: 05394 36423**

HIGHFIELD HOUSE

COUNTRY HOTEL

AA ★★ RAC ★★ ETB ♣♣♣ Highly Commended

Set on the hillside in 2 acres of gardens overlooking the picturesque village of Hawkshead and magnificent fells beyond, Highfield House Hotel offers the warm welcome and friendly hospitality that you expect for a relaxing Lakeland holiday.

Enjoy warm, gracious accommodation: we have eleven spacious en-suite bedrooms, all carefully decorated and furnished with those little extras to help make your stay a truly comfortable one. Unwind in the snug bar or spend a gentle evening in front of a cosy fire in our guests' lounge.

Taste fine traditional and modern cuisine, complemented by a good selection of wines. The 4 course menu changes daily offering a tempting range of the freshest, local produce and recipes, including a superb vegetarian alternative. But save space for our delicious and indulgent puddings! We are happy to cater for special parties and are open to non-residents for dinner and light lunches.

Whatever you want from your holiday, Highfield House offers the perfect base. Call us and we will be pleased to help with all your questions.

Proprietors: Pauline and Jim Bennett
Highfield House Country Hotel,
Hawkshead Hill, Ambleside, Cumbria LA22 0PN.
Telephone: (05394) 36344

HAWKSHEAD

Ann Tysons Cottages

Ann Tyson's House

Wordsworth Street, Hawkshead. **New Barn Conversion**. We offer bed and breakfast accommodation for up to six guests. All bedrooms are centrally heated, two are en-suite, all with colour T.V. and tea/coffee making facilities.

Ann Tyson's Cottage. Vicarage Lane, Hawkshead.

Very old Lakeland Cottage, early home of Wordsworth, the poet from 1779 - 1787, oak beams and large open brick fireplace...coal provided..oil fired central heating. accommodation consists of large lounge with colour TV/ Dining area. Kitchen, two bedrooms with double beds and hand basins. Bathroom on ground floor. Sleeps 4/5 people.

Ann Tyson's Top Cottage

Much smaller...open fire, oil fired central heating. Accommodation consists of cosy lounge with colour T.V. dining area, shower room with toilet and hand basin. Kitchen, Two bedrooms (one twin, one double) Sleeps 4.

Both cottages are available for Winter Breaks between November-February.

All enquires to:

Ann Tyson's Cottages
Vicarage Lane, Hawkshead, Cumbria. Tel: 05394 36405
Members of the English Tourist Board and of the English Lake District Hotels and Caterers Association.

BROOMRIGGS Cottages & Apartments
In some of the Prettiest Locations in The Lake District.

Esthwaite Cottage.
This is a large detached cottage situated two miles south west of Hawkshead village, overlooking Esthwaite Water. Traditional stone built property set in its own gardens on the edge of Grizedale Forest. Sleeps 5/6

The Barn South, Cunsey, Far Sawrey.
The Barn is a traditional stone built beamed property recently restored to a high standard. Magnificent views over Windermere Lake, with a footpath leading from the property directly to the lake shore. Sleeps 5

Stable cottage, Satterthwaite
A newly converted stable. Situated on the edge of Satterthwaite Village in the heart of Grizedale Forest. Detached in its own gardens, overlooking fields, fells and forest...Sleeps two.

5 Kings Yard, Hawkshead
One of a group of cottages on the edge of Hawkshead village, which has recently been completely refurbished. Small enclosed patio, garden (with furniture) and parking for two cars.

High Longmire Cottage, Oxen Park.
Detached, oak beamed olde worlde farm cottage in a secluded, quiet part of the Lake District. Set in its own gardens with patio/furniture, overlooking fields and fells. Sleeps 6-8 persons.

Broomriggs -Hawkshead.
A number of privately owned flats available for self-catering holidays. The apartments have been converted from a beautiful country house set in an elevated position overlooking Esthwaite Water, and all have magnificent views. Eight apartments available sleeping from 2 to 6 person.
Details/Brochure:

Mrs.J.R. HADDOW & MRS. F. TAYLFORTH
BROOMRIGGS, HAWKSHEAD, NR.
AMBLESIDE, CUMBRIA LA22 0JX
TEL: 05394 36280 & 46534
Open all year for self-catering accommodation.

The Barn Studio
The Square
HAWKSHEAD, AMBLESIDE, CUMBRIA LA22 ONT

It has taken just two years to convert this long established Pottery into a highly successful and popular art studio.
At one time it was believed to have been a haunt of Wordsworth's, during the time when this older property was the home of a wealthy wool merchant.

Visitors today will discover an enormous selection of local artists paintings and prints. On display throughout the extensive showrooms will be seen the work of Judy Boyes, Jill Aldersley, David Elliott, Brian Eden, and Anne Sudworth, as well as etchings by Stephen Whittle.

__PICTURES__

__PRINTS__

__GIFTS__

__BOOKS__

__ARTISTS MATERIALS__

Visitors will note that a great deal of the work is linked with he areas of Hawkshead, Coniston, Tarn Hows and Haweswater.
Also to be found is a wide selection of artists materials, together with an attractive card display.
A tasteful selection of handicraft, many of them unique and typical of Lakeland
Postal delivery to all parts of the world.

R.S. & E.M. Fife Tel: Hawkshead (05394) 36434

DRUNKEN DUCK
Barngates, Ambleside, Cumbria, LA22 0NG
Tel: 05394 36347

Commanding a magnificent view of lake and mountain scenery, and the centre of many beautiful woodlands and tarns, the Drunken Duck is an inn with a difference. Every modern convenience and comfort offered by large hotels is to be found at this 400 year old inn which is pleasantly situated midway between Ambleside, Hawkshead and Coniston and the Langdale Valley.
A gem of Lakeland, Tarn Hows, is only two miles away, and Barngates is an ideal centre for walking and climbing. The inn possesses a good private trout lake. Lake and river fishing for sea trout and brown trout are to be found within easy distance of the inn for a nominal sum.
During the winter months the Coniston Foxhounds and the Windermere Harriers meet at or near the inn and hound trails are in August and September. An 18 hole golf course is at Windermere seven miles away.
A fully licensed free house, the Drunken Duck still retains the character of a rural hostelry and is open all the year round.

Good food and wine amid comfortable surroundings and a friendly atmosphere are to be found at the Inn. Excellent meals include such dishes as Cumberland Sausage casserole; Celery,Stilton and Walnut pasta; Gressingham Duck. Rolls and ploughmans are also served at lunchtime
The legend of the Drunken Duck dates back to Victorian` years when the landlady found her ducks stretched out in the road, presumed they were dead and began to pluck and prepare them for dinner, Under such treatment the ducks soon proved they were alive and well. Down in the cellar a barrel had slipped its hoops and the beer had drained into the feeding ditch. The landlady, full of remorse provided the birds with knitted jerseys and kilts of Hawkshead yarn, until their feathers grew again.

Hawkshead's biggest tourist attraction

The Hawkshead Countrywear shop is a popular landmark on the tourist trail.
Ramblers are impressed by the extensive selection of outdoor clothing and footwear. Local people appreciate the value for money and choice of casualwear - our stock changes with the seasons and is always up-to-date.
Tourist parties are always excited by our in-store Innovations shop. It's full of bright gift, household product and personal accessory ideas.
So make sure you take in the Hawkshead Countrywear shop - the biggest of its kind in the Lakes. We're open 7 days a week on Main Street.

Every visitor will receive a free copy of the latest Hawkshead catalogue.

Main Street, Hawkshead Village, Cumbria.
Tel: 05394 36633

HAYTON

Map ref.G.4.
Location 2 miles south-west of Brampton.

Hayton is a village just over two miles south-west of Brampton,and seven miles from Carlisle.
On a bluff amongst the trees at one end of the village will be seen a substantial farmhouse...all that remains today of Hayton Castle, and which was beseiged in the Civil War, built up again in the same century, and then for 300 years was the home of the Musgraves. Here in 1735 was born Sir William Musgrave, one of the early trustees and benefactors of the British Museum, to which, upon his death, he left some valuable biographical tracts. Better known still was Sir Thomas Musgrave, who was born two years later. He made a great name for himself due to his bravery.Once at Germanstown, the British outpost near Philadelphia, he was surprised by a large force of Americans, but entering upon a stone house with his few soldiers he held it till help came. A military medal was struck showing this house and it appears again on his engraved portrait in the British Museum.Sir Thomas was the last British Commandant of New York.He died a General, and was buried in 1812 outside the famous London church of St.George's, Hanover Square.

HERDWICK SHEEP.

Herdwick Sheep are farmed commercially only in the Lake District...the legend is that the breed we know

today are descended from a small flock of about two dozen animals that swam ashore from a Spanish galleon which was wrecked at Drigg, Near Ravenglass.They were claimed by the Lord of the Manor and their ability to thrive productively on the high hard fells of the Lake District led to them being distributed amongst the local farming communities and eventually spreading to most of the high fell area.
The breed remains unrivalled in surviving on the bleak fells and mountains. A visit to any of the Western Dales Shows will convince anybody of the tremendous pride and shepherding expertise still being applied to the Herdwick.
The National Trust and other Cumbria landowners insist on the retention of the Herdwick on some of their tenanted farms. Indeed the late Beatrix Potter, authoress of so many children's books was during her life a great supporter of the breed.Her sheep were exhibited by her shepherd and entered under the name of Mrs Heelis...her married name.
The Herdwick enjoys a tremendous reputation as a producer of meat with a flavour.In fact many farmers who are keepers of more prolific breeds of sheep on a commercial basis on good farms are known to buy two or three Herdwicks to fill their own deep freezers.
The Herdwick is a slow maturing sheep which is typical of any animal that survives on a very spartan diet. This slow growth and later maturity gives a flavour to the finished product that excels by comparison with the quick growth of more delicate species, and subsequently since they cook easier, the result is a more tender chop or joint...as anybody who has tried can verify.

HEVERSHAM & LEASGILL

Map ref. G.12.
Next nearest Town or Village "Milnthorpe"
Location. 1` mile north of Milnthorpe

Heversham & Leasgill nestle at the foot of a hill called The Head, six miles south of Kendal, close to Milnthorpe, where it enjoys views of sea and mountain.The village is generally accepted to have derived from a 7th century Anglian Chief...Haefar, giving the village a history of some 1300 years. The restored mediaeval church of St.Peter is the oldest recorded church in what used to be known as Westmorland dating back to the 9th century...as can be testified by the fine stone-work in the porch,and its Anglian cross-shaft in the churchyard. The villages other distinction is the famous Grammar School founded in 1613. The founder of the school was Edward Wilson, descendants of

whom still live in the district.For much of its history it has been a private day and boarding school for boys, producing a number of eminent scholars...one of whom was Ephraim Chambers...of Chambers Dictionary fame..the fore-runner of modern encylopaedia's..published originally in 1728.
In a field next to the school the old village cock-pit can still be seen.
The oldest residence here is Heversham Hall, parts of which date back nearly a thousand years when it was originally the headquarters of a steward appointed by St Mary's Abbey in York to farm lands which the Abbey owned hereabouts...remaining under their control until 1539.In 1614 the Wilson family purchased the Hall, and in fact it is still in their ownership today, even though they actually live at Dallam Tower in Milnthorpe.One of its rooms has a grand Tudor roof ,and two of its notable possessions are an oak staircase and an oak table 13 feet long and four centuries old.

HINCASTER.

Map ref. G12
Next nearest Town or Village "Milnthorpe"
Location,3 miles north of Milnthorpe.

Hincaster is a small hamlet three miles north of Milnthorpe and five miles south of Kendal.At one time the village would have been on the main route to Kendal,passing through the villages of Ackenthwaite, Hincaster .Sedgwick and Natland.These days the route is the A6 road.
In the mid 19th century a high demand for gunpowder led to the old families of Strickland and Wakefield supporting the development of a gun-

powder mill.In 1880 a Mr Swinglehurst had control of the works.The works continued until 1920 when they moved to Gatebeck.Today only the mill race walls remain.
The canal from Stainton to Kendal was first planned in the 18th century, and eventually reached Kendal in 1819.The quarter of a mile tunnel at Hincaster is interesting in that it was here that the horses which drew the barges were led over the hill and the bargee's 'clogged' the barges through the tunnel by pushing with their boots on the tunnel roof.Today the canal is dry, and in parts paved for walkers, but there has been talk for years of the canal one day being re-opened.

HOFF.

Map ref. I.8.
Next nearest Town or Village "Appleby"
Location. 2 miles south-west of Appleby.

Hoff is a small hamlet just over two miles south-west of Appleby, straggling the B6260 road, which itself connects Appleby to Kendal. The name is thought to be of Viking origin.
Just west is Orton Moor through which runs a huge scar of limestone...amongst which will be seen many signs of settlement of early man.

Close by is the 'New Inn' though it actually dates back to the 17th century, and next door is a house with the date 1698 engraved upon the wall, which at one time at the end of the 1800's..was a workhouse.It is believed that the upper floor was used for spinning and weaving.
At Douglas Ing, near Hoff Bridge, at the beck which flows near the boundary, a violent battle took place between the Scots and English during the reign of Richard 11. Its almost difficult to imagine such a scene these days, as it is more a haven for the red squirrels, deer, herons, and kingfishers, than the site of a battlefield.

THE BLUE BELL

at Heversham

The Blue Bell Hotel

The Princes Way, Heversham, Milnthorpe, Cumbria LA7 7EE
Telephone: 05395 62018

The Blue Bell Hotel has been part of the village of Heversham for over five hundred years, starting life as the Vicarage in 1460. Its chequered history has seen it used as a ladies seminary, school dormitory, private residence, boarding house...and since 1956 as a hotel.

Situated in a rural setting and yet so accessible at the gateway to the Lakes, the Blue Bell Hotel is the perfect setting for a relaxing break, small conference or overnight stay.

Your comfort being of prime importance, the 21 individually styled bedrooms, all with private facilities, have remote control colour television, radio, direct-dial telephone and hospitality trays.

Good food and fine wines are the backbone of this successful and well-known hotel. Dining at the Blue Bell, whether it be in our Lakeland Restaurant or in the bar, is not only popular for residents but those who live locally. As many of the guide books will tell you, the restaurant offers a choice of attractive table d'hote or mouth-watering a la carte dining, and the bar offers wholesome food and snacks with the traditional atmosphere of an English country pub.

You can always be assured of a warm, hospitable welcome, excellent value and the wish to make you as comfortable as possible. We

hope to cater for you as we do for the many who return time and time again.

Overnight accommodation...two-night breaks available. Christmas and New Year break details available upon request.

HOLME

Map ref. G.12.
Next nearest Town or Village "Beetham"
Location. 4 miles south-east of Milnthorpe.

Holme is in the south of the County, halfway between Kendal and Lancaster, and very close to the Lancashire boundary.

The village is bordered on the east by Clawthorpe Fell.Farleton Knott here rises to a height of over eight hundred feet.
Here too, at one time barges would have been seen on the Preston to Kendal canal, bringing coal from the Lancaster pits.
Holme Mill, some half a mile from the village was, as its name implies, originally a corn mill, later a flax mill which was operating until as late as 1975.

Abbeyhorn of Lakeland

Established 1749

Tel/Fax 0524 782387

Now you can experience for yourself what it is like being a horn worker in the 20th century. for here, as you will soon discover...the processes, and in some cases, the tools, have not changed since the time when the horn works was first established in the 1700's...in the days when the monks of Llanthany Abbey in Monmouthshire worked with the same material.
To give you a brief insight into horn and its many uses, ABBEYHORN today produces well over

Holme Mills, Holme

150 different lines in horn goods, even making one-off items commissioned by customers to suit their individual needs. On spoons, tableware, walking sticks, combs, brushes, deskware, jewellery, as well as many other items too numerous to mention.
Horn has it all...It is a by-product of beef cattle, no species is endangered or threatened with extinction are used.

FACTORY SHOP.....FACTORY TOUR.....GROUP VISITS.

HOLME ST CUTHBERT.

Map ref. C5
Next nearest Town or Village "Beckfoot"

Looking across the lowlands and the sea to the hills of Scotland is this scattered village with a sandstone church of the last century replacing the chapel it had before the Reformation.It is plain and spacious, with a simple tower and turret. To the north are the scant remains of Wolsty Castle, made strong in 1250 and used by the Abbots of Holme Cultram as a safe for their treasures.Last century pottery and coins along with everyday items of the Romans were discovered here.

Beckfoot nearby lies on the coast, and based on fairly recent excavation it would appear that here too the Romans had built a fort as part of their coastal defences.In fact the site of a chain of defensive towers and fortlets indicate considerable Roman presence here in the past. To the south, can be seen often at low water, the remains of a submerged forest. Further south is Mewbray, once known as Old Mewbray.
The village is a collection of 17th century cottages and farmhouses, at one time in its way a busy metropolis.
Today only the Inn...The Lowther Arms...still survives...together with the forge...which has been transformed into a restaurant.

HOWGILL.

Map ref.H.11.
Next nearest Town or Village "Sedbergh"
Location. 3 miles north-west of Sedbergh.

Howgill is a hamlet three miles north-west of Sedbergh. The road from Sedbergh to Howgill is an old Roman road going past the site of a Roman camp...and continues on to Tebay.

Its only mill at one time was engaged in the manufacture of woollen goods and employed over a hundred people.Though closed in 1870, the building(though derelict) still stands, together with the flume which provided the water power.

MAKING HAY

There are many old houses hereabouts, often with their original features.Two still have the original beef-hawks ,one time used for drying beef 'Beckstones' can still be seen (used for the baking of oak-cake).

Unusual here is the sight of slave chains on Hole House Farm, where the encumbent of that time was engaged in slave trading for many years. There is a story attached to this house which is worth repeating.One of the family returned from a journey to the West Indies bringing a lovely wife and her devoted black slave. In a fit of temper he murdered her, and the slave hearing her screams rushed to her assistance and also met a violent end. A lady in grey is said to uphold the husband's homicidal reputation by rustling along the shadowy oaken corridors, and when moonlight streams through the long window, stands gazing to where the Lune splashes over its rock bed. Her little negro slave, his chains rattling pathetically, takes her place in the restless house on the darker nights, when the wind howls bleakly through the pines.

The same house incidentally is believed to be the birthplace of Roger Lupton the Founder of Sedbergh School in 1525.

The hills and dales here are popular with fell walkers and hikers alike.There are many quiet lanes and footpaths which frankly can only be seen on foot. The views,as to be expected, are magnificent.

HUTTON IN THE FOREST.

Map ref. F.6.
Nearest Town or Village "Skelton"
Location. Approx 6 miles north-west of Penrith

Hutton in the Forest is located some six miles north-west of Penrith.Here surrounded by fine woodlands and growing on the site of the ancient Forest of Inglewood is the village's simple church with its double bellcot. It stands all alone at the end of a road lined by high Scotch pines, and its great house still stands in seclusion among magnificent trees.

From the Penrith road there is a glimpse of the mansion, the home of Lord and Lady Inglewood, its turrets and battlements contrasting oddly with the part designed by Inigo Jones. Like other Cumbrian homes it has grown up around an ancient tower, which was added to in Elizabethan and Jacobean times.

The house's story begins with the legend of Sir Gawain and the Green Knight, and then continues into the Middle Ages with the DeHotons. In the early 17th century they sold out to the Fletchers, rich merchants from West Cumberland from whom, about a century later it was inherited through marriage by the Fletcher Vanes, within whose family it has remained ever since.

In the church there is a mediaeval coffin stone, carved with a cross and little pictures of a chalice and a missal.The oak lectern is in memory of a man who ministered here for 56 years last century, and there is a memorial to Sir George Fletcher of 1700 who was 'Knight of the Shire nearly 40 years'and built part of the great house.

HUTTON ROOF.

Map ref. H.12.
Next nearest Town or Village "Kirkby Lonsdale"
Location. 2 miles west of Kirkby Lonsdale.
Gala days/festivals.Skelton Agricultural Show.
Hutton Roof Country Fair. Last Saturday May.

Hutton Roof is a parish some two and a half miles west of Kirkby Lonsdale, and includes the hamlet of Newbiggin.

It lies high in the rolling countryside with narrow lanes ,surrounded by woodlands and rocky outcrops of limestone. Once the village belonged to St Marys' Abbey now in ruins at York, and it must have had a church in mediaeval times.It had a chapel built in the 18th century and the present church was built in the 19th.

The village is best known for its crags which lie to the west of the village, and for the outstanding example of limestone pavements. The crag in fact is designated an area of Special Scientific Interest.

St Johns is a small but beautiful church located at the northern end of the village adjacent to the old school buildings.A former vicar was a deserved celebrity during the First World War. Theodore Bayley Hardy was a Chaplain to the Forces, and was awarded a Victoria Cross for his gallantry.He unfortunately died in 1918, just three weeks before the Armistice was signed, from wounds received in the battlefield.

The Country Fair and Fell Race is held here at the end ofMay. The race covers seven miles across Hutton Roof crag, Newbiggin Fell, and Farleton Knot, and finishes in the village field.

INGS.

Map ref. F.10.
Next nearest Town or Village "Staveley"
Location. 2 miles east of Windermere
Gala days/festivals.Lake District Sheepdog
Trials.Thursday after 1st Monday in August.

The hamlet of Ings is situated two miles east of Windermere Station, just off the A591 Windermere to Kendal road.

It is difficult to imagine that less than 100 years ago this village was an important staging halt for the coach and horses who dropped off their mail here.Gone is the Roman cobbled 'highway' true; but the houses and the church in particular still retain their quaint original character of bygone days.

Wordsworth loved this little place, and gave it immortality in his poetry.

Here will be found High House with a great round chimney and walls nine feet thick, and on Hugill Fell are fragments of a British village about 160 yards square, You can still see its wall, and traces of hut circles, along with a stone with curious cup markings.

One of the first men to investigate this ancient village was the botanist Peter Collinson who was born at Hugill Hall in 1694, a great lover of these fells.A celebrated antiquarian,he was a great authority on insects and flowers.Amongst his friends were Sir Hans Sloane and Benjamin Franklin.

A few stones of the old church of Ings are in the new church and an arch is hidden away in a farm, but the new church,like the almhouses with their lovely gardens, have a story of their own, for they were Robert Bateman's offering to the village which was kind enough to give him his opportunity to make a fortune...which he certainly did. He built the church in 1743 and gave it a floor of Italian marble.It is a memorial to the Dick Whittington of Ings whose portrait will be seen in the nave of the church.It is certainly a wonderful story of how poor boy became rich, but regretfully his story ended unhappily, for less than a year after the first stones were laid he was killed by an Italian Captain as he was sailing home in one of his own ships.

The Watermill Inn here dates back over 250 years and started life as a wood mill and joiners' shop (which it remained until as recently as 1960) where everything from cartwheels to coffins were made.

IREBY.

Map ref, D.6.
Next nearest Town or Village "Uldale)
Location. 18 miles south of Carlisle.

Ireby is a picturesque village 550 feet above sea level, and is a former market town, some seven miles south of Wigton, and 18 miles south of Carlisle. It is situated just outside the Lake District National Park.
Ireby has shrunk from being a little market town to a village these days, with its old Moot Hall still here and its old market cross restored after being long in ruins.
Though receiving its charter in 1237...and by the 17th century an important corn market...today little trade survives.Only two pubs remain (originally four). One is the Sun...once frequented by John Peel who lived in the neighbouring hamlet of Ruthwaite,and the other the Black Lion. One of the pubs now long gone was the Tun Inn at which dancing was quite popular.Dances of the region were the Cumberland Square Eight, the Long Eight, Ninepins Reel, Circassian Circle...all of which resemble Scottish country dances.
The oldest building here is the 'Old Church' which is situated in a field about one and a half miles from the centre of the village.It is a 12th century building but only the chancel still survives.It is still consecrated however, and a service is held here annually.It has been superceded by St James Church built in 1845. The new church has however an ancient font with four carved roundels, and two old stones built into the walls of the porch.One stone is carved with a pair of shears and some crosses, the other has an ornate cross and a sword, the memorial of John de Ireby who lived 700 years ago.
Lovely views of Skiddaw hereabouts.

IRELETH & ASKAM IN FURNESS

Map ref. D.13.
Next nearest Town or Village "Dalton-in-Furness"
Location. 7 miles from Barrow in Furness.

Ireleth is situated on the southern banks of the river Duddon, just a half mile east of its neighbour Askam in Furness, and seven miles from Barrow-in-Furness.The village dates back to the 17th century.
In the 17th century a free school was founded here when locally born Giles Brownrigg gave land and established a trust to endow a school for the children of Ireleth. St Peters Church here has an outstanding view of the Duddon Estuary.
The small township of Askam in Furness owes its origins to the establishment of a large ironworks built to exploit the finding of iron ore nearby. Smelting began in 1867 and continued through until 1919.
Askam in Furness is noted for having a long fine beach, with a profusion of flora and fauna. Additionally it is one of the prime breeding sites in the country of the rare (and protected) natterjack toad.

Towns & Villages of The Lake District and Cumbria

is part of series of "Towns and Villages" in Great Britain published by

Village Publication

IRTHINGTON.

Map ref. G.3.
Next nearest Town or Village "Brampton"
Location. 3 miles north-west of Brampton.

Irthington is a parish on the banks of the river Irthing, three miles north-west of Brampton, and seven miles east of Carlisle.Included in the parish are the villages of Laversdale,Newby,Newtown, together with the hamlets of Ruleholme and Old Wall

The village lies astride the Stanegate Roman road which ran from Corbridge to Carlisle, and many Roman remains and coins have been found here.Only recently a Roman well was unearthed at White Flatt.Not far away are the quarries in which the Romans hewed stone 1800 years ago, while the remains of one of their forts was found last century at a spot known as the Nook.

Many farms and cottages here date back to the 17th and 18th centuries...many having peat cutting rights. The church is dedicated to St Kentigern, who it is thought preached at the Holy Well in the 6th century.The church is of Norman origin. A memorial window here is dedicated to Robert Bowman who died in 1823 aged 119 years. Buried here too is Cavalier Randal Mulcaster of Stonewall...Laversdale's 'Randie with the Long Sword'

A Norman baron...Robert de Vaux had his stronghold on the mound behind Nook Farm, and in 1169 gave Irthington Church as part of the endowment for the new Lanercost Priory.In 1201, King John is known to have stayed here in the old castle...though a mound, often covered in daffodils, is the only sign nowadays that a castle even existed.

Growing in the hedge will be seen a tiny white double rose, and there is a legend that states that where-ever it grows,Prince Charlie's men were welcome 'be it a castle or a clachan'.

IRTON WITH SANTON.

Map ref.C.10.
Next nearest Town or Village "Eskdale"
Location. Approx 4 miles east of Seascale.

Irton with Santon is a scattered parish , along with the hamlets of Santon,Hall Santon, and Santon Bridge, nestled between the hills and the sea. About two miles long and one and a half miles wide it is bounded by the river Irt and Mite...the Irt at one time being famous for its pearl producing mussels...regretfully no more.

Evidence exists here of an Anglo -Saxon settlement here dating the village more than a 1000 years old. In fact there has certainly been a church on the site of St Pauls Irton since the 13th century, being built on an elevated position with spectacular views of the Wasdale Valley. In the churchyard will be found an ancient Celtic 8th century 10 feet high sandstone cross,ranking only second to that wonderful cross at Gosforth.

This solid little church was re-fashioned last century and has a fine tower with an imposing turret above the battlements. Its eight bells must echo far and wide among these hills and vales.The tower archway is screened by attractive wrought iron gates, and the attractive chancel arch has black marble shafts.

Amongst its many memorials there is a marble tablet with cannon and anchor in memory of one Skeffington Lutwidge who commanded a ship in an expedition of polar discovery in 1773, and it is interesting to learn that serving under him on HMS Carcass was a certain 14 year old midshipman by the name of Horatio Nelson.

Approximately one mile away is the Manor House of Irton hall...a mansion built around a pele tower.In the grounds is a huge oak tree where it is said Henry VI hid in 1464 when seeking refuge during the War of the Roses..The Hall still has its embattled tower and some other remains of the 14th and 16th centuries. Santon Bridge, located on the banks of the Irt at Bridge Inn is where the well known 'Biggest Liar Competition' is held annually.Santon Bridge is where the crystal waters of the River Irt come rushing over a rocky bed from Wastwater, the deepest of all the lakes.

IVEGILL
Map ref. F.5.
Next nearest Town or Village "Calthwaite"
Location. 8 miles south of Carlisle.

Ivegill is a village situated some eight miles from Carlisle on a crossroads linking Carlisle to Penrith,dating back as far as the 15th Century.
The two main houses here were at one time the homes of Quaker families.One being Bernard Barton at Ive Bank, and the other the Newby Family at the Grange. The Grange is reputed to be also the Quaker Burial ground and today is a well preserved 16th century farm.

At High Head a castle stands in ruins following a fire of 1956, and close-by,situated in the fields, is the old chapel of ease..built in 1358 and in the mid 19th century used as the parish church.Lovely views of the Caldbeck Fells, and the Lake District hills.
To the east is a further settlement of farms known as 'The Beacon'...named apparently because it was used as a link in the chain of bonfires lit to warn citizens of Carlisle of the coming of the Armada during the reign of Queen Elizabeth 1.

KABER.
Map ref. J.9
Next nearest Town or Village "Brough"
Location.5 Miles from Kirkby Stephen

In 1664 Kaber was the scene of the Kaber Rigg Plot...a rebellion against Charles 11 led by Captain Robert Atkinson, of Watergate Farm in Mallerstang.The rising failed and he was hung,drawn and quartered at Appleby...tragically a messenger carrying his reprieve was delayed at Stainmore.

KELD & THORNSHIP.
Map ref. G.9.
Next nearest Town or Village "Shap"
Location.1 mile of Shap.

A hamlet near Shap, on the banks of the Lowther. Close to the entrance is a 16th century chapel, thought to have been built by the monks of Shap Abbey. It was apparently rescued from total destruction by various owners who from the 17th to the 19th century used it as a dwelling house.In 1860 it was described as 'the ruins of a small chapel, which serves as a cow-house', a fate from which it was finally saved when in 1918 it was given to the National Trust which has since restored it to its original purpose. Today it is once again open to visitors.
At the larger hamlet of Rosgill with Hegdale is the bridge above which the Swindale beck joins the River Lowther. Rosgill Hall was originally a Manor House owned by the de Rosghyll and Salkeld families.

Mary's Pillar to be seen here, is in fact a memorial erected by Thomas Castley to his daughter Mary, who died here at the tender age of 24. Mary apparently used to visit this spot regularly, from where she would have had a splendid view towards the entrance to the Mardale valley,Haweswater, and the surrounding hills.

Looking from Mary's Pillar,is Mardale, a once thriving village until 1935 when it was submerged to provide a reservoir for Manchester Water Supply.The stones of the Grammar School were removed to build a house a mile or more from the valley, opposite Thornthwaite Hall.Remains of the people buried in the valley were re-interred at Clifton, and the Mardale plot in the Shap church-yard. During very dry summers, the water has been known to shrink until the 'lost village'can become visible once again.

KENDAL.

Map Ref. G.11.
Bus services. Cumberland Buses 41, 41A, 42, 42A,43,44,45,46,47,530.531,535,730,735,540,552, 553,555,556,561,564,567,568
Trains. Nearest Oxenholme.
Tourist Information Centre. Town Hall
Location. 12 miles south east of Windermere.
Early closing. Thursday.
Market days Weds & Sat.
Gala days/festival
Northern England Goat Club Show. Spring Bank Holiday.
Westmorland County Show. 2nd Thursday September.
Lune Valley Mink Hounds Show. 2nd Sat.May.
Endmoor Country Fayre.Last Sunday June.
Northern Int.Festival of Mime. 4th Friday April (for 4 days)
Kendal Folk Festival.August Bank Holiday weekend.
Kendal Festival of Jazz and Blues. 2nd Sat Nov.(for 15 days)
Kendal Gathering. August 4th for 23 days.
Kendal Torchlight Procession. 2nd Friday Sept.
Kendal Sheepdog Trials. Last Sun August.
Kendal Bonfire & Fireworks Display. 5th Nov.
Mary Wakefield Music festival. Bi-Annual...Late Spring.
Kendal Art Society Annual Exhibition - Mid August.

Kendal is a main market town and a gateway into the Lake District. It's motto 'is 'Wool is my Bread'...and so it was for several centuries. 'Kendal Cottons'...coarse woollen fabrics, were once famous since the 14th century. 'Kendal Green' a heavy woollen cloth early became famous for its hard wearing quality,and Shakespeare immortalised it in his 'King Henry 1V'. Beside cotton, 'Kendal Bowman' have,of course, also to be mentioned..skilled archers with longbows made of yew trees.

The town is built largely of the limestone on which it stands, and some of the older buildings are timber framed.Within and close to the main thoroughfares are to be found the oldest part of the town, consisting of a unique combination of 'yards' or 'courts', with narrow cobbled pavements.These narrow yards were, according to one local tradition, built as a matter of necessity in order that the inhabitants could barrricade themselves against the Scottish Border raiders...or according to another tradition, built in order to provide easy access for purposes connected with the woollen industry. Much of the character of the houses still remain...long narrow windows, steps leading to quaint doorways, overhanging upper storeys, slated roofs, and chimney stacks at strange angles. Certainly a distinctive feature of Kendal is undoubtedly the numbered yards tucked away as they are through so many archways and alleyways, and once the focus of local small industry. 'The New Shambles' for example is a case in point, running between the Market Place and Finkle Street, and was purpose built originally for the many butcher's shops...They moved from the Old Shambles(behind the Fleece Inn) because of complaints about insufficient slope for drainage purposes.

Opposite the gates to the parish church is what is known as a 'Ginnel' (an old Westmorland name for a narrow entrance), and which leads up to Anchorite Well, so named because of a one time religious order of Anchorites who lived in cells here...cells made of stone with small openings through which they would communicate with the outside world.

Just south of the town is Kendal's Roman fort of 'Alauna' located at Watercrook.The first Norman defensive tower was a 'motte and bailey' which was a wooden structure on a man-made mound. The mound can still be seen west of the town centre near the old Westmorland hospital. CONT.

ART GALLERY

The River Kent runs southward to the estuary at the northern end of Morecambe Bay and marks the dividing line between the old part of the town and Castle Hill, on which stands the remains of Kendal Castle, parts of which date back to the 12th century. In the 16th century it was in the ownership of Thomas Parr, and his daughter Katherine Parr was born in the castle. She became, as most people know, the last, and only surviving wife of Henry V111. She married him in fact on the 12th July 1543, and in total lived with him for three years, six months and five days...a Queen in name only..she was never actually crowned. Henry V111 was Katherine's third husband, and after his death she re-married for a fourth time.

At the end of the 11th century, Kendal was made a Barony by William Rufus, and later it was made into three parts part of which came under the control of Ive de Taillebois.

The town has certainly seen many dark days, from the devastating Scots raids....the one in 1210 led by the Earl of Fife for example, being recorded as 'one of the bloodiest and most lamentable days ever known in Kendal'...to fire and floods. In 1598 and 1623 came the Black Death too.

A local story here is that when the Pretenders army was passing through Kendal they prepared to raid the Angel Inn, but were prevented from doing so by the appearance of an angel (or ghost?) who drove them away.

Another old pub The Pack Horse Inn on Stricklandgate proudly accommodated King James 1 in 1617.

There are six bridges across the Kent in Kendal, consisting of three fine examples of stone construction, a girder bridge and two footbridge's.

The parish church of the The Holy Trinity was rebuilt in 1768, though it actually dates back to the 13th century, and its claim to history is the fact that it is the second widest church in the country...complete with five aisles. By the church gates is 'The Ring-o-Bells', the only public house to be built on consecrated ground..in 1741.

A story linked to the church relates to a Colonel Briggs, a staunch Parliamentarian and Justice of the Peace in Kendal, ...held in considerable awe by the local inhabitants. In 1644, at the end of the Civil War he besieged the house of a Royalist..Major Philipson of Holme House,

CASTLE DAIRY

Windermere for eight days until it was relieved by Huddlestone Philipson. A short time later it is said that the major went into Kendal with a small body of men to seek his revenge upon Briggs..and hearing that he was in church, rode up and down the aisle on his horse, with his sword drawn. Unable to see his adversary he was leaving the building when he was unseated from his horse by one of the congregation, and this so angered the major that he slew the man. Major Philipson's helmet to this day still hangs in the church.

Another calamity hit the church in 1210 when townswomen and children gathering in the church were all massacred by marauding Scotsmen.

Not at the same time fortunately, but at one time in the past , the church charged people who did not attend services a fine of one shilling (five new pence). Churchwardens were expected to round up villagers and apparently did so enthusiatically. In 1741 the 'Ring-o-Bells' pub was built thus allowing the churchwardens to refresh themselves, probably at parish expense.

An old custom linked to this, and other Kendal churches, and still seen on occasions is the tying of the church gates by children, only to be released by the scattering of coins to hopeful youngsters. This custom was widely observed throughout the North, as was another which required a bride and bridegroom to leap over a form on leaving the church...

In the churchyard there exists a gravestone showing that one Martin Stevenson died on the 17th October 1782, aged 117 years. It is said that he began life with 16/-(.80 new pence) and died with

KENDAL

WEIR RIVER KENT

funds in excess of £18,000...a fortune in those days.

Sandes Hospital in Highgate (near the Town Hall) was built in 1659 and houses today, as always, elderly persons. Within the gateway is an old iron collecting box beneath which is the words 'Remember the Poor'

The Town Hall, though a comparatively modern building, is itself full of interest. The tall clock tower has a magnificent carillon which automatically plays English, Welsh, Scottish and Irish airs six times daily.

In front of the Town Hall will be seen the old 'Call Stone'...the original base of the Market Cross, from which from time immemorial successive monarchs of England have been proclaimed to the villagers.

The foundation stone of White Hall Buildings (now the Town Hall) was laid in 1824. Under the foundation stone will one day be discovered a copy of each of the Kendal newspapers of that day, together with a facsimile of the Corporation Seal enclosed in glass.

The Mayor's Parlour at the Town Hall contains a valuable collection of relics of George Romney, including many of his paintings, along with Katherine's Parr Prayer Book. This little book measuring just two and a half inches by one and a half inches, and bound in silver, was discovered in an antique dealers in London, and purchased by a Kendal resident for £500.

Near the Post Office is the YWCA but in 1745 in

this building it housed the Young Pretender, who stayed the weekend when on the way south to try to gain the crown. Retreating from Derby shortly afterwards he again stayed with Justice Thomas Shepherd the owner. Two nights later the Duke of Cumberland in hot pursuit, occupied the same house (and bed?)

Today two small, but traditional industries survive here...the making of snuff, and the famous Kendal Mint Cake, which has long been carried in every mountaineers pack.

A few other facts of interest about the town... In 1830, 20 ale-houses opened in Kendal..Possibly linked to the fact that at the time ale was 4d(2 new pence) a quart....The Working Men's Institute, at the corner of Market Place, was a one time theatre. In fact it was the first Theatre to be built in Kendal in 1758 to be precise.Also look out for the building in Stricklandgate (now an estate agents office) with the beady-eyed bristly hog protruding from the wall. The building dates from the 17th century, and was known originally as Blackhall. Its the last surviving relic of Kendal's brush industry.

Castle Dairy near the Railway Station, is one of Kendal's (if not the north of Englands) oldest buildings, and well worth a visit, especially on a Wednesday afternoon when it is the only time of the week that it is open to the public. It is still inhabited and can be inspected.It is an interesting example of Tudor domestic architecture, being rebuilt in 1564.Some parts of it are however much older, the doorways for example date from the fourteenth century.   CONT.

KENDAL CASTLE

Wonderful.

The history of the garden centre reaches as far back as 1810, when a nurseryman by the name of James Meldrum set up a small horticultural business in the ancient old town of Kendal. Clarence Webb bought this from him in the mid 1800s. Indeed, it was Clarence Webb who introduced the Webbs Wonderful Lettuce, back in the late 1800s, renowned throughout the world for its large, deliciously crisp heart. Developments continued in 1922, when James Webb bought and turned a hayfield into an established growing area for what were to become his nationally acclaimed prize blooms of dahlias and chrysanthemums. The nursery then went into its second generation with James' son, Geoff taking over the management of the business, bringing it together to its present site on Burneside Road. From here, he developed it into the immensely successful and popular garden centre it is today. Webbs has now branched out into its third generation with Geoff's daughter Judith, and her husband Bill Stocker. As the longevity of its history suggests, the garden centre provides an extremely well founded and diverse service to the gardening world, which we hope you will continue to enjoy.

Since Clarence Webb introduced the world-famous 'Webb's Wonderful' lettuce, back in the late 1800s the name of Webbs' has become synonymous with quality and value in the garden and in the home.

With expert advice always on hand, plus acres to wander round. Webbs' Garden Centre is now the ideal rendezvous both for the serious gardener and the interested visitor.

Allow plenty of time to stroll round the nursery beds; to enjoy home-made snacks in the gardener's cafe and to visit the gift shop where you'll find an abundance of artificial flowers, toiletries, ceramics, greetings cards and novelties - all perfect mementos of a Kendal visit.

And with plenty of shelter over much of the gardening stock, you can expect a warm and dry welcome, whatever the weather.

Enjoy a visit to Webbs - the garden centre with a history to be proud of!.

Open 7 days including Bank Holidays.
Closed Christmas Day.
Coaches welcome, even at short notice.
Usual coach driver facilities

**Webb's Garden Centre
Burneside Road
Kendal, Cumbria LA9 4RT
Telephone (0539) 720068
Fax: (0539) 727328**

PARISH CHURCH

The Castle dairy incidentally was originally the milk farm for Kendal castle and is particularly noteworthy for two carved inscriptions..the letters A.G and the date 1564 on a massive carved oak bedstead denoting Anthony Garnett..the proprietor. The name 'Garnett' means a garner or keeper of the grain stores...so no doubt the Garnetts of old were responsible for the farm produce of the dairy which supplied the owners of Kendal Castle in Henry V11I's time.The dairy was in use when Katherine Parr lived at the castle.It is now unquestionably the oldest habited house in the area.

No feature on Kendal would be complete without mention of George Romney, the famous artist.

Romney was born at Dalton-in-Furness, over 230 years ago and was first apprenticed to a cabinet maker. At odd moments he sketched visitors to the workshop and his skills were eventually noticed by the Cumberland artist Edward Steele. During an illness he was nursed by a compassionate young girl whom he eventually married.Promptly he neglected her while he travelled over the north of England sketching and doing portraits for small fees.Following this he left her with two children in Kendal whilst he went to London where he achieved great fame as a portrait painter. It is on record that in twenty years he only paid two visits to his wife and children.When at the end of the century he broke down in health and became little more than a hypochondriac, he suddenly remembered his wife in Kendal, and returned North again.His wife received him with loving greeting, and for the last three years of his life she was a tender and unwearying nurse to him. He literally exhausted himself with his work.Scores of his pictures were left unfinished.In his hey-day his highest fee for a portrait was 120 guineas...though one of his portraits later sold for 60,000 guineas.

On the northern side of town, and north of the church are the grounds, now a public park bordering the River Kent, of Abbot Hall, built on the site of an Abbot's House, which stood here in the middle ages. The present house, built in the middle of the 18th century by George Wilson, was planned by John Carr of York whose portrait hangs in the house. Bought by the Corporation in 1896 it remained uninhabited for 50 years until a trust restored the building to its 18th century elegance as a fine example of Georgian architecture incorporating art gallery and cultural centre, displaying permanent and changing exhibitions of work by artists and craftsmen.On the walls today are paintings by Sir Thomas Lawrence, Peter de Wint, Romney, and Kendal born Daniel Gardner...an 18th century painter notable for his small portraits in pastels and oils.

TOWN HALL

Abbot Hall,
Kendal, Cumbria LA9 5AL
Telephone: 0539 722464

ART GALLERY

Situated in a Georgian country house just off the main street of a bustling north country market town, Abbot Hall has established itself as one of the best small museums in the country, with choice collections of eighteenth century and modern British art. Built in 1759 for Colonel George Wilson, and set in parkland overlooking the River Kent, the house has been attributed to the architect John Carr of York

Colonel and Mrs. Wilson made certain that the interior decoration of their new house matched the elegance of its Palladian exterior. They commissioned their portraits from the Kendal based artists, amongst whom George Romney was on prominent display.

Another important collection here is centered on John Ruskin who lived for the last three decades of his life at Coniston. Many examples of his work can be seen here hanging in conjunction with Turner's "Passage of the Mount St. Gothard".

Throughout the rooms can be seen examples of furniture made by Gillows of Lancaster. The Scott Family Gallery here shows work produced by succeeding generations of artists within the Lake District over 250 years. Differing visions of Lakeland hills and tarns are shown in a number of works from the 18th century through to the 19th century in works by Constable, Blacklock, and Edward Lear...to the present day with examples by Sheila Fell, Delmar Banner and Andy Goldsworthy.

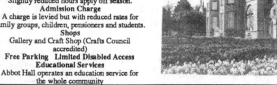

Opening Times
Main Season:
Monday - Saturday 10.30 a.m. - 5.00 p.m.
Sunday 2.00 p.m. - 5.00 p.m.
Slightly reduced hours apply off season.
Admission Charge
A charge is levied but with reduced rates for family groups, children, pensioners and students.
Shops
Gallery and Craft Shop (Crafts Council accredited)
Free Parking   Limited Disabled Access
Educational Services
Abbot Hall operates an education service for the whole community

KENDAL MUSEUM

Kendal Museum, Station Road, Kendal LA9 6BT

Telephone: (0539) 721374

OPEN DAILY

Monday-Saturday 10.30 - 17.00

Sunday 14.00 - 17.00

Shorter opening hours during Winter.

Please telephone for details

The Kendal Museum collection is one of the oldest in the country. It was begun by Mr. Todhunter who set up an exhibition of curiosities in 1796 for which he charged an entrance fee of "one shilling per person; children, workmen and servants 6d each".

In the 1830's the collection passed into the hands of the newly formed Kendal Literary and Scientific Society which established a museum and added to the collection with the aid of such eminent members as John Dalton, Adam Sedgwick, Richard Owen and William Wordsworth.

The museum was described as having 'the finest local collection in the country' a reputation we feel is still justified today. In 1913 the collection moved to its present site, a former wool warehouse to form the nucleus of Kendal's first municipal museum.

Since then the collections have grown with the support of the local people notably Col. E.G. Harrison who gifted most of the specimens of world wildlife.

A Wainwright was the Hon. Curator for many years, a permanent display of his life and original works are now on view. There are now three galleries with splendid new displays of local and world wildlife, local history and archaeology. In 1986 the museum received the Judges' Special Prize in the Museum of the Year Awards.

MILLERS BECK

MILLER'S BECK is a delightful converted 17th century Corn Mill, situated in open countryside just outside of Kendal. The mill still retains many of its original features with the mill race tumbling through the garden combining "Olde Worlde" charm with comfortable accommodation.

The bedrooms are en-suite with colour television and tea/coffee making facilities. Guests have use of the conservatory dining room and two gallery sitting area's overlooking surrounding hills and farmland. Also within the mill are two self contained catering apartments each with own access. All linen is provided and there are no meters.

MILLERS BECK is owned and run by Angela and Norman Hodgson who extend a warm welcome to all.

MILLERS BECK COUNTRY GUEST HOUSE. MAIN A65 Nr. STAINTON, KENDAL. TEL. 05395 60877

FAIRWAYS GUEST HOUSE

Proprietors: Eric & Mavis Paylor

102 WINDERMERE ROAD, KENDAL, CUMBRIA LA9 5EZ Telephone: 0539 725564

Victorian Guest House on main Kendal/Windermere Road All rooms en-Suite. T.V. Tea/coffee making facilities. Traditional 4 poster bedroom. Private Parking. Non-Smoking
Golf nearby.......Lovely Views.......Handy for touring Lake District.........Open all Year.

WINMAUR GUEST HOUSE.
90 Windermere Road KENDAL, CUMBRIA LA9 5EZ
Tel: 0539 720253

Small family run guest house, with en-suite rooms, all having tea/coffee making facilities. Colour T.V. 4 Poster Beds
Ideal base for touring lakes and Dales. Handy for golf course and town centre. Full English breakfast served.

NEWLANDS GUEST HOUSE.

37, MILNTHORPE ROAD, KENDAL LA9 5QG Tel: 0539 725340

"Open door to a comfortable, friendly Victoria House.
Quality breakfast including home-made marmalades. Evening meal by arrangement. Private Parking. Two Crowns. Tourist Board Approved.

More than 150 years ago Mr. W. Quiggin started up a confectionery business in Douglas on the Isle of Man. It was here that Lettered Rock with the words "Welcome Prince Albert to Mona" through the centre was presented to the Prince in 1847. Mr. Quiggin had four sons who were all involved in the business there and in 1872 one of them came to Cumbria and started manufacturing in Kendal.

Quiggins made up to 60 different kinds of sweets in their early days. These included such lines as Coconut Ice, Bullseyes, Indian Rock, Mona Cough Drops and Mint Pennents. They now concentrate on the famous Kendal Mint Cake and Cumberland Rum and Brandy butters.

Kendal Mint Cake is known for it's energy giving qualities and is much sought after by mountaineers and explorers. The energy is created by the sugar and glucose content of the product which is broken down and absorbed into the bloodstream to invigorate the customer. The following is an extract taken from a letter sent to Quiggins by the leader of the "Yorkshire Nepal Himalayan Expedition"; "The Mint Cake when eaten seemed to be converted into energy almost immediately and we were able to undergo very strenuous activity for long periods without any further nutrition. It was a very essential part of our diet".

I know of no other food that would satisfy the exacting and difficult requirements of high altitude climbing so well"

Quiggins were the first to enrobe the Mint Cake in Chocolate and with the introduction of chocolate have now diversified into the manufacturing of a large range of hand made chocolate confectionery. Within this range are a variety of flavours of Chocolate Truffles, Chocolate Covered Marzipans, and a selection of moulded Chocolate Animals. Some of these lines have been designed especially for the Restaurant and Hotel catering Market. Quiggins prides itself on being a family business that provide high quality products and excellent service to its customers.

Specialities:
KENDAL MINT CAKE - CHOCOLATE MINT CAKE - CUMBERLAND RUM AND BRANDY BUTTER - LAKELAND VIEW PACKS - HAND MADE CHOCOLATES & NOVELTIES
Available from Selected shops throughout Cumbria
Telephone: KENDAL 0539 720668/733699

 **K SHOES** *How it all began . . .*

On 3rd June 1842, a young man of 21 made his first entry in a brand new leather bound ledger. It read: "Robert Miller Somervell" and the entry "To Cash £1.10s." On a second page he recorded his first sale: "to Thos. Clark, Newcastle-upon-Tyne - Goods to the Value of £1.19s.0d". Bearing in mind that the ledger comprised some 570 pages, it said something about his confidence and optimism. He had started his business in Kendal two months earlier with stock supplied by his brother William, himself a leather merchant in London.

In those days all shoemaking was done by hand in the home - there was no such thing as a shoe factory - and there were 200,000 shoemakers in the UK, each able to make, on average, 7 pairs a week. In Kendal there were 30 shoemakers and Robert's business was to supply them with leather. Within a year he had a list of 138 customers having travelled by stagecoach to shoemakers and saddlers throughout the Lake District, Yokshire and Lancashire.

By 1849, having been joined by his brother John, he began to manufacture cloth gaiters, made necessary in those days of unmetalled, muddy roads, and in 1855 started making ladies leather uppers using the new American sewing machines perfected by Elias Howe and Singer.

Despite the introduction of the new machinery, the attachment of soles and finishing were still carried out in people's homes. Some finishers found they could earn extra money by selling the high quality Somervell leather soles and substituting cheaper grades. The brothers' overcame this problem by stamping the letter "K" for Kendal on all the leather they supplied. This mark is still the only registered single letter mark in the British Trade Marks register. In 1899 Robert Somervell died at Windermere. He left behind him a business with a national and international reputation with appointed stockists throughout the UK and many countries overseas and a workforce of 600 people in regular employment.

The largest selection of K branded footwear including substandards & discontinued lines in the country . . .

 PLUS Large selection of CLARKS shoes for all the family and a tremendous selection of walking boots, trainers and outdoor clothing always available.

COFFEE SHOP
For tea, coffee & sandwiches
A chance to take the weight off tired feet!

 **K SHOES FACTORY SHOP**

NETHERFIELD KENDAL TEL 0539 721892
ALSO AT ASKAM-in-FURNESS & SHAP

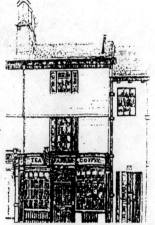

KENTMERE.

Map ref. F.10.
Next nearest Town or Village "Staveley"
Location. 9 miles north of Staveley,
Gala days/festival.Kentmere Sheepdog Trials.
Last Sunday August.

Kentmere is a peaceful valley community, lying some nine miles north of Staveley.
The river Kent which lies below High Street is reputed to be the fastest flowing river in England.The Kent provided water in the past for water power for a corn mill at Low Bridge,Kentmere, and the Saw Mill at Saw Mill Cottage, though there are traces of other mill and smelting sites hereabouts.

Perhaps only a few of the thousands of the visitors who see the smooth and graceful peak of Ill Bell on its western side from Windermere see(or suspect) that rugged drop on its eastern side into Kent Dale. River Kent the one Cumbrian river reaching the sea entirely through the county so placidly at Arnside, has its highest springs in the midst of the most lonely grandeur.

The oldest house here is Kentmere Hall dating from the 14th century...the home of the Gilpin family (in)-famous for killing the last wild boar in England in 1325..Today it is a farm , with regretfully its 14th century tower slowly crumbling away. It has a vaulted cellar and stairway to the battlements.Here lived in total 12 generations of the remarkable Gilpin family. Little now is left of their home, but their names are woven into our history.They grew up in this remote valley to be preachers, artists, writers, and doctors, men of rare capacity, one of them at least among the choicest spirits of his day, and one of them Bernard Gilpin by name, became known as the Apostle of the North.

The ancient church stands at the head of a marsh.It has a yew which has kept sentinel in this lonely place for about 500 years.To this spot they brought St Cuthbert in his coffin on his way to Durham, here the Saxon saint lay in the church all night.But there is nothing now of those days. The church is 16th century, the painted reredos in red and blue is modern, two brightly painted angels stand guard at the altar. The tower is 19th century.

KESWICK.

Map ref. D.8.
Next nearest Town or Village "Threlkeld"
Bus service. Cumberland Buses Route 34, 35, 36, 555,556, 79,105,X5,
Tourist Information Centre.Moot Hall.Market Square.
Plus;Keswick Discovery Centre, 31, Lake Road.Keswick...and National Trust.Lakeside.
Location. Junction A.591 & A.66.Approx 15 miles west of Penrith.
Early closing. Wednesday.
Market Day. Saturday.
Gala days/festivals.
Keswick Agricultural Show. Bank Holiday Monday.August.
Keswick Carnival. Nearest Sunday to June 17th.
Keswick Victorian Fayre. 1st Sunday December.
Keswick Convention. 2rd-3rd Saturday in July.
Threlkeld Sheepdog Trials(Nr Keswick) 3rd Wednesday August.
Keswick Jazz Festival. 3rd Week May.

Keswick (Kesewic in Ad 124)...meaning 'cheese dairy' is the undisputed hub of the Lake District.Literally from no other centre of Lakeland are so many lakes and a variety of fell walks so easily accessible.Its veritable girdle of fells include Skiddaw, Saddleback, Helvellyn, Scafell, Robinson and Grisedale Pike.
It was once a mining town with much of its early history written about by many fine writers over the years.
Keswick is rightly famous too for its excellence of lead pencils...being in fact the birthplace of the industry, during the end of the 18th century and early 19th century pencils were made entirely by hand...By the 19th century, it was the coming of the railway which effectively started the tourist industry here.

In the market square is the town's best known building...the Moot Hall, dating from 1813 and now housing the local Tourist Information Centre.It has one of the oldest one-handed clocks in the country. In the tower of the Hall hangs a

KESWICK

bell bearing the date 1601 and the letters H.D.R.O. which is said to have come from the ancestral home of the Derwentwater's on Lords Isle.

In the past the Moot Hall has been used as a court-house, market, prison, museum and Town Hall.

The town has held a market charter from the days of Edward 1, and at one time was famous for its bull-baiting...thankfully abolished in 1835.

The oldest building hereabouts is St Kentigerns Church (better known as Crosthwaite Church) located about a half mile out of town. Though built in 1553 it has been built on the site of a much earlier church. It contains a 14th century font, and a fine recumbent effigy of Southey...who lived for forty years at nearby Great Hall, was made Poet Laureate in 1813, and is buried here in the churchyard. His memorial incidentally was written by his friend William Wordsworth.

MOOR HALL

In this churchyard that Southey loved so much was also laid to rest in 1920 Hardwicke Drummond Rawnsley, a vicar here for 34 years, but better known as the famous canon who did so much, along with Miss Octavia Hill in becoming one of the founders of the National Trust. Through his watchfulness and enthusiasm many gems of Lakeland are forever safe, and it is indeed fitting that he should lie almost within sight of some of the great scenes he saved.

St John's Church is a more modern building on the edge of town and has a prominent landmark...its spire!. From its terraced walk there is a delightful view of meadow, wood, lake and fell, with Brandlehow and Silver Hill beyond the lake, covered with bushy foliage up to the bracken-clad slopes of Catbells and Maidenmoor. Sir Hugh Walpole, the famous Lakeland author lies buried in the churchyard overlooking the lake.

Keswick's reputed oldest inn is the George Hotel. Many great smuggling deeds were reputedly plotted here.

Another inn, the 'Royal Oak' was according to a slate plaque near the doorway frequented by Robert Southey, Samuel Taylor, Harley Coleridge, the Wordsworth's, Shelley, Thomas de Quincey, Christopher North, along with other Lakeland poets and writers. Here Sir Walter Scott wrote part of his 'Bridal of Triermain' and here too Lord Tennyson and Robert Louis Stevenson were visitors while the

'Skiddaw Hermit' and John Peel were frequently to be seen.

Whilst in the Market Square look for the black and white building, which frankly looks as if it might be a church. It is in fact the Old Court House and Prison which dates from 1695, though it was rebuilt in 1813.

A short distance along the road is the Post Office. Next door was where the poor-house once stood. It was founded in 1644 by Sir John Bankes, a local man who rose to become Lord Chief Justice and a Privy Councillor.

Amongst Keswick's most attractive features are the High and Low Fitz Parks through which flows the River Greta, coming from Thirlmere.

Derwent water is a few minutes walk from the town centre. The view from Friars Crag into the jaws of wooded Borrowdale is a short way from the boat landing and is certainly one of Britain's classics. The lake is three miles long, and a mile wide. The lake incidentally has four islands. St.Herbert's Isle in the centre was traditionally the retreat of the Saint-friend of St.Cuthbert.

A visit to the Museum and Art gallery in Keswick is a must for all literary lovers. Manuscripts of Wordsworth, Southey, Coleridge, Ruskin and Walpole will be found here. Amongst the museums further items is a set of musical stones collected from Skiddaw. This is the amazing Rock, bell and

Steel Band of Joseph Richardson, consisting of about 60 stones, 60 steel bars, and 40 bells, the longest stone measuring more than a yard and the smallest bell being about two inches across. All are mounted on a huge piece of furniture ready to be struck by hammers, the long stones giving the lowest notes and the small bells the highest. Four men are needed to play this extraordinary instrument. Turner paintings are here too (donated incidentally by an American) .Look for Southey's original manuscript 'The Three Bears' forerunner of 'Goldilocks and the three Bears;'

Derwent Island is the largest of the lake's four islands and lies just a mere stone's throw offshore. It was once a sanctuary for the German miners of old, and was bought in 1778 by one Joseph Pocklington...an eccentric. He literally covered his island with bizarre buildings which were then used as a background to his regattas and mock battles on the lake. In 1884 the Marshall family occupied the house for over a hundred years. Then in 1951 ownership was transferred to the National Trust.

Castlerigg Stone Circle just outside of Keswick has got to be a must on everybody's itinerary. It is undoubtedly one of Englands most spectacular Neolithic monuments. It is a circle of some 48 standing stones, 90 feet across and with the tallest being 7feet two inches high. They date from around 2,000 years B..C.

For all its associations with greatness...a 40 year residence of Robert Southey and Samuel Taylor Coleridge's family...Greta Hall at Keswick is one of the least known houses of historical interest in Cumbria.

Possibly this is because it is not so easily found, for it is perched on a hillock several hundred yards from one of the main streets of the town, and is surrounded by trees and shrubs. Greta Hall is not officially open to the public but visitors who make appointments are usually allowed to look around. This 190 years old house, where two of England's most famous poets lived and worked, is now part of Keswick School and the home during term time of some 40 young girls. William Jackson, who had the house built, was a wealthy carrier. He devised a double mansion and lived in half of it himself, letting off the remainder to the Coleridge's and the Southey's.

If any of the poets returned they would not be too unfamiliar with the appearance as well as the

atmosphere, for the house contains furnishings, paintings and bric-a-brac connected with them.All the rooms are named after their former occupants.Southey's Parlour, Hartley's Parlour, The Apple-Room and Mrs Wilson's kitchen...which still has the original stone-flagged floor.

Robert Southey's study and library, a large room on the first floor which overlooks the lower part of town, now contains rows of brightly coloured beds. Robert Southey was 30 when he came to Keswick in 1803 and here apart from his travels abroad, he lived for 40 years..very much a friend of all the Lakeland poets and certainly one of the best of them. He was born in Bristol in 1774, his father being a tradesman there.An aunt brought him up and he was a youthful prodigy.At the age of eight he had read all of Shakespeare and had the ambition to be a poet. The story goes that an Uncle who lived in Lisbon sent him first to Westminster School, and then later to Oxford.He was apparently turned out of the school because he wrote an essay making a much needed protest against the violent thrashing of the scholars!

Finally further mention should be made of Derwent Water.Certainly it is Keswick's great attraction, and second only to Windermere in popularity,

CASTLERIGG STONE CIRCLE

although it avoids the larger lake's bustle and noise...in fact a ten mile per hour speed limit applies. Its surrounding scenery too is more dramatic and can be more impressive when viewed from Friar's Crag, with the high hills to the west, the crag walls to the east and the Jaws of Borrowdale ahead.It is well wooded and the colour changes in spring and autumn are sublime. The lake has a normal depth of 72 feet

Derwent Water has always been a 'highway', and there is a regular boat service with 'request stops' at jetties.For information the lake contains trout, perch and pike.

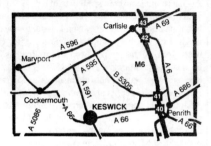

**FORGE LANE, KESWICK,
CUMBRIA, CA12 4NX
07687 73612**

Riverside Workshop is a former watermill on the bank of the river Greta on the eastern outskirts of Keswick. It is shared by three woodworkers who produce exclusive handmade furniture and woodturning.

The Three craftsmen, Graham Cave, Peter Goldthorp and Andrew Webb work in a variety of traditional and modern styles and share an old fashioned insistence on quality workmanship. By careful design and attention to detail, and by taking time to find out exactly what their customers want they create furniture that is cherished and will last for generations.

Most of their work is made to order, but there is a small showroom where prospective customers can see some finished pieces on sale and browse through photographs of previous commissions.

This is an ideal place to visit if you want to commission a unique and lasting present (perhaps for a wedding) or if you just want a special piece of furniture that you can hand on to your children. It is advisable to phone before visiting.

GREYSTONES

Ambleside Road,
Keswick on Derwentwater,
Cumbria, CA12 4DP
Telephone 07687 73108

Greystones is an attractive and spacious Victorian stone built house, situated in a quiet location opposite St. Johns church, but is ideally placed for the town, lake and fells.

The Hotel has been personally run by Eileen and David Davenport for ten years over which period they have built up a reputation for a warm and friendly atmosphere, this coupled with stylish and comfortable accommodation having all the facilities you would expect, makes an ideal base for your stay in Cumbria.

David has an extensive knowledge of the area and has many ideas for helping you enjoy the area, whether walking or driving. Keswick being in the centre of the fells is ideally situated for travelling to any part of the Lake District National Park. The Pennines, The Border Country, Hadrians Wall and Scotland are all within easy reach.

Greystones is Highly Commended by the Tourist Board, Highly Acclaimed by the RAC, Recommended by the AA and is personally recommended in independent publications by Hunter Davis and Melvyn Bragg.

NEWLANDS
ADVENTURE CENTRE
Stair, Keswick,
Cumbria CA12 5UF
Tel & Fax:
Braithwaite (07687) 78463

"Newlands" is the modern name. It used to be called the "Stair Mill" and many local people still refer to it by this name. It is at least two hundred years old, and when the poet William Worsdworth and his sister Dorothy wandered up the valley, crossing the old humped bridge, they must have heard the distant thunder of the big water-wheel as it turned the machinery for making cloth. The cottages alongside, were built to house the workers of those days.

Today situated in the heart of the Lakeland Fells, the Newlands Adventure Centre offers the perfect ingredients for excitement and adventure with some of the best facilities available in Great Britain.

GHYLL SCRAMBLING
Wild, wet and lots of Fun! This is a great way to sample our local mountain streams and waterfalls!

SAILING
Take to the water in our 5 metre Wayfarers under the watchful eye of an instructor. With an ever present safety boat, this is a great way to learn a popular sport.

ARCHERY
A basic introduction to a very popular sport. Strictly supervised, yet still leaving room for the element of fun that all sports require. Who knows, you may be the next Robin Hood?

ORIENTEERING
Equipped with map, compass and brain power, it is up to each individual to help get their team round set courses amongst the local fells.

CLIMBING & ABSEILING
A truely native Lakeland sport, rock climbing and abseiling really is the safe challenge for one and all.

PONY TREKKING
Discover Lakeland at a natural pace. We can arrange advanced tuition and all day trekking which can give an insight to stable management and pony care.

ASSAULT COURSE
Given the stamp of approval by a whole host of assult course experts, this is a confidence builder for both the chimps and the gorillas!

MOUNTAIN BIKING
Explore the fells and byeways of Lakeland with outstanding views over the Helvelyn Range.

NEWLANDS CHALLENGE
A series of initiative and problem solving exercises designed to develop teamwork, communication and leadership skills.

Our accommodation consists of:
One hundred and twenty beds in comfortable dormitory accommodation, separate leaders' rooms and facilities. Ample showers and toilets, drying room, games room, tuck shop, extensive grounds and secluded riverside wood. Full English Breakfast, packed lunch, three course evening meal (vegetarian and special diets catered for). All specialist equipment and clothing.

Red House Hotel

Underskiddaw
Nr.KESWICK
CUMBRIA CA12 4QA
Telephone Keswick
(07687) 72211

Red House was built as, and called, Oakfield House in 1850 by the Spedding family whose principal seat in the area was Mirehouse on the shores of Bassenthwaite - decendants still live there today. Much of the land alongside Skiddaw had been divided between four families - the Vanes, Speddings, Walshes and Fishers. Oakfield was built on land exchanged in 1838 between the Speddings and Sir John Walsh (later Lord Ormathwaite) and was a very elegant country mansion built adjacent to farm buildings. There still remains the evidence of early agricultural use - the sandstone slabs where pigs were salted and ventilation slits in the walls of former stores.

For a quarter of a century or so Oakfield was rented by various families who enjoyed a gracious lifestyle, employing up to a dozen live-in staff plus others who came in daily to maintain the house and grounds in impeccable order and look after the needs of the "family". In 1883 Mrs. Ballantine Dykes - a widow from Dovenby Hall near Cockermouth - bought Oakfield, integrated all the buildings, extending some and building a new coach house and stables to form a lovely country residence which was then named "The Red House".

There followed a further period of gracious living with houseparties a-plenty, and, what a lovely setting! In 1909 the house was bought by the Falcons, followed in 1918 by Mrs. Evelyn Rathbone from Liverpool who kept it as a country retreat, for occasional use, until she sold it to the Nicholson family in 1928 - Sir John was knighted for his works in designing Singapore Harbour.

In 1943 Red House was acquired by Vernon Birkbeck who turned it into an hotel for gentle folk. We are only the third family to own the hotel in over fifty years of operation. The whole house feels as if it has enjoyed a century and a half of happiness

Today, Red House Hotel offers a taste of life in those days gone by - comfortable accommodation, deliciously tempting food reminiscent of that associated with a country house at the turn of the century, warm relaxed atmosphere and friendly service. We have also revived the concept of houseparties which are proving to be successful. Complete seclusion is assured in our wooded grounds where a gentle stroll is rewarding with stunning views of many Lakeland fells. Come for a break soon and enjoy the relaxation of this true Country House Hotel -
once visited always hooked!

Seymour House

36 LAKE ROAD
KESWICK - CUMBRIA - CA12 5DQ
TEL: (07687) 72764
FAX: (07687) 71289

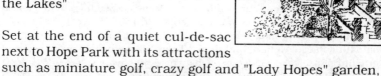

A traditional Lakeland stone and slate house situated midway between Keswick Town centre, with its many good shops, pubs, and restaurants not forgetting Derwentwater "The Queen of the Lakes"

Set at the end of a quiet cul-de-sac next to Hope Park with its attractions such as miniature golf, crazy golf and "Lady Hopes" garden,

Seymour House is owned and run by Andy Peters who can offer you comfortable accommodation with a choice of ten bedrooms. We can offer family rooms for up to five people, down to a single room, four of the rooms having en-suite facilities.

A home cooked three course meal is available at 6.30pm and a full English breakfast at 8.30 a.m. Packed lunches too are available, though we do ask guests to order in advance.

All bedrooms have colour T.V., tea/coffee making facilities and are heated. We can also offer drying room facilities when required.

A recent addition to our services is 'Discovery breaks'...Outdoor activities for everyone to choose from: rock climbing, abseiling, fell walking, ghyll scrambling, mountaineering, Nordic skiing, Kayaking, canoeing, windsurfing and sailing....

Kindly phone/write/fax for our fully detailed brochure.

The Perfect Place to Come Home to

Lake District Timeshare Lodges

Imagine the relaxing holidays you could enjoy from one of the luxurious Lakeland style lodges at Keswick Bridge.

Here you can see how secluded we've made them, nestling between trees close to the banks of the River Greta. So come and see for yourself...we think you'll be tempted to make one your holiday home in the Northern Lakes. Keswick Bridge is a superb private development of luxurious Scandinavian lodges situated in

sheltered woodlands on the bank of the River Greta in Keswick-on-Derwentwater, Cumbria.

Thanks to the concept of holiday ownership, the dream of owning your own luxury holiday home in this most sought after area can now become a reality for the week or weeks of your choice in the year

A Resort Member Of **INTERVAL INTERNATIONAL**
The Quality Holiday Exchange Network

Keswick Bridge
Brunnholme Road, Keswick, Cumbria CA12 4NL
Telephone Keswick (07687) 73591

There are three styles to choose from: The 'Skiddaw' is a one bedroomed lodge which sleeps 4 people most comfortably, the 'Blencathra lodge has two bedrooms and sleeps 6: while the 'Helvellyn' has three bedrooms and sleeps 8.Each is built to the most exacting standards, immaculately furnished and professionally maintained and managed all year round, with 24

hour services on site at the Management Lodge. This cosy hamlet of holiday residences is beautifully secluded, and yet surprisingly convenient for all the facilities which the unspoiled market town of Keswick has to offer. Superbly designed and constructed. Keswick Bridge represents the perfect opportunity for you and your family to own the holiday retreat of your dreams. Available for whichever weeks you desire, one of these outstanding homes will undoubtedly become the focal point for memorable family holidays now and for years to come.

Lairbeck Hotel
KESWICK

Lairbeck Hotel was orginally a country house built in 1875 as the family home of Mr James Reddie Anderson. A barrister and eminent local dignitary. 'J.R. Anderson' was also an important person in the life of John Ruskin, who it is believed visited Lairbeck.

Enjoying magnificent views of Skiddaw and surrounding countryside, the Lairbeck Hotel offers impressive accommodation in a secluded position and surroundings.

Kathleen and Colin Lisle, the resident proprietors, have personally refurbished the hotel to a high and imaginative standard. Retaining the county house theme many of its original features have been carefully and lovingly restored such as the magnificent main staircase which gives the reception area a prestigious and classic feel.

As a reminder of its country house history the Lairbeck Hotel has given its rooms their original names. You may, for example, be given the 'Housekeepers Room', or possibly the 'Maids Room' even the 'School Room'. Why not reserve (in advance though) the impressive 'Drawing Room'.

Each of our 14 rooms have been individually decorated and furnished so that you can enjoy their character and proportions. What is constant in all the rooms is the fine quality of fittings and tasteful furnishing thus ensuring your stay is comfortable and enjoyable. Most of the rooms have splendid views of Skiddaw, the surrounding countryside, or the hotel grounds and garden.

All rooms are en-suite, with complimentary tea and coffee making facilities and colour television. Some of the rooms have direct dial telephone too.

Children of all ages are welcomed and catered for.

The attractive dining room also provides the guest with a pleasant view of the hotel gardens. Be it a full English breakfast, a packed lunch or the five course evening meal, the wonderful home cooking is enjoyed by the many regular guests. The food is painstakingly prepared and cooked, with fresh local produce being used wherever possible, and the menu's are complemented by specially selected wines. The standard is such that Lairbeck Hotel is recommended in Good Food Guides.

The lounge and bar offer guests a comfortable place to relax, make new friends, or enjoy a pre-dinner or after dinner drink.

Just the place to reflect upon the events of the day or to plan those for tomorrow.
AS SEEN ON 'WISH YOU WERE HERE'

VICARAGE HILL, KESWICK, CUMBRIA CA12 5QB
Tel: (07687) 73373

Lairbeck Hotel - so peaceful, it breathes rest and comfort

KINGS MEABURN & MAULDS MEABURN.

Map ref. H.8.
Next nearest Town or Village "Morland"
Location. Approx 6 miles north-west of Appleby.

The River Lyvennet runs almost parallel to the Eden here. Along its banks are these two charming unspoilt villages.

In the 12th century the two manors belonged to a brother and sister Hugh de Morville and Maud de Veteripont...Hugh was one of the Knights who murdered Thomas a 'Becket in 1170.

He was later forced to forfeit his lands to King Henry 11.

The village is a haven for wildlife, due to the rich variety of habitat within so small an area. Trees will be seen to grow precariously from cracks in the rock face, which also provide homes for the numerous small animals hereabouts. Parts of the cliffs called Jackdaw Scar are host to a noisy colony of jackdaws. This is a conservation area and most of the houses are built of local stone. Many of the houses date from the 17th century, some in fact still have their mullioned windows.

KIRKANDREWS UPON EDEN.

Map ref. E.4.
Next nearest Town or Village "Burgh by Sands"
Location. Just over three miles west of Carlisle.

Kirkandrews upon Eden is a small village located some three miles west of Carlisle near the mouth of the River Eden.

The Eden is a salmon river, with fishing rights being held by local families

Despite the village name, there is in fact no 'kirk', and when exactly the church, dedicated to St Andrew, disappeared, nobody knows, but the churchyard still exists.

Roman remains have been found hereabouts, understandable when you consider Hadrains Wall passed through...though little remains today.

KIRKBAMPTON.

Map ref. E.4.
Next nearest Town or Village "Thurstonfield"
Bus service. Cumberland Buses Route 71
Location. 2 miles south-west of Burgh.

Kirkbampton is a village two miles south-west of Burgh, and six miles west of Carlisle.

The village is designated a conservation area and contains a Grade 1 and four Grade 11 listed buildings...Croft House Farmhouse, Laurel House, the Post Office, together with Solway View House. The Rose and Crown Public House was built in 1799 and stands near the church.

All about are remains of defensive work which protected the English against the Scots in days of old.... noted is a one acre field with a double ditch and a double rampart. In the churchyard lies a Scottish raider, his gravestone fixed to the south wall. He is said to have been found asleep in a field by a villager who took up the sword at his side and slew him.

The parish church was dedicated to St Peter, and is an ancient Norman structure. Over the north entrance door is a finely sculptured tympanum, of which only three examples now exist in Cumbria. There is a fine Norman lancet, one with a modern portrait of Peter, and a 700 year old trinity of windows with our Lord and minstrel angels..

HIGHLAND LADDIE,

Glasson, Kirkbride,
Telephone: 06973 51839

The Highland Laddie has been a coach-house and an Inn now for over 400 years, making it one of the longest established of its kind in the North of England. It is unusual in so much that unlike so many of its contemporaries it didn't start out in life as a farm-house, and further the entire property was built out of stone which at one time formed Hadrian's Wall...and which probably, in part, makes the pub so popular with the many walkers who explore the entire length of this famous Roman landmark nearby.

Though unfortunately not available to see, mine hosts Beryl and Sid Hepworth wll delight in telling you of the days when the cellar was a slaughter house and had a natural beck running through the centre. These days Highland Laddie is very much a family run establishment. Totally refurbished recently, it offers a quiet intimate atmosphere, with a wide selection of beers...including four Real Ales...sufficient to quench all visitors thirsts.

The recently opened, and separate Restaurant is, in itself, worth travelling many miles for. In fact any of our regulars come from as far away as Carlisle, the 'especialite de la Maison is undoubtedly the locally caught salmon and game. The salmon incidentally being caught in the Solway, rather than as is so often the case...farmed.

All our food is home-made, including the bar meals, using locally grown fresh produce. Our proud boast is that "No one has managed to finish their entire meal"

KIRKBRIDE.

Map ref.D.4.
Next nearest Town or Village "Newton Arlosh"
Bus service.Cumberland Buses Route 71
Location. 10 miles east of Silloth.

Kirkbride is a very pretty village north-west of the Solway Plain.The village is the centre of a farming district, once noted for Clydesdale Horses and short horn cattle,
The church of St Bride is known to date back to at least 1189...with much of the stone in the building coming from the Roman Wall...certainly many of the stones have traces of Roman handiwork. British, Roman and Anglo-Saxon remains have been found in the vicinity in the church, together with a Roman street and forge.
There is much old work in the church's rough stone walls, a simple Norman doorway, two deep Norman lancets, and a sturdy Norman chancel arch of a very rare kind...for it has altar recess at each side.. In the east window of the chancel are

three figures of St Columba, St Patrick, and St Bridget..Bridget being the patron saint..she was the renowned abbess of Kildare, who in her youth wove St Patrick's shroud..An ancient sculpture of the Entombment hangs on the wall of the chancel arch, and in the sanctuary is a holy-water trough carved with the lamb...it was found not so many years ago in the rector's garden..The font is believed to be about 600 years old.
A lonning leading from the church is called Wine Lonning...believed used for smuggling wine into England and salt to Scotland.It is thought too that the same lonning was used by Roman soldiers and monks to take their horses to water at St Bride's Well, and Monks Dyke.
Just to the north is a field which is known locally as 'Bloody Field'...and where a battle is said to have taken place.Because of the blood shed here the grass remains green even in times of drought.
At one time Kirkbride had its own airfield, and in 1938 it was ferrying aircraft from Canada and USA.Today though the hangers are still apparent though they are now used as warehouses.

Kirkby in Furness.

Map ref.D.12.
Next nearest Town or Village "Broughton-in-Furness"
Trains. Railway Station
Location.5 miles south of Broughton-in-Furness.

More correctly known as Kirkby-Ireleth. Situated on the east side of the Duddon estuary; Kirkby in Furness is actually a string of tiny hamlets or villages following the line of the A.595.Soutergate, Sandside, Beckside, Wallend, Marshside and Chapels.
The Manor of Kirkby-Ireleth belonged to the deKirkby family...from the days of the Norman conquest until the 18th century.They lived at Kirkby Hall for ten generations.The Hall, dark and sombre with its large round chimneys and mullioned windows, dates from Tudor times, and is the oldest house in the parish.These days it is a working farm. Though the village is small and scattered it is nevertheless famous in its own right.Its Norman church for example has a quaint bodiless effigy which attracts a lot of attention, together with an ancient font.
Within one mile is 'The Kirk', a ring embankment at which games used to be played at Easter until the early part of the 20th century.
Seen hereabouts are some fine examples of nineteenth century carved inscriptions on the walls of cottages and stables.Called 'date' stones, these indicate the (then) occupation of the tenants, and the age of the property.
The influence of slate quarries is also particularly noticeable in this area, and in fact it was the availability of water transport in the Duddon Estuary at the end of the 1700.s that actually ensured their development,putting them eventually as one of the leaders in output and ensuring large quantities of slate being shipped to Bristol, Chepstow, London...and in the nineteenth century, also to the West Indies.

LONGLANDS CARAVAN PARK
KIRKBY - IN - FURNESS
"Where luxury & comfort is standard'

Longlands Holiday Home Park is ideally situated on the western fringes of the Lake District, and because it is nestled on the hillside above the villages of Kirkby-in Furness, it offers panoramic views of the Duddon Estuary, Black Coombe and the Western Hills.

All caravans here are gently terraced on the side of the hills, ensuring each has individual views in one direction and having views of the western hills to the rear.

All sites are well spaced and all have full mains services, and are well served with roads and adequate parking space.

A heated open-air swimming pool and children's paddling pool are a distinct advantage to visitors and owners alike. There is no clubhouse here however, the park being suited only to lovers of the countryside, coupled with peace and quiet.

Within close reach is Askam in Furness, a small agricultural town close to the sand dunes and salt marshes...itself a favoured nesting place for wild fowl and sea-birds. 20 minutes away is Lake Coniston a favourite haunt of walkers...and within just four miles is the fine market town of Ulverston.

Other attractions include the Duddon Estuary, Furness Peninsular, Ravenglass Scenic Railway...even the sixteenth century Holker Hall (home of the Cavendish family since 1756) is easily reached within 30 minutes.

Outdoor heated swimming pool and paddling pool. Nine hole mini golf course...free admission village bowling green. Free admission to the village tennis courts...Mountain bikes available. Free admission to the Gardens and Grounds of Holker Hall

TELEPHONE:0229 889342

KIRKBY LONSDALE.

Map ref. H.12.
Next nearest Town or Village "Casterton"
Bus service. Cumberland Buses Route 567
Trains.
Tourist Information Centre. 24,Main Street.
Location. Approx 15 miles from Kendal..West.
Early closing. Wednesday.
Market day.Thursday.
Gala days/festivals.
Victorian Fair. First weekend in September.
North West Shears Annual Event. 3rd Sunday
June.

DEVILS BRIDGE

Few places can lay claim to more picturesque surroundings than the town of Kirkby Lonsdale.It has a most charming and romantic appearance, the River Lune flowing from the fells down delightful slopes, flashing here and there over rocks, then onwards with a sweeping curve past the church and town above, through the golden glade and wood.

The Devil's Bridge here is a remarkable structure composed of three beautiful fluted arches.It gets its name because an old legend tells us that it was built by Satan himself (in three days).

Kirkby Lonsdale is a very ancient 'settlement'. Romans, Saxons, Normans and Danes at some time or another have carved their name on the town. It was included in the Domesday Book under the name Cherchebi, meaning 'a village with a church'. Appropriate really for the parish church of this town is a treasure.There is a mixture of late Norman work, the outstanding feature being the Norman carving on some of the nave piers...long connected with the work of masons at Durham Cathedral, and dated 1100 (very early indeed for this region)

Situated by the River Lune the town has imposing views over the Lune Valley...enough in fact to inspire Turner to paint one of them, and prompted Ruskin to describe the scenery as some of the loveliest in Europe. The market dates from 1227, when a Kings' Licence was obtained for it, and has continued to be held on a Thursday since that time.The old market place which contains the market cross was thought to be too small,and so the present market place was built in 1822.

Of all the outdoor possessions of this village none is more valued than the old bridge over the Lune. It is the oldest bridge in what used to be known as Westmorland, built early in the 15th century, it has three beautifully ribbed arches, one forty feet above the river,all a triumph of simplicity and grace.Since 1673 it has had an inscription which calls on all who cross to 'Fear God,Honour the King', and for centuries it has been used by knights and pedlars, monks and soldiers.

Kirkby Lonsdale is best explored on foot. On the outskirts of the town there are plenty of larger houses..Biggins Hall of the 16th and 17th centuries.Tearnside Hall of the 17th and 18th centuries.Large houses in the town too, some with extensive gardens partly hidden by high walls. The major house is Underley, built in1820.One time owned by William Thompson,

KIRKBY LONSDALE

Alderman of London, his daughter married into the nobility by marrying Lord Kenlis, Marquess of Headfort.

The town boasts splendid public houses and inns. The Sun for example, is late 17th century in part (probably older) with a projecting upper storey on pillars which cover the pavement. The Red Dragon and Green Dragon (nowadays known as The Snooty Fox) each from the 17th and 18th centuries, with excellent interiors. The Royal on the prominent west side of the market place is a 17th century Inn re-built in Victorian times after a disastrous fire. Market Street, Mill Brow, Firbank.... all are littered with very good examples of 17th-19th century houses, and the alleys and passageways allow one to wander at will. Abbot Hall in Michelgate is a remarkable house of the 16th century and causes interest to passers by on the way to the river.

Queen Elizabeth School was founded as a free Grammar School in 1591. A sum of £100 had been left towards the endowment of a school, with a similar sum being raised by the inhabitants, and the school was founded under the control of 24 Governors. It was formerly free to all boys in the town and neighbourhood, for languages, but a payment had to be made by those who were taught writing and arithmetic.

RUSKINS VIEW - PAINTED BY TURNER

Thurland Castle hereabouts, built in the reign of George 111, stands on the site of a much older building. One time home of the Tunstall family...most famous being Sir Brian Tunstall the stainless knight'who fought at Flodden and commemorated in Sir Walter Scott's 'Marmion'...later besieged by Parliamentary forces, and only surrended after nearly three months of struggle.

The Old Market Hall still has its original wrought iron gates and the high domed windows on the first floor.

Recently a limestone path walk has been established between Kirkby Lonsdale and Arnside, which is already proving very popular with visitors and residents alike.

Red Dragon Inn

Main Street
Kirkby Lonsdale
Tel: 05242 71205

The red Dragon Inn is situated in the Main Street in Kirkby Lonsdale. The Inn which is a 17th century coaching house has been modernised without losing any of its 'olde world' character. It has a welcoming log burning fireplace, a comfortable bar/lounge and a well appointed dining room in addition a private function room has a steady demand for parties and meetings.

Personally supervised by Miss Jane Fletcher and her family the premises are very much 'family run'. They cater for everyone that comes into the premises, vegetarians, children and people who may want 'something different'.

The wide menu offers an excellent choice of over 20 meals to choose from and a further selection of sweets 'Specials' are served lunchtime and evenings seven days a week.

Traditional Sunday lunch plus full menu is available every Sunday and bookings can be made in advance.

Jennings ales (Cumbria's oldest brewery) is available from the imposing bar together with an excellent choice of draught lagers. Murphys, Guinness and ciders. The Inn also has a selection of excellent bottled and imported beers and lagers and a carefully selected wine list.

For the weary traveller and holidaymaker, many of whom may find this inn ideally locaed in the town centre, and take the opportunity to book into the Red Dragon Inn's refurbished bedrooms. Most with en-suite and within reach of everybodys pocket. Double, single and family rooms are available all with satellite channels T.V. plus hospitality tray. All guests are provided with a choice of breakfast menu.

The opportunity to appreciate a family friendly atmosphere at the Red Dragon Inn, along with a visit to Kirkby Lonsdale makes this secluded yet easily asccessible Market Town very attractive.

KIRKBY LONSDALE GOLF CLUB

A challenging 18 hole par 70 course in parkland on the ancient Underley estate on the banks of the River Lune.

Situated on the east bank of the river, the course is crossed by Barbon Beck and its 6,224 yards of fairway, greens, tees, rough and hazards seek wherever possible to follow the natural lie of the land. The course construction has been carefully planned to involve the minimum interference of man and machine. Gently undulating, the course covers an area of some 166 acres and is set amongst some of England's most beautiful scenery. Kirkby Lonsdale Golf club was first established in 1910 and has now become well settled into its fourth home. The Club is run, efficiently, by the members for the members and in so doing the aim is to retain all that is best in the finest traditions of the game.

Visitors are, of course, doubly welcome to share our surroundings and hospitality. You are invited to call or telephone to obtain details of our fees, and special offers for parties or individuals. We provide reduced green fees, for 2 to 5 days play mid-week for individual visitors, and there are attractive packages available for parties of 8 or more players which include a snack lunch and two or three course meal in the evening to finish off a first class day's sport.

Why not contact our Secretary's office - Tel: 05242 76365 or pay us a visit? We are just three miles from the famous "Devil's Bridge" at Kirkby Lonsdale, on the A683 road to Sedbergh.

KIRKBY LONSDALE GOLF CLUB,
Scaleber Lane,
Barbon,
Kirkby Lonsdale

MAIN STREET, KIRKBY LONSDALE, CUMBRIA.

Tel: (05242) 71308

Most people flock to this attractive seventeenth-century inn to sample its renowned home-cooked food, but anyone seeking good bed and breakfast

5 Bedrooms, all with private bathroom.
Free House with real ale.

Bar and restaurant meals.

Car Park.

Listed in the A.A.'s "Britains Best Pubs".

Recommended by Egon Ronay.

Special dishes cooked daily using local produce.

accommodation in this delightfull part of the county, will be delighted with the comfortable guest rooms, all of which have private facilities. Breakfast is served in the comfort and privacy of one's own bedroom. As most visitors will know the area is ideally situated for touring the Lakes and Dales, and the view of the Lune Valley from here was once described by the nineteenth century artist and social reformer John Ruskin, as one of the loveliest in England.

Sellet Hall Gardens Near Kirkby Lonsdale

SELLET HALL is situated on the south side of the A65 just outside of Kirkby Lonsdale, on the Burton-in Kendal, Hutton Roof Road through Low Biggins.

The Lune Valley is undoubtedly one of the most beautiful parts of England, and certainly SELLET HALL

makes full use of its setting, as many visitors have remarked. It is both a nursery, specialising in herbs, together with a very attractive garden disposed in rooms linked by enticing vistas. Yew hedges and walls of fine local stone divide the spaces some of which are laid out as flowery parterres.

Apart from a wide range of herbs, the nursery also sells trees (in particular maples) shrubs, bamboo's and a choice selection of auriculas.

The house is of Tudor origin on a site inhabited since the ninth century...though it is not open to the public

GARDENS OPEN MARCH - OCTOBER
Daily 10am - 5pm or by appointment

NURSEY & SHOP OPEN ALL YEAR ROUND
Tea & Coffee are available at anytime.
Fuller menus if booked in advance.

KIRKBY STEPHEN.

Map ref. J.9
Next nearest Town or Village"Winton"
Bus service.Cumberland Buses Route 561
Trains.Railway station (Carlisle-Settle Line)
Tourist Information Centre.Market Square.
Location 5 miles South of Brough
Early closing. Thursday.
Market day. Monday.

Formerly the centre of the knitted stocking industry, today Kirkby Stephen is a small Cumbrian market town set in countryside of exceptional natural beauty. It lies at the head of the Eden valley between the Lakes and the Herriot Country of the Yorkshire Dales National Park.

The market square is surrounded by an ancient collar of cobblestones which marks the area once used for 'bull-baiting'.Many of the attractive buildings in the town centre are listed as being of historical importance, especially the restored knitting gallery. Nearby is the old Trupp Stone where tenants paid their tithes in days of old. There is no doubt that Kirkby Stephen's roots dig deep into the past.Within a radius of some ten

miles or so there must be up to forty tumuli of various types proving that this fertile valley was home to people in prehistoric times, in fact the massive burial mound Raiset Pike goes back to the Neolithic period of 2500-2000 years BC and various axe-heads and artifacts found locally date man's presence here into the Stone Age (7000 BC). The first village community here would probably have been Viking, its name derived from the Norse words 'kirke' and 'bye', meaning church town

Kirkby Stephen can boast one of the finest churches in the County...St Stephen's, dating from the 13th century, with monuments as curious as any. Near the font on entering you will see the famous 'Bound Devil', the figure of Satan, chained and horned, a fragment from some grave stones of the Viking period.Also the effigy of the famous Lord Wharton (1568) a very efficient, though cruel, keeper of the Border in troubled times. Sir Thomas made his name with the sword, enlarged his Hall in Tudor times, founded the Grammar School in 1556, and was the ancestor of Philip Wharton who made his name with the Bible. Their old home was Wharton Hall, now a farm, but once a stately place with a massive gatehouse dated 1559 and a banqueting hall where James 1 came to dinner. Amongst the ruins of the 14th and 15th century buildings today are a

PENDRAGON CASTLE

1050 Bibles in a number of English counties, and each year to this day a number of children in the Eden Valley receive a Wharton Bible. It was Philip Wharton who helped to bring William of Orange to England, and his splendid portrait by Van Dyke is well known.

The effigy of another knight in the church is thought to be a Musgrave. There are many old stones in the church including a 10th century cross-shaft.

The church of today is like a small cathedral, a noble building with traces of Saxon and Norman work. It is one of the largest in the county with a stately nave notable for its length and its magnificent 13th century arcades under a modern clerestory.

Kirkby Stephen was one of the centres of "Pilgrimage of Grace' a rising in 1536 against the religious changes of Henry Vlll. The rebels marched on Carlisle but were defeated and 6,000 gave themselves up. In the following year an attempt to arrest the leaders who had taken refuge in St Stephen's church resulted in a much more violent march but its ultimate failure saw seventy four of the rebels executed. Five of the executions took place in Kirkby Stephen.

chapel and the great kitchen in a corner of the courtyard. The Wharton's were here in the days of Edward 1 and rose to importance in Tudor days. When the English Bible came it was a Wharton who left money here for the distribution of

This market town has many attractive nooks and crannies to explore, a super little riverside walk complete with old bridge, and in summer a mass of local children enjoying the water, together with plenty of old buildings, many of them covered in grey rendering to hide their age and cracks and rough stonework. Several of the old industrial premises

KIRKBY STEPHEN

remain, though nowadays they are either business premises or private houses.

Five minutes down any of the narrow ways from the Market Place and you can reach the River Eden. Cross by the old pack horse bridge and you have numerous enjoyable walks along the riverside, by ancient paths used by drovers for centuries, or through the picturesque hamlet of Hartley to the higher fells and the mysterious Nine Standards.

On the outskirts of town lies the popular Stenkrith park. Here the Eden drops into a deep gorge known as Coop Carnal Hole and flows over a fantastically worn bed of hard Brockram rock. There are three nature Reserves within a five miles radius of Kirkby Stephen together with settlements of the Iron Age and the Castle of Pendragon...home of Prince Uther Pendragon, father of King Arthur.

REAR CHURCH PATH & GARDENS

Pendragon Castle is said to take its name from Uther Pendragon. The castle too is said to be the place of his death...beseiged in his stronghold by Saxon enemies, he initially succeeded in repelling all attacks until the enemy, frustrated in their attempts to storm the castle, poisoned the well from which he obtained his water. The 12th century pele tower is believed to have been built by Sir Hugh de Morville (famous, or better still in-famous) as one of the knights who murdered Thomas a Becket in Canterbury Cathedral.

Travellers making their way north over Shap at nights often report seeing a giant of a man mounted on a large horse which is careering around the countryside...said to be Uther Pendragon.

The castle too has its own ghost. An unseen (but not unheard) spirit guarding the treasure buried deep by Uther Pendragon's wizard Merlin.

HEREDITIES Bronzed Cold Cast Sculpture

For more than 5,000 years, Bronze metal has been the dominant medium for sculptural art, for it was, and indeed still very much is, the only way in which a sculptors' talents can be reproduce in multiple form. Bronze has always been hot cast. The metal being heated, melted, and poured into a mould. In the 1950's advances in modern technology made it possible to put into production the concept of mixing atomised metal powders with polyester resin, to produce a metallic appearance which was in every aesthetic way entirely comparable with poured bronze.

Heredities were the finest in the world to pioneer this new technology. Indeed it was the first Company to use the process commercially...in the manufacture of small quality figurines. Today we boast a range of over 80 fine quality sculpture, covering a wide range of subjects by leading international artists...all at affordable prices.

Our entire range, along with the work of Jean Spouse, David Geenty, Doris Lindner, Marc Ricketts, and Brian Ormerod can be seen in our showrooms here in Kirkby Stephen, as well as at selected crafts and gift centres throughout Cumbria.

HEREDITIES LIMITED, KIRKBY STEPHEN,
CUMBRIA, XA17 QY
TELEPHONE 07683 71543 FAX 07683 72041

Kirkby Thore.

Map ref.H.7.
Next nearest Town or Village "Temple Sowerby"
Bus service. Cumberland Buses, Route 100
Location.4 miles north-west of Appleby.

Kirkby Thore is a village four miles north-west of Appleby, offering magnificent views across the Eden Valley...eastwards to the Pennines, and westwards to the lakeland Hills.

Much excavation is taking place here in and around the Roman fort and settlement of Bravoniacum.This settlement was at the junction where the military road from York to Carlisle joined the Maiden Way, which ran through Kirkland and Alston across the Tyne at Whitley Castle, and through Gilsland to the Roman Wall and Bewcastle.

In the loveliest corner of this village, which has the Pennine escarpment for a background, are groups of white-washed cottages and lofty trees near a small hill called the Cross. Here is the parish church of St.Michael which was begun by the Normans, with stones from the Roman camp. A fine pulpit, an ancient bell and fragments of old glass are among the best possessions of the church.The 15th century glass pieces in the south window in the chancel and in the north aisle enrich the windows with bright colours.The oak pulpit is in an unusual position on the right hand side of the nave and is dated 1651, it has been skilfully carved with flowers, foliage and figures. The bell said to be the largest in Cumbria, hangs in an iron frame and strikes the hour for the clock in the tower.It was cast in York in 1450 and is believed to have rung in the tower of Shap Abbey long before the monks were turned out by Henry V111. Probably very likely as the last Abbot of Shap was also the Rector of Kirkby Thore.

Kirkby Thore Hall hails from the 14th century though there were many additions in the 16th century.

KIRKLINTON.

Map ref. F.3.
Next nearest Town or Village "Longtown"
Location. 4 miles south-east of Longtown.

Kirklinton is a parish some four miles south east of Longtown...anciently the kirk of the barony of Levington.
The church was dedicated to St Cuthbert in 1734 though it is believed a church has stood on the same site far earlier than this. It is one of the resting places of St Cuthbert's body, during the wanderings of the Lindisfarn monks. Saxon gravestones along with Norman are in the belfry, and the fine Norman chancel arch has been set up again as the tower arch.
Because of its location near the head of the Solway, regularly pack horses, pedlars ,cattle,farm produce, and homespun cloth would all pass on the drove roads through Kirklinton. Smithfield lies on the Roman road which ran between the Roman stations of Caststeads...known in Roman days as Uxeloudunum...near Brampton and Netherley, near Longtown.
Hereabouts was born George Graham whose astronomical instruments were as wonderfully made as the clocks of his uncle Tom Tompion.Born here in 1673 he was apprenticed at 13 to a London watchmaker...as a young man he was befriended by Tompion, considered by many as the father of English watch-making, who made him his assistant. He died in 1751 and lies in the same grave as his uncle in Westminster Abbey.
The original school known as 'Cobble Rose' was situated in the field opposite The Robin Hood pub. Firs End School was built at the end of the 19th century at the sole expense of Joseph Dacre of Kirklinton Hall.
Years ago the village was commercially important...for as many as fifty carriers laden with bacon,grain ,and butter regularly passed through from Newcastle to Longtown...with much of the produce being sold locally.In fact the area was given the name 'Little Smithfield' after the London market, and today is officially called 'Smithfield'
A Quaker meeting house was built at Sikeside in 1688 when Kirklinton became a centre for dissenting Quakers after the Civil War. It was closed in 1931.
Nearby is the ruins of Kirklinton Hall, one time home of the deBoyvill family, later the Appleby family, and finally the famous Dacre family.Originally when first built the hall was called 'Clough Hall' a name echoed in nearby Cleughside and Longcleughside. (a 'clough' was a ravine and all three of the buildings here follow the course of a stream which runs into the Lyne)
The last Dacre at the Hall was Joseph Dacre who celebrated his birthday on the day of the consecration of the church..Three weeks later he advertised the furnished Kirklinton Hall to let, along with out-offices, the garden, a paddock, and the fishing and shooting over several hundred acres. The estate was eventually sold to John and Mary Frederica Saul who changed their surname to Kirklinton-Saul.; Their son George Graham Kirklinton was born in 1853 and inherited the estate in 1868. He greatly enlarged the Hall and became the High Sheriff of Cumberland in 1898. He died in 1927 and his wife in 1936. The estate was broken up and the Hall had various owners after that...Rossall School, requisitioned by the RAF, used as flats, and finally was made into a Country Club/Casino which then closed in the late sixties.
Today it is in ruins having had a disastrous fire in recent years. Owned by St Cuthberts Traditional Catholic Trust who have great hopes of restoring it to its former glory in years to come.

KIRKLINTON HALL

The Cliff Inn,

Kirklinton

To the casual visitor the 'Lyne Valley' may well seem far from obvious. You won't find any steep side to delineate it, and the road certainly doesn't lie alongside the river. Instead it crosses repeatedly by bridge (and ford) until the visitor could quite easily become thoroughly confused.

Little is actually known about the history of Kirklinton before 1100 AD. Certainly evidence of prehistoric remains have been uncovered at Standingstone Rigg and Cross Bank Hill, and it is said that Roman stones were used in the building of St. Cuthbert's Church, Kirklinton...but at the beginning of the twelfth century Ranulph de Meschines granted the barony of Levington to Sir Richard de Boyville who built a castle here. Levington meant 'the town on the Lyne' and this in time was corrupted to Kirklevington. From whence the name Kirklinton eventually arose. Nothing today though remains of the castle.

In the centre of all this history stands the old, but beautiful CLIFF INN hostelry.

The Cliff Inn offers a warm welcome to visitors and local alike...in fact there can't be many days when the bars don't appear to be crowded. No expense has been spared recently by the present owners in the transformation of the pub. Totally refurbished, and decorated inside and out with the kitchen and dining room being their pride ad joy.

The accent is on informality from the visitors point of view, meals are not just served in the dining room, but on those warm balmy days in the gardens also. The presentation is meticulous, with a comprehensive range of meals with many specialities. Needless to say local produce is used extensively.

Telephone: 0228 75409

KIRKOSWALD.

Map ref. G.6.

Next nearest Town or Village"Lazonby"

Location. Approx 20 miles south-west of Carlisle,

Kirkoswald is situated in the fertile Eden valley, where the raven beck from the Pennines slopes down to the flat valley floor. It has been a market town since it received its charter in 1201.It is one of the most charming little villages in Cumbria, nearly all built of red sandstone and delightfully embowered in trees. Hereabouts are found things left behind by the Romans and the Saxons, and the village has a grim memory of the Scots who raided and burned it three times, including once after Bannockburn.

The houses which are of varied shape, size and style, straggle up the slope alongside the formerly cobbled street. Many of the streets in fact were built using stone from Kirkoswald castle, which at one time was a powerful mediaeval stronghold built in the 11th century, soon after, in fact, the Norman conquest.Like so many others in Cumbria, it was devastated by the Scottish border raiders, and has been re-built and fortified many times.

Today, still protected by a deep and wide moat (with water in it) the chief ruins are a wall with vaulted dungeons, and a fine turret 65 feet high, complete except for its battlements.Within is a much-broken spiral stair.Traces of the gatehouse site are still here, and there are considerable remains of the towers 500 feet apart, each with a basement and two floors above. The active life of the castle was about 500 years, for it was founded in the 12th century and dismantled in the 17th. Its famous collection of portraits of English kings went to Naworth , where regretfully they were destroyed by fire.

Almost everywhere one goes around town you will be confronted by history.The oldest relics include a Bronze Age burial urn associated with nearby Long Meg and her daughters. The cobbled market square is still today the heart of the village, complete with its old stocks preserved alongside.One of the Inns still has its old bull baiting rings in the cobbles of its fore-court.

Nearby Nunnery House Hotel is a one time sanctuary where nuns are reputed to haunt the place to this day. One of Edens 'best kept secrets' is to be found half-way between the villages of Kirkoswald and Armathwaite...to the east of the Eden.Known as Nunnery Walks...no walker can fail to be amazed at the 'hiddden gorge' with its high waterfall.Stretching to the river Eden this beautiful wood is a delightful place to walk and to explore.Views of the gorge and fells can be obtained safely from the woodland above.

An interestingly named house called'The College' was the home for 400 years of the Fetherstonhaugh family.The house started life as a college for priests in 1523, and contains fine oak panelling in the hall and staircase. The house has the remains of an immensely strong.pele-tower , and in the lower part of the house more comfort and light has been provided by a projecting bay window.The house came to the Fetherstonhaugh's in 1590 and has belonged to the family ever since.Over the centuries successive owners have added to its collection of old china, glass, pictures, furniture and curio's, including relics from more warlike days. The house is private however, and is not open to the public.

The beautiful ancient church of St Oswald has many mediaeval grave slabs together with an early cross head. To the rear of the church is a small hill on which is a detached belfry...these days a Victorian replacement of the original structure which dated back to Henry VlII's time. Apparently the bell tower was placed in this spot so that the sound of the bell would be easily heard by the parishioners.

Below the west window of the church is St Oswald's stone well whose water comes from a stream flowing under the nave, it is one of the odd features of this exterior, another is the porch with its projecting gable and its massive weatherwork beams resting on two great wooden supports on low stone bases.

The village takes its name from St Oswald, King of Northumbria, who according to legend, toured the pagan north with St Aidan in the 7th century.They stopped at a well on the site of the present church and converted the local inhabitants to Christianity. To the left of town, below a band of trees is Nether Harescough, a typical fortified farm designed to repel the Scots and cattle thieves.Nether Harescough is famous for its 'luck', a small glass bowl of dark claret with a white rim. Nothing is known of its origins.'Lucks' are thought to be connected with Celtic and Scandinavian 'magic cauldrons' precursors of the holy grail legends.

Nunnery House Hotel

all nine bedrooms in the hotel have views either to the east, and the pennine fells, or to the west where sheep graze in the open felds of the rolling Eden Valley. Choose from the Honeymoon Suite with its four-poster bed and en-suite facilities, or our individually furnished double or twin rooms, most with en-suite facilities.

In the evening why not have a leisurely drink before dinner and draw on Alf's fund of information about the area.

Meals are served in the pannelled dining room. the food is English in sytle and includes plenty of fresh local produce. Cumberland sausage, local lamb and cream from one of Eden's Jersey herds are complemented in the summer by fresh fruit, vegetables and herbs from the large walled garden beside the house. Vegetarian food is the speciality of the house.

After dinner, relax in the lounge by the large wood burning stove, or take a summer evening stroll in the grounds. Your visit is unlikely to pass without a sighting of our resident owl or the deer which regularly stroll across the lawn in front of the house. The friendly atmosphere of the house and the peace and quiet which surround it can guarantee you an enjoyable stay.

In addition...Day trippers are cordially welcome to explore Nunnery Walks, and visit our new Craft Centre.

Believe it, or not, the house (as the name implies) really was a nunnery... from soon after William the Conqueror landed in 1066. The Benedictine nuns who were here had a harsh life, with very little money...in fact £2.14s.5d each to be precise per year...which was meant to cover food, clothing, and the costs of the Nunnery. In comparison, monks at Furness Abbey had over £24 each a year. King Edward IV apparently took pity on the nun's plight and made a substitute charter for them, but the Prioress Issobel complained that this did not give them all the privileges they had priviously held. In 1480 she claimed to have found an old charter of 1088, giving right such as freedom from trolls throughout England, and granting the rare right of sanctuary...Today it is believed that the document was almost certainly a forgery, but nethertheless she believed and in fact her claim was backed up by a nearby sanctuary stone (also probably a forgery).

There were never more than a dozen nuns here, and by 1536 only the prioress and three nuns were left. The Nunnery was abandoned, although nuns are reputed to haunt the place to this day. In the 18th century the house as re-built and the Aglionbys who then owned the property, laid out the now famous and popular Nunnery Walks....

Todays owners Alf and Joan Armstrong look forward to welcoming you to "Nunnery House", today, a small country house ets in its own grounds, and which includes the spectacular Nunnery Walks.

The Hotel is situated in the Eden Valley between the villages of Kirkoswald and Armathwaite, just 15 minutes drive from the M6 Motorway at penrith or Carlisle.

For further information please telephone:

Lazonby (0768) 898537
Nunnery House Hotel
Staffield, Kirkoswald, Penrith,
Cumbria CA10 1EU

LAMPLUGH.

Map ref. B.8.
Next nearest Town or Village "Loweswater"
Location. 4 mIles North West of Cleator Moor

Lamplugh is a parish some two miles east of the Marron valley. The parish extends for about six miles from the north to south, and three miles from east to west.

The church has been dedicated to St. Michael, and stands on the site of an old chapel. The vestry here was previously part of the Lamplugh family mortuary chapel.

The church however has been much renewed, but some of it can be seen to be some 600 years old, and there is a charming little window with two carved faces. One of the old memorials is to Thomas and Francies Lamplugh, the other being to their daughter who was born in 1693 and died within a few months of her wedding.

In 1747 one Richard Brisco of Lamplugh Hall bequeathed a yearly rental of £12 payable out of Skelsmoor lands...to be distributed amongst poor widows and the school. These days, Lamplugh Hall, now a farmstead still has an ancient feature at its entrance...an archway bearing the Lamplugh family crest with the date 1595.

The row of houses at Cross gates originally housed the navvies who constructed the reservoir at Cogramoss. A building near Brook House housed Lamplugh's first school. Later the school was used to house the local hearse, and somewhat naturally became known as 'Hearse House'. These days the building is used to store hay.

LANERCOST & BANKS

Map ref. G.3.
Next nearest Town or Village "Brampton"
Location. 2 miles north east of Brampton.

A parish, with church, north-east of Brampton. Undoubtedly the focal point of this parish is Lanercost Priory, situated in the fertile Irthing valley, and built in the 12th century. Second only to Furness Abbey in interest as ruins, though it stands in far more delightful countryside.

Like so many of its counterparts it has had many famous visitors amongst whom was Edward 1 who stayed here often..in 1280,1300,and 1306, followed by Robert Bruce in 1311. During the Middle Ages it saw many turbulent times. In 1346 it was invaded and ruined by David, King of the Scots. The Priory buildings are late 12th century and consist of a great church with cloister and crypt now used as a museum for Roman antiquities...all found locally.

The interior of the nave gains its effect from a handsome 13th century arcade and a singularly beautiful clerestory whose arches are rich with ornament inside and out. A blocked doorway in the aisle makes a frame for the celebrated Lanercost Cross, the shaft of which is here with part of a Latin inscription, saying it was made in 1214, in the seventh year of the Interdict, Innocent 111 holding the Apostle See , Otto being King of Germany, Philip King of France, John King of England, and William King of Scotland.

In the north transept under an arched recess is the oldest tomb in Lanercost, that of Sir Roland de Vaux. It was another Robert who founded the priory in 1166. In the same transept is a chapel, perfectly vaulted, where there is an impressive 15th century altar tomb with bold carvings of shields held by angels and curious winged animals. Here too lies Lord Humphrey Dacre of Naworth Castle, and his wife who was a kinswoman of Katherine Parr.

Men and women have worshipped at the priory for hundreds of years...and still do. Services are still held in the nave of the beautfiul priory church...now converted into what must be one of the most splendid parish churches in the country.

Hadrian's wall runs through the parish. Though pillaged over the centuries there is still a well preserved turret at Banks. Besides being an impressive monument it offers wonderful views across the Pennines.

LANGDALE.

Map ref. E.9.
Next nearest Town or Village Elterwater & Chapel Stile
Location. 4 miles west of Grasmere.

The most popular valley in the Lake District.
The valley consists of two dales which join at Elterwater and are separated by Lingmoor Fell, otherwise known as Great Langdale and Little Langdale.
Here will be found some of the most inviting hills and crags.Starting with Chapel Stile (the valleys village at the foot) the long ridge of Blea Riss is to the north, and Lingmoor to the south.These are followed by the very distinctive Langdale Pikes...Harrison Stickle at 2,403 feet and Pike o'Stickle at 2,323 feet. (Stickle incidentally means pointed), and is easily recognisable from so many viewpoints in the Lake District.
The two Langdale valleys, because of their isolation and importance as part of a clandestine route from the coast had, at one time, a great popularity with the smugglers of some two centuries ago. Pack-horses would have brought the spirits over the mountains and down the lonely valleys. Close to Little Langdale Tarn is an old farmhouse which was notorious locally as a smugglers hideout, while lower down the valley is Greenbank Farm, the home of the famous contrabandist and moon-shiner...Lanty Slee....An Irishman, he became a great Lake District character and his appearances

in the Ambleside courtroom were apparently hilarious as he kept his native wit well exercised.Lanty had many illicit stills hidden in obscure locations about the fells...the secret of their positions dying with him in 1878.
A story attached to him is the one that relates to the day an excise officer called to search his home. He was detained for some time by a lady who sat elegantly in her crinoline, receiving him in a little room over the porch. It was all very friendly, and she finally rose to say 'goodbye' the keg she just happened to be sitting on 'happened'to be completely empty...The menfolk of the house had drilled a hole through the floor and keg, and every drop of the contents had been drained away..
'Little Langdale lies south of the great Langdale valley, and is connected to it by a rugged moorland road which surmounts the pass linking the two valleys and runs by the Blea Tarn. This was the 'little lowly valley'of Wordsworths 'Solitary'...the philosophic hermit who chose to live in isolation in this valley.His home was a farmhouse (Bleatarn House) situated close to the tarn. For the view described by Wordsworth you will have to climb the crags above the summit of the pass.
Although the Langdale Pikes may fail to top several other peaks in the vicinity, the steepness of their flanks, and the arrogant rock castles of their summits, give them a challenging individuality unmatched elsewhere.This is a paradise for climbers and scramblers.The sheer sides of the Pikes are renowned for the quality of the climbing they provide, and there are ascents on the Langdales which range from easy to hard...very severe. Gimmer Crag is undoubtedly the most popular climbing ground, it is situated to the west of Dungeon Ghyll, opposite Harrison Stickle. Its Kipling Groove is considered to be amongst the hardest climbs in the district.
Budding archaelogists will be interested to learn that it was here on the scree slopes below Langdale Pikes that Neolithic man found that he could shape the rock fragments into stone axes.In fact these axes were shaped roughly on the terraces beneath the crag of Pike o'Stickle, as well as at the head of the steep scree that falls towards the windy trough of Mickleden.The site was only discovered in 1947, and the ledges here are littered with roughly-shaped axes and broken cast offs.

LANGDALES & WINDERMERE

Little Langdale was possibly the one time home of a Scandinavian settlement. Directly behind Fell Foot Farm is a flat topped, almost rectangular mound, and on the steep sides will be seen a short flight of grassy steps. W.G.Collingwood called it a 'thing'mount...better known as a meeting place of Viking Councils, and was possibly the seat of government for both of the Langdales.

STICKLEBARN
Tavern and Eating-House

GREAT LANGDALE
NEAR AMBLESIDE
CUMBRIA LA22 9JY
TEL: 05394 37356

STICKLEBARN
BUNKBARN ACCOMMODATION

Situated at the very heart of the famous Langdale valley, 7 miles NW of Ambleside, beneath Harrison Stickle and Pavey Ark, the Bunkbarn is probably unique to Lakeland as it is privately owned and available to the general outdoor public and traveller on foot.

Converted from a traditional stone barn and stable in the Spring of 1986 using local builders and craftsmen, every effort has been made to retain the exterior integrity of the building whilst providing interior facilities and furnishings to the very highest standards, Its completion allows us to offer sleeping accommodation to augment the already establishes bars and all day food service offered in the adjacent Sticklebarn Tavern.

The Sticklebarn is beautifully situated amidst some of the finest mountain scenery in England, at the very foot of the famous Langdale Pikes and Dungeon Ghyll waterfalls.

Nature lovers, mountaineers, ramblers and climbers will all find something to satisfy their ambitions and for those who wish to spend a quiet restful holiday, the unspoiled beauty of Langdale makes it an ideal centre.

Greenhowe Caravan Park
Great Langdale, English Lakeland

Greenhowe is a permanent Caravan Park with Self Contained Holiday Accommodation. It provides no accommodation for touring caravans but subject to availability Holiday Homes may be rented from 1st March until mid-November.

The Park is situated in the heart of the Lake District some half a mile from Dungeon Ghyll at the foot of the Langdale Pikes, a little over two miles from the lovely village of Elterwater, and within a few miles of Coniston, Lake Windermere, Ambleside and Hawkshead, and just about one mile hike to the Stoneage axe factory.

It is a quiet secluded, beautifully wooded and approached by a short private road off the B5343 which runs to the head of the valley. It is an ideal centre for Climbing, Fell Walking, Riding, Swimming, Water Skiing or just a lazy holiday.

Winners of the Rose Award for the last 12 years.
ETB Grading "Very Good"

Greenhowe Caravan Park,
Great Langdale, Ambleside
Cumbria LA22 9JU
Telephone: (05394) 37231
Fax: (05394) 37464

LANGWATHBY.

Map ref. G.6.
Next nearest Town or Village "Edenhall"
Trains. Railway Station
Location. 5 miles north-west of Penrith.

ST. PETERS

Deep in the heart of the Eden Valley and surrounded by beautiful countryside which the valley is renowned for...it has not surprisingly been called 'Englands best kept secret'
Langwathby is a village five miles north-east of Penrith, and is situated between the River Eden and the Carlisle-Settle scenic railway line.
Before the erection of the stone bridge over the Eden in 1685 there was a Wath (ford) which was the longest across the Eden...hence the name Langwathby. In those days it was the main crossing for horse transport from the East fellside to Penrith. It was as recently as 1968 that the stone bridge was washed away to be replaced by a steel structure.
Round the broad green, farm buildings stand close together, many of the weathered sandstone walls very substantially built.Centuries ago they had to keep out border raiders.Among the red houses stands a small red church with a double bellcot , and with stairs from its porch to an upper room, where is an old oak chest.A window from this vestry looks down into the nave which has roughly-shaped beams in its roof, and on the west wall are pieces of mid 17th century armour once used by the village militia. There are two breastplates, awide brimmed helmet and some other pieces from the store which most villages kept in those days.
Look for Beck Mill Gallery, once a ruined mill, now converted to a delightful arts and crafts centre.

LAZONBY

Map Ref. G.6.
Next nearest Town or Village "Kirkoswald"
Trains. Railway Station
Location. 7 miles north-east of Penrith.

ST. NICHOLS CHURCH

A village in the Eden, seven miles north-east of Penrith. A busy place when thousands of sheep are sold here periodically, it stands above a fine curve of the Eden, with houses looking away to a splendid sandstone bridge of four arches, and with many old possessions...a weathered stone which was part of the village stocks, and an ancient cross crowned by a cube with a little cross tilted back to make a sundial. The shaft is believed to be around 800 years old.

Many British artifacts, burial mounds, even a Bronze Age fort have been found in the village over the years. The Roman fort of Voreda was close by at Plumpton. Yet another link to Arthurian legend here...in the north-west corner lies Tarn Wadling, now drained, linked strongly to the story of gawain and the Green Knight.

Many of the houses here date from the 17th and 18th centuries, with most properties being built of hard red sandstone from the local quarries.In fact Liverpool's Anglican Cathedral has steps made of Lazonby stone.

The church of St Nicholas though consecrated in 1863 has had a church on the site since 1272 when Sir Hugh Morvill gave it to Lanercost Priory.It still has its original churchyard cross. This 19th century church is built rather oddly on the side of a great pyramid hill.It has an Elizabethan altar cup, and there is a fragment of a mediaeval gravestone in the churchyard.

Three miles north-west of Castleriff is the site of a moated ruin.

The big cave near Baronwood, known as Giant's Chamber, is said to have served as a place of refuge when the Scots came over the border.

LEVENS.

Map ref G.12.
Next nearest Town or Village "Heversham"
Location. 5 miles south of Kendal.
Gala days/festivals..Levens Sports. 4th Sat June.

The village of Levens, formerly known as Beathwaite Green, straggles along the southern tip of Scout Scar, and overlooks the Lyth Valley on the west.

The old Norse name for Levens is "Lauf-ness' which means 'The Leafy promontory', as it lies in rich pastureland.

The church with its light coloured spire, stands out as a landmark.Built in 1828 by Mary Howard of Levens. who also built the school for girls in 1810. Later this, with the boys school was amalgamated into the present school building.

The first chapel in 'Beathwaite' was built in 1795. The building still exists (though now is two flats) and ranks as the oldest Methodist buildings in South Lakeland. One of the oldest buildings hereabouts is Nether Levens farm built in the 16th century.It has an open hall with a huge fireplace surmounted by a giant chimney.

The great house, one of the wonders of Lakeland is Levens Hall. it is set in extensive parkland enclosed in the 14th century, where the river meanders among fine oaks and beeches, here are broad avenues and shady paths, a sanctuary for wild life where about 100 Norwegian black fallow deer graze.

The Hall is the largest Elizabethan house in Cumbria, but some of the fabric, the centre of the building, is part of an early 13th century peletower built by a deRedman as one of a chain of fortified houses extending to Arnside, places of refuge against the Scots. Open to the public,here will be seen a wealth of exquisite oak panelling, wonderful plastered ceilings, magnificent chimneys, panelled rooms, and deep friezes, the whole house filled with 17th and 18th century furniture and set in an evergreen garden of almost incredible loveliness.

The front door opens straight into the Elizabethan Hall in which Sir James Bellingham was proud to display the coat of arms of Elizabeth 1. Here are firearms and armour used by the people who have lived at Levens. In the house are relics from the time of Waterloo, a watch given to Colonel Henry Percy by the Duke of Wellington, and a clasp from the cloak of Napoleon.

The house has long been noted for its pictures which include paintings by Constable,Cotman, Ruben's and Bicc di Loringe. Don't overlook seeing one of Drakes Bowls, which was used during a game at Plymouth Hoe at the time of the Spanish Armada. The splendid topiary gardens, laid out in 1689 by Monsieur Beaumont(gardener to James 11, and the same man who laid out the gardens of Hampton Court) remain much as originally planned, and is said to be the finest topiary garden in England,laid

LEVENS

out so that it might be impressive at all seasons with yew and box cut to every conceivable shape, fine beech hedges and herbaceous borders aglow with colour in the summer.

A colony of ghosts inhabit Levens hall...One the 'Grey Lady' often seen stepping out in front of cars...though nobody is there when the driver goes to look...said to be the ghost of a gypsy woman turned away empty handed by the mistress of Levens Hall many years ago.

Also the 'Pink Lady' is a kindly lady ghost wearing a mop cap and print dress...appearing only when children are around.

The phantom of a black dog frequently appears often trotting alongside two visitors. One can see him...the other can't!

In the centre of the village is an oldbank barn, originally a shippon and haybarn.Today it is the village institute, and an attractive well kept building.

Lindale in Cartmel.

Map ref. F.12.
Next nearest Town or Village "Cartmel"
Location. 2 miles north of Grange over Sands,

Lindale in Cartmel is a village just two miles north of Grange over Sands, off the A 590 Kendal to Barrow Road at the foot of Newton fell...the southerly limit of a range of low, rolling hills to the east of Lake Windermere.

The village is rescued from its comparative obscurity by its associations with John Wilkinson 'the father of iron'. He was born in a cart as his parents were on their way to market at Clifton (near Penrith), an event which apparently made the local folk prophesy that he would 'Som tyme bee a girt man". In 1741 at the age of 12 he moved to Backbarrow with his father, and seven years later be bought a forge and furnace at Wilson House...sandwiched between the River Winster and the present main road from Lindale to Levens bridge..Here his first invention was the box iron...using an old mill in Lindale for processing purposes.Probably his most ambitious local undertaking was to dig a canal into the peat mosses alongside the Winster, and on this he floated what

is claimed to be the world's first iron boat, using it to obtain peat for fuel, and the underlying clay for brick manufacture.

His home a Georgian mansion situated at Castle Head, half a mile south of Lindale was built in part by Irish labourers, after being summoned from their slumbers with an ancient bell which Wilkinson had obtained from Cartmel Priory. Castle Head, its battlemented garden was neglected for many decades but has been restored to its former glory when the building became a training college for Roman catholic priests. The bell which Wilkinson obtained from Cartmel is now in Lindale church.

Many fascinating corners can be explored in this old village which was first mentioned in 1191`. Until the building of the roads across the marshes around 1800 it was little more than a secluded hamlet, but after this date it quickly rose in importance and acquired three coaching inns. George Fox spoke at Lindale to a congregation which was at first hostile...but after became 'convinced'

The writer Mrs Gaskell lived here whilst she wrote 'The Sexton's Hero'

Overlooking the village is Ravensbarrow Crag, and Eller How Tower, a mock ruin erected in the 19th century.

LINDAL IN FURNESS.

Map ref. D.13.
Next nearest Town or Village "Urswick"
Location. 5 miles south of Ulverston.

Lindal in Furness is an ancient settlement recorded in 1220 as a Grange of Furness Abbey, located six miles away.
Church Farm dated 1635 and the church of St Peter's 1875. Lindal Moor Farm which overlooks the green originated in the 1600's.

The area was once a maze of railway tracks and open cast pits and shafts, when iron-ore was mined in the middle of the 19th century to the beginning of the 20th century.
The village extends both sides of the busy A590 Barrow road. On one side is a long row of three storey 'cottages' built originally for railway workers and miners. Note the 'Railway Inn' nearby. Heavy subsidence has been known to take place here and locals still talk of the day at the end of the 19th century when an engine disappeared into a 200 feet hole...never to be seen again.

LINSTOCK.

Map ref F.4.
Next nearest Town or Village "Carlisle"
Location. Just over two miles from Carlisle northeast.

The village of Linstock...formerly spelt 'Lynstock' lies just two and a half miles north east of Carlisle close to the banks of the River Eden, and only a short distance off the line of the Roman Wall. Though small with only about 150 inhabitants, the village nevertheless boasts a castle. Today only the tower and the moat remain, but in the 16th century, Linstock Castle was still intact and offered a good defence against the border raiders, especially the Armstrong's...a Scottish Clan...though they eventually almost totally destroyed the castle. Edward 1 is known to have stayed here in 1307.
The present owners are the Wannop family...it is said that the ghost of Bishop Irton who died in 1283 roams Linstock Castle every year on the anniversary of his death.
Drawdykes Castle on the Roman Vallum is also nearby. Built around a pele tower by the Aglionby's in 1676.

LITTLE SALKELD.

Map ref. G.6.
Next nearest Town or Village " Langwathby"
Location. 6 miles east of Penrith.

A small village on the east bank of the River Eden, halfway between Appleby and Carlisle...six miles east of Penrith.

Two small village greens separated by the approach road to Salkeld Hall, one time seat of the ancient family of Salkeld, built prior to the Civil War. The story goes that Colonel Lacy who purchased the Hall in 1790 had a batman who deserted the army and came here, so rather than give his servant in to the military, the Colonel instead gave him the task of hewing out of the solid rock some caves on the river bank...about a mile north of the village, and which to this day is known as Lacy's Caves...and consequently somewhat of a tourist attraction in itself.

This faithful servant also built a bridge (in his spare time?) over a rivulet which divides the parishes of Hunsonby and Glassonby.

In 1725 an attempt was made by Colonel Lacy to use the stones of Long Meg and her daughters nearby...as mile posts. However just as work was about to begin a great storm blew up and the workmen fled believing the Druids were angry at the desecration of their temple.

On the opposite bank of the river is St Michael's Well near the supposed site of a village called Addingham, which was 'drowned' when the river changed its course in the 12th century.

Look for the village smithy under the oak tree on the village green. and which is still in use today.

Near Sunny Gill is the old corn mill...in existence on the same site since 1345, and up until 1974 had been in the ownership of the Atkinson family for over 300 years. Today it is still water powered and produces wholemeal flour.

Here on a hill is a famous family perhaps twice as old as Christianity itself; Long Meg and her Daughters, Cumbria's Stonehenge, they make up a stone circle 400 yards round, the biggest in the land after Stonehenge.

High above the village they stand, at a magnificent viewpoint where many of the Cumbria mountains are in sight.There are 67 in the family circle, many of the stones being exceptionally large and almost all shapeless. Some are higher than man, and are 10 to 15 feet round. A few are now level with the ground.Some are rocks of greenstone, others are limestone or granite. Long Meg herself stands alone a few yards away 18 feet high and 15 feet round, and weighing it is thought about 17 tons. She is roughly tapering and slightly round-shouldered, and facing here are her four big daughters, making a sort of crude gateway.

LONG MARTON.

Map ref.I.7.
Next nearest Town or Village "Dufton"
Location. 2 miles north of Appleby.

Long Marton village is situated some two miles north of Appleby.

The ancient name of the village was originally written as Mereton, literally meaning 'a homestead' by the mere.

Its early Norman church lies well to the south of the village and offers many interesting features..not least the fact that it is the only church in England dedicated to St Margaret and St James. Its position almost certainly indicates that it was originally built to serve two hamlets Long Marton itself,and nearby Brampton.

The nave and parts of the chancel of the red sandstone church were built about 800 years ago and in the Norman tower three bells hang on an ancient frame, one was cast in 1500 and another a century earlier, A staircase in the tower leads to the gallery where there is an early 17th century Communion Table.

Its interesting to note that the graves of several gypsies who happened to die whilst in the area for the ever popular Appleby Horse Fair (held every year) are in the churchyard. Surviving friends and relatives still tend their graves.

Across the beck is the site of the old corn mill, and at the top of the hill approaching the village on the opposite side is the spacious Marton Hall...home of many rectors of the parish.

LONG SLEDDALE.

Map ref. G.10.
Next nearest Town or Village "Burneside"
Location. West of the A6 , approx 6 miles
north of Kendal.

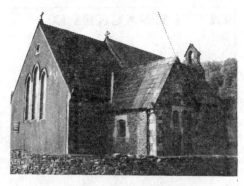

ST. MARYS PARISH CHURCH

A secluded valley with a lane, seen in springtime, winding through mists of bluebells and alive with grey wagtails. Above the village is Goat Scar, and on Harter fell are the beginnings of the little River Sprint, which goes down to meet the Kent near Kendal.

Legend has it that in the 18th century the most famous wizard, or wise man of the Lake District was a Dr Lickbarrow, who lived in Long Sleddale.Even though he practised the black arts so it is said, he was nevertheless a regular churchgoer.The powers of the doctor were often called upon to find lost or stolen valuables.

Kilnstones nearby was once inhabited by monks and in the 1600's provided hospitality for pack-horses and travellers on their way to Scotland.Two of these packhorse bridges still survive.

The first St Mary's church was built in the 13th century, but the current one here is well worth investigating.It has, amongst other things, an 18th century oak locker and an Elizabethan chalice.

Look for Yewbarrow Hall which incorporates an old pele tower.

LONGTOWN.

Map ref. E.3.
Next nearest Town or Village "Kirklinton"
Bus service.Cumberland Buses Routes 84, 101
Tourist Information Centre. Community
Centre.Longtown.
Location. Approximately 12 miles north of
Carlisle.
Early closing. Wednesday.

ST. MICHAELS WELL

Longtown is the last English 'settlement' before Scotland, on the west coast route.Its a small place, and interesting for having been a planned town in the 18th century, when the Rev.Dr Robert Graham, owner of the local great house and estate of Netherby, laid out a town of four streets and squares, and a tiny port at Sarkfoot to serve it.

The entire area is steeped in history from its past as the 'Debatable Land', a virtual buffer state between England and Scotland.

While unrest dates back to the time of Hadrian's Wall, the 13th century saw the first major quarrels.People from both countries grazed stock here but pulled down any building the other side erected in 1551.Both countries declared their intention to lay waste the area, giving citizens the right to rob,burn, and murder. In 1552 the land was divided between England and Scotland, but raiding, as to be expected, continued.

The name Longtown first appears in 1584.The village was far more important in the days of stage coaches when the main route to Edinburgh passed through the village. In those days there was a cattle market (charter 1306) which was a rival to Carlisle. The attractive five arch bridge built in the 1700's spans the River Esk, and which is famous for salmon fishing.

On the left of the town at Esk Street, stands the Moot Hall and Council rooms which once housed the old school. This was built as a school for 60 children of poor parents.

Fauld Mill is a watermill which once ground corn for the parish, with equipment supplied by the Graham family.

Longtown is situated in the parish of Arthuret, and for centuries had laid claim to connections with the legendary King Arthur. In fact in 1669 the rector wrote 'Arthuret has its name from the famous King Arthur, King of the Ancient Britons' in whose time there was a battle fought here...probably on the moor of the same name'

The battle to which he refers took place in the 6th century and according to legend 80,000 were slain. Another battle involving Arthur's mentor. Merlin, took place just north of Longtown...at Carwhinley. Arthurian expert Dr Norma Goodrich has actually named Arthuret as the last resting place of the monarch.

The old parish church of St Michael is also at Arthuret. It was re-built in 1609. There is an interesting gravestone erected to one Archie Armstrong who was a jester to Charles 1. Appropriately enough he was buried here on the 1st April 1672. Just outside the walls of the church is St Michaels Well, a Holy spring dating back, it is believed to 1609. It is really a spring trickling into a bowl below a sandstone arch. Worn sandstone steps lead down to it, testifying to long usage, including baptisms from 1860 to 1951. It was probably a holy spring for many centuries prior to its current form, especially as the area is associated with the 6th century St Kentigern, which is often linked with water.

The first church here may have been founded by St Kentigern in the 6th century, but the earliest records date from 1150 when it was connected with Jedbergh convent. It was destroyed twice in the 14th century. In

LONGTOWN

the late 16th century the church displayed a register of those paying blackmail money to one of the reivers, who would then refrain from raiding that person's land.

Beyond the Esk is the Solway Moss, possibly the site of a battle in 1542. The Moss is worked for peat, used in horticulture and industry, some once being sent to Japan for use in whisky-making.

The moss is rich in wildlife, including charcoal-grey roe deer and red grouse.

In town, at the foot of Esh Street, is the site of the old ford on the main road to Scotland, where tradition tells us that Bonnie Prince Charlie and his Highland army crossed on their way to Carlisle in 1745. With the river in full spate, swollen by rain and high tides, the 200 pipers waded through the strong current up to their necks in water. Once safely on the other side the pipers started to play, and the army danced reels until they were dry again. This incident is reputed to be the origin of the pipe tune 'Wi a hundred pipers an 'a'.

It was Dr Graham who helped to bring the Carlisle-Edinburgh railway line through Longtown. From 1802 many people became weavers for the mills in Carlisle and many sheds were built behind the houses. One road called ;'The Shades' was originally "The Sheds'.

Netherby Hall can be seen from the main road, and stands on the site of a Roman fort. It is not often open to the public, but Daffodil Sunday in the Spring is an opportunity to see the grounds. As the ancestral home of the Grahams, it featured in Sir Walter Scott's exciting poem "Young Lochinvar'.

Across the Esk and even nearer to the main highway is Kirkandrews Tower, a smaller Graham strong-hold, is a typical sixteenth century Border pele.

LORTON.

Map ref. C.7.
Next nearest Town or Village "Braithwaite"
Location. 5 miles south of Cockermouth.
Gala days/festivals/Melbreak Hunt Show
.4th Saturday July.
Vale of Lorton Sheepdog Trials.
3rd Saturday July.

PEEL TOWER

Lorton is a chapelry in the valley of the Cocker, considered the prettiest of the Lakeland valleys. ...Certainly John Wesley thought so in 1752 when he wrote 'Lorton, a little village lying in a fruitful valley, surrounded by high mountains, the sides of which are covered with grass and woods, and the bottom watered by two small rivers'
Today the countryside remains much the same. The village itself retains much of its traditional character with slate roofed houses mostly between 150 and 300 years old.
The village it will be seen is sign-posted High and Low Lorton, though it is doubtful if they are more than four hundred yards apart.
The well known Jennings Brewery originated here in 1828 but moved to Cockermouth in 1887, and where today it operates at Castle Brewery. The original brewery maltings still exist, though its now the village hall.
Interestingly enough the village hall is known as Yew Tree Hall in recognition of the large yew tree behind reputed to be over 1,000 years old. The tree was immortalized in 1803 by William Wordsworth in his poem 'Yew Trees'. In fact this tree is an important part of Lorton's history, for George Fox, the Quaker preacher, preached here in 1652 stating that 'the tree was so full of people that I feared they would shake it down'.

Lorton church dedicated to St Cuthbert, an early 19th century Gothic building though there has been a church on the same site for over 800 years.
The Methodist chapel here, once called the Wesleyan Preaching House, is a tiny one-roomed building where John Wesley preached to a large and serious congregation in 1752, 1759, and 1761.

Lorton Hall is one of the few pele towers to have strayed in amongst the central fells. It is 15th century, with 17th and 19th century additions.

LOWESWATER.

Map ref. C.8.
Next nearest Town or Village "Buttermere"
Location. 8 miles south of Cockermouth.
Gala days/festivals. Loweswater & Brackenthwaite Agricultural Show. 3rd Thurs Sept.

Looking over Crummock to Buttermere is said to be one of the loveliest views in the north of England.

The lake is a little one, but pretty in the way woodlands come down to its southern edge.
Its not really a village...its more a straggle of houses between Loweswater Lake and Crummock Water. The lake takes it name from the wood lane around its shores and means 'leafy lake'.
Apart from fell walking, the two main things for which the village is famous is the Melbreak Foxhounds and the Agricultural Show.
The church of St Bartholmew was built by the villagers in 1827.

LOWICK.

Map ref. E.12.
Next nearest Town or Village "Colton"
Location.7 miles east of Broughton-in-Furness.
Gala days/festivals.Lowick & District Agricultural Show. 1st Saturday Sept.

The village of Lowick Bridge forms a ribbon of houses on the road leading to the church and the Red Lion Inn.

Lowick Green is situated in a most attractive setting with a church dedicated to St Luke. Records indicate that a chapel was erected here prior to 1577.
Spectacular views of the 'Vale of Lowick'...panoramic views of the whole valley with the Blawith, and Torver Fells behind, and in the distance, Coniston Old man, Dowcraggs, and Wetherlam.

LOW ROW.

Map ref. H.3.
Next nearest Town or Village "Lanercost"
Location. 4 miles east of Brampton.

Low Row in the parish of Nether Denton is four miles east of Brampton, and was originally High Row, Middle Row, and Low Row.
The village shop was built over a hundred years ago...made of tin and completely lined with wood.Today its exactly as it was then...a tourist attraction in its own right! Its still complete with

rows of small drawers for dried goods, and the coffee grinder and old scales are still on view.The present owner is the third generation to run the business.

There is in Low Row a charitable trust known as the William Hodgson Trust. This was formed in 1856 when a William Hodgson donated a field to the parish whereby the rent will be given to the poor.The field was sold in the 1980's and the yearly interest on the money is given to pensioner's and widows of the parish.

LOWTHER.

Map ref. G.8.
Nearest Town or Village "Clifton"
Bus service. Cumberland Buses Route 107
Location. On the A6 5 miles south of Penrith.
Gala days/festivals. Lowther Horse Trials &
Country Fair.Weekend - Early August

LOWTHER PARK

Lowther is a village situated directly on the A6, some 5 miles south of Penrith.

Lowther is the parish name, with the villages of Lowther, Lowther Newtown, Hackthorpe, Melkinthorpe, and Whale settled well within its boundaries.

The river Lowther is the westerly boundary to the beautiful park, with the magnificent facade of the castle to the south.

Lowther is somewhat synonymous with the Lowther family. The old home of the Lowther family was originally Lowther Hall, the main part of which was burnt down in 1720. For a while the family lived in the west wing until the early 19th century, when the magnificent castle was built...designed incidentally, by Sir Robert Smirke. Lowther Castle today is now only an empty shell, an imposing facade left to disguise the ruin of a once mighty mansion. Lowthers have lived there since 1421 and more than a century before that they achieved a position of power in the Government, a role they placed in various capacities in every age for over 600 years.Political fortune and family prosperity went hand in hand and by the early 19th century they had acquired vast wealth and estates becoming one of the most powerful landowning families in Northern England, and rejoicing in the title of Earls of Lonsdale.It seemed an appropriate time to create a family seat worthy of such affluence and aristocratic eminence and in 1806 Robert Smirke was commissioned to design it.In the next five years arose one of the most remarkable inventions of the architect's imagination ever seen in this country, described by a Victorian admirer as 'unquestionably the most magnificent edifice of which Westmorland can boast, combining in itself the majestic effect of a fortification with the splendour of a palace', with numerous towers of different shapes and elevations, crested with bat-tlements and pierced with slit windows.The northern front was in the style of the 13th or 14th century with ramparts boasting parapets, and turrets, fortified gateways and towers, while the southern front was in'Gothic Cathedral style" with pointed mullion windows, delicate pinnacles,niches and cloisters.

The grandeur of the interior was equally overwhelming and the grounds were laid out in beautiful formal gardens with lakes,canals and bridges all exquisitely carried out.Avenues of beech, sycamore and yew led the eye towards a wonderful panorama of the Cumbrian hills.The shell of Lowther Castle demolished nearly forty years ago basically because it was so large...it had almost as many rooms as there are days in the year. Its most famous occupant was Hugh, the Fifth Earl of Lonsdale, nick-named the Yellow Earl because of his yellow carriage, and enormous fleet of yellow cars.He entertained Kings and Queens, Emperors,and Crown Princes, on a lavish scale and had all the dividing walls in the park demolished to make it larger than the neighbouring Greystoke.

In 1956 the roof was removed leaving only the shell of a fairy-tale like castle to bear witness of the immense power and influence of the Lowthers.Today the estate is used as a caravan site and wildlife park, where deer,Highland cattle and St Kilda sheep roam. There are two ghosts associated with Lowther Castle. One is believed to be the 1st Earl of Lonsdale or

LOWTHER

'Wicked Jimmy' as he was better known. His wicked temper was said to be the result of losing his one true love, a lady whom he could not marry as she was of lowly birth. Upon his death his body was confined under a large rock, but his ghost still haunts the stables, grounds and hall.

.....and...any dark night a coach and horses may be seen driven at a mad pace from the Castle and careering around the countryside...beware!

Lowther Church is an ancient building dated somewhere between 1175 and 1300. On the mound to the left of the entrance is where the 5th Earl of Lonsdale is buried. He was known as a noted huntsman, steeplechaser, yachtsman and boxer. As President of the National Sporting Club he founded and presented the 'Lonsdale Belt' for boxing. The Earl was also the first President of the Automobile Association and permitted his family colours to be used by the Association...hence the familiar yellow of the AA signs. He died in 1944 aged 87 years.

The present home of the current Earl is Askham Hall.

Norse hog back gravestones have been discovered in the churchyard dating back to AD 950 which can be seen in the church porch. The mausoleum is where some of the Lowther family have been buried over the years, and the church as to be expected is full of memorials to the family. Also buried here is Jacob Thompson, the artist who died in 1879. He painted landscapes and portraits and was provided with the house called 'The Hermitage' in 1840 by the then Lord Lonsdale.

The 18th century Lowther village is situated between Lowther Newtown and Hackthorpe. In 1682 the old village of Lowther was pulled down by Sir John Lowther, as it was in front of Lowther Hall (the site now of the present castle),,,which he wanted to enlarge.

Between Lowther village and Hackthorpe on the A6 is the Lowther endowed school, founded in 1635 by Sir John Lowther, together with Richard Lowther and John Teasdale (Rector of Lowther).

Mention should also be made of the beautiful Lowther Leisure Park, situated as it is in 150 acres of parkland. Superb attractions, scenic miniature railway, imaginative adventure play area, boating lake, and sporting activities, provide a wonderful day out for people of all ages.

MALLERSTANG.

Map ref. J.9.
Next nearest Town or Village "Nateby"
Location.South of Kirkby Stephen.

Mallerstang is a quiet and unspoilt valley.This is the place where the last wild boar in England was killed in the 16th century.

It is a narrow steep-sided valley between Wild Boar fell and High Sea, both over 2,300 feet. Here on Black Fell Moss the River Eden is born close to the border of Yorkshire.

The charming church of St Mary built in the 14th century.Stained glass window is dedicated to the Saints of Northern England, together with the coat of arms of Lady Anne Clifford.Visitors should note the set of shelves next to the door which in the past held loaves of bread for the poor of the valley. Surprisingly the bread is still distributed today under an 18th century charity.

The church was another of the buildings restored by Lady Anne in 1663. Apparently she often travelled between Appleby and Skipton making stops on the way at Pendragon Castle.The castle is now a ruin which lies just below Outhgill.

This 12th century castle .sometimes referred to as the most romantic ruins in Cumbria, was at one time rebuilt by Lady Anne. Legend says it was the home of Uther Pendragon..the father of King Arthur.

MARDALE.

Map ref. G.8.
Next nearest Town or Village "Shap"
Location. Difficult to locate as doesn't exist any more.

The village of Mardale has to be totally different to the other towns and villages in this book, as being the only one you cannot actually see...and consequently has the reputation of being not only the quietest...but also the least visited.

The village of Mardale once stood at the head of the valley now occupied by Haweswater.In the past it was famous for its dairy produce...at one time sending up to 3,000 pounds of butter each week to the markets in Manchester.

It was in 1929 that everything changed for the residents when Manchester Water Corporation began the building of the dam, in order to raise the level of Haweswater.By 1940 the residents were moved and the valley flooded.

The old school (founded in 1713) was dismantled and rebuilt at Walmgate Head, and today is a private residence..The Dun Bull Inn...one time home of the Mardale Shepherd's is now underwater, as is the old bridge and the church...'a church so small that the parson could touch any of his congregation from the pulpit'.

Most of the Mardale church fittings were removed to other churches and remains from the graveyard were exhumed and re-interred at Shap or elsewhere.' The road which formerly ran along the side of the north-west shore of the lake too was submerged, and a new road nearly five miles long was constructed on the south eastern side to take its place.

The only time since those days when the village has been seen was in the drought conditions days of July 1984, when the interest was such that it needed policeman in attendance to control the crowds of sight seers.

An interesting historical point of the village is that in 1209 Hugh Holme established himself as King of Mardale, with his descendants assuming the title until the death of the last direct descendant in 1885.

MARYPORT,

Map ref. B.6.
Next nearest Town or Village "Flimby"
Bus service. Cumberland Buses Route 30, 58, 300 (Clipper)
Trains.Maryport Railway Station.
Tourist Information Centre. Maritime Museum.Senhouse Street.
Location. A.596 Carlisle/Workington road.
Early closing. Wednesday.
Market day. Friday.
Gala days/festivals. Maryport & District Carnival. 2nd Sat.July.

MARYPORT

Maryport is a small industrial town on the west coast.Though already a port in Roman times, the town and port were first properly planned and developed in the 1750's by Humphrey Senhouse, owner of Netherhall, and the Manor...with the intention of making it a rival to the hugely successful port of Whitehaven...just down the coast.The town incidentally was named after Senhouse's wife..Mary.

It soon became an important port..shipping coal and iron.One local man who made his mark was a Thomas Henry Ismay who founded the White Star Line..the livery of which is still plainly visible on the wreck of the Titanic in 1985 when cameras photographed it on the sea bed.

The main docks were built in the 1850's and 1880's and some of the local publications of the time show how the narrowness of the river meant that breach launchings had to be made...with the ensuing swamping of watching crowds, including the schoolchildren given the day off to watch the event. The harbour was finally closed to shipping in 1961.

Nowadays the South Quay has been remodelled to provide a broad esplanade.What was once the hurly-burly of dockside commercial activity is now a complex of waterfront shops, restaurant, offices, a harbour square, and various specialist shops.The'greyhound' sailing ships which once weighed anchor have now given way to pleasure craft berthed in the modern marina.

After a visit to the harbour and port, complete with its Maritime Museum....why not visit the hill on which the Roman Museum stands, and which provides an ideal viewpoint of the transformation of Maryport

A Roman fort Alauna, north of the Ellen, was first excavated in 1766 and again in the 1960's.It was occupied in the 5th century.At Netherhall is a collection of altars, one of the finest in the country by all accounts, taken from an original fort.Additionally, south of the town is a conspicious mote...an 11th or 12th century castle, of which virtually nothing is known..

The Netherhall mansion , once the home of the Senhouses, is still there today, but in need of attention.Originally a pele tower of the middle ages with extensive 19th century re-building.

Many of Maryport's finest sons have been seafarers.One remarkable centenarian was Joseph Peel who died in 1790 aged 106.In his youth he had sailed in the same ship as Alexander Selkirk...the original Robinson Crusoe, when that unfortunate man was marooned on his Pacific Island.Peel is buried in the parish churchyard.

MARYPORT DOCKS

MATTERDALE.
Map ref. F.8.
Nearest Town or Village "Troutbeck'
Location. 12 miles south-west of Penrith.

The name Matterdale is derived from 'Matterdock'
meaning the madder, a red-rooted plant, that was
once used to make dye.
Matterdale is a parish that runs the length of a
peaceful valley from the main Penrith to Keswick
road to Ullswater...famous for Wordsworth's
daffodils.

'I wandered lonely as a cloud,
That floats on high o'er vales and hills,
When all at once I saw a crowd
a host of golden daffodils
Beside the lake, beneath the trees,
Fluttering and dancing in the breeze.'

......a dale of scattered farms and cottages, with at
one end lying the hamlet of Matterdale End, and
at the other the attractive village of Dockray.
Happily it is known exactly where and when
Wordsworth had this lovely vision, and also who
it was who gave him eyes to see it, and helped him
to interpret it. It was his sister Dorothy. On April
15 1802, the two were staying with Thomas
Clarkson at Eusemere, near Pooley Bridge. As we
know from Dorothy's entry in her Journal for that
day, after their midday meal they set off to walk
along the western side of the lake. When they had
passed round the foot of the lake they rested
awhile in a boathouse. They rested again about
two miles further on, in Watermillock
Lane. Having passed Gowbarrow Park and entered
the wood beyond, approaching Lyulph's Tower
they saw a few daffodils and fancied the lake had
floated the seeds ashore, so close were the flowers
to the water.
But, says Dorothy, "As we went along there were
more and yet more, and at last under the boughs of
the trees we saw that there was a long belt of them
along the shore, about the breadth of a country
turnpike road. I never saw daffodils so
beautiful. They grew among the mossy stones about
and above them, some rested their heads upon these
stones as on a pillow, for weariness, and the rest
tossed and reeled and danced and seemed as if they
verily laughed with the wind, they looked so gay,
ever glancing ever changing"
Matterdale church was built in 1685, though itself
replaces the original smaller church first licensed
in 1573...and today is a typical Cumbrian building
of greystone walls, low pitched slate roof, ancient
beams, and small oblong nave windows.
Simple and dignified it was once a chapel of
Greystoke, and inside it is light and homely, The
sandstone font stands in an old square singing seat
and has had some odd adventures. It was turned out
of Greystoke church more than 200 years ago, it
was used as a cheese press at a hamlet along the

road, and it was put up in this churchyard as a sundial before it found its way into the church.

The Royal Hotel in Dockray, built in the 16th century is famous in its own right for it is said that Mary, Queen of Scots stayed here, and also William and Dorothy Wordsworth.

The famous huntsman Joe Bowman was born at Matterdale in 1850.'Auld Hunty' as Joe was commonly called has been immortalized in a famous hunting song written by Dr Walker who lived at Southport.

MELMERBY,

Map ref.H.6.
Next nearest Town or Village "Gamblesby"
Location. 4 miles north-west of Langwathby.

Melmerby is a small picturesque village situated some four miles north-east of Langwathby, and ten miles east of Penrith, on the edge of the Eden valley...nestling at the foot of Hartside Pass.

It is delightful village at the foot of the Pennines where the road between Penrith and Alston begins to climb Hartside, which rises to 1900 feet on the top of the escarpment. Not far away the Roman road called Maiden Way goes over the fells northward to the Tyne valley. Parts of the road are still traceable where fragments of the original paving are visible. Almost every house here overlooks the village green...itself dissected by three becks with many wild woodland flowers. Each house-holder here has grazing rights, mostly used by horses, though in the past it was more common to see large flocks of geese grazing.

It will be noted that many of the trees in the village have been planted as windbreaks against the cold winter Helm Wind.

The old church of St John the Baptist situated on the edge of the village dates back to 1332 (at least). It has a three decker pulpit and gallery, together with a mediaeval cross-slab and piscina.

The school here was built in 1860 and has a church-like clock tower.

The residents of Melmerby Hall...the Manor House...own several properties and farms in the locality...there has been a Lord of the manor here since the reign of Henry III.

Bakery • Licensed Restaurant
Craft Gallery

Egon Ronay Healthy *Eating Out Place of the Year* 1987
Sunday Times Organic Food Award Winner, Royal Show 1991
Egon Ronay *Tea Place of The Year* 1992
Caroline Walker Award 1992
ADAS/ Sunday Telegraph
Best Speciality Food Award 1993

The Village Bakery was established in 1976 to turn organic English wheat stoneground by waterpower at the local watermill into tasty and nutritious food, producing a wide variety of breads, rolls, pies and cakes. An 18th century stone barn overlooking Melmerby's undulating village green has been converted into a restaurant and bakery with a wood-fired brick oven. Increasing demand for the bakery's products led to the construction in 1991 of a new bakehouse incorporating a larger and more efficient brick oven, fired with the renewable resource of wood. This wood heat not only bakes the bread and warms water for the bakery, but in addition a greenhouse surrounding the brick oven is used to propagate plants for the organic small-holding which supplies the restaurant daily with fresh vegetables and fruit.

THE VILLAGE BAKERY
MELMERBY, PENRITH, CA10 1HE
Tel: 0768 881515

N.B. Our mail order service supplies individual customers wherever they live with a selection of delicious baking. If you would like further information, please write or telephone.

MIDDLETON.

Map ref: H12
Next nearest Town or Village "Barbon"
Location. 5 miles south of Sedbergh.

Set in beautiful countryside, Middleton is bounded on the west by the river Lune with Middleton Fell rising to the east.
Its northern boundary is at Rawthey Bridge where the Lune and Rawthey meet,
At one time a Roman road ran through Middleton and a Roman milestone can still be seen on a hill near the church. An inscription MPL 111 is believed to be the distance(in Roman Miles) to Carlisle.
The church of the Holy Ghost though built in 1878, stands on the foundations of an earlier building dating back to 1634.
Close by is Middleton Hall, once a Manorial residence, now a family farm. It was the home of the Middleton family for centuries. It is a fine 15th century house close to the river.It has a massive outer wall and wide doorways into its spacious courtyard.Its great hall has fine windows and an arched fireplace 400 years old, and another room has much old woodwork over the mantlepiece. Perhaps its chief treasure is a medieaval oak door beautifully panelled and studded with iron.
Middleton is mentioned in the Domesday Book as among the possessions of Torfin.
Two rather attractive old inns..The Swan and Middleton fells (originally the Railway Inn).

MILBURN.

Map ref. H.7.
Next nearest Town or Village "Newbiggin"
Location. 3 miles north-east of Temple Sowerby.

Milburn is a village set around a rectangular green three miles north-east of Temple Sowerby. making it a classic example of a mediaeval fortified village.
The parish is the most northern in old Westmorland and the village has retained its original plan laid down in the 12th century.Always in danger of being destroyed by raiders from Scotland its houses were built facing a spacious green to make a protection for cattle.At each corner of the green are narrow entrances which were walled up each winter, a custom that continued until 150 years ago. Access to the village was made by 'throughgangs'...narrow, easily defended gaps between the houses.
The village green has been used as common land for centuries with some of the present inhabitants still retaining their grazing rights.The maypole still to be seen is believed to have been erected on an ancient Celtic burial site.
Just outside the village is Howgill Castle dating back to the 14th century.Much of the castle has undergone many architectural changes over the centuries. with a great deal of the interior of the two pele towers being beautifully restored, together with the adjoining watermill and currently in regular use.Until comparatively recently the house of an extensive sheep farm, Howgill Castle was originally planned as a semi-fortified house in the 14th century. With walls ten feet thick and two huge towers on each side of a central hall, it still retains something of its early grandeur.
The whole of the south-east front was altered in 1733 but some of the 16th century windows were retained.In the middle of the 18th century Colonel Honeywood, an officer in the Duke of Cumberland's army, owned the castle. It was to this place that he was brought home severely wounded, after the skirmish on Clifton Moor near Penrith, with a rearguard force of Highlanders retreating northward in December 1745. He recovered to be an MP for Appleby for 30 years.
The church of St Cuthberts dates from Norman times, and is built of red sandstone.
An old custom here was Butts Hill Nights when local lads on Saturday nights would remove gates and set them around Butt Hill. Other household goods, such as brooms, buckets, etc would be set around the maypole to be subsequently relieved by the owners the following day.
Built into the wall of Underwood House, within a mile of the church is a Roman inscribed stone, taken from a nearby quarry, and relates to the work of the 20th legion.

MILLOM.

Map ref. C.12.
Next nearest Town or Village "Kirksanton"
Bus service.Cumberland Buses Route 16,15,511,507
Trains.Millom Railway Station.
Tourist Information centre. Millom Folk Museum.
Location. 8 miles south of Broughton in Furness.
Early Closing.Wednesday.
Gala days /festivals.Millom and Broughton Agricultural Show.Last Saturday in August.

Millom was once a small village complete with its Norman castle. To many visitors the town seems out of character with its setting, set as it is in a sparkling landscape of sea, sand and mountains. The estuary of the River Duddon bites deeply into the Millom coastline, and to the north the land rises sharply to the summit of Black Combe Fell.

In the 19th century, it became a boom town.Rich iron ore deposits were discovered south of the town at Hodbarrow in 1843. By 1880 the mine was producing over 300,000 tons of ore annually. The decline (to many regretfully) came in the 1920's

There is a rather pleasant folk museum here which effectively tells the Millom story...its history of the mines...the development of the iron trade.

Millom was the birthplace of Norman Nicholson...the Lake Poet, and the town figures prominently in his poetry and books.
Nearby at Haverigg is an extensive RSPB reserve on the old iron mine site at Hodbarrow, and which shares an artificial lake with a water ski centre. Very many species of sea birds can be seen here.

The parish church of Holy Trinity dates back to the Norman period...in fact during a recent restoration, fragments of a cross shaft and head were found in the north wall of the chancel...the workmanship clearly dating it as late 11th century.
The 14th century Millom Castle stands in a position where lines of approach were limited, and observation easily maintained, and was originally the Hudleston family home. (John Hudleston was the man who administered the last sacrament to Charles 11 at his bedside.)

In its great days the castle stood in a fine park , and though never very big it was very strong, some of the walls still left are seven feet thick.The Lords of Millom wielded power of life and death over a very wide area, and we are vividly reminded of this in what is known as the Gallows Field not far away.

The castle was largely destroyed around 1460 during the War of the Roses, but during the 16th century the pele tower was built and today is the only part of the castle which is inhabited...as a farmhouse!

OLD AND NEW MACHINERY

MILLOM FOLK MUSEUM

BROCKWOOD HALL

THE PERFECT PLACE.....THE PERFECT SETTING....

WHICHAM VALLEY Nr. MILLOM, CUMBRIA LA18 5JS
Telephone: (0229) 772329

Brockwood hall is a handsome Victorian country house, which has been tastefully furnished and decorated to an exceptional standard, situated on the southern edge of the lake District National park. Surrounded by 26 acres of delightful gardens where rhododendrons, azaleas, and camellias provide an exquisite array of blossoms in the spring months. Brockwood Hall is situated in a densely wooded elevated position especially attractive in autumn when the leaves turn magnificent shades of red, yellow and gold.

This woodland is teeming with wildlife, including fox, roe deer, and of course the badgers, who can be watched from a special observation hide. A fantastic nature trail in fact starts from the well equipped children's play areas.

Close to the hall with it's bar and dining room facilities, yet hidden among the trees, are thirty award winning Norwegian style lodges, designed to blend into the woodland setting. Brockwood is undoubtedly the perfect place for getting to know the Lake District with its fascinating landscape which changes constantly throughout the year. Four styles of Norwegian designed lodges, sleeping from 4 to 6, are available, the Derwent two bedroom with patio, Maple 2 bedroom with sauna, the Helvellyn two bedrooms, large lounge, sauna and verandah and the Windermere's, 3 bedroom 11/2 bathrooms and large lounge & verandah. Timber built, blending subtly into their rural setting they are nevertheless within easy reach of the Hall, Leisure Centre and play areas. All are detached and situated to give varying degrees of privacy or view. Each is fully heated, triple or double glazed and well insulated. They are just as cosy in winter as they are comfortable in summer. The interior of each lodge is pine clad, traditionally furnished and carpeted. Each has a modern fitted kitchen with ample cupboards and modern tiled bathrooms. All have colour television, video recorder and telephone.

Situated in the heart of the resort is the leisure centre. Its focus is a heated pool and whirlpool spa, which overlooks a large patio and lawns leading onto the childrens play areas. Sauna, sunbed and exercise rooms are all available. All the leisure centre facilities are included in the realistically priced rental tariff. Brockwood is open all year round, and our short breaks offer excellent value getaways with the choice of days tailored to suit your needs.

....and for those with a healthy appetite a warm elcome awaits you in our restaurant. Here we serve good food and wine in a friendly relaxed atmosphere, thus ensuring that you have a truly memorable evening "away from it all". We have created a wide choice of dishes to suit most tastes. Every night our house menu offers something for everyone from home-made chicken and mushroom pie to the famous Brockwood Mixed Grill, whilst along side this, our home-made daily specials represent excellent value for money.

MILNTHORPE.

Map ref.G.12.
Next nearest Town or Village "Heversham"
Bus service Cumberland Buses Route 552
Location. 10 miles south of Kendal,Lancaster road.
Early closing.Thursday.
Market day. Friday.
Gala days/festivals.Burton,Milnthorpe and
Carnforth Show.Last Thursday in August (held at
Carnforth)

Milnthorpe sits astride the A6 between Kendal and Lancaster, north to south and Arnside to Crooklands west to east.

A market town from the 13th century, close to the Kent estuary..it was one time Westmorland's only port. The river Bela skirts the south-west corner of the village, running past the comb mill (still manufacturing combs today) and through the Dallam Tower Park..Dallam Tower built 1320.....on its way to meet the estuary. Until as recently as 1880 the Bela was navigatable as far as the Strands, now a riverside walk.

In the 18th century a main source of industry here was the importation of sulphur and saltpetre for the gunpowder works of the South Lake District...afterwards exporting the gunpowder to Liverpool.

Architectural features of the village are the folly at St Anthony's Hill, known as St Anthony's Tower (or the Summerhouse) and the Market cross on the square.The 'cross' as such doesn't exist anymore, but a weather-worn 'crying'stone for proclamations does. In the past it also served as the whipping post for local wrongdoers. At the end of the square is the fountain, once the main village well...the spring can still be seen underneath the grating.

There are still several greens dotted around the village, the largest one being in front of the Victorian church of St Thomas.

HOBBY CERAMIC STUDIO

MORESBY,

Map ref. A.8.
Next nearest Town or Village "Whitehaven"
Bus service. Cumberland Buses Route 27
Location. Just over 1 miles from Whitehaven.

One and a half miles from Whitehaven stands Moresby Hall...though today it is a private guest house

Anyone well versed in the mysterious Druid Lore would be advised to pay a visit, for says legend, a vast fortune lies buried here somewhere...guarded so it is said by fairies...and the information only being released to someone who has that special Druid knowledge.

However there are two other pre-requisites necessary before that special person can lay claim to the fortune.

Firstly he must be there at the right time, that is on the one night of the year when an enchanted lake forms in the vaults beneath the house, from the fairy fountain, and secondly he must hear the dirge-like song wailed by the swan who glides across the lake, lamenting the extinction of the Moresbys.

The person fortunate enough to fulfill all three conditions will then have the power to enter the vaults, stop the flow of water, and retrieve the treasure....Now,that doesn't sound too difficult does it?

Apparently there has been a settlement at Moresby since these days of the Roman occupation...possibly long before. The Romans built a fort here but were so strongly influenced by the Celtic culture that they built altars not only to their Roman Gods but to the Celtic Gods Rosmerta and Sylvanue too.

With the departure of the Romans and the arrival of the Christian missionaries Moresby again found itself in a sphere of influence for one of the nunneries dedicated to St Bridget was founded here in the sixth century.

The present day church of St Bridget lies within the ruins of the Roman fort and at one time an underground secret passage connected the church and Moresby Hall. The church is a formal little place with many pictures in its windows, and paintings on the pulpit of Christ teaching and Matthew and Paul with their books. On each side of the chancel arch is a bishop's head. A holy-water stoup, a stone coffin lid marked with shears and a cross, and a stone-head, all came from the old church, whose 13th century chancel arch stands in the churchyard.

The Moresby family (the name incidentally means 'Maurices Place') came into prominence after the Norman Conquest. The Moresby of the day found it expedient to offer his loyalty to the new ruling House in exchange for the priviledge of retaining his land and property. From that point on the Moresby's never looked back. Advantageous marriages and loyal service to king and countries didn't do them any harm either...and increased their holdings. Several of them made their mark in other ways too, such as the Moresby youth who ganged up with other wild individuals and raided Fountains Abbey, making off with a haul of gold plate and jewels. He was apparently hastily packed off to the wars where he distinguished himself at Agincourt.

A few generations later a daughter lived to inherit Moresby...a pattern that was to be repeated in Tudor times. The heiress was unfortunate in her choice of husband, for he became romantically involved with Anne Boleyn, and Henry VIII certainly had no compunction in sending him to a similar fate that had befallen others who had upset him. It was this lady's son who sold Moresby Hall to the Fletchers of Cockermouth.

The Fletchers must have had a soft spot for the Royal Stuarts of Scotland...One earned fame in 1568 when Mary Queen of Scots sought refuge in England after the Battle of Langside. Because Cockermouth was unfit at that time to offer accommodation to the illustrious refugee, Henry Fletcher was asked to provide lodgings for her. He went the extra distance, he also gave her a rich velvet gown in which to receive all the wealthy folk from the district who called to pay their respects, a kindness which paid off in the next generation for Mary's son James knighted Henry's son when he became James 1 of England.

MORLAND.

Map ref. H.8.
Next nearest Town or Village " Newby"
Location. 5 miles west of Appleby.

The village of Morland in the Eden Valley is situated five miles west of Appleby and eight miles south-east of Penrith.To many it is a picture postcard village.

Morland's St Laurence's church has the only 11th century Saxon tower in Cumbria still in use today...worth visiting if only for that reason. It's the two lower storeys that date from the 11th century...the upper storeys from the 16th and 17th centuries.

Inside is a beautifully carved coffin lid, with leaves growing from the stem of its cross, which looks little older than the day it was carved nearly 700 years ago. The foot has a 17th century bowl and a carved pyramid cover as old as itself, but its stem and base are mediaeval, as is some ironwork on the north door.Some old timbers are in the roofs, and from the 17th century come the altar rails, some panelling in the aisles, a chest, and a poor box dated 1648. The splendid carved oak in the chancel is the work of a man who lived before America was known in Europe, a man with a rare sense of humour for his 22 heads are as quaint as anything seen in the county...kings, queens, bishops,monks,angels, patriachs, and a demon in their midst.

In 1362 the village obtained a grant to hold a weekly market, together with an annual fair. It was in addition an important coaching centre.The main street..,Water Street, follows the beck and mill race.There are two small footbridges and a yard which lead to the village green.Near the beck stands the old Quaker Meeting House (now a private house).

Look for several old lime kilns which can be seen hereabouts.

One lane here is where to celebrate the defeat of the Armada, the churchwardens ordered the founding of a new church bell.At the end of the lane is a lovely old house known as 'Little Appleby'.The name is derived from a story in the Middle Ages when a plague struck Appleby and a grant was given for the Appleby Gypsy Fair to be held in Morland for the duration.

There is an abundance of wildlife in this area, along with red squirrels and deer.

Beside the church, the oldest property here is a farmhouse dated 1709. It lies over the bridge and waterfall and has a semi-circular horse engine house (or ginn gann) where a team of horses walking around powered the earlier threshing machines.

One of the most delightful houses in the district is Newby hall, now a farmhouse ,standing above the village of Newby...it has well-kept lawns and a flagged pathway through a colourful garden that leads to the main door. Above, set in a red sandstone panel is the much-weathered 17th century coat of arms of the Newison family and on a lintel are initials and the date 1685. The Hall between two wings has its original arched fireplace, nine feet wide, and in the kitchen is a bake-stone,once a feature in Cumbrian houses.Many of the rooms are panelled and have exceptionally thick walls.

MUNGRISDALE.

Map ref.E.7.
Next nearest Town or Village "Threlkeld"
Location. 10 miles north-west of Keswick.

Mungrisdale is a village east of Saddleback...at least it's a village as far as visitors are concerned...to the locals it is beautiful, unspoilt Cumbrian valley and which includes not only Mungrisdale, but also the smaller hamlets of Bowscale and Mosedale.

On three sides it is protected by steep green fells, and on the fourth it looks away from Lakeland to gentle hills and the woodlands of Greystoke. Whitewashed farm houses stand against a background of blue hills and Glenderamackin Beck tumbles down from Scales Tarn to flow by the village on its way to join the Greta.

Bowscale was at one time on the itinerary of the gentry visiting the lakes. They would travel by carriage along the gated road from Keswick, and then walk up the long track above the valley to view Bowscale Tarn. The tarn is set in a wild and rugged place surrounded by majestic crags.

The story goes that because of its position surrounded by high quarry like ridge, together with its great depth, it is possible to see the stars in the tarn at midday. The tarn is also famous for its two immortal fish that are said to live in the waters. In the mid eighteenth century local people watched in amazement as on one occasion troops of soldiers marched across the fell top, then on a later occasion the troops were mounted. These surprising sights were not over in a flash, they took up to two and a half hours in the late

ST. KENTIGERN

evening. The observers were so ridiculed, that about ten years later, in 1746, when there was a lot of troop movements in Scotland, and the same phenomen appeared, they watched for a while then mustered all their neighbours to join in. Twenty six people swore to a magistrate what they had seen and that they were sober, honest people.

The church here was built anew a few years after the spectres were seen, and it has hardly changed since. It stands by the roadside, very plain and white with a little porch which has a cobbled floor, an old oak door opens to a light interior which has a view from every window. Some of its possessions from an earlier church are the 15th century bell, the Black Letter Bible of 1617, and the panelled three-decker pulpit. There is a row of old hat pegs on the wall, a quaint little font like a pillar, and a tablet to Raisley Calvert whose son Raisley was 'nursed by Wordsworth'

Near Howe

If you are looking for that quiet away from it all holiday, then Near Howe and Grisdale View are the ideal answer. Standing just one mile off the A66 trunk road, it is easily accessible and yet isolated enough to ensure you of the peace and tranquillity you are seeking.

Near How is a traditional old Cumbrian Farmhouse standing in 380 acres of rolling moorland in the midst of the Cumbrian Fell Country.

There are seven bedrooms, most of which have their own facilities, a comfortable residents lounge with colour television, a games room, a smaller lounge with a well stocked bar and for the cooler evenings a large open log fire.

Or - Self catering

Grisdale View is one of three cottages beautifully converted from an old barn with views over the fells. The cottages have also been furnished to a high standard.

You will have the run of the large well tended garden of Near Howe Hotel and also the use of the well stocked bar in the hotel in the evenings.

Accommodation: Comfortable living room with kitchen, dining area, cooker, microwave, fridge/freezer, toaster. Bathroom - bath with electric shower over, W.C., wash basin and shaver socket, heater, fully carpeted throughout. Two bedrooms; one double and one with two single beds which make into a double if need be. All beds have duvets.

There is one large laundry which you have the use of the washing machine and tumble drier are coin operated.

Cumbrian Farmhouse Comfort

The resident proprietors Mr. and Mrs. Weightman ensure you of a warm, country welcome and will help in any way they can to make your holiday as pleasant, comfortable and relaxing as you desire. They are also justifiably proud of their home cooking, with every meal freshly prepared and using, wherever possible, produce from the surrounding farming community. All meals are served in their beautifully appointed and homely dining room.

If you are having days off touring, there are a number of good places for a light lunch or a bar lunch or, if you order the evening before, Mrs. Weightman will provide you with a packed lunch.

Children and pets are very welcome and we hold a full fire certificate.

Mungrisdale, Penrith, Cumbria, CA11 0SH
Tel/Fax. 07687 79678

MUSGRAVE.

Map ref. J.9.
Next nearest Town or Village "Brough"
Location. 2 miles south-west of Brough.
Gala days/festivals. Rushbearing Ceremony
1st Saturday July.
Industrial and Horticultural Show..
Beginning Sept.

Musgrave is a parish situated in the upper Eden Valley, and is divided into the two townships of Great and Little Musgrave. Its just two miles west of Brough and a mile to the east of the A66. The village stands on a hill and commands fine views of the Eden Valley and the Pennines.

The parish church of St. Theobald was built in 1845, and is the third to be built here. The tower contains two pre-Reformation bells supposedly cast early in the 15th century and bearing Latin inscriptions.

It is thought that the old manor house once stood in a field next to the farm, these days known as Hallgarth. The field contains some of the best examples of the pre-historic cultivation terraces, known as lynchets, to be found in the country.

The manorial rights granted by William the Conqueror were dissolved in 1914.

NATEBY & WHARTON.

Map ref. J.9.
Next nearest Town or Village "Kirkby Stephen"
Location. 1 mile south of Kirkby Stephen

A hamlet in a deep valley one mile south-east of Kirkby Stephen near Stenkrith Bridge. The villages lies in the upper Eden valley and are joined by a footbridge.

At the centre of Nateby is a small village green with a shady sycamore, commemorating the victory of World War 1. Facing the green The Black Bull inn proudly wears its old AA plaque informing motorists that it is 266 miles to London.

The oldest building in Wharton is Lammerside Castle, now a ruin, believed to have been built in the 13th century to guard the pass between Wild Boar Fell and High Seat. It was built by the DeQuerton's. Over the years the name has changed to the present Wharton. A second stronghold was built further down the Eden. This is now Wharton Hall and it began life in the 15th century when it was built by Hugh de Querton. Today it is a fortified farmhouse with gatehouse and courtyard...it is however privately owned and not open to the public.

For historians it should be noted that the most colourful of the Wharton's was Thomas, who prospered in the reign of Henry V111. In 1560 Thomas made himself a deer park by enclosing land from Wharton over to Ravenstonedale and turning out his tenant farmers.

NATLAND & OXENHOLME.

Map ref. G.11.
Next nearest Town or Village "Kendal"
Bus service. Cumberland Buses Routes 41, 41a, 553
Trains. Oxenholme Railway Station
Location. 1 mile south of Kendal.

A chapelry south of Kendal, which embraces the two villages of Natland and Oxenholme.

Both share St Mark's church in Natland, and are dominated by Helm, a hill of Silurian rock 605 feet above sea level.

There is a Wishing Tree that stands along the footpath bordering the western side of Helm. For innumerable years persons passing under this tree would make a wish, and at the same time place a small stone in the wall under the tree. Tradition says that any backward glance at the tree invalidates the wish.

St Mark's church is comparatively new having been built in 1910, though it did replace earlier churches on the same site. There is something substantial about the church with its tall tower and even taller stair turret, and inside there is dignity in the spacious nave and strength in the graceful arches, and in the enormous pillars supporting the walls of the tower.

St Mark's Boys Home for Waif's and strays' was an important feature of the village. It is now run as a holiday centre for disadvantaged children...under the control of the Children's Society.

The Lancaster to Kendal canal on the west side of the village was at one time busy bringing coal to Kendal. Unfortunately it has now been filled in, and parts of it are popular footpaths.

Oxenholme meaning 'a place where oxen came to drink' made its debut as a village with the opening of the mainline railway to Scotland from the south.

The story of the village goes back to the days when the Romans had two camps close by. One was a sort of look-out post built on the ruins of a British fortress on Helm Hill, where there is a glorious view, the other was a bigger station 500 feet long and 400 feet wide, protected on three sides by a loop of the River Kent known as Watercrook. Of this stronghold, a great Roman post in Agricolas day, a few green mounds remain, and hereabouts have been found many treasures, among them an inscribed gravestone and an altar now in the British Museum. The gravestone has a quaint inscription to a soldier of the 20th Legion, and ends with the odd threat that anyone putting another body in his grave will be fined.

NEAR & FAR SAWREY,

Map ref. E.11.
Next nearest Town or Village "Hawkshead"
Location. 2 miles south of Hawkshead

The two Sawreys are approximately half a mile apart, and about two miles from Hawkshead. Basically they consist of a few large Victorian houses and farms.Besides the road route the other way to get there is by ferry across Windermere.

The village of Sawrey, can in one respect, call itself modestly famous, for it was the home of Beatrix Potter.
For the last thirty years of her life, long after Peter Rabbit and the other nursery masterpieces were written, she lived there ,the retired but busy life of a wealthy farmer, in the long, low but unpretentious house known as Castle Cottage.

But Castle Cottage was not her first home in Sawrey, nor the one she loved best.She moved into it when,late in life, she married a country solicitor, and thought that the luxury of more space was due to her middle-aged husband William Heelis. From the upper windows of Castle Cottage she could see across the apple trees and the Post Office meadow to that little farmhouse that, as visitors will soon discover, cannot be seen from the road..a roughcast, slate roofed building which looks away from the village and is cunningly hidden behind the Tower Bank Arms...the little farm that she had bought with her first earnings...and which she could never afterwards bear to alter or relinquish. Its name is Hill Top.

"BUCKLE YEAT" IN BEATRIX POTTER'S BOOK

Most of the people who come to Hill Top today, now that it belongs to the National Trust and is subsequently open to the public...all do so because they loved Beatrix Potter's books when they were children, and have an affectionate impression at the back of their minds of the kind of surroundings in which those books were written.If they remember them really intimately, they will see that Hill Top *is* the farm of Jemima Puddleduck, that it *is* Tom Kitten's house, that the front door is the very one at which Cousin Ribby knocked, and that the long narrow garden path *is* the identical path the policeman came up looking for Pigling Bland.

..In fact no less than six of her nursery classics are intimately concerned with Hill Top Farm and Sawrey. Beatrix Potter loved Hill Top so much that when she married at the age of forty-seven she could not bring herself to alter it. Instead she bought Castle Cottage, a few hunded yards away and al-

SAWREY
HOUSE COUNTRY
HOTEL

SAWREY HOUSE COUNTRY HOTEL offers you a very special combination of comfort and elegance set amidst the stunning beauty and tranquility of the Lakeland fells. This delightful Victorian house looks down over three acres of garden to Esthwaite Water below a view shared by Beatrix Potter herself during the many years she lived at neighbouring Hilltop.

Our centrally heated hotel is open all the year round, truly a place for all seasons, from the brilliance of early spring, through the peace of an English summer, to autumn's gold and winter's frosty majesty.

Inside the hotel, enjoy a drink before dinner in our comfortable lounge bar, while next door in the spacious dining room take care lest the panoramic views distract too greatly from the delicious food....and afterwards, retire to the elegant lounge for coffee and conviviality or perhaps outside for an evening stroll or game of croquet on the lawn.

Our homely comfortable bedrooms are attractively furnished, and most have private bathrooms. We provide for children of all ages in our family rooms and well-behaved dogs are also most welcome and may be brought into the bar. One ground floor bedroom is also available.

We cook for pleasure, your pleasure! We'll set you up for the day with a hearty Lakeland breakfast, and the daily four course dinner menu also caters for vegetarians and those with special dietary needs. We will gladly supply packed lunches on request.

As proprietors, we run the hotel entirely ourselves, offering a personal service to all our guests. Situated in a quiet valley but close to the heart of the lakes. Sawrey House is also an excellent centre for walking and touring the area and provides an ideal setting for special celebrations and functions. We are open for Christmas and the New Year.

Come to Sawrey House Hotel and look upon the very same spectacular scenery which inspired Beatrix Potter years ago. Here you will find the peace of those bygone days in which to enjoy quiet luxury, excellent food and caring hospitality. Why not join us for a while?

Our Potters View Tea Parlours open seven days a week, for morning coffee, light lunches and afternoon tea.

Near Sawrey, Ambleside,
Cumbria LA22 0LF
Tel: Hawkshead (05394) 36387

SAWREY
HOUSE COUNTRY
HOTEL

Beechmount is a large spacious country house beautifully situated in the picturesque village of near Sawrey, where Beatrix Potter's intriguing house "Hill Top" stands close by to "The Tower Bank Arms", a delightful olde worlde, village inn serving good food and fine Cumbrian ales.

Beechmount provides extremely good accommodation in a relaxed, comfortable and friendly atmosphere. All bedrooms have individual heating, electric blankets, tea/coffee making facilities, colour televisions, radios and hairdryers. Some with superb, panoramic views over Lake Esthwaite to the Langdales in the distance, en-suite rooms are available. Downstairs there is a large guest lounge and of course the lovely dining room where we serve from a wide choice of large sumptuous wholefood breakfasts. For those who enjoy the peaceful countryside, there are delightful walks from the door, within minutes you can be up in the hills with spectacular views, beautiful tarns, lakes and woods or go across to Grizedale Forest with its fascinating walks amongst most unusual wooden sculptures. Beechmount is just 2 miles from Lake Windermere car ferry and 2 miles from Hawkshead.

You will find Beechmount an excellent place in which to stay for a break or for a Cumbrian holiday.

BEECHMOUNT

Country House Accommodation
Near Sawrey, Hawkshead, Ambleside,
Cumbria LA22 0JZ. Tel: (05394) 36356

CONT.

tered that instead...keeping Hill Top as a sort of sanctuary and private burrow of her very own, where she could potter about at will and conceal her odds and ends and personal treasures. And there, you will still find many of them. The four poster bed for example, the family Bible. Her French dolls are there, together with miniatures and photographs of the children for whom many of her books were originally written. The dolls house in the upstairs room is not the original, but inside will be found the actual dolls house food that Tom Thumb and Hunca Munca stole.

Besides Hill Top also to be visited is St Peter's Church nearby built in 1869. A walk from here to Esthwaite is recommended. Its the quiet lane so loved by Wordsworth as a boy.

"OLD SMITHY" IN BEATRIX POTTER'S BOOK

NENTHEAD.

Map ref. J.5.
Next nearest Town or Village "Alston"
Location. 5 miles south of Alston.
Gala days/festival. Nenthead Rose Queen
& Carnival 1st Sat June.

A village and chapelry five miles south of Alston and for centuries the centre of a thriving lead mining industry, together with its association with the finding of silver and zinc in the region. Those strange lumps and hollows on the hillside you will see bear witness to the work of the miners as do many mine entrances still to be seen around.

For around 400 years lead was the sole industry...thousands worked in the valley, and the influence of John Wesley made the area a stronghold of Methodism. Nenthead was the second village in Cumbria to have street lighting.

All around you here is the grandeur of the mountain scenery and the impressive list of records which it claims to hold...Here with the high road climbing to about 2000 feet, everything seems to be the highest of its kind in England.Here you will find the highest house, the highest vicarage,the highest parish church, and a methodist chapel claiming to be nearer to heaven than any other place of worship in the country.

The church, worth investigating, has a reading desk with two poppyheads 600 years old, and there is a little 14th century work in the altar rails.The organ incidentally has been made from a barrel organ, and still has some of the old machinery, with a list of the ten tunes played.

Hereabouts the River Nent rises, and we see it flowing among rocks and trees on its way to Alston. A waterfall is seen from the road, and there is an underground canal not far away.

NEWBIGGIN on LUNE.

Map ref. I.9.
Next nearest Town or Village "Ravenstonedale"
Bus service. Cumberland Buses Route 508
Location. A.685. Tebay to Kirkby Stephen road,
Gala days/festivals.Ravenstonedale Agricultural
Show. 3rd Saturday August.

A village near Ravenstonedale, 18 miles from Kendal and in the shadow of Howgill Fells.

Here there is still evidence of the industry of the Sempringham monks and their cross-wise ploughing,cultivating the land.On Chapel Butts they practised archery.They also had a fish pond, the sluice of which was discovered earlier this century when the beck was being lowered. These men were garbed in cassocks of sheep's wool with white cloaks, and St Helen's Well, edged with blue forget-me-knots, still bubbles up in the field where so many years ago they lived out their quiet and useful lives, educating the peasants and de-

fending them against marauders, since in these times the parish was still feudal.

Later, the Manor of Ravenstonedale, of which Newbiggin is a part was ruled by a 'peculiar Court', consisting of '24 Worthy men' drawn from the four 'Angles' of the parish.

At Betsy Croft in the centre of the village, a spinning gallery remains, restored to something like its original, with an outside stone stairway and adjacent room where the greasy pungent fleeces were stored until the whirr of the spinning wheel began. Before and during the 19th century, as in Ravenstonedale itself and all surrounding villages, much knitting was done, and men and children, as well as the women folk were busily engaged in knitting coarse but warm garments.

Here too is a small single storied building at one time the communal bakery...where housewives would bring their bread to be baked.Low Yard was the venue for a market held twice weekly.

NEWBY.

Map ref. H.8.
Next nearest Town or Village"Morland"
Location. 10 miles south-east of Penrith.

Once known as Newby Stones, Newby is situated just over a mile from Morland and is one of the townships of that parish.

It is thought that the name relates to the several old limestone quarries to be found along the Lansmere Road, and west of the village in Stonehills.

The hamlet consists of little more than a collection of several farms and some older stone cottages. An old Quaker graveyard is close by. Newby Hall once the Manor House is still here, though these days is a hotel. Its worth investigating the grand fireplace and Jacobean windows.

At Cross House a plague stone has been set into the garden wall. During the plague in the late 16th and 17th centuries, vinegar was put into the plague stone to wash and disinfect the coins prior to collection by suppliers.

Roman remains have been found hereabouts indicating occupation here for many centuries.

NEWBY BRIDGE

Map ref. E.12.
Next nearest Town or Village "Backbarrow"
Bus service. Cumberland Buses Route 518
Trains. Lakeside & Haverthwaite Railway near.
Tourist Information Centre. Fell Foot Country Park (National trust)
Location. 10 miles south of Windermere.

HAVERTHWAITE RAILWAY

Newby Bridge is in the parish of Staveley in Cartmel, on the banks of the Leven, where at one time the monks of Cartmel Priory had a flour mill. It has had a long history, all of which has been powered by water from the river. The long closed mill has changed many times from its beginnings in the early days, when very young orphans from Liverpool and London were the major work force. After the mill closed down it was eventually taken over by the Lancashire Ultramarine Company, and finally by the well known company of Reckitt & Colman. Both of these companies made industrial blue for laundering purposes, the dust from their tall chimneys (now demolished) used to stain everything around blue.

The most famous and long lasting of local furnaces was also sited here. The Backbarrow Iron Furnace, with the famous John Wilkinson as ironmaster opened here in 1711, and its remains can still be seen by the traveller curious enough to turn off the bypass here.

It was here at Backbarrow that young John Wilkinson (1728-1808) began his amazing career which was to make him the greatest ironmaster of the eighteenth century, and a seminal figure in the Industrial Revolution. He worked with his father at Backbarrow, where he invented the box iron...much esteemed by laundresses for making the fancy lace frills of the period, and where he experimented with iron boats on the River Leven, an idea he was to develop later on the River Severn, the first practical iron boats the world had seen. Today the mill building has been tastefully turned into the Whitewater Hotel and time-share lodges, collectively better known as "The Lakeland Village'.

Just up the hill near where the Victorian School was located, is the 'headmaster house' still known locally as 'The School House'. Also nearby is Bigland Hall, home of the one-time squires.

One mile north of here is the Stott Park Bobbin Mill, a working mill and museum of woodland industries., and of course not to be over-looked is the Lakeside and Haverthwaite Railway which operates steam trains in summer from Haverthwaite to connect with the passenger ships from Windermere.

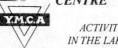

ENGLISH HERITAGE
Stott Park Bobbin Mill Cumbria

Set amongst magnificent scenery near Windermere, Stott Park is a living monument to one of the small but crucial technologies that drove the Industrial Revolution.

Built in 1835, the mill was typical of many mills all over Lakeland which grew up to supply the cotton and weaving industry of Lancashire with vast quantities of wooden bobbins. Over the years it turned its versatile lathes to wooden objects of all kinds, and continued in use right up until 1971.long after many of its contemporaries had disappeared. Now preserved as a working museum, Stott Park provides a remarkable opportunity to see a demonstration of 19th century machinery and techniques. When you enter the mill today, it is as though you have stepped back a hundred years, to experience at first hand the conditions in which the bobbin-makers worked. You can see how entire tree trunks from the Lakeland forests were fashioned, under one roof, into finished bobbins, on machines once driven by Lakeland streams.

The mill now features a working static steam engine which can be seen in operation and is typical of the kind which once powered the machinery in tandem with a water turbine, thus replacing the original water wheel.

SPECIAL FEATURES
Steam engine, bobbin turning, guided tours (about 30-45 minutes) Exhibition: colour guide book.

FACILITIES
Access for visitors in wheelchairs to ground floor: toilets: car park.

ADMISSION 1994
1 April - 31 October : Open daily 10am-17.45 (or dusk if earlier)

Last tour 5.00pm. Steam engine operates on Tues/Wed/Thurs with some additional days. Telephone for details.

Adult £2.20 Concessions £1.65 Junior £1.10

15% Discount on groups over 11.

Free Admission normally available to organised groups of students.

HOW TO GET THERE
On Newby Bridge Hawkshead road 1/2 mile N of lakeside on W shore of Lake Windermere Bus: 518 (Ulverston-Ambleside) to within 1 1/2 miles

For further information (and details of days when steam engine operates) Call 05395 31087.

Oak Head Caravan Park
Ayside
Grange-over-Sands
Cumbria, LA11 6JA
Tel. 05395 31475

Holiday Caravans for sale and to let
(1 Bungalow to Rent)
Touring Caravans & Tents welcome

THE CARAVAN PARK is licensed for 71 statics, 30 tourers, 30 tents. It is wooded, quiet, select secluded and very pleasant, set in the picturesque fells of South Cumbria. It is situated on the A590 main road. Two miles south of Newby Bridge, and sixteen miles from M6 Motorway, junction 36. The Caravan Park is sign posted on the side of the A590 main road. 4.5 miles Grange-over-Sands; 11 miles Windermere; 10 miles Bowness.

The nearest railway station and open air swimming pool are at Grange-over-Sands.

The site is well situated for touring all the places of interest in the Lake District, also within easy driving distance of Morecambe and Blackpool.

ACTIVITIES - Boating, fishing, sailing, canoeing, horse-riding within two miles of the site. Free access to Lake for boats, 5 miles, public slipway charged at Windermere and Ambleside. Tours from Haverthwaite to Ambleside via old steam trains and boats on the lake. **ON SITE** - Flush toilets - mains water, hot and cold water to hand basins, hot showers, deep sinks and spin dryer for laundry. Caravans are not crowded; on their own private stand with car space.

Shop - Shop and Garage - one mile from site.

Don't miss our privately owned old car collection.

Whitewater Hotel

The Lakeland Village, Newby Bridge,
Cumbria LA12 8PX
Telephone: 05395 31133 Fax: 05395 31881

Enjoy gracious hospitality and attentive service at the Whitewater Hotel

Originally a mill, this centuries-old building has fulfilled many varied roles as a landmark of the locality, but none so glamorous as its transformation into the Whitewater Hotel. Its stone and slate construction is characteristic of the Lake District, and an impressive five storeys now boast all that is best in modern hotel design and decor, There are 35 bedrooms, consisting of single, double, twin, triple, family and and king size with the largest bedroom boasting a four poster bed. Some have balconies overlooking the river. All the bedrooms have bathroom and shower en-suite. The emphasis is on comfort with furnishings of the highest standard. Remote control television and satellite, direct dial telephone, radio, tea and coffee making facilities and a well-stocked refrigerated mini bar are provided.

In the hotel restaurant which overlooks the terrace and fast flowing waters of the River Leven you can enjoy the delicious meals selected from our extensive menu supplemented by our varied wine list. You have a residents' lounge and bar in which to relive your day over a quiet drink. Experience the traditional atmosphere of the Fisherman's Bar. This popular meeting place also provides bar meals which you may wish to enjoy either in the bar or on the riverside terrace. On certain evenings during the week live entertainment is provided. The hotel has ample parking space for residents and guests.

The Cascades Experience!

The health and Leisure Club occupies a purpose-built complex next to the Hotel, and offers a variety of exercise and sporting activities with expert advisers, together with a health spa staffed by fully trained beauty therapists. As a resident, you have free use of the heated indoor swimming pool and whirlpool, and the fully equipped exercise studio. Relax in the spacious lounge areas, or on a sunbed. It is sheer bliss to slip into the temperature-controlled, ozone-purified waters of the indoor leisure pool...invigorating to experience the whirlpool...so relaxing to recline in a sunlounger by the poolside or on the riverside terrace. Overlooking the pool is the lounge where light meals and refreshments may be enjoyed throughout the day.

Luxury at the gateway to the English Lakes

NEWBY BRIDGE HOTEL

Newby Bridge Hotel occupies a commanding position overlooking the southern shores of Lake Windermere. It is probably one of the oldest hotels in the region and retains a wealth of period features.

Guests can either eat in the glorious old bar which is very popular with locals or in the oak panelled restaurant.

All meals are prepared from fresh local ingredients wherever possible and you can be sure of a first class meal at a reasonable price. There are special vegetarian and children's menus.

All bedrooms offer the following facilities:
* En-Suite bathroom or shower
* Tea & Coffee making facilities
* Remote control TV with satellite channels
* Direct-dail telephones
* Radio
*Alarm call facility.

NEWBY BRIDGE HOTEL has its own mooring on Lake Windermere which is available for the use of Hotel residents. Guests may also take advantage of the Hotel's fishing rights at no extra charge....a wide variety of fish including salmon have been caught here! Other attractions within five minutes' drive of the Hotel include the steam trains at Haverthwaite and the Lake Windermere Steamers which sail from the pier at Lakeside. Golfers are very well catered for...there are three 18 hole courses nearby, Grange, Ulverston & Windermere.

Newby Bridge, Near Ulverston,
Cumbria LA12 8NA
Telephone: 05395 31222

NEWTON ARLOSH.

Map ref. D.4.
Next Town or Village "Kirkbride"
Bus service.Cumberland Buses Route 71
Location. 2 miles south of Kirkbride.

Newton Arlosh...meaning 'New town on the Marsh'..owes its existence to the misfortunes of Skinburness...which was swept away by sea in 1301, and the inhabitants moved to a safer spot. Sometime called Longnewton, due to its being a long straggling village, this 'settlement' was originally founded in 1301 by the monks of Holm Cultram Abbey.It is situated on the B5307 road between Abbeytown and Kirkbride.

ST. JOHNS CHURCH

The main feature of the village is undoubtedly the church of St John the Evangelist.Erected in 1303 by Holm Cultram Abbey it is thought that it was built on the foundations of an existing church...St Ninian's of around AD400. The present church is noted for its pele tower, which originally served as a refuge. By 1580 it was in a bad state of decay, but fortunately restored to its present condition in 1844.

The church door it will be noted is only 2 feet seven inches thick, and it is said that at a wedding the first of the bridal pair out of the church will be the boss.

NIBTHWAITE.

Map ref. E.11.
Next nearest Town or Village "Lowick Bridge"
Location. Southern tip of Coniston Water.

This idyllic village is situated on the east side of Lake Coniston, and inspired much of the writing of Arthur Ransome.

It has always been an important village. The monks of Conishead Priory used to fish from the lake in the 12th century. Later the lake was used for transporting various items including charcoal slates and gunpowder. There were many landing places stretching from Water Park to the fields below Allen Tarn where the goods then continued their journey down to the port at Greenodd,

On the return journey it was common to be carrying pig iron for Langdale and saltpetre for Elterwater.

Lower down the lake is the hamlet of Low Nibthwaite, and today consists of little more than a group of houses and Nibthwaite Grange.

In 1735 however it was a bustling industrial centre complete with smelting furnace, foundry and forge. It was from here , as well as from Dixon Ground in Coniston, that cannonballs were made for the Duke of Cumberland's use in the '45 rebellion.

Later, on the same site, bobbin manufacture was the order of the day, which continued until the 20th century.

NICHOLFOREST.

Map ref. F.2.
Next nearest Town or Village "Longtown"
Location. 10 miles north-east of Longtown.

Nicholforest consists of several small hamlets...Catlowdy, Warwicksland, Scuggate, Stoneygate, Penton and Bushfield.

The area was once a great forest between England and Scotland, and today still has many trees watered by the Liddel and the Kershope coming down from the Cheviots.

Historically too, its very interesting. Back in the 16th century the Borderland was divided into six 'Marches', three being on the Scots side and three on the English side. Nicholforest being part of the West March.. Kershopefoot in the northern corner was a recognized venue for the feuding Scots and English Reivers to meet on days of truce.

The oldest building hereabouts is Stonegarthside Hall a one time Border stronghold, and the seat of the Forsters. It is now a listed building. Many visitors will find interesting the dungeons below the massive edifice. In one of the four feet thick walls is a heart shaped aperture through which you can see virtually the whole extent of Liddesdale.

The hamlet lost its old church last century when the pleasant new one was built with an apse and a small slated spire on a wooden belfry.

OLD HUTTON

Map ref. G.11.
Next nearest Town or Village "Natland"
Bus service. Cumberland Buses route 568
Location. 5 miles south-east of Kendal.

Old Hutton is approximately five miles south - east of Kendal and consists of five small hamlets...

Holmescale Farm is the oldest house in Old Hutton, and has been in the Robinson family since 1904.

Bleaze Hall dates back to 1600...the Jacobean period. It was apparently built by a Roger Bateman, who it is said made his money as a cloth manufacturer in Kendal. In one of the attics there is a 'dobbie stone' which is a charm to prevent evil spirits or ghosts from disturbing the house.

It was a noble house built in the last years of Queen Elizabeth 1. Much of the grandeur of Bleaze hall has gone, but it has an imposing front, beautiful plaster ceilings, and rich woodwork, one of its spacious rooms has oak panelling with elaborate figures and foliage, and a mantelpiece of Stuart times.

Beckside has got to be a 'must' for all visitors. No one can help but admire the picturesque scene with its lovely waterfall. The waterfall is part of the river running through the village and is known as Peasey Beck, though below Old Hutton is called the River Bela.

In the hamlet of St John's View is the school, public hall and St John the Baptist church. The church incidentally has in its possession a silver chalice dating back to 1495.

In the hamlet of Church View is a house that has a plaque proudly announcing that John Wesley slept one night here as he was on his way from Leeds to Whitehaven.

ORMSIDE.

Map ref. I.8.
Nearest Town or Village "Appleby"
Location. 2 miles south-east of Appleby.

Ormside is a village just two miles south-east of Appleby and eight miles from Kirkby Stephen. The Norman church of St James on the river bank is without doubt one of the oldest in the Carlisle Diocese. Relics of early Christian burials, together with a Viking sword have been found in the churchyard, though their most exciting find was what is now known as the Ormside Cup...a beautiful example of Anglo-Saxon metalware dating from the 8th century. It is made of gilded silver, richly decorated with vine scolls, birds and animals. Currently on display at the Yorkshire Museum, York.

There are some fine examples of Cumbrian farmhouses hereabouts, two of which bear dates of 1683 and 1687. Entrance to the houses in those early days would have been through the adjoining barns.

Near to the church is Ormside Hall, originally built as a place of defence with its 14th century pele tower. It was the one time home of the Hilton family who lived here for over 100 years since 1620. nearby is a large sycamore tree, growing in steps, and known locally as the Cross tree. It is thought that it was the place of a preaching cross at one time, and later when the cross was broken and removed to the churchyard, the sycamore tree was planted.

In Lodge Garden will be seen a magnificent cedar tree which is said to have been brought back from Lebanon in General Whitehead's hat.

At one time there was a hospital for infectious diseases (opened in 1899) which later became a T.B Unit then a geriatric hospital. These days the site has been converted into a tourist centre...The Wild Rose Caravan Park.

ORTON.

Map ref. H.9.
Next nearest Town or Village "Tebay"
Bus service. Cumberland Buses Route 561, 577
Location. 10 miles south-east of Shap.

Orton is a small market town established since the reign of Edward 1, in the 13th century...in fact the All Saint's Church still has many mediaeval remains.

Nearby, at Crosby Ravensworth are the remains of a large late iron age settlement at Ewe Close, reputed to be one of the finest in the North of England.

Orton village, though small, is well sign-posted off the A685 Kendal to Kirkby Stephen road. Little activity goes on here and its very much a village which has hardly been touched in the past 700 years. Today, visitors could be just as likely to be visiting the chocolate factory here, or the tea-rooms..as history itself.

Orton's main claim to fame is that the Duke of Cumberland stayed in the village at the time he was chasing Bonnie Prince Charlie in 1745...successfully too, for Charlie never returned, wandering through the Highlands with a price of £30,000 on his head before eventually escaping to France. The ale-house he stayed at was re-named

ORTON

'The Duke of Cumberland'..but unfortunately no longer exists. The building however, can still be seen in Orton.After his defeat at the battle of Culloden in 1746, the Stuart Pretender,made his way to the west coast of Scotland in an attempt to flee to France. Whilst he waited for transport, two French ships arrived, bringing him some 35,000 gold coins. As English ships had been sighted, the gold had to be taken ashore and hidden hastily so that the Frenchmen could escape.The coins were later retrieved and split into six casks which were stored at several sites. It is known that some of the money was later collected by the Prince's followers, but it is certain that much of it remained unfound, and to this day still lies buried waiting to be recovered.

The village, for some unexplainable reason has a reputation for longevity, and a remarkable number of its inhabitants have reached a century and one even lived to the grand old age of 106.

There are two halls,both at the south end of the village.Petty Hall is Elizabethan and once belonged to the Birkbeck family whose initials GB and MB and the date 1604 are on a panel over the doorway. A strong oak beam in stone sockets is still used to fasten the heavy door. On the opposite side of the road stands Orton Hall built in 1662, and for many years the home of the Burn family.

Once known as 'The Fleece', today the George Hotel is located directly in the centre of town, and is very much the centre of activity for the villagers. Twice yearly, for example the fox-hunt meets here

(December and January) ...and without horses incidentally...which at least gives the foxes a sporting chance.

The village seems to attract large numbers of walkers, mainly due to Wainwright's coast to coast walk (St Bee's Head to Robin's Hood bay, Whitby) which passes this way.

The background of Orton Scar is a pleasant setting for the village.In fact if you approach from Appleby you will have a magnificent view of the Howgills and Lune Gorge, with the hills of Fawcett Forest and Shap Fells in the distance.

Orton lies at the foot of the hill and overlooking the village is the beautiful old parish church of All Saints. The large tower dates from the year 1504. Inside will be found many relics of past ages, one is a large box said to have been hollowed out of a tree grown in Lowther Park...and probably the original parish chest....and another is the old bread charity chest into which loaves were put out for the poor of the parish.

At the northern end of the village is Mill House which had a water wheel which at one time was the largest in 'Westmorland', with four stones for grinding.There is a date of 1693 on a cupboard in the house, which also served as the Post Office.

George Whitehead, who with George Fox was one of the founders of the Quaker movement was born here in 1636.

George Hotel
Orton, Penrith Telephone: 05396 24229

Orton is a small village established since the reign of Edward I in the 13th century...in fact the All Saints Church still has many medieval remains here.

The road from Crosby Ravensworth to Orton is one of the loveliest in East Cumbria, passing superb limestone scenery. Orton was the birthplace of George White (1636-1723), who, with George Fox, was one of the founders of the early Quaker movement. The church has a massive 16th century tower built for defence..a necessary precaution. On Orton Scar a beacon used to be lit to warn local people to tend their flocks and herds and seek safety from the Scottish raiders.

Nearby are the remains of a large late iron age settlement at Ewe Close, reputed to be one of the finest in the North of England.

Orton village, though small is well sign posted off the A685 Kendal to Kirkby Stephen road. Little activity goes on here and its very much a village which has hardly been touched in the past 700 years. Its main claim to fame is that the Duke of Cumberland stayed in the village at the time he was chasing Bonnie Prince Charlie in 1745. The ale-house he stayed at was re-named 'The Duke of Cumberland'...but unfortunately no longer exists as a pub. The building however, can still be seen in Orton.

Once known as 'The Fleece', today the George Hotel is located directly in the centre of the village. Twice yearly the hunt meets here. Wainwrights coast to coast walk (St. Bees Head to Robin Hood Bay) attracts vast numbers of walkers to this pub as it is directly on the route.

The owners Peter and Val Graveson have been in residence since 1992, having been local farmers until then. Peter looks after the bar, whilst Val has settled comfortably into the catering side.

Seven rooms are available for overnight stays allowing visitors to make use of the outdoor activities in the close vicinity...rock climbing, abseiling, scrambling, mountain walks...even canoeing, A nice open fire, pool and bar skittles ensure a relaxing pub in convivial company.

PAPCASTLE & BELLE VUE.

Map ref. B.7.
Next nearest Town or Village
Location 1 mile North -West of Cockermouth.

Papcastle is a village one mile north-west of Cockermouth. Here was the Roman fort of 'Derventio'...now nearly obliterated by buildings and the road...worth looking for though..
The barrack block and commandants bath house was excavated in 1961-2 and the large fort of just over six acres appears to have housed a cavalry unit. Regretfully stones from the fort have been plundered over the years for building in the surrounding areas...Cockermouth Castle is a good example of that..To date the fort has never been fully excavated.

Papcastle village is much the same as it was some 200 years ago. The name originates from 'Pips Castle'...namely the castle built here by one Gilbert Pipard...though no trace of the castle now exists. A mile off the line of the Roman road to Maryport is a marked footpath known locally as 'Wet Lonning'.

PATTERDALE.

Map ref. F.8.
Next nearest Town or Village "Glenridding"
Bus service.Cumberland Buses Route 108
Location. Approx 12 miles south of Ambleside.
Gala days/festivals.. Patterdale Sheepdog trials.Sat AugustBank Holiday

Patterdale, or to give it its ancient name St Patrick's dale...so called because according to legend the saint having been shipwrecked on the Duddon sands made his way to the dale, and stayed long enough to baptize the local inhabitants.There is a well dedicated to him in a wall by the roadside at Glenridding.
Crossing the lake of Ullswater at Glencoin the parish boundary continues almost unbelievably for about fifty miles over the fells. At the valley bottom the road links the hamlets of

Hartsop,Patterdale,Glenridding, Deerdale and Grisedale, each of which has its own dale.

The Kirkstone Pass rises at the other extremity with Dovedale Red Screes, and Cawdle Moor. Hartsop shows much evidence of its old importance with its 'spinning galleries' and lead mining remains.

John Mounsey, the so-called 'King of Patterdale' lived at Patterdale Hall. His main claim to fame was leading a party of dalesmen to Stybarrow Crag when Scottish marauders were expected. He later sold the Hall to the Marshall family.

Opposite St Patrick's church is 'The Butts' where archery was practised and the stocks would have stood.

The beautiful Grisedale valley is behind Patterdale Hall. Above this valley is the famous Striding Edge...a knife-edge ridge leading on to Helvellyn...over 3000 feet!

It was up here , on what deQuincey called the awful curtain rock, that Charles Gough was killed in Trafalgar year, his faithful dog watching by his body for three months.The story has been told by Scott and Wordsworth. High on Tarn Crag, a few yards before Grisedale Tarn comes into sight, is a rock with an inscription recalling that here Wordsworth came on his last walk with his brother John, not long before John, who was commander of the 'Earl of Abergavenny' went down with his ship. Five miles north is 'Aira Force' in all probability the Lake District's most famous waterfall eighty feet high. Also worth visiting is Lyulp's Tower an 18th century building on the site of a possible pele tower. Its the scene of Wordsworth's 'Somnambulist' At Glenridding in 1927, the reservoir at Kepple Cove burst, and over a quarter of a million gallons of water flooded into the valley, and at the same time sweeping 25,000 tons of rubble into Glenridding beck.The devastation as can be imagined, was enormous.

Patterdale has had a goodly share of characters over the years.Lanty (lancelot) Patty lost his wife and took most of his family to live in a cave near Goldrill bridge.It was named Lanty's castle. Lanty was buried on August 8th 1865, aged 96 years.

The Reverend John Mattinson reached the age of 96 in the year 1765.During his lifetime he was paid a stipend that started at £12 per year, and rose to £18 per annum!

He lived very well, brought up four children without benefits of any kind, and managed to leave £1,000. John Walton of Bridgend was master of the Old Hartsop Foxhounds. This function brought him no lasting fame, but he was widely known for his aversion to soap and water.He prided himself on being the dirtiest man in Patterdale, and left instructions in his will that he was to be buried as dirty as he was found at death.

PENNINGTON.

Map ref. D.13.
Next nearest Town or Village "Ulverston"
Location. Just over i mile from Ulverston south-west.

Pennington is a parish just over a mile from Ulverston, and consists of an area some three and a half miles by one and a half miles. It is recorded in the Domesday Book.

There are various hamlets and villages in the parish, including Harlock, Trinkeld, Carkettle, Walthwaite, Rathmoss, Horace, Holebiggerah, Cross-a-Moor, Swarthmoor,and Loppergarth...the latter having derived its name from a leper hospital.

Near Castle Hill...with its great ramparts overhanging a ravine, was the one time seat of the Pennington family back in the 14th century.The ramparts appear to have enclosed an early mediaeval house, built of wood and clay.

The church in parts,dates back to 1150 and outside the graveyard walls will be found the ancient parish stocks, which would not have been used since 1837 when an Act of Parliament put an end to stocks as a punishment. (That's on the assumption that somebody in authority got round to telling the villagers).

During the reconstruction of the church in 1826 a stone was uncovered which is attributed to the Bronze Age and connected with pagan worship.The inscription on it is thought to show that it originally belonged to Gamel de Pennington who was the donor of the church during the reign of Henry 11.(1159-1189). The stone is the only one of its kind in the country, and today has been re-located into the west wall of the font.

Close by at Ellabarrow and Conynger Hurst is an iron age internment.

PENNY BRIDGE

Map ref. E.12.
Next nearest Town or Village "Greenodd"
Location. 5 miles north of Ulverston

The name Penny Bridge...at the mouth of the Crake, the outflow of Coniston Water...is a surname, not as so many think..a coin.

In April 1735 the will of one Henry Lindow made provision 'towards educating and bringing up at school the poor children belonging to Egton-cum-Newland.with books.,school wages, boarding, or clothing and clogs'. The sum provided for this was £138, a considerable sum in those days.

Like the church, the increasing population of the villages of Greenodd and Penny Bridge had created the need for a school specifically for the area. So, during the years 1780-81 a schoolhouse was built 'upon ye common of pasture called Arrad', today known as Sandhills.

The actual cost of the building was met by voluntary contributions from the inhabitants of the villages and the Squire William Penny offered £5 a year to the Schoolmaster. The last master of the school incidentally was a William Hartley who apparently combined his school duties with those of being a tinker,umbrella-maker, and musical instrument repairer.

During this period the building seen today as Sodhouse Farm was actually a Higher Grade School, the teacher being the incumbent of St Mary's...the Rev James Burn.

Originally the villages of Greenodd and Penny Bridge obtained their spiritual support from Ulverston';s parish church ,as it was the nearest. In the early 1700's however it was decided that besides the school, it was obvious that a chapel of their own was also needed. Fortunately this need was met (again) by the Squire William Penny (of Penny Bridge Hall)..Lord of the Manor of Dunnerdale and Seathwaite. The chapel was built at a cost of £733. two shillings and eleven pence,though part of this money was reclaimed by the selling of pews for approximately £2. each.

In the Kendal Weekly Mercury dated Saturday May 3rd 1735 the following....'died, James Wilson aged 100 years.Four years earlier Timothy Coward died aged 114 years and still living...Roger Friars aged 103 and in perfect health'.

HAMLET OF PENNY BRIDGE

PENRITH.

Map ref. G.7.
Next nearest Town or Village "Greystoke"
Bus service. Post Bus plus Cumberland buses route 100, 104, 105, 106, 107, 108, 109 X5
Trains Penrith Railway station.
Tourist Information Centre. Robinson's School,Middlegate.
Location. Junction of Keswick,Alston & Carlisle road.
Early closing. Wednesday.
Market Day. Tuesday & Saturday.
Gala days/festivals.
Penrith Agricultural Society Show. 4th Saturday July.
Eden Valley D.T.C. Obedience Show. 3rd Saturday July.
Fell Pony Stallion Show. 2nd Sat May.
Fell Pony Society Breed Show. 1st Sat August.
Castletown Gala Week. 1st Monday June (for 1 week)

The name Penrith derives from the old English for 'The Chief Ford".

An ancient market town, with a charter dating back to 1223, recognisable by its many red sandstone buildings it is a popular shopping destination in Eden, known for its sophisticated arcades and traditional markets.
The castle of Penrith is situated,logically enough, in Castle Park, and dates mainly from 1390. It was built by Strickland...Bishop of Carlisle, who, it should be added, was also fortifying Rose Castle.It was the one time residence of Richard 111, then Duke of Gloucester. He lived in the castle when he served as Lord Warden of the Western March.He married Anne Neville.History shows that he died in 1485 at Bosworth.
Just down the street is Great Dockray, with the Two Lions Inn (home one time of Gerard Lowther) not overlooking the Gloucester Arms dating back to the 15th century. An overnight stay here on one occasion for Richard 111.
The parish church of St Andrew cannot boast of being such an age having been built in the early 1720.s...though its tower is much older.The alleys around it and the shops form the pleasantest part of town.The church has an interesting collection of relics including mediaeval tombstones,old crosses, together with many other pre-Norman items...Legend has it that the grave of Owen

PENRITH

Caesarious, the 10th King of Cumbria is here too. The body of the church is 18th century.The lowest parts of the tower are 13th and the top was probably built two centuries later by Warwick the King-maker, who was Lord of the manor of Penrith. His sign was the ragged staff, and of the eight he put on the tower as pinnacles only one is left now. The interior has all the dignity of .ts day. The pillars supporting the panelled gallery are remarkable be-cause each is a single stone ten feet high and four feet round, from a Cumbrian quarry worked by the Romans. The chancel walls are decorated with very dark paintings done about a century or more ago by Jacob Thompson who was born at Penrith and became known in London as a landscape painter.

Many treasures older than the present building are in it. There are two old fonts and stone figures of a 17th century lawyer and his wife, in the vestry wall there is a striking row of fine Tudor memorials carved with shields and letters, one being the stone of a border hero whose name was used to frighten the children. One is a king wearing his crown , the other two are Richard Duke of York with his yellow hair and beard,and his wife Cicily Neville with jewels in her hair, and a remarkable pair they were.He was the Yorkist heir slain at Wakefield after which his head was crowned in mockery and impaled on the walls of York.She was the 23rd child of Ralph Neville Shakespeare's Earl of Westmorland. Two of their children became kings of England, a third married Henry V11, making this old couple the ancestors of every British sovereign.Two of their grandchildren were the little princes murdered in the Tower.

The Penrith Grammar School was re-founded in 1564 by Queen Elizabeth 1 having originally been a mediaeval school attached to Bishop Stricklands chantry in 1395. The school today is part of the comprehensive.

OLD STORE

Penrith Museum is well worth visiting, it is housed adjacent to the Tourist Information Centre, in the 300 year old Robinson's School. The lintel over the door of the School shows a date of 1670...though many local historian's believe the building itself goes back much further than that. The name Robinson relates to one locally born William Robinson who made his fortune in London. He left £55 a year to the town when he died in 1660 of which £20 was specifically for 'education and up-bringing of girls'. The poorest scholars here used to wear badges with the letters PS which permitted them to beg on the streets.Reports of those days show that the pupils had a miserable time at school suffering frequent beatings,...often without reason, and eleven to twelve hour working days. The school continued until as recently as 1970 (presumably without the beatings).

Walking around town visitors will notice the vari-ety of little squares, which like Kendal could be blocked off in time of crisis...Scottish raids for example

A square plague stone, looking rather like a great font in which the townsfolk washed their money in vinegar when paying for produce brought in from the countryside, stands in the garden of old people's homes in Bridge lane.The stone would be in use about 350 years ago.

Plague hit Penrith at the end of the 16th century killing we are told some 2,260 people.

Look for Arnison's store. At one time this was the site of a Moot Hall which consisted of five shops with courtroom and prison underneath. A plaque on the wall today states that William Wordsworth's grandparents William and Ann Cookson lived here.

When William Wordsworth was five years old he attended Anne Birketts Dame School in St Andrew's Place. It was here that he first met a local tobacconist's daughter ...one Mary Hutchinson who was to become his wife some 27 years later.

Musgrave Hall opposite Robinson's School, was the one time town house of the Musgraves of Edenhall.Today it is a British Legion Club...though the family coat of arms can still be clearly seen on the building.

Other well known names associated with the area are John McAdam who was known for his contri-

ROBINSON SCHOOL

bution to road construction and lived at Cockell House, in Drovers Lane.

Anthony Trollope was a regular visitor to the town staying at Carleton Hill.

And overlooking the town is the famous Penrith Beacon, which dates back to the Border wars and one time blazed out a warning of marauding Scots.It was last lit in 1745.

Wetheriggs Country Pottery & Museum
CLIFTON DYKES PENRITH CUMBRIA

One of the very few genuine country workshops in Britain which can trace its origins back to the Industrial Revolution. The pottery was founded in 1856 and until the last war, household, agricultural, and horticultural items of a functional nature accounted for almost its entire output. In those days the range was a fairly narrow one and in fact it was often possible to produce a thousand pots in a day.

Over the last thirty plus years there has been somewhat of a quiet revolution at the Pottery. It has had to change over to making decorative, but nevertheless useful articles. Scores of different pots are now produced and the variety of designs is enormous. The most traditional item i the old salt pot with a hole in its side, which these days is generally bought as a curio, though it can still be used for keeping salt dry, The majority of the pots have somewhat of a wiggly white marking which is something of a trade mark. The most popular basic colour however is blue, with a turquoise shade.

Visitors are very welcome at Wetheriggs. A tour of the buildings usually ends in the extensive showroom where a wide range of exciting items are on display, Many visitors will find another building here equally interesting. It houses a beehive kiln, which used to take 36 to fire and used six tons of coal at a time. It could hold up to four thousand pots at a time though.

MAKE YOUR OWN POT
Have a go yourself, great fun for al the family

GIFT SHOP
Splendid gift shop where all our products can be purchased along with other gifts and accessories

HUDSONS COFFEE SHOP
Enjoy a bite to eat and drink in our charming victorian parlour

PLANT CENTRE
A selction of attractive plants and gardening accessories available in this charming centre

VIDEO
Learn about the history, restoration, and future plans of this unique piece of Britain's heritage.

OPEN EVERY DAY FROM 10,00AM *Tel: 0768 62946*

Beckses Caravan Park

Penruddock Penrith, Cumbria CA11 0RX

Tel: Greystoke (07684) 83224

A small pleasant site on the very fringe of the Lake District National Park, within easy reach of the M6 Motorway (6 miles). Ullswater (4 miles) Keswick (12 miles), offering modern facilities for those wishing to pitch their own caravan or tent, or hire a luxury fully equipped static or touring caravan.
Toilets
Showers
Chemical Disposal Point
Conveniently Placed Stand Pipes
Laundry facilities
Site Shop (open 8.30 to 10 am & 4.30 to 6 pm)
Hard Standing available Kiddies Play Area with swings etc.
Pay phone on site
Calor and Camping Gaz Stockist
Caravan Accessories
Garage Repair Facilities Adjoining
M.O.T. Station
Electricity Available for Touring Caravans
Automatic Washing Machine
Tumbler and Spin Dryer
Within easy reach of...
Outdoor Heated Swimming Pool, Pony Trekking, Fishing
Fell Walking, Local Pubs, some with restaurant facilities

A.A.
3 Pendant

Asociated Member
English Lakes Counties
Travel Association

Caravan Club
Recommended

UNITS FOR HIRE

Caravans
Choice of 6 berth Statics with main services:- Electric Lights and Fridge, Gas Cooker and Fire, Toilet, Black and White T.V., Separate Double Bedroom and Bunk Bedroom, Kitchen Area and Lounge, Choice of 12ft 4 berth to 16ft 4/5 berth Tourers, either on site or self tow. If available.
All vans fully equipped with Crockery, Cooking Utensils, Cutlery, Blankets and Pillows in statics only (own sheets and pillow slips to be provided)
No meters on Electricity, Gas or Water, Parking beside caravans
Touring vans for self tow or on site equipped as above but without blankets or pillows on self tow bookings.

PENRUDDOCK & MOTHERBY.

Map ref. F.7.
Next nearest Town or Village "Greystock"
Location. 7 miles west of Penrith.

The villages of Penruddock and Motherby are known to be the old Celtic settlements situated some seven miles west of Penrith,
Motherby is in the parish of Greystoke, and Penruddock is in the parish of Hutton and is located in the grounds of the National Park.
Up until 1927 the railway connecting Penrith and Keswick ran between the two. Now long closed, though the ruins of the station still remain, as does various stretches of the embankment and some bridges.

Hereabouts will be found numerous farmhouses, which at one time were little more than hay lofts with living accommodation below. High Farm dates back to 1695. A chest, known as the Penruddock Kist was found here, and upon opening was found to contain all the old deeds relating to the village. This Kist is now in All Saints church, whilst the documents are held in the Carlisle archives.
It is thought that the Presbyterian or Puritan movement reached here in 1654. The present church built in 1789 is the third oldest Presbyterian church in England.

PIEL ISLAND.

Map ref: D.14.
Next nearest Town or Village "Rampside"
Location. Approx 5 miles from Barrow ...by boat!

One of the Furness area's more colourful places....Foudrey Island...better known as Piel Island...taking its name from the castle.
Piel Island was probably visited by the Celts and later by the Romans during their conquest of Britain. The first recorded name for the island came from the Scandinavian settlers to the area. The name Foudrey or Fotheray may have come from the Old Norse 'foder or fouder', meaning fodder and 'ay or oy' meaning island. Therefore it is safe to assume that Foudrey may have been used as a foddering place for the settlers grazing animals.
In 1127 the island was given to the Savignac monks as part of their original land grant for an Abbey from King Stephen. After the Savignacs merged with the Cistercians in the middle of the century, Furness Abbey started to grow, and the need for a safe harbour was felt. Somewhat naturally Foudrey appeared to be the perfect solution.
In 1212 King John granted the Abbey a license to land one cargo of 'wheat, flour and other provisions' in order to stave off a famine caused by the failure of the local harvest. Thus the first wooden tower was built on the island. An unlimited cargo license was granted in 1232 and again in 1258...the Abbey's own ships came under Royal protection.
The current motte and bailey 'castle' with its defense ditches was built in the early part of the fourteenth century and was the largest of its kind in the northwest. It was probably intended to be used as a fortified warehouse to keep cargoe's safe from pirates and other raiders. The Abbey soon discovered that it did not keep just the pirates out, the 'Pile of Fotheray' also kept the King and custom's men at a distance. It was widely known at that time that the Abbey was active in the smuggling business. It was during this period that the island was probably the home of one Adam of Beaumont and his outlaws (1346-1363) The Robin Hood and his Merry Men of their day.
Although Piel Island was held by King Henry V for a short period, the Island continued to be a focal point for the smuggling trade in Furness until 1487.
On June 4th of that year Lambert Simnel, a merchant's son, under the guidance of the Earl of Lincoln, landed at Piel. Simnel claimed that he was the Earl of Warwick and therefore was the rightful King of England. With his army of German and Irish mercenaries, Simnel set off across Furness to march on London. He did finally arrive in London but only as the prisoner of Henry V11, after being defeated by the King's forces at the Battle of Stoke on June 16th.
The island and harbour continued in use for shipping as the iron industry grew in Furness. Houses for pilots and a public house were built on Piel in the

late eighteenth century.
Today the landlord of the Ship Inn is traditionally known as the 'King of Piel'. The title comes from the time of Lambert Simnel when he declared himself king. This tradition has also given rise to the 'Knights of Piel'. In the Ship Inn is an old oaken chair and anyone who sits in it becomes a 'Knight of Piel'. The 'knighthood' ceremony must be performed by the 'King' or another 'knight'. The new Knight must then carry out his duties which include buying everyone a drink, being a moderate smoker,

an ardent lover of the opposite sex, and of good character.
One of the rights of a knight is, if he finds himself shipwrecked on Piel he may go to the inn and demand a night's free lodging and as much as he can eat and drink!
The castle was given to the townspeople of Barrow by the Duke of Buccleuch as a memorial to the men who were killed in the First World War. Piel Castle can be visited by ferry from Roa Island or Rampside during the summer months.

PLUMBLAND.

Map ref: C.6.
Next nearest Town or Village "Bothel"
Location. Just over a mile south of Aspatria.

Plumbland is an ancient parish some one and a half miles south of Aspatria, looking back towards the Scottish hills.
The site of a neolithic settlement nearby indicates habitation going back centuries, particularly as the Roman road from Old Carlisle to Papcastle passes by within a mile.
There are four 'Manors' in Plumbland,... Plumbland itself, together with Arkleby, Parsonby and Wardhall. Arkleby has an elegant anglo baroque hall which dates from 1725 and which incorporates an earlier pele tower, complete with spiral staircase. Today little remains of Old Wardhall, unless you count the pair of gate-posts standing in a field.

St Cuthbert's Church though built in 1871 replaced a Norman church built in 1130. It is known to have been used as a sanctuary during the invasion of William the Lion in 1173. It is also thought that there was a Saxon community here as far back as the 8th century. Two Viking hog-back stones can be dated AD980.
By two cottages a mile away is the shapely old mulberry tree up which Thomas Dykes, an ardent Royalist, hid after the battle of Marston Moor, his wife and daughter bringing him food from Ward Hall...the home no longer there. The old tree hid him safely, but later he was captured and died a prisoner in Cockermouth Castle.
A traditional craft still undertaken here is the making of shepherd's crooks.

PLUMPTON.

Map ref: G.6.
Next nearest Town or Village "Skelton"
Location. 5 miles north of Penrith.

A village five miles north of Penrith on the A6 road. It has had a long history....Voreda, a Roman fort stood just a mile north at Castlesteads, and was considered of some importance...garrisoned as it was by a fully armed and mounted troop which would have been guarding the Roman road from Chester to Hadrian's Wall on the border...in fact the Church Lane is said to stand on the line of the old Roman road.
One can trace the outline of the ramparts with the stones of one of the gates still in place and today there is cattle grazing where the great buildings once stood. Not far away is a stone-lined Roman wall. Just before Trafalgar a gold fibula decorated with bears and griffins was found here, and just before Waterloo were found five Roman altars carved with figures of gods.
Life was going on here in the second century, and these ramparts are from those days.
The little church with an embattled tower here is perhaps the first Cumbrian church of the 20th century, a neat and trim place with no east window, the nave and chancel divided by an iron screen and covered with a wagon roof carved with roses, red and gold ones over the sanctuary.
In mediaeval times the area hereabouts was called 'The Manor of Plumpton Parks' and stood within Inglewood Forest.

PIEL ISLAND / PLUMBLAND / PLUMPTON

POOLEY BRIDGE

POOLEY BRIDGE.

Map ref. F.7.
Next nearest Town or Village "Stockbridge"
Tourist Information Centre. The Square.
Location. 7 miles south-west of Penrith.

Pooley bridge is situated at the foot of Ullswater
and is combined with the parishes of Barton and
Martindale. The village itself consists of not a lot
more than greystone houses two hotels and a few
shops.
The 'Pooley' part of the name is Norse for 'the hill
with a pool'. The bridge part was not added until
around 1800.
The River Eamont flows out of the lake and runs
through farmland to Eamont Bridge,eventually
reaching the River Eden. An attractive 16th century bridge crosses the river and leads to the main
part of the village.
Opposite to the church is a row of very old houses
one of which was a blacksmith's, and there are
traces of a stand for the grindstone and a well for
the cooling of irons.
To the south is Eusemere once the home of the
anti-slave campaigner Thomas Clarkson.

"POOLEY BRIDGE

Mrs Clarkson was one of Dorothy Wordsworth's
closest friends, and the poet and his wife used the
house as the starting off point for many of their
Lakeland excursions.
On the northern side of the river is the hill
Dunmallet..a name which means 'hill of
slaughter'...though nobody seems to know why.
On the summit is an iron age fort...which might
possibly give food for thought however.
At the lakeside is the site of Tristamont, thought to
have been the home of Sir Tristram, one of King
Arthur's Knights.
Scattered about the moor will be seen many pre-
historic cairns.

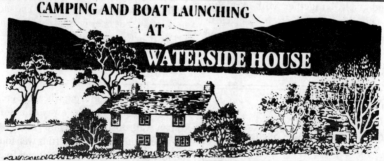

Sharrow Bay
COUNTRY HOUSE HOTEL

Sharrow Bay Country House Hotel is on the extreme edge of Ullswater, the waves actually lapping the terrace wall. The hotel stands on a wooded promontory backed by Barton Fells. The building is of soft grey stone with large windows and a loggia above the terrace.

From the front windows, the views are of lake, woods and mountains with the Helvellyn range filling the far distance. Beside the house is a private jetty and boathouse. There are 12 acres of gardens and woodlands, and half a mile of lake shore where guests may wander at leisure.

Guests can enjoy boating, swimming, fishing and of course walking or climbing, but above all, Sharrow is a haven for those who wish to relax completely in peaceful and beautiful surroundings. The old world garden offers a wide variety of glorious and outstanding vistas of both lakes and fells.

Sharrow Bay Country House was built in 1840 and up until 1949 was a private house.

The style of building is unusual for the area and has an interesting continental flavour, such as one would find in the Italian Lakes, angled low roof ridges and wide eaves on its lakeside elevation.

On entering Sharrow Bay Country House Hotel, one soon realises the significance of the title. Here is a house with a unique unhurried atmosphere. The decor and furnishing never fail to please the eye and add to the overall atmosphere of peace that pervades both house and grounds.

There are two comfortable lounges and two beautifully appointed dining rooms. The picture window in the drawing room offers an ever changing scene across the lake to the Martindale Fells from daffodil time to Autumn, with is symphony of golden and russet leaves.

Sharrow Bay Country House Hotel has 29 bedrooms, 10 of them being in the lodge annexe and cottages, and seven in Bank House. In the main hotel at present, eight bedrooms have private bathrooms and we have four cottage suites.

All bedrooms are central heated, some rooms have lake views while others enjoy views of the fells and beautiful trees. All bedrooms are furnished with the same individuality and comfort as the public rooms, and each bedroom has been given a name rather than a number, being associated with Sharrow when created as a hotel. Our internationally renowned cuisine emphasises traditional British dishes, created with imagination and served with graciousness and care by our excellent staff, some of whom have been at Sharrow for more than twenty five years.

LAKE ULLSWATER
POOLEY BRIDGE PENRITH CUMBRIA CA10 2LZ
TELEPHONE 0˜684 86301 and 86483 FAX 0˜684 86349

PORT CARLISLE.

Map ref. D.3.
Next nearest Town or Village "Bowness on Solway"
Location. 12 miles north-west of Carlisle.

At one time sailing boats made their way by canal from Port Carlisle to the heart of the city of Carlisle. Boats were towed to the city a journey taking around one hour forty minutes, and enabling Carlisle to be reached within a day by sea from Liverpool.
Try to find the old harbour wall today though...
It was the idea of marine architect William Chapman. The Carlisle and Annan Navigation Company was formed in 1819 and four years later a canal was opened. It was 11 miles long, had a drop of 60 feet and was navigated by eight locks. It connected with steamer services to Liverpool and Annan .
Unfortunately there was never enough traffic to keep it profitable, and it was eventually and effectively killed off by the railway. U.S.A. President Woodrow Wilson's Carlisle born mother left from here when she went across the Atlantic. Solway House, the fine mansion in the middle of the terrace was the hotel where they waited for their boats.

PORTINSCALE.

Map ref.D.8.
Next nearest Town or Village "Braithwaite"

Portinscale is a village one mile west of Keswick on the north west bank of Derwentwater. It is a gateway to the beautiful Newlands Valley and the west bank of Derwentwater where breathtaking views can be seen all the way to Grange in Borrowdale.
The only two marinas on Derwentwater are found just south of the village, Derwentwater marina and Nicol End, where canoes, rowing, and sailing boats can be hired. The ferry which frequently circulates the lake calls at Nichol End.
Half a mile south of the village is the magnificent mansion of Lingholme where the gardens are open to the public from Spring to Autumn.
The name Portinscale comes from the Anglo-Saxon word 'Portcwene' meaning prostitute, and the meaning 'a small house'. So the original sense of the name was 'The Harlots House'!!
The most famous local here was one John Graves...three times Lord Mayor of Manchester.

NEWLANDS VALLEY

Upon retiring to Portinscale he decided to build a mansion in keeping with his position, and decided on one of Gothic grandeur on the edge of the lake...even though he was repeatedly warned that the ground was far too boggy to hold such a weight....As to be expected the ground sank taking his mansion with it!

Derwent Cottage

Portinscale, Keswick,
Cumbria, CA12 5RF
Telephone: Keswick (07687) 74838

Derwent Cottage is no mere cottage, say the resident proprietors, Mike and Sue Newman, for the original dwelling dating from 1745 was greatly extended during Victorian times. It is set well back from the road in mature established grounds of nearly one acre with terraced lawns and stately conifers. From the grounds there is a splendid view across to Skiddaw, the highest mountain in the Northern Lake District, whilst the gravel drive allows for eight cars to be parked.

The accommodation, which has full central heating, double glazing and is carpeted throughout, consists of five spacious double rooms all with en suite facilities (both bath and shower). Each is individually and elegantly furnished and has a colour TV, radio alarm clock, beverage making requirements, a hair dryer and an electric blanket as well as plenty of drawer and hanging space and towels. The beds are all at least five feet wide. In the private wing of the house, there is a smaller room with an en suite shower room and a standard double bed along with all the other facilities.

The bright dining room has tables usually laid for two which can be put together in numerous combinations to accommodate any number up to a house party of twelve. Each table is laid with crisp linen, shining silver cutlery and sparkling crystal ware. At 7,00pm daily a four course, candle lit 'table d'hote' meal of fresh, home cooked food is served, followed by coffee and chocolates, all to the accompaniment of background classical music.

Vegetarian and special dietary needs can be catered for with prior notice ie at time of booking. The menu of the day is displayed at breakfast time in the dining room and should any guest feel that they are unable to eat a course, then an alternative can be arranged on request. A four course buffet style breakfast is available between 8.30 am and 9.00 am when a wide selection of traditional food is available. There is a bar, with a wide selection of wines and drinks, and a lounge where maps and books are available to allow guests to get to know the area better and plan their days. During the cooler evenings open fires are lit in these rooms, producing the only smoke allowed in the house! Derwent Cottage is a Non-Smoking establishment. Children over twelve years of age are welcome, but pets are not. There is a pay phone for the use of guests.

Derwent Cottage is not a typical hotel, Mike and Sue treat all visitors as personal house guests and a stay at the house, ideally a week, enables each guest to become exhilarated by the scenery and fully refreshed and rested in this peaceful location.

ETB 3 Crowns Highly Commended..

PRESTON PATRICK & PRESTON RICHARD.
Map ref. G.12.
Next nearest Town or Village "Milnthorpe" Location. 4 miles south east of Kendal.

Located some four miles south east of Kendal, Preston Patrick and Preston Richard together form one ecclesiastical parish, but were formerly in the parishes of Burton in Kendal and Heversham. Prerston Patrick consists of the hamlets of Gatebeck, Goose green,Millness, and Nook...though there are various houses in the Domesday Book referred to as the Manor of Torfin.

Preston Richard is listed as Preston Uethred, getting the Richard much later. It comprises the hamlets of Crooklands, Milton,Low Park, and Endmoor. The whole area has changed enormously over the years, though all have stories to tell of the past.

At Gatebeck for example, was the gunpowder works said to have been the best in Cumbria, and which only closed down as recently as 1937. An old tramway used to run from Gatebeck down to Crooklands, and then onwards to Milnthorpe.The retorts used for charcoal making can be seen in their new occupation...acting as gateposts to the caravan site along the Gatebeck road.

On the various roads there are many old milestones and boundary stones, quite a few made of cast iron, believed to have been made at Gatebeck around 1826. A house at Cow Brow, close to Nook, bears the name 'Toll Bar'

An Abbey was actualy founded here in 1119, though don't expect to see any remains, as the Abbey was later moved to Shap.

St Patrick's church stands on a hill to the west. There is still a Friends Meeting House and burial ground here, and Carnsgill Farm has strong connections with the Quakers.

At Crooklands there used to be coal wharfs, cinder ovens, stables and a mill. Today only the old coaching Hotel remains, together with what's left of the mill...now a car repair business.

RAMPSIDE

Map ref. D.14.
Next nearest Town or Village "Barrow in Furness"
Location. 3 miles south-east of Barrow.

A lovely village on the shores of Morecambe Bay, three miles south-east of Barrow and nine miles from Ulverston.

St Michael's church, though built in 1840 stands on the site of an older chapel...which in turn stood on the site of a Saxon burial ground.Many artefacts have been found in the churchyard,proving that the Vikings were here at one time.

George Fox the Quaker, who married Margaret Fell of Swarthmoor Hall, came and preached here. The unusually named Concle Inn was built on the site of a gravel pit once known as 'Conk Hole'. Filled with saline water it was used by people from far and wide for the therapeutic bathing it offered. Rampside Hall, the late 16th century home of the Knipe family has twelve chimneys,known locally as the "Twelve Apostles'.Local folklore has it that in the early 16th century a young man wanted to marry, but the lady's father would only give his permission when the lad had built a house with 12 chimneys.The building was completed as requested, and each wedding anniversary would see smoke issuing from all 12 chimneys.

On Roa Island lived the Trinity House pilots. There has been a lifeboat station here for over 100 years

A spur of land 'Foulney Island' is a bird sanctuary.In the Walney Channel is a small island known as Sheep Island where are the remains of an isolation hospital. In the old days...i.e. sailing ship days, and when yellow fever was common place...captains had to fly a yellow flag if infection was aboard...at which point the sick would be taken off and put into hospital.

RAVENGLASS,

Map ref. B.10.
Next nearest Town ior Village Drigg"
Trains. Ravenglass & Eskdale Railway.
Tourist Information Centre .Ravenglass & Eskdale Railway: Station.
Location. A.595. Millom-Whitehaven road.

Ravenglass is an ancient and delightful Cumbrian coastal village, situated at the junction of the rivers Esk,Irt,and Mite, where they form an estuary flowing into the Irish Sea.

Throughout the 17th and 18th century this little urban centre enjoyed a good coasting trade for its ships could in those days dock right by the single main street for loading and unloading.The proximity of the Lakeland fells, the lower cost involved for shipping, and its handiness in avoiding expensive Whitehaven, encouraged the growth of the village.

In Roman days,Ravenglass was the second largest port in Britain. ...in fact it was the only natural harbour on the west coast between the Dee and the Solway.Additionally the Romans under their General Agricola, built an important fort here in AD 79, known as Glannaventa...though little remains of the fort these days. 'Walls Castle' was the

RAVENGLASS RAILWAY

bath house for the fort and can be visited just outside the village. Its interesting to note that it has the highest standing walls of a Roman ruin in the north of England...they are over twelve feet high in parts. Roman cement can still be seen clinging to the inside of the walls even today,

It is thought by many that the fort had associations with King Eveling and King Arthur.Today. you can if you wish still find Neolithic flints on the sand dunes.

The village received a market charter in the 1200's, drawing large numbers of people to its annual fairs and markets

Today the village is more famous for its railway...the Ravenglass and Eskdale Railway, better known as 'La'al Ratty'. The R & ER operate a steam train service starting from this picturesque estuary and winding its way through the fells to the terminus at Dalegarth in the heart of Eskdale.Such is the prospect of riding in open carriages over this seven mile route, from the coast to the mountains, so to speak..that it attracts thousands of tourists almost daily during the season.

Muncaster Castle...the home of the Pennington family since 1208 is just a short distance away.

The castle grounds in themselves have been one of Cumbria's principal attractions for very many years, and thousands have flocked in spring and summer to see the massed rhododendrons and azaleas in the castle park.,but equally as many visit to see the wonders of this beautifully kept castle too.

The Penningtons, owners of the castle throughout its long history have been one of the great families of 'Cumberland' since the 11th century, and their forebears lived in Walls Castle before building in the 13th century the pele tower which was the corner-stone of the present castle.

The castle in its present form is relatively modern, no later than the 18th century, but the pele tower with walls ten feet thick, still stands on the right of the castle facade.

Probably the most magnificent room on view to the public is the library, a vast octagonal chamber which soars up through two floors of the castle with a fine brass-railed balcony running all round to bring thousands of rare books within reach.

Several of the bedrooms are open to the public, including what is referred to as the'Kings Room'.Solid carved oak Elizabethan four-posters are the focal points in these rooms and two of them have carved stone Elizabethan fireplaces which were brought by the Pennington's from dismantled homes many years ago. Among the treasures on show are some excellent old tapestries, the best, by far, being four small framed pieces, hung in the bedroom corridor, depicting allegorical scenes including the destruction of Sodom and Gomorrah, Lot's wife and all.

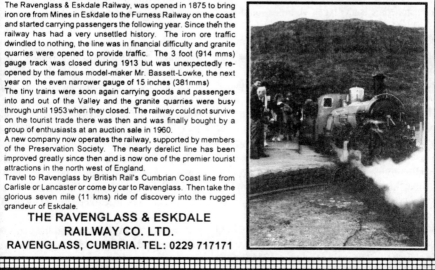

MUNCASTER CASTLE

Set in an idyllic corner of the English Lake District, with a breathtaking view of Eskdale from the Terrace...once described by John Ruskin as "Heaven's Gate"...MUNCASTER CASTLE has something for everyone. The castle has been the home of the Pennington family since the 13th Century. The Pele tower stands on Roman foundations and was extended through the centuries to form the castle as it is seen today.

A walk through the castle brings you seven centuries

of glorious history. The 40 minute guided 'walkman' tour, written and narrated by the present owner Patrick Gordon-Duff-Pennington, contains a wealth of interesting and humorous family anecdotes which adds immensely to the enjoyment and creates a unique atmosphere in which to view the superb antique furniture, portraits by famous artists, beautiful tapestries and many other articles of historical and artistic merit.

A walk through Muncaster's gardens and woodlands will provide unceasing joy to anyone who loves nature. The gardens are spectacular, enjoying as they do a world wide reputation for their outstanding collection of azaleas and rhododendrons, with many varieties first propogated here. There is also a wide variety of rare and beautiful trees and exotic plants. A trip to our well stocked Plant Centre is a must, where you can purchase top quality plants at modest prices. The gardens are also home to the Owl Centre, which strives to conserve owls world-wide. Daily at 2.30 p.m. (April to October) a talk is given on the work of the Centre and, weather permitting, the birds fly. Here too is the Stable's Buttery where light meals and refreshments are available, together with a gift shop for you to browse around.

Ravenglass, Cumbria CA18 1RQ
Tel: 0229 717614/717203 Fax 0229 717010

RAVENSTONEDALE.

Map ref. I.10.
Next nearest Town or Village "Newbiggin-on-Lune"
Location. 5 miles south-west of Kirkby Stephen.

Ravenstonedale is a village five miles south-west of Kirkby Stephen, and formerly a market town. The dale is surrounded by hills, with the Howgill fells to the south-west and the Wild Boar Fell rising to over 2,300 feet to the south-east.

The village is virtually within hailing distance of Yorkshire, and is almost hidden among the magnificent fell country of the Pennines and in this land of high hills and delightful valleys are the streams of the young Eden and Lune. Through the village, Scandal Beck flows over a pavement of tilted limestone, and on the side of the valley near by ancient man has left traces of his earthworks and dykes.

The village has been occupied, literally, since prehistoric times as witnessed by the many dykes and mounds (known locally as 'giants graves')

The church of St Oswald erected in 1744 (on the site of an earlier church). It has a fine three-decker pulpit, complete with a seat for the parson's wife. The church has a window in memory of Elizabeth Gaunt who was burnt at Tyburn in 1685 for sheltering a fugitive from Monmouth's rebellion...she was in fact the last woman in England to die for their Protestant faith.

A few fragments of the original church, which had a separate tower with a 'refuge bell' have been incorporated in the fabric of the present building. The interior has a number of surprises. Dark oak pews face the central aisle, a feature seen in only four other parish churches, and Robert Mounsey who was the vicar for over half of the 18th century must have got used to the idea of seeing his congregation facing each other instead of looking east as in most churches.

In bygone days local affairs in the village were controlled by the 'Peculiar Court'. Sessions were held in the parish church, the steward of the Lord of the manor presided over a jury of 24 local men, and Gallows Hill in Wharton Park is a reminder of their power, and where up until the early part of the last century, felons were hanged for a variety of crimes as well as murder.

About the year 1200 Gilbertine Monks came from the priory of Watton in Yorkshire, and settled in Ravenstonedale. They built a small establishment adjacent to the old church from whence they administered the area. It is only recently that the ruins of this monastery have been excavated from the church's graveyard, and subsequently re-dedicated in 1989 by the Archdeacon of Carlisle.

Beside the Black Swan Hotel at the corner of Main Street note the spinning gallery which is still excellently preserved, and is mute testimony to the days when the village was renowned for its knitting at the early part of the last century, much as it was for butter towards the end of the last century.

RENWICK.

Map ref. H.5.
Next nearest Town or Village "Croglin"
Location. 12 miles north-east of Penrith.

The village of Renwick is situated some 12 miles from Penrith and an equal number from Brampton. A quiet village, nestling in the shelter of the Pennines in what can only be described as beautiful, dramatic scenery. Small and bleak it clings to the side of Thackmoor, while giving its name to another Fell, down which torrents tumble into the fir trees.

Most of the buildings here date from the 18th and 19th century...in fact, unusual for Cumbria, only five houses have been built in the village this century. Visitors to the village will notice some interesting features such as beehive shelters built into garden walls, along with some fine old barns. Since the 14th century, the memorial rights of Renwick have been held by Queen's College, Oxford.

The little church of All Saints has ancient foundations..in all probability, Celtic. The tiny church, with double bellcot and with nave and chancel under one roof, was rebuilt last century, but kept its two-decker pulpit, and a bell which has fallen silent after 500 years.

In the churchyard a great stone table stands by the door and near it are the remains of an old cross and on a green mound a mile or so away are fragments of stone walls in places ten feet high, all that is left of Haresceugh Castle after 600 years.

WCF COUNTRY CENTRES

The Country Store That Offers...

Choice, Quality and Value

in

PET FOODS - EQUESTRIAN - GARDENING
COUNTRY CLOTHING & LEISUREWEAR

plus

ALL FARM SUPPLIES REQUIREMENTS

At a WCF Country Centre Near You

Crawhall, **BRAMPTON** (06977) 2566
Allenbrook Road, Rosehill Trading Estate, **CARLISLE** (0228) 818058
Station Street, **COCKERMOUTH** (0900) 822249
Mintsfeet Rd North, Mintsfeet Ind. Est., **KENDAL** (0539) 723684
Brunswick Road, **PENRITH** (0768) 62207
Station Road, **WIGTON** (06973) 45061

EVERYONE WELCOME AT:

ROSLEY

Map ref. E.5.
Next nearest Town or Village "Welton"
Location.10 miles south-west of Carlisle.

The village name stems from 'Ross Lea' and means a place where horses grazed...no doubt linked to the fact that it was originally the site of a very old horse and cattle fair.

The church is in the centre of the village, and has just recently celebrated its 150th anniversary.

One cottage here has been built around two old trams from Carlisle.

RUSLAND.

Map ref. E.11.
Next nearest Town or Village "Oxen Park"
Location. 8 miles south of Hawkshead.

Rusland Valley 'This beautiful and secret valley' as it has been known to be called by many, runs from Rusland Beeches through to Satterthwaite and the Grizedale Forest, and lies between Coniston Water and Lake Windermere.

At one time the monks of Furness Abbey owned all the valley, and following the closure of the Abbey by Henry VIII the monks left a little chapel at Satterthwaite. Over the years it has been rebuilt several times, until finally in 1840 it was consecrated a church.

Visitors today will discover that the main occupation of the valley is agriculture and forestry, though there are still some excellent examples of its past when the monks were active here with their 'bloomeries' and smelting hearths. The best preserved tannery in England can be seen here, as well as pitheads, pot ash pits and copwood kilns.

St Paul's Church at Rusland stands high on a rocky eminence overlooking the entire valley. Many people visit it to make a pilgrimage to the graves of Arthur Ransome and his wife Eugenia. Also several of the Romney family are buried here too, the painter at one time having lived at Whitestock Hall..Also here is Rusland Hall dating from the 17th century, and built by the Rawlinson family. Within walking distance is Grizedale Forest. here you will find the largest site-related 'Sculpture in the Forest' exhibition in the country and which in 1986 was awarded a prize for the most outstanding contribution to art in a working environment.

RYDAL.

Map ref.E9.
Next nearest Town or Village "Ambleside"
Location. Just over one mile north of Ambleside.
Gala days/festivals. Rydal Sheepdog Trials 2nd Week August

Rydal lies on the main Ambleside to Keswick road, just one and a half miles north of Ambleside. Rydal means 'the valley where rye was grown' Though a small village its attractions are many. Here during the latter part of his life (1813-1850) lived William Wordsworth, Rydal Mount being the fourth and last, of his Lake District residences in adult life. For 37 years he lived here and here too he wrote nearly half the poems he published in his day. Here he built up his fame and gathered his friends about him. Here DeQuincey came, and Hartley Coleridge to name but two. The house is open to the public, and as to be expected attracts many thousands of visitors each year.

Wordsworth bought a sloping field here... Rashfield, ostensibly to build a house. The house never materialised so he renamed it 'Dora's Field' after his daughter. The main feature of the land comes to light in the spring, masses of daffodils and narcissi.

DORA'S FIELD

RYDAL

Rydal Hall has to be the most outstanding building in Rydal. The LeFleming's came to live at Rydal Hall in 1575....before the advent of the Lake poets the notable people of Rydal were the Flemings who had held the Rydal Hall estate for four centuries. Sir Daniel, a stout royalist, became after the Restoration an equally active repressor of such people as Quakers and Dissenters, and was knighted. Not far off is Wordsworth's Seat, a little rock where he loved to look across the lake, and at Fox How is the house built by Dr Arnold of Rugby, where Wordsworth would often look in for a chat. It was Arnold who gave nicknames to the three roads from Rydal Water to Grasmere. One was Old Corruption, another Bit-by-Bit Reform, the other Radical Reform.

The chapel of St Mary was actualy built by Lady Le Fleming, she even laid the foundation stone in 1824. Up until this time local people had had to rely on using the parish church at Grasmere for funerals, and even today a well known walk here is still known as "The Coffin Trail'. Its where coffins were carried over the rough road under Nab Scar to Grasmere. Visitors to the church will notice that the gallery in the church was reserved solely for the use of the LeFleming family, whilst Wordsworth and his family occupied the pew in front of the pulpit.

Rydal's chief natural attraction is its small lake...Rydal Water...a modest little lake fed from Grasmere by the river Rothay. At one time it was known as Rothaymere. The lake is steeply conscripted between the rocky hill Nab Scar on the north and the expansive plateau of Loughrigg Fell on the south. It is a beautiful situation traversed by the central highway of the Lake District for more than half a mile along the northern shore of the lake, which is shallow with extensive reed beds encumbered with reeds, but its situation and its placidity much admired.

This area, between Rydal and Grasmere is very popular with walkers. White Moss Common and Viewpoint were mentioned by Dorothy Wordsworth in her journal for 1st June 1802.

RYDAL HALL

We went to look at Rydal. There was an alpine fire-look red upon the tops of the mountains...we saw the Lake in a new and most beautiful point of view between the two little rocks. This White Moss, a place made for all kinds of beautiful works of art and nature, woods and valleys, fairy valleys and fairy tarns, minature mountains, alps above alps".

White Moss House built in 1730 was bought by William Wordsworth for his son Willie, and the poet often rested and composed poetry in the porch on his wanderings. He had moved to Rydal Mount at this time, but buying White Moss House gave William voting rights in Grasmere, which he used to help prevent the extension of the railway line from Windermere to Grasmere. The Wordsworth's owned the house until the 1930's. Today it is an internationally renowned small hotel and restaurant.. One of the oldest houses here is Cote How, it has a spinning gallery and dates from the 15th century. Fox How, another beautiful house, was built by Dr Arnold, one time Headmaster of Rugby School.

Nab Cottage, a typical Lake District farmhouse has the date 1702 over the door. Wordsworth's great friend Thomas deQuincey lived here. Today it is a delightful guest house.

ST. MARYS CHURCH

LAKE DISTRICT TRAIL RIDING CENTRE

Cote How

Rydal, Nr. Ambleside

Cumbria LA22 9LW

Tel: 05394 32765 Prop Mrs. C. Norton.

Come trial riding in our beautiful countryside.
We can offer a variety of riding holidays from - learn to ride weekends for
complete beginers to four days on the trial for more experienced riders.
You can even bring your own horse and stay on a B & B basis.
The centre is also ideally situated for walkers.

Comfortable and homely B & B accommodation. with oak beams and
large bedrooms. Tea/Coffee making facilities in all bedrooms.
Genuine English breakfast

Open all year.

SCALES.

Map ref. D.13.
Next nearest Town or Village "Baycliffe"
Location. 5 miles south-east of Ulverston.

A very pleasant Furness village with houses and cottages of all shapes and sizes. The name 'Scales' is of Norse origin, and means 'a shepherds hut' (or cattle shed) so it is quite likely the invaders penned their sheep or stabled their cattle at Scales.

This agricultural hamlet known as High and Low Scales used to belong to a family called Reay who were given the land in the twelth century by Scots King William the Lion as a reward to the first Reay for his fleetness of foot.

When his royal patron was pursuing the deer, Reay could outstrip both dogs and horses. The family seat was Gill House in a wooded glen beside the Langrigg Beck. It was built about 1830 by a John Reay, perhaps the first oldest son to break the tradition that they all had to be called William. At any rate the Gill must be one one of the few haunted houses to have its spooks officially recorded by the Government. It happened during the last war when the hauntings ......obviously by pro-Nazi ghosts...stopped the house being used as a Women's Land Army Hostel. Mediums declared the trouble-makers to have been a Satanist and a wife-murderer. Their activities ceased when the house was unoccupied for some years after the war. The present owners report nothing untoward these days.

There used to be many trades operating here but today 'trade' as such, consists of three farms. The Parish hall was a malt kiln at one time, and at the rear will be found three store huts, used for cattle shelters at one time. It is thought that cock-fighting took place here, each has a hole in the top allowing the public to look down on the proceedings. The school incidentally was at one time a tithe barn.

Two village greens, one of which has a pinfold...i.e. a pound for stray animals.

SCOTBY.

Map ref. F.4.

Next nearest Town or Village "Wetheral"

Bus service. Cumberland Buses Routes 74, 75

Location. 4 miles east of Carlisle.

Scotby lies about a mile beyond the eastern boundary of Carlisle, on high ground, and separated from the city by the M6 motorway.

It lies between the Eden and Carlisle, a delightful village with a green, white houses with porches and the tower curiously placed at the south-east end of the 19th century church.

The centre of the village forms a rough rectangle, with railway lines forming the north and south sides, and streams forming the east and west sides. There is a pleasant mixture of old and new houses around the green.

Scotby has developed over the years from an ancient settlement made by Scotsmen, clearing part of the ancient forest of Inglewood.

By the end of the 17th century Scotby had become one of Cumberland's earliest Quaker villages. The house opposite the pub was in fact the farmstead of their leader William Bond. A Friends Meeting House was built here in 1718 on the Wetheral road corner, it had its own graveyard.

In 1781 Elihu Sutton a local landowner established a tannery beside the stream and coal vaults. This provided labour for the community until its closure in 1930.

Ghosts are reputed to haunt Scotbys oldest houses and there are reports of a phantom horseman who races the road to Wetheral.

SEASCALE.

Map ref. B.10.

Next nearest Town or Village "Drigg"

Bus service. Cumberland Buses Route 06, 12

Trains. Railway station.

Location. Midway between Whitehaven and Millom.

South along the coast from Whitehaven and Workington, Seascale still has a popular following, partly due to its rail link and fine sandy beach, and a backdrop of splendid accessible mountains. It s still a lovable little seaside place for many things...for its fine open stretches of sand and for the beauty of the hills and mountains which rise magnificently in the east. Monarch of all the fine array is the wild twin-peaked mountain mass which climbs 12 miles away to the highest point in England, Scafell Pike, 3,210 feet above the sea.

There's been two distinct stages in the towns development over the years. The first would have been the coming of the railway in the 1850's, when it could be said Victorian Seascale really began, complete with bathing machines, ice-creams, deck chairs...even donkey rides.

It was the outbreak of war in 1939 which brought to an end the holiday trade, and from the mid 40's an atomic station was set up at Sellafield close by...(though then it was known as Windscale)

Following the war the holiday trade started up all over again though this time it was the Sellafield workers and their families who were enjoying all that Seascale could offer.

The spacious church stands proudly at a high corner of the village, near a war memorial cross carved with vines and knotwork. Hardly older than the 20th century, the nave has five round bays built in Norman fashion.

An old farmhouse a little way off was built as the manor house in the 17th century, and there is also in the neighbourhood about a mile away, one great stone standing near the golf links, the only stone remaining of a prehistoric Circle of the Stone Age, the others sunk into the ground. Quite near is yet another circle of standing stones, their purpose still remains a mystery however.

Over the years as we all know, Sellafield has expanded enormously, and the visitors these days are the thousands who visit for an exciting tour of the site.

SEATON.

Map ref. B.7.
Next nearest Town or Village "Workington"
Bus service. Cumberland Buses Route 47
Location 3 miles north of Workington.

Seaton is the largest village in Cumbria, though at one time it was just a small mining community with brickworks and a few farms; though today the mines and brickworks have disappeared.

Villagers will tell you that in 1752 John Wesley, the founder of Methodism preached a sermon on the village green and proclaimed he was standing on the greenest turf in the country.

In the centre of the village stands the parish church. St Paul's which celebrated its centenary in 1982.It is built of local stone, in Gothic style.

Its an attractive spot with many excellent views. Seaton Mill Farm, for example, is situated on the banks of the River Derwent and has an old mill wheel.

SEBERGHAM

Map ref.E.6.
Next nearest Town or Village "Caldbeck"
Location. 2 miles north of Caldbeck.

Sebergham is a parish in Inglewood on the river Caldew...said to have been first settled by the hermit William of Wastall in the 12th century.His cell is supposed to have been on the site of St Mary's Church.

Called 'Sebberam' locally, it is charmingly set among the hills at the northern end of the Pennine fells which rise majestically a few miles away. Its houses cling to the steep banks of a lovely glen where the River Caldew flows under an old stone bridge taking the road to Penrith.

The church stands away from the village in Churchtown with a small group of 18th century houses for company.

The valley through which the Caldew flows is thickly wooded with steep sides until it widens into pastureland on the outskirts of Sebergham.At this point will be noted a huge boulder with a crack across and about a foot deep. Locals like to tell the story of a young man who was courting one of the Miss Denton 's...daughter of the local land-owner. She refused to marry him,until one day he vowed to saw through the boulder and would not stop until she consented to marry him...after sawing a foot deep, one assumes she must have relented!

It was here that the international civil engineering firm of Laings had its beginnings. It was David Laing along with his younger brother who after travelling from Dumfries were lucky to find some building work in the district.They prospered so well that David married local girl Jane Mason and moved into the Old Rectory. By 1867 it was necessary to move the business to Carlisle, from whence it prospered until it became the size it is today.

Be warned..Upon leaving Sebergham, visitors must climb a steep hill. To the south is Sebergham Brow a 1 in 8 climb, and to the north Doctor Brow, which is worse 1 in 6. Incidentally Dr Brow is so named in memory of a local doctor who was coming down it in his pony and trap when the horse shied, turned the trap over, and consequently killed the doctor. Near too is Warmell Hall, originally a pele tower acquired by the Denton's in 1496.

SEDBERGH,

Map ref.H.11.
Tourist Information Centre. 72, Main Street.
Location. 10 miles east of Kendal.
Early closing. Thursday.
Market day.Wednesday,

It is rather an anomaly to find this recognisably a Dales Yorkshire town under Cumbria,but since 1974 this part of Yorkshire has been firmly included in Cumbria...even though the Yorkshire

"ENTRANCE TO ST. ANDREWS CHURCH

SEDBERGH

Dales National Park claims it.

This attractive old market town, with its cobbled streets and attractive 'olde worlde'atmosphere has been developed at the confluence of four valleys and four rivers where the ancient trade routes merged. The town is somewhat dwarfed by some of Alfred Wainwright's favourite fells...the mighty Howgills. Dating from Roman times, Sedbergh still shows clear evidence of the influence of the subsequent Saxons, Vikings, and Norman's.

Firmly based as a market centre for the rural district, Sedbergh also had...stocking making,woollen workers,smithying,the odd small mill.By walking around the old yards behind the main streets and seeing the cottages all of which date from 1790-1850 this will become apparent.

Sedbergh's main claim to fame has to be its public school...founded in 1525.Many of the Sedbergh School old pupils have left their international mark over the years, the most recent being Will Carling, Captain of the England Rugby team . The original school building is now a library. William Wordsworth's son was a pupil here too, and Hartley Coleridge was on the staff for a time.

"HIGH ST.

Overlooking the town is the site of Castlehaw, an ancient motte and bailey castle built originally to repel the rebellious Scottish hordes.

Historian's visiting the area may be interested to learn that George Fox, founder of the Quakers preached in both the courtyard of St Andrew in the heart of town,and at the nearby Brigflatts Quaker Meeting House which itself dates from 1675, and interestingly enough is the second oldest meeting house in existence. It is also reputed that Bonnie Prince Charlie hid in a seven feet wide chimney which is still to be seen, before escaping in disguise with the pack horses taking away the woollen goods.

COBBLE COUNTRY
—Holidays—

SELF CATERING COTTAGES * APARTMENTS * B & B CAMPING * HOTELS
SITUATED IN UNSPOILT SURROUNDINGS

We are the specialists in providing a wide range of accommodation of all forms to suit the needs of any person or group requiring a visit to the beautiful Sedbergh and District area.

Ideally situated just 5 minutes from Junction 37 of the M6 Motorway, we are just inside the **YORKSHIRE DALES NATIONAL PARK** and yet only twenty minutes journey from the **LAKE DISTRICT NATIONAL PARK.**

Sedbergh Town has remained relatively unspoilt by the demands of the modern age, but has managed to develop a style that is becoming ever more attractive to the discerning visitor.

The completion of an attractive development of holiday accommodation in 1994 which features one third of its rooms as meeting the "Tourism for All' ACCESSIBLE standard is further proof of the way Sedbergh is looking to the future. Indeed 50% of those ACCESSIBLE Rooms will meet the exacting standards of CATEGORY 1 and is only the second establishment in CUMBRIA to offer this to the traveller. We would like you to visit us and sample our hospitality and look forward to your call

63, Main Street, Sedbergh, Cumbria

LA10 5AB

☎ 05396 21000.

P.S. We hope that you probably do not need the additional incentive of a chance for a free Holiday in our area but details will be sent with every enquiry unless you request us specifically not to send them.

SEDBERGH SCHOOL

Sedbergh School was founded in 1525 by Roger Lupton, a Provost of Eton, who persuaded the young King Edward V1 that a school wasdesperately needed "in the North Country amongst the people rude in knowledge". In the 19th Century it was

one of the leading Grammar Schools in the North of England and like so many old Grammar Schools it was reconstituted in the mid-19th Century by a powerful governing body who laid the foundations of the school's modern achievements.

Of the original school the handsome library (1719) is the oldest remaining building. Two of the boarding houses are located in the town on Main Street and Back Lane while the remainder of the extensive buildings and grounds are located to the South of the Parish Church. Visitors are welcome on the campus.

Of all the leading schools in Britain Sedbergh School can justly boast of the unrivalled beauty of its setting. As the school song records "The hills that are built around us...make the Sedbergh man!" Sedbergh men have gone on to make their mark as musicians, artists, actors, parliamentarians, explorers, and sportsmen - indeed their are few areas of national life today where former pupils of the school do not occupy a position of distinction, and few of these who ever forget the haunting image of "Winder's clear-cut outline against an evening sky". While acknowledging its proud traditions and debt to the past the school has kept pace with the rapid changes of the modern world and offers its pupils the most up to date facilities for education and recreation. The school is Independent and accepts boys for entry from the age of eleven. Scholarships and Bursaries are available.

Visitors wishing to find out more about the educational opportunities offered by the school are invited to contact the Admissions Officer -

Tel Sedbergh (STD 05396) 20535

SEDGWICK

Map ref. G.11.
Next nearest Town or Village "Natland"
Location. 4 miles south of Kendal.

Sedgwick is situated some four miles south of Kendal, close by the River Kent.
The original village buildings are mostly gathered around the area of the Post Office and along the main road. One of the most interesting pieces of architecture in Sedgwick is the canal bridge built by John Rennie.
It was in 1869 that the village was altered considerably,when the Wakefield family from

POST OFFICE

Sedgwick brought the gunpowder industry to the area, and additionally built many of the cottages for their estate, and many others of their workers. A local builder today by the name of Willacy is a direct descendant of the builder who undertook so much of the work in the village.

It was on the Sedgwick House tennis courts that the first competitive festival in the country took place. The Mary Wakefield Music Festival is now held biennially in Kendal..

SELSIDE.

Map ref. G.10.
Next nearest Town or Village "Kendal"
Location. 4 miles north of Kendal.
Gala days/festivals. Selside/Grayrigg Agricultural Show. 1st Thursday September.

Just north of Kendal will be found Selside, somewhat of a hilly area with many scattered farms and houses most of which date back a large number of years.

Selside has one hamlet...namely Watchgate..which has a grand total of twelve houses and a blacksmith's. At one time a Roman road ran through the parish and over the notorious Shap fell, and in parts can still be traced. Watchgate, Gateside, Leagate, and Hallowgate were old settlements alongside. Half a mile away is Toll Bar Cottage which was originally built to collect the tolls along the Turnpike road.

FELL WALKING

St Thomas's church overlooks Selside Hall which is a fine Elizabethan farmhouse which started life as a 14th century pele tower.

In 1730 a John Kitching gave land and money for a Whitwell and Selside school, this can still be seen, but is now a private residence.

SHAP.

Map ref. G.8.
Next nearest Town or Village "Keld"
Bus service. Cumberland Buses route 107
Location. 15 miles north of Kendal A.6.
Early closing. Thursday and Saturday.
Market day. Monday.
Gala days/festivals Shap sheepdog trials. 4th Saturday June.

OLD MARKET HALL

Shap is located directly on the A6 road, at over 800 feet, south of Penrith, and until the building of the M6 extension was a busy town. In fact a hundred years ago Shap was a stop-over place for the weary traveller arriving on horse back or stage coach...if you look carefully you will still see the steps at each end of the village where passengers would have alighted.

Although Shap has for long been on an important routeway, the Romans bypassed the site of the village around which are many traces of the Stone Age.

There are stone circles at Oddendale, and Gunnerkeld and standing stones were disturbed when the A6 road cut through Carl Lofts to the south, to the north west is the Thunder Stone. Travellers may turn off the main road and see the ruins of Shap Abbey in a sheltered valley. They make a fine picture with a background of the distant Mardale fells and the beautiful River Lowther. The Abbey was founded 800 years ago by Thomas Gospatric and fell into ruin soon after. It was surrended in 1540 and Lord Wharton took the valuable lead from the roofs of the buildings. Not even the gateway is standing, but fragments remain of the 13th century church, with stones of the 13th century and a noble tower built about 1500. Although the Abbey buildings would be well concealed in the narrow valley, the west tower, largely intact, looks out over the green moorlands, its great arch a frame for the hills beyond. There are a few fragments left of the presbytery, among them a tomb of the 14th century, the incised cross indicating the grave of one slain in battle, and it is thought that this may be the tomb of Robert de Clifford who was killed at Bannockburn.

Not too far away is Stuart House where Bonnie Prince Charlie is supposed to have lodged on the 17th December 1745, as his bedraggled army retreated towards the border during the Jacobite Rebellion.

When the Abbey was plundered in the 17th century, stone was brought to the village to build the market hall, and at the same time a charter was granted. The arches of the old hall have long since been filled in, and from in later years being a Dame school, then the Parish Rooms...it now houses the village library.

On a hillside above the village is a small enclosure where the dead from Mardale churchyard were re-buried when the church was demolished before the waters of Haweswater reservoir covered the area. Around the walls of the enclosure are a number of plaques from the church in memory of the Holmes family...the 'Kings of Mardale'.

Today Shap has lost its avenue of stones, its stagecoaches, its packhorses, its market, its Abbey, its Spa, even its famous landmark. Shap Thorn described in Wordsworth's guide as 'planted on the top of the hill for the direction of travellers' is now a prominent group of ash trees. But its quaint little market cross is a cosy library, its coaching inns are as welcoming as ever.

For many years people came to Shap Wells to bathe in or drink the water of the Spa Well. These waters include some sulphur and have a smell which was once described as being similar to a musket barrel being discharged! The waters are in fact very similar to those of Leamington and Harrogate, the principal constituents being calcium chloride and sodium chloride with some magnesium sulphate (better known as Epsom salts). These days, the well, unfortunately is no longer in use, though water may still be obtained from the spring on the river bank.

One of the most interesting chapters in the Hotel's history occured during the Second World War when it became a prisoner of war camp for German Naval and Luftwaffe Officers, many of whom, to this day, still return to the hotel. It is even reputed that Rudolph Hess was held prisoner here.

There are many features at Shap Wells Hotel today upon which our guests comment. Some speak of the log and peat fires which burn in our public rooms, or the attentive local staff...or the personal supervision of the Metcalfe family and their manager, along with the location of the Hotel in what has been described as "Britains Healthiest Spot". All these combine to produce the warm, relaxing and friendly atmosphere for which Shap Wells Hotels is rightly renowned.

The Hotel's bedrooms' which are furnished in individual styles, have radio, intercom, auto-alarm, and baby listening services. Of these the "prestige' rooms in our Bretherdale Wing are furnished to executive standards, with direct dial telephones, televisions, tea and coffee making facilities...even hairdriers. The public rooms of the hotel which include the Riverside Lounge and the adjoining Birkbeck Restaurant enjoy splendid views over the river and surrounding moors. Here you may enjoy an aperitif before a leisurely dinner chosen from our a la carte or table d'hote menu's...or just sit and relax over a pot of tea, taking in the wonderful scenery...Other public rooms include the Fell Bar, which is a pub style lounge, the Salterwath Lounge, and the Lonsdale Suite...

THE SHAP WELLS HOTEL, SHAP, PENRITH, CUMBRIA. TEL: 0931 716628

Kings Arms Hotel
Free House
SHAP Village, Cumbria
Telephone 0931 716277

Shap is a high point for many on the famous Coast-to Coast Walk across Britain, although not only for its geography and geology! The friendly welcome, the four-poster beds, great breakfasts at the Kings Arms Hotel make the inn something of a "walkers paradise".

The walkers say it gets better as it goes along and that, if their stay at Shap is anything to go by, they can't wait for the next stage of the walk" say licensees, Judith and Clarry Collins. The couple have set themselves the dual priorities of providing home comforts for guests with their six letting bedrooms, which include two four poster beds, two twin and two family rooms and of ensuring a real village pub atmosphere in the bar.

The Inn dates from 1700 and has had a varied career - in fact - Bonnie Prince Charlie stayed here on his flight back to Scotland...and prior to being re-instated as one of Cumbria's mot popular pubs some 20 years ago, was for a time being run as an antique shop . Today though the main theme of the Kings Arms Hotel is as a genuine, traditional pub and lively village social centre. Live music provides an attraction every alternate Saturday night, and there are excellent facilities for pool and darts. Dominoes is another popular activity and the inn runs monthly Sunday "chip-out" events popular with both the strong following of regulars and with visitors.

Clarry Collins is responsible for their famous full English breakfasts, which include no less that seven items. According to regularly repeated comments in the visitors' book they are 'the best breakfast you will get anywhere".The Kings Arms is a free house and offers hand-pumped real ales including Stones bitter, Websters Yorkshire bitter and Wilsons mild. The inn stands alongside the A6 road and is only a couple of minutes away from the M6 junction 39 at Shap.

SILECROFT.

Map ref. C.12.
Next nearest Town or Village "Kirksanton"
Location. 3 miles from Millom.

Silecroft village lies on a long road between the main coast road and the sea, just three miles from Millom.

Not one style of house here, but a variety of stone houses, farm buildings, bungalows, and terrace houses, most of which were built originally to house the railway workers together with the employees of the small local ironworks.

The oldest house here has a well in its kitchen. Cobble walls line the streets between the houses, and it still has its own railway station.

The beach here is safe and popular with visitors and locals alike...beach combing is a popular sport, often turning up early Roman flints.

Silecroft has its own hill...Black Combe, lying to the north, and which besides being a perfect beacon hill, also acts as a shelter from the worst of the winter weather.

SILLOTH.

Map ref. C.4.
Next nearest Town or Village "Beckfoot"
Bus service. Cumberland Buses Routes 38, 38a.
71
Tourist Information Centre. The Green.Silloth.
Location. 10 miles south of Allonby.
Early closing.Tuesday.
Gala days/festivals..Silloth Carnival..Bank Holiday Monday.Aug.
Silloth Victorian Weekend.

Silloth...the name derives from 'Sealathe...meaning a barn for the storing of grain, ...and was the port used by the monks of nearby Holm Cultram Abbey for the export of wool .

Until 1857 Silloth was a tiny fishing hamlet.it was then that work commenced on building a port, to be served by a branch railway from Carlisle...the port being planned originally to rival Whitehaven. No difficulty in finding financial backers in those days..one of the foremost being J.D.Carr, a major bakery owner of the region...and now of course a household name...Today the dock covers six acres and the expanse of water roughly measures 600feet by 400 feet. Visitors will normally find one or two ships tied up here.

When the rail link with Carlisle opened in the 1850's a competition was held to design a new town, which was won by a Liverpool firm of architects. Consequently Silloth retains its Victorian 'spa' style atmosphere with an attractive seafront and purpose built docks.

Many parts of Silloth are as attractive as any Cumbrian town...the street with the fish dealers...all the buildings red brick and Victorian...the fine parish church. Its an attractive district overlooking the Solway and Scotland in the distance with a great expanse of beach.

Silloth is much favoured by the Cumbrians on fine summer weekends. It never became another Blackpool, but it does have what the more popular resorts lack...a fine green between the buildings and the promenade.

The 18 hole golf course beside the shore here was the home course of Miss Cecil Leitch (1891-1978) the most celebrated woman golfer of all time. Other famous players were the late Duke of Kent, and Kathleen Ferrier, the great contralto. A plaque on the wall of the National Westminster Bank in Eden Street, marks the place where her short married life in the town was spent.

SKELSMERGH.

Map ref. H.11.
Location 2 miles north of Kendal on Shap road.

Skelsmergh lies a short distance north of Kendal and is bounded on three sides by the waters of Mint,Kent, and Sprint.
The name is derived from a Norse settler by the name of Skjalmar.
Skelsmergh hall which at one time was the home of the Leybourne family for over 400 years actually has its origins in the 14th century, and even today still retains its 15th century pele tower.
It was in 1745 that the Catholic Leybournes lost their property due to their support for the Jacobite rebellion. It has a 15th century pele tower,an oak staircase, much handsome panelling and a chest in which the Lord of the Manor would have kept his armour. Today Skelsmergh Hall is a farmhouse.
Another fine house is Dodding Green which was first built by William Dodding nearly 600 years ago. At one time mass was celebrated here in secret in an attic chamber...certainly until 1791 when a small chapel was allowed to be built. The house has many secret cupboards where priests are said to have hidden and in the library are many precious books some printed less than 40 years after Caxton's day.

Once upon a time a Roman road passed through the area en route from the fort at Watercrook (south of Kendal) to the fort in Borrowdale... crossing over the River Mint. This old packhorse bridge which in recent years has been widened, forms a lovely stone arch.

At one time there were flourishing watermills at Oakbank, Beck Mills and Stock Mills which ground corn, sawed timber and also produced bobbins and woollen cloth.

The busiest one of all was at Mealbank (in the parish of Scalthwaiterigg) where more than 500 people were employed until the mid '40's.

Many of the mills still stand though in all cases they have either been converted to another business use, or turned into a comfortable home.

SKELTON.

Map ref. F.6.
Next nearest Town or Village "Greystock"
Location. 6 miles north-west of Penrith.
Gala days/festivals.Skelton Show. 3rd Saturday in
August.

SPIRE HOUSE

Skelton lies six miles north-west of Penrith off the
B5303 Wigton Road.
The church here of St Michael's dates back to the
13th century.In fact its most famous visitor was
King Edward 1 who whilst on a hunting trip north,
took communion at the church (in 1299) even
leaving seven shillings (35 pence) in the collection
box.

arches still to be seen.

Hutton in the Forest is the historic home of Lord
Inglewood and dates back (via its pele tower) to
the 14th century.In the middle ages it was held
direct from the King by 'money rent' and the duty
of holding the King's stirrup when he mounted his
horse at Carlisle Castle.
Half a mile from Skelton is Hardrigg Hall, one of
the old fortified houses now a farm. Its strength lay
in a tower now ruined..there are broken walls and

Skelton Show which has been held here on the 3rd
Saturday in August now for over 100 years is the
largest horticultural and agricultural show in the
north-west of England. It is held at Hutton in the
Forest.

Only one pub remains today. The Dog and Gun
(once known as the Sportsman)

SKELWITH BRIDGE.

Map ref. E.10.
Next nearest Town or Village "Ambleside"
Location. 4 miles south-west of Ambleside.

'Skelwith' comes from the old word Schelwath, meaning (appropriately) ford by the waterfall.
One time the boundary between Lancashire and Westmorland, Skelwith Bridge is really just a hotel and a handful of houses by a road junction...where the B5343 to Langdale branches off the A593. A few yards off this 'A' road here are the Kirkstone Galleries, the showroom for slate products made from stone quarried near the Kirkstone Pass, annexed to it is a coffee shop, restaurant, and gift shop. A path sign-posted through the yard of the slate workshops leads to the river and to Skelwith Force, not the tallest Lakeland waterfall at a mere 20 feet, but the fall bearing the greatest volume of water. It is through this narrow gap formed by glacial action that all the water from the high fells around the Langdales rushes after heavy rainfall...definitely the best time to view (and photograph). 'Force' incidentally, is the local name for a waterfall.
Concentrated within a half days walk from Skelwith Force is a variety of scenery that it would be difficult to match anywhere else in the Lake District...Elterwater the exquisite Loughrigg Tarn, and the charming setting of Colwith Force are examples of the pleasures in store.

SMARDALE.

Map ref. I.9.
Next nearest Town or Village "Kirkby Stephen"
Location. 3 miles west of Kirkby Stephen.

Smardale is situated some three miles west of Kirkby Stephen, and is one of the oldest inhabited areas of Cumbria, containing remnants of prehistoric village settlements.
As villages go they don't come much smaller than Smardale. It consists of six houses and two farms, one of which is a 13th century fortified Hall. It is rather an unusual design being a long narrow rectangle with round towers at each of the four corners.
Near the Scandal beck is known to be a mediaeval settlement...it is near the ford which leads from Smardale to Crosby Garret. At one of the settlements is the locally called 'Giants Graves' which could have been ancient burial grounds.

Here are two railway viaducts, one of which is used by the Settle to Carlisle railway line. It stands 130 feet above ground and was built in the 1870's. On the lane outside Smardale Hall is the entrance to one of Cumbria's Wildlife Trust's most prized nature reserves Smardale Gill.
Because of the diversity of limestone grasslands and woodlands, rare butterflies and plants, the reserve is listed a Site of Special Scientific Interest. The woodland is mainly ash and birch, with some oak, rowan and coppiced hazel. In spring and summer, primroses, violets, helleborines and orchids flower in the banks and beneath the trees. Also to be seen are roe deer and red squirrels, pied flycatchers and long tailed tits.
For almost 2,000 years people have been working this land. High above the valley floor lies the remains of an ancient Romano-British settlement and dotted over the open slopes will be seen the remains of charcoal burner's hearths.

SLAGGYFORD.

Map ref. I.5.
Next nearest Town or Village Alston
Location. 1 mile north of A.689 Alston to Greenhead.

Slaggyford Village is situated about a mile north of the A.689.
The name means 'muddy ford'. The Pennine Way goes through the village...part of it in fact along the old Roman Road (otherwise known as 'The Maiden Way), on its way northwards from Alston to Greenhead...a favourite walk with many of Cumbria's visitors.
The area is actively known as Knarsdale and take its name from the Knar burn which flows from the western fells into the South Tyne.
Knarsdale Hall is situated about a mile or so south of the village. It is a 17th century farmhouse with stone slab roof and mullioned windows, which

THE KIRKSTONE GALLERIES

In a lovely setting on the Banks of the River Brathay at Skelwith Bridge on the A593. from Ambleside to Coniston.
Here is the place to find something different.

This is the home of Kirkstone, a natural sea green stone of volcanic origin. Unique to The Lake District it has been quarried here since Roman times. On display are the many ways in which Kirkstone can be cut and shaped to produce everything from patio paving and kitchen worksurfaces to table mats and clocks, even earrings.

There is much more to see. The Galleries feature a collection of home furnishings, crafts and gifts reflecting the best of contemporary taste. Different room settings establish the style from conservatory through to kitchen, with unusual furniture, Kirkstone tables and colourful soft furnishings.

Elegant wine glasses, original tableware and pretty paper napkins spark ideas for home entertaining. Soft lights from an unusual lamp, or a centre piece of candles and perhaps a bowl of silk flowers. For the cook all manner of kitchen paraphernalia from a sharp little knife to the specialist home made pasta maker

For kids we have plenty of pocket money items they can choose for themselves alongside games, puzzles and soft toys. Our stationery room features cards for all tastes, plus beautiful wrap, books and journals. Visit in autumn and you'll find plenty of ideas for Christmas.

Take a break in Chesters Coffee Shop and enjoy a delicious frothy Cappucino or a strong Espresso. Choose from a varied selection of home made cakes such as Westmorland Crunchie or Banana Toffee Flan.

During the summer months meals are served on the patio alongside the river Brathay. Lunchtime menus include filled rolls, pates and rich, substantial home made soups. English country wines, fruit cordials and lagers are available.

Chesters is a popular spot for locals and visitors alike who appreciate the excellent quality of the produce and the delightful setting. Open all year round for good food in the heart of Kirkstone Galleries.

OPENING HOURS
April to October 10 am - 6.00 pm
November to March - 10 am - 5.00 pm
7 days a week throughout the year.

Skelwith Bridge, Ambleside, Cumbria, LA22 9NN
Telephone: 05394 34002

SLAGGYFORD /SOULBY / SPARK BRIDGE

appears to have been built on the mound of an earlier Norman castle. It still shows the remains of a moat around it. These days a more recent farm-house adjoins the old building.

There is a ghost story connected with this old hall which concerns a laird whose young wife fell in love with her husband's nephew. The young man's sister learned of the affair, and the guilty pair, fearful that she would betray them, seized her one stormy night, and plunged her into the moat. The old man, upon being awakened by the howling of the dogs, saw his niece standing by the kitchen door wringing water from her hair, but at the sound of his voice the apparition disappeared. The young apparition disappeared , and was seen no more, and the young wife died of brain fever after revealing the guilty secret . Her ghost is said to haunt the hall until this day.

Just a half mile away from the Hall is the church of St Jude, which though built in 1838 does in fact stand on the site of a much older church. In fact there are a few Saxon memorial stones let into the walls of the present building.

The only pub in the village now is the Kirkstyle Inn.

SOULBY

Map ref. I.9.
Next nearest Town or Village "Crosby Garrett"
Location. Just over 2 miles north of
Kirkby Stephen.

Soulby is a small village lying some two miles north west of Kirkby Stephen. The name is derived (as so many Cumbrian village names are) from the Old Norse meaning 'Short valley'

The village contains no buildings of great antiquity, though many of the houses have door lintels or tablets bearing 17th and 18th century dates. The oldest building will be the parish church of St Luke which dates from 1663. It was originally a 'chapel' of the church of Kirkby Stephen, for it was not until 1873 that Soulby became a separate parish.

Just half a mile above the village stands the old water mill...remains of the mill race are still notice-able.

The village has a wide village green in the centre, and close to the beck, complete with what was until 1938 the villagers only water supply...the village pump...in its ivy covered limestone enclosure.

The beck is spanned by an attractive but sturdy three arched stone bridge erected in 1819.

SPARK BRIDGE

Map ref. E.12.
Next nearest Town or Village "Colton"
Location. 5 miles north of Ulverston.

Spark Bridge nestles along the banks of the River Crake...(the river which flows from Conisiton Water into Morecambe Bay) and is situated just five miles north of Ulverston.

Somewhat as the name implies it was at one time the scene of bustling activity. There is certainly evidence of early iron smelting hereabouts and a bloomsmithy was erected in 1710...though there is strong evidence to suppose it was there a lot earlier than that. In 1761 it was converted to an iron furnace from whence it despatched much of its products from the (then) port of Greenodd to Scotland, Wales and Ireland.

In 1848 the countryside demand was for bobbins, consequently the forge was demolished and a bob-bin mill built instead, and which not only produced bobbins for the textile industry, but also pill boxes, brush heads, and spinning tops. Demand regret-fully ceased to exist in later years, and in 1983 the mill closed its doors for the last time. Several of the buildings can still be seen today as can the timber drying sheds.

The village still has one 'craftworker' in situ. That is a woodman who carries out the business of coppicing, besom making and bark peeling.

Two pubs in town. The Royal Oak Inn in the village, and just outside, the Farmers Arms (with its spinning gallery and huge round chimneys)

STAINMORE.

Map ref. J.8.
Next nearest Town or Village "Brough"
Location. A.66. Scotch corner to Appleby road.
Gala days/festivals.Brough Agricultural Show.
4th Thursday August.
Brough Cumbria Hound and Terrier Show.
3rd Sunday June.
South Stainmore Sport and Hound Trail.
2nd Thursday June.

Stainmore, so small that you will be hard put to find it on your map. But exist it does, and it will be found on the A66 'The Stainmore Pass' bordering Yorkshire and Durham, where some of the most spectacular limestone fells in the Pennines give way to moors of millstone grit.

Before the roads were made the pass carved by retreating glaciers millions of years ago, was the natural place to cross the Pennines. The Romans built a road over Stainmore, and a heavy cavalry garrison was stationed at Brough to protect it .It was certainly of great importance to the Romans when marching from York to the Wall and Maiden Castle.
Stainmore's history is long and illustrious. During excavations weapons and tools have been found, dating from the Bronze and Iron Ages. Maidens Castle thought to have been a small square Roman fort on the old Roman road north of the A66 and not far from the summit of the pass. A Roman signal station at Roper Castle or Round Table may have been built on a site going back some 3,000 years and used for religious rites.

Near the summit of Stainmore is the stump of a cross known as 'Rey Cross' which in the 11th century marked the boundary between Scotland and England...itself erected as a grave monument in the 10th century. A popular theory is that it was erected originally to the memory of the last Danish King,Eric Bloodaxe, killed in a battle on Stainmore in AD 954.

Nearby, and visible for miles around, Brough Castle looms as dramatically over the landscape today as it has done for centuries. Built on the earthworks of a former Roman fort, the ruins form

part of a chain of castles standing guard over what was once a crucial trade route across the Pennines. Besieged and burnt by the Scots in the 12th century, rebuilt but left to fall derelict again in Tudor times, the castle rose from the ashes under the skilful ownership of Lady Anne Clifford in the 17th century.

Sir Cuthbert Buckle, Lord Mayor of London in 1593 endowed a school at South Stainmore with £8 per year allowance in 1594. The school house was built by local inhabitants. Although the church consecrated in 1608 is still in use today, the school closed as recently as 1970 and is now a residential outdoor centre.

Tree worship was at one time a way of life in Brough. On twelfth night the holly tree would be suitably illuminated with rushlights or candles, and carried through the town, where later it would be thrown amongst the crowd. The younger and more daring members of the crowd would then attempt to seize it and carry it off to rival inns where drinking and dancing continued far into the night.

It is to a Norman family that the ghost of the headless horse-woman of Stainmore belongs.
Apparently on one of the Saxon raids, the Saxons made off with the daughter of the Norman Fitzbarnard.
A particular Saxon decided he would keep her for his wife, but before he was able to tie the knot, a Norman rescue party literally snatched her from his grasp. The Saxon understandably furious of being deprived of his intended hotly rode into the middle of the Norman raiding party laying about everybody with his sword...and in the confusion cut off the head of the girl!...Ever since her headless body has careered around Stainmore on horseback.

Beyond Stainmore, near Mortham's Tomb is an old border pele tower, and connected with it a grim legend. Hundreds of years ago a certain Lord Rokeby apparently in a fit of temper caused by jealously, murdered his wife in the glen below the tower, and the bloodstains which cannot be effaced are still to be seen on the steps.It is said they were caused by the blood dripping from his dagger as he mounted the stairs after committing the crime.

STAINTON WITH ADGARLEY.

Map ref.D.13.
Next nearest Town or Village "Scales"
Location. Approx 1 mile from Dalton.

Stainton with Adgarley lies one and a half miles from Dalton-in-Furness, and about halfway between Barrow in Furness and Ulverston.

There are many old farm cottages around, quite a few dating back to the early 18th century, the oldest of which is adjacent to Stainton Hall, and is believed to have been converted from the Halls stables.

Stainton Hall (the Manor House) itself, is a most impressive building. It is believed that the ancestors of George Washington actually built the Hall though as yet this has not been proven. The Hall is distinctive for its mullioned windows and huge high chimney stacks. Part of the Hall was demolished by cannon fire during the Civil War.

The village green at Stainton was one of the centres for cockfighting and to this day the remains of the cockfighting ring can still be seen.

Within the village and boundary evidence exists of a Bronge Age burial ground together with Bronze Age and Neolithic settlements have been found. Two pubs hereabouts...the Farmers Arms and the Miners Arms, each indelibly showing the areas connections with farming and iron-ore mining.

STAVELEY.

Map ref. F.10.
Next nearest Town or Village "Windermere"
Trains.Staveley Railway Station.
Location. 4 miles north of Kendal.

The village of Staveley, meaning a wood or glade where staves were cut, lies midway between Kendal and Windermere, nestling at the foot of the Kentmere Valley.

Staveley is a large, and to many people, attractive village of 700 years, retaining much of its heritage. At one time it was a minor market centre with a charter granted in 1329, but Kendal usurped its trade. Later the village became a focal point for the bobbin industry with five mills in the Kent and Gowan valleys, these have gradually closed over the years, though wood turning and paper making still survives.

The Burne-Jones window is the great possesion of the long and handsome chancel in the 19th century church. It shows the Crucifixion and the Ascen-

TOWER STAVELEY

sion with angels grouped on a starry background. Only the noble tower of the 15th century church remains, a magnificent monument to its builders, its west window set between lovely niches. Other relics are a mediaeval font, a 17th century chest, and old glass fragments of heraldry and a half figure of a man.

It was Sir William de Thweng who was originally granted the market charter. He also then held a fair on the 17th, 18th and 19th of October each year. Sir William also founded the chapel of St Margaret, as mentioned above.

In the centre of the village stands the rather impos-ing late Victorian building 'The Abbey' built originally to serve as a hotel when the railway was brought through Staveley to Windermere. These days it is a residential home for the elderly.

In the past it was bobbins that really made Staveleys fortune. All the ingredients were available...water power, technical skill, wood and of course business knowledge. After 1819 the Kendal-Lancaster canal made transport to the large Lancashire mills much easier, and 'King Cotton' made Britain and Staveley rich, with the coming of the railway in 1847 speeding up the process.

ST BEES,

Map ref. A.9.
Next nearest Town or Village "Egremont"
Bus service.Cumberland Buses Route 20
Trains. Railway Station.
Location.5 miles south of Whitehaven.

St.Bees is a small village on the west coast of Cumbria, and lies five miles south of Whitehaven. Tradition has it that it got its name from St.Bega, an Irish lady who fled in the 7th century from Ireland to avoid an unsuitable marriage, and landed on the beach by chance, and founded a nunnery. It is thought that the Nunnery was destroyed by Viking raiders, but in the 12th century a Norman Priory was built on the same site. The Dissolution by Henry V111 just left the church of St Mary. There are Norman details to be seen, the most striking ones being in the doorway with three orders of columns and zig zag patterned arches. Most of the chancel has been walled off and used by St Bee's School.

The most interesting possession of St Bees is an ancient relic of the nunnery itself, a remarkable stone believed to date from the 8th century. It is to be seen between the churchyard and the vicarage where it forms the lintel of an alcove. It is carved with an ugly dragon turning to snarl at a tiny armed figure attacking it from behind. One end of the stone is decorated with plaitwork, and with the knotwork at the other end is a very curious carving which looks like a boar's head. Standing in the alcove is another relic, a stout stone cross on which the bearers of a coffin would rest their load.

Among other stones here are a stoup, a piscina, and a mortar all of the 12th century. Others are probably part of still older cross shafts with primitive carving and one is the upper part of a 10th century shaft decorated on each side. with chain and scroll. There are coffin stones 800 years old, carved with crosses and swords and shears.
The church has one of the most perfect old registers in the County, the entries beginning in fine writing in 1538.

In company with the church is the school, attractively built round three sides of a quadrangle.One wing is the original 16th century building, and over the doorway is a stone with the arms of its founder Archibishop Grindal, who gave the church one of its three Elizabethan chalices.Archibishop Grindal was born in a house on Cross Hill, just off Finkle Street.
The village main street has many ancient houses of much interest to visit and there is an extensive sandy beach.

In the 1980's when excavations were taking place near to the priory, a lead coffin was found. It contained the mummified remains of what is believed to be a knight of the 13th century.The body has since been re-interred and the shroud, which covered the body is now on display in Whitehaven Museum.
A bird sanctuary is situated at the top of St Bees, and here will be found guillemots,puffins,terns, razorbill,kittiwake and herring gull.
A mile or two away is St Bees Head with lighthouse and field patterned crown, thrusts a blunt nose out into the Irish Sea.Its red sandstone cliffs honeycombed by weathering offer convenient nesting ledges during the summer months to noisy throngs of birds.St Bees Head is an ideal stroll, providing very fine views of coastal scenery.Beneath it incidentally there is a cove at Fleswick where interesting pebbles and crystals can be found.

The Coast to Coast walk, devised by A.W. Wainwright in 1973,starts from the Irish Sea at St Bees and stretches 190 miles across the north of England to the North Sea at Robin Hood's Bay. This is an enjoyable and challenging walk with the route passing through three National Parks, the Lake District, The Yorkshire Dales and the North Yorkshire Moors. The walk has been divided into 14 daily stages to suit walkers of average ability.

St. Bees School

St. Bees School was founded in 1583 by Edmund Grindal, Archbishop of Canterbury, and for nearly four centuries remained a school for boys only. Since 1979, St. Bees has been fully coeducational and accepts boys and girls aged 11 - 18 as full boarders, weekly boarders and day pupils.

Approximately 40% of pupils are boarders, and weekly boarding is an increasingly popular option. Lessons take place from Monday to Friday and an extensive transport system is provided for day pupils and weekly boarders. Full boarders have a varied and imaginative weekend programme which is available to other pupils on a voluntary basis.

All pupils follow the same broad curriculum during the first three years; 16 GCSE courses are offered and 16 A level courses.

The School has excellent sports facilities including a 9 hole golf course, courts for tennis, squash, badminton and Eton fives, an indoor heated swimming pool, multigym, shooting range and large multi-purpose sports hall.

The Lake District National Park is very close at hand for climbing, fell walking, wind surfing, canoeing and camping. Outdoor pursuits, including the Duke of Edinburgh Award Scheme and St. Bees Challenge Award form an integral part of the curriculum. Music, Drama, CCF and community Service all thrive and there are numerous clubs and societies.

A Business Management Centre was opened by HRH The Prince of Wales in March 1993 and represents a unique initiative, linking the school with the educational needs of commerce and industry. The latest facilities for information technology and modern language teaching in the school are closely associated with a conference and management training centre for the business community.

Further information can be obtained by contacting The Registrar,
St. Bees School, St. Bees, Cumbria CA27 ODS
Tel 0946 822263   Fax: 0946 823657

SWARTHMOOR.

Map ref. D.13.
Next nearest Town or Village "Ulverston"
Location. Approx 1 mile south of Ulverston.

The small (but expanding) village of Swarthmoor is located in the parish of Pennington and sits astride the A590 Ulverston to Barrow road. Much of the land here is actively owned by the Society of Friends...the Quakers in other words.

It was in 1652 that George Fox first came to Swarthmoor...and was in due course allowed by Judge Fell to use Swarthmoor Hall as a meeting place. In fact they became close friends, and after the Judge died, George Fox married his widow..Margaret. The property was to change hands later, and it became a farmhouse for a while. Since 1954 Swarthmoor Hall has been owned by the Society of Friends and is now open to the public.

In 1850 there was in fact no houses whatsoever in Swarthmoor..Just farms. A few cottages were then built to accommodate the workers from the iron ore mining industry.

These days the village has grown and has joined with the hamlets of Cross a Moor and Trinkeld....it even has two pubs The Red Lion and 'Miners;.

The public houses were, of course, watering places in the days of the miners. Across the road is Rufus Lane...at one time a locked gate barred the path, the key being held by the Red Lion. The name 'Rufus' is derived from 'Rough House Lane' from the days when miners walked from Swarthmoor to Lopper garth on pay day, and often met men from Loppergarth on their way to Swarthmoor pubs...as to be expected a 'rough house' often ensued.

In the Post Office wall is to be found a Quern, a stone used for grinding corn by hand...it was probably last used during the period of the Bronze Age..Look for the pieces of fossilised trees also to be seen here.

TALKIN.

Map ref.G.4.
Next nearest Town or Village "Brampton"
Location. 4 miles of Brampton.

Talkin is within easy reach of the M6 motorway and the A69 Carlisle to Newcastle road. The village stands where the land rises to 600 feet from the Irthing Valley and flattens out before rising steeply to the fells.

In the past agriculture was the main occupation, coal was also mined in the fells during the 19th century and miners would have lived in the village. Disused limestone and stone quarries can still be seen hereabouts, including indications that the Romans at one time quarried here.

In 1552 there were strong regulations for the protection of the community, being a border town. Nightly 12 men were required to guard a point where the River Gelt could easily be crossed by moss troopers intent on stealing cattle and laying waste crops and homesteads. Most of the watchmen had the same name...Milbourne, originally spelt Milburn (in 1224). The name is believed to have originated from Mill Burn which flows through the village. During the period 1639-1733 there were ten Milbourne families living in Talkin. The last of the Milbourne families died in 1939.

Two pubs hereabouts 'The Hare and Hounds' and "The Blacksmiths Arms'

Biggest attraction here is Talkin Tarn Country Park which offers 165 acres of woodland and pasture.

TEBAY.

Map ref. H.10.
Next nearest Town or Village "Orton"
Bus service. Cumberland Buses Route 561
Location. On A685 Kendal to
Kirkby Stephen road.

Tebay is a long rambling village situated midway between Penrith to the north and Kendal to the

south, close to the junction of the Birkbeck river and the Lune river.

The hamlets in the parish are Ellergil, Gaisgill, Redgill, and Roundthwaite. At Redgill at one time lived a man known as William Farrer who had two professions...surgeon and magician. He could apparently read the stars, cast horoscopes and possessed the power of circumventing witches and of course casting out evil spirits

The Cross Keys
Tebay, Cumbria

Comparatively new (in historical terms that is) the town of Tebay only achieved prominence towards the end of the last century, when the railway of the London, Midland, and Scottish company snaked through The Lune Valley on its way to Scotland, a railway centre was built where 'Bank' locomotives were kept to assist the express trains, both freight and passenger, over a long hard pull of the notorious Shap Fell. It became an important junction and terminus for the branch line to Kirkby Stephen and points south. The branch line was closed some years ago and the track removed with Tebay station being demolished in 1970.

Long before he days of steam trains though, The Cross Keys has provided hospitality to many a traveller, be it cattle drovers or the many stage coaches passing this way.

Centrally located for the Lake District, Eden Valley and the Yorkshire Dales, The Cross Keys provides an ideal place to stay. It is said (though no one has yet proved it) that Mary Baines (the Witch of Tebay) who died in 1811 is still a frequent (ghostly) visitor. Though long gone, tales still linger of her ability to transfer herself into a hare. She was credited with possessing prophetic powers, and after the style of Mother Shipton, of Knaresborough, foretold that carriages without horses would one day go over Shap Fells!.

Her reputation owed as much to her extreme ugliness as to the success of the spells she cast. The smell of brimstone kept visitors away from her cottage, whilst menacing cats (black as jet) prowled around.

Standing on the A685 (in the Kendal direction) not far from junction 38 on the M6, John and Jean Connor happily provide todays more 'human' visitors with a homely relaxing atmosphere in extremely pleasant surroundings. Overnight visitors are offered a choice from six double bedrooms (of which, two are family sized),. The surrounding fells of the lesser known Howgills provide very many picturesque walks and drives. The River Lune, which has long been noted for its Salmon, sea trout and trout fishing flows close by and permits are available from the Cross Keys.

A good selection of food is available both in the dining room and the bar. Our extensive menu covers a whole spectrum of delightful food to satisfy the most fastidious. Look out for the 'Blackboard' specials

Stop by....you'll be glad you did

Telephone: 05396 24240

TEBAY / TEMPLE SOWERBY / THIRLMERE

Several places of historical interest hereabouts. In the Galloper Field of Old Tebay is the Brandery, or Brandreth Stone, where it was customary at one time to brand the cattle. near Low Borrow Bridge are the ruins of a Roman fort. Which appears by its size that it could have been an area of considerable strength. Also here is a rounded hill or mound called 'Castlehow'. so called because it is thought that a castle stood here at one time..though no record of it can be traced. Strangely enough the field nearby is known as Castle Green. The round turret and conical spire of its church standing below Langdale Fell on the road from Appleby to Kendal is seen afar off. The building was provided by railwaymen for the men who lived and worked on the lines among the fells and is faced with local Shap granite with brick lining the interior walls. There is a large apse at the west end and very substantial timbers in the roof. Its stalls, pulpit and reading desk are made from American walnut, and its handsome font is carved out of a single block of granite, richly ornamented.

The old school which was endowed by a Robert Adamson in 1672 is now closed, and these days the building is a County Venture Hostel.

TEMPLE SOWERBY.

Map ref. H.7.
Next nearest Town or Village "Cliburn"
Location. A.66 Penrith to Appleby road.

Temple Sowerby is a village between Penrith and Appleby, close to the A66, rejoicing in the name 'Queen of the Westmorland Villages'. It is a village set around a village green, and gets its name from the Knights Templar who once owned Sowerby Manor, though later the Knights Hospitallers were Lords of the Manor until the middle of the 16th century when the Dalston family gained possession...in fact their heraldry can still be seen inside Temple Sowerby House(also known as Acorn Bank) and a carved stone on the north wing has the initials of John and Lucy Dalston, along with the date 1656. Acorn Bank today , though owned by the National Trust, is occupied by the Sue Ryder Foundation...the grounds and herb garden contain the largest collection of some 250 species of culinary and medicinal plants in the North of England.

To the south of town is the small and delightfully preserved hamlet of Morland. Its church has the only Anglo-Saxon tower in the County.

Near Acorn Bank stands ancient Millrigg, now a farmhouse, it is dated 1597 and stands close to Crowdundle Beck which here forms the original county boundary. Close to its confluence with the Eden one of the largest bridges in the valley spans the river on four arches of red-sandstone. It replaces a structure which was washed away in a great flood around 180 years ago.

THIRLMERE.

Map ref. D.9
Next nearest Town or Village "Keswick"
Location. A591 Gramere - Keswick

Thirlmere is a near four mile long lake (turned reservoir) in a strikingly beautiful woodland setting under the shadow of the Helvellyn range which rises abruptly from the lake's eastern side. Just south of Thirlmere is the oldest highway in the Lake District...Dunmail Raise. A large cairn marks the boundary of old Cumberland and Westmorland. It is said that under the cairn lies Dunmail, Wordsworth's 'lost king of rocky Cumbria'. Legend credits him with being the son of Owain, and leader of the last desperate resistance against the Anglo Saxons in 945AD.

Dunmail was apparently killed here and his body covered with the rocks and boulders which you see today. Apparently the story goes that as he fell mortally wounded, he cried to his men not to let the golden crown fall into Saxon hands...urging them to hide the crown safely until the day that he returned. His followers threw the crown into Grisedale Tarn and that is where it remains to this day. Every so often though, his warriors return, retrieve the crown, and return to the cairn. After first knocking, the voice keeps coming back "Not yet, my warriors, not yet...wait awhile". After which the crown is once again returned to Grisedale Tarn.

At Thirlspot and Wythburn nearby is where Wordsworth would meet up with his famous contemporaries and set off up Helvellyn, amongst whom would often be Humphrey Davy (of the miners lamp fame) and Sir Walter Scott.

Armboth, which is marked on most OS maps, was a hamlet which disappeared under the reservoir when the valley was flooded.

Another well known legend from this village is the 'Legend of Armboth Hall' For many years there was an innocent looking farmstead known as Armboth House on Armboth Fell above Thirlmere, which was said to be haunted. On one All Halloween, a wedding feast was being prepared for the daughter of the house, but in the midst of the preparations a man came rushing in to tell the family that the bride had been pushed into the lake and drowned.

It is said that every year on this particular night lights are seen and neighbours say that just as the bells start ringing, the ghostly figure of a large dog can be seen swimming across the lake. The plates and dishes clatter and the table is spread by unseen hands. That is the preparation for the ghostly wedding feast of a murdered bride who comes from her watery bed in the lake to keep her nuptials. There are however no record as to who the unfortunate bride was, nor for that matter can be traced any record of the foul deed.

THORNTHWAITE.

Map ref. D.7.
Next nearest Town or Village "Braithwaite"
Location. 5 miles north-west of Keswick.

Thornthwaite is a village at the head of the Bassenthwaite Lake at the foot of Whinlatter Pass to Lorton...on the northern fringe of Thornthwaite Forest...it is in the parish of Thornthwaite cum Braithwaite.

The mother church of the parish is St Mary's built in 1746 close to the site of an earlier church. It stands amidst pastoral scenery...the main door is reached through an archway of yew trees. Many old tombstones worth investigating,

Possibly the most prominent landmark is the white-washed Bishop Rock. The legend goes that in the year 1783 the newly appointed Bishop of Derry was travelling to Whitehaven on his way to Ireland. He stopped at the Swan in Thornthwaite, and whilst having a few drinks bet his new found friends that he could ride his pony to the top of 'Barth' and 'Lords Seat'. He reached the top alright,

but the pony stumbled, killing the rider. He was buried at the foot of the scree at the rock known as 'The Clerk'. The landlord of the Inn had the rock white-washed, and in fact it is still done annually by the Keswick Mountain Rescue Team. The payment for this service until comparatively recently was a shilling and a quart of ale!.

Nearby is a small hamlet..Seldom Seen (the origins of the name are lost in history, but one doesn't have to think too hard as to how it got its name) This small hamlet is 'dominated' by the roaring chapel beck which crashes over the large boulders. In the past the power of the water was harnessed and producing enough energy for working the Rachel Mine, as well as driving the plant at the Saw Mill.

Other than farms, the lead mine used to be the chief source of employment in the area, with miners being housed at Seldom Seen.

There is a visitor centre on Whinlatter Pass. also look for the Thornthwaite Gallery which is an attractively converted 18th century barn, and which deals in fine arts.

THRELKELD.

Map ref. E.7.
Next nearest Town or Village "Scales"
Location. 5 miles north-east of Keswick.
Gala days/festivals. Threlkeld Sheepdog
Trails 3rd week August

Threlkeld is basically a string of cottages and farmsteads on the Keswick road, together with the outlying hamlet of Scales. Both names are Scandinavian in origin and probably derive from the Norse settlement of the Lake District in the 10th century.

Its a pleasant little village with two inns..The Horse and Farrier dated 1688 and the Salutation Inn, both cheerful places much frequented by climbers and fell walkers.

Threlkeld Church was built in 1777, although the unusual little squashed tower is probably 17th century in origin.A neat stone-seated porch leads into the church with its tiled floor and interesting possessions.There are two bells at least 500 years old, a well-worn Black Letter Bible of 1613 and a handsome modern font made of Threlkeld granite. The church records go back to Queen Elizabeth 1's time and tell of the quaint local custom by which a person making a promise of marriage promised also to pay five shillings (25 new pence) to the poor if he or she broke the contract.

The area is also popular with budding archaelogists. A Roman settlement existed here and was occupied from the 3rd to the 8th centuries A.D. Today this Threlkeld site ranks amongst the most instructive in the Lake District. The elementary features of the view, the mountains that lie around, are probably not very different from the time when the settlement was inhabited more than 1500 years ago. Apart from the site of this old British village, the Celtic period of this area has left its mark in the name of the mountain that dominates the scene...Blencathra,

Blencathra rises steeply above the Great valley to the east of Keswick, from which there are excellent views of Thirlmere and Derwentwater.

The old farm called Threlkeld Hall and the mountain slopes near by have between them a memory which takes us back to the Wars of the Roses. The original Threlkeld Hall was the home of Sir Lancelot Threlkeld, who used to say that of his three great houses one was for pleasure, another for profit and warmth in the winter, and this one to provide him

with tenants to go to the wars. He married Lady Clifford, whose cruel first husband had been slain at Towton and whose young son Henry Clifford was in danger of his life from the Yorkists. Today the only remaining signs of the original building are a raised pile of stones and a largely filled in moat to the south of the present farmhouse.

A busy period in the life of Threlkeld was during the time 1880-1900 when a total of 10,000 tons of galena and 13,400 tons of zinc was produced here.

With a value exceeding £120,000 (a princely sum in those days) it brought a rapid (though short-lived) prosperity to the area. About a hundred men in the village worked in the mines and the refining sheds. What was once a small hamlet quickly became a typical mining village...an appearance incidentally, which it still retains to this day.

The area is of course the home of the Blencathra Hunt...one of Lakeland's most famous packs.

THURSBY.

Map ref. E.5.
Next nearest Town or Village "Wigton"
Location. 6 miles from Carlisle south-west.

Six miles from Carlisle along the A595, Thursby is an important road junction, for here the A596 leaves the Roman road and branches off to Wigton, Silloth, and Maryport.

It take's its name from 'Thor's by'...Thor, the Thunder God of the Saxon's, whose temple is reputedly near by at Kirksteads.

The Green where the village school used to stand, is situated at this point. Its most celebrated scholar was Thomas Bouch, who was born at Thursby in 1822, and grew up to become a railway engineer who helped plan London's first tramway system and many railways in Scotland including the one over the Tay Bridge. This bridge was regretfully the scene of one of the most appalling disasters in British railway history however. The bridge was officially opened in May 1878, and in 18 months a train with 70 passengers was crossing the bridge in a gale of 150 miles an hour when an over-whelming blast carried away 400 yards of the structure and flung the train and its passengers into the river. Not one person escaped, with some of the bodies being found up to four miles away.. A Government report declared that the bridge was badly designed, badly constructed and badly maintained, and that defects in the structure must sooner or later have brought it down. Broken by the calamity, the unfortunate engineer died at Moffat in Dumfrieshire in October 1880.

The old school came about due to the kindness of one Thomas Tomlinson who left money in his will of 1802 for the teaching of ten poor children in the parish. Two customs which were once familiar to all pupils at the school was the 'barring out' of the headmaster at the approach of the hay harvest to secure holidays...and the giving of the Christmas Goose to him.

As Christmas approached a neighbouring farmer would be asked to keep the chosen bird until the last day of term when two senior pupils would collect it, tie a bow of ribbon and a card around its neck and then put it through one of the windows of the school...so the goose would be seen walking round the classroom to the delight of the younger pupils.

The skyline here is dominated by St Andrew's church, which though Victorian does in fact stand on the site of two earlier ones, namely a 7th century wooden church, and a second built by David 1 of Scotland. One gravestone here is for the Rev Mason, who was rector of Great Orton when he died, and a curate of Thursby when a younger man. His grand-daughter Mrs Beeton achieved her claim to fame when she wrote her book on 'Household Management'

There has been a village...in the early days digni-fied as a town, here since 1300 and the nineteenth century church has many memorials inside to the Brisco family who at one time lived at the now demolished Crofton Hall close by. There is a story about an underground passage between the church and the hall and a ghostly grey lady who travelled by it. She was apparently a child murderer and is supposed to be buried in a railed enclosure near the church door. Another tale is that two brothers, both giants, lived on the wooded hill called Torkin, west of the village.

THURSTON FIELD

Map ref. E.4.
Next nearest Town or Village "Carlisle"
Location. 5 miles west of Carlisle.

Thurstonfield is a village in the parish of Burgh-by-sands, five miles west of Carlisle, and two miles inland of the Solway Estuary.

At one time there were seven farms, a corn water mill, a tannery, and the Greyhound Inn. In or around 1900 Mrs Stordy...a Quakers family from Moorhouse, built a number of larger brick houses. Mrs Stordy at 'Red House' kept the famous Thurstonfield Harriers.....a pack of hounds known from Silloth to Caldbeck and Carlisle.
Cockfights (illegal) took place at the cock-pit alongside the Methodist church.

THWAITES.

Map ref. C.12.
Next nearest Town or Village "Millom"
Location. Midway between Millom and Broughton-in-Furness.

The parish of Thwaites consists of three hamlets,,,,'The Green', Hallthwaites, and Ladyhall. It is situated on the Duddon estuary, midway between Millom and Broughton-in-Furness.
Evidence shows that the area has been populated for a very long time. In fact Neolithic man lived here, and is thought to have built the stone circle which can be seen at Swinside. Remains of their round dwellings can additionally be seen at Thwaite Fell.
On a hill above Hallthwaites is the parish church dedicated to St Anne. The first of the church's to

stand here was built in 1725 originally as chapel of ease for Millom. In 1805 the 'new' church was built complete with steeple and two bells.
Until 1826 the parson was also the schoolmaster. The Rev John Ormandy was the last in the area to hold the dual post and actually received a grant from Queen Anne's Bounty.
From the Middle Ages until the early 20th century there were several industries in the parish and deriving the power they needed from the river Duddon or the Black beck. At one time there was a bloomery in the woods (near Duddon bridge) which was established in 1737. Fortunately a great deal of the earlier buildings are being preserved and are open to the public. There was also a thriving woollen mill dating back to the 16th century at Hallthwaites. Some of the carpets and blankets, woven and dyed are still in use in the district even today.

TIRRIL & SOCKBRIDGE.

Map ref. G.7.
Next nearest Town or Village "Penrith"
Location. Just over two miles south west of Penrith.

A small streams runs through these two villages..Though both stand on the B5320 road two and a half miles from Penrith and three miles from Pooley Bridge at the foot of Ullswater.
Sufficient history is attached to these two villages to make them a 'must' on everybody's itinerary.
In the village is a house dated 1699 originally built for a Reginald and Elizabeth Dobson. The property was later sold to Richard Wordsworth who was Receiver-General at the time of the Jacobite Rebellion. Richard's son John was William Wordsworth's father, but as history informs us the

family had moved to Cockermouth by the time William and Dorothy were born. Somewhat understandably the house has been re-named 'Wordsworth House'
Also here is Sockbridge Hall, a 15th century Manor House believed to be standing on the earliest dwelling in the area...though these days it is a busy farm. Sockbridge Mill, also one time very active is on the banks of the river Eamont, and is today a successful fish farm where it is possible to buy (or catch) fish.
The village of Tirril too has had its fair share of famous people. Thomas Wilkinson for example...the poet and friend of Wordsworth who was very active in the Quaker movement. In 1773 a Quaker Meeting House was built in Tirril and was used constantly for over 100 years. Today though it is a private house.
In the graveyard next to the house is the grave of

Charles Gough who was killed in a fall whilst climbing Helvellyn. His dog stayed beside his body for three months until he was rescued. This incident is recounted in Wordsworth's poem 'Fidelity'

Visitors may notice a stone standing at the side of the B5320 road to Sockbridge bearing the inscription Big Jim R.I.P. 1773. Nobody knows who Big Jim was...Man, horse or dog?

TORVER.

Map ref. D.11.
Next nearest Town or Village "Coniston"
Location. Just over 3 miles south-west of Coniston.
Gala days/festivals. Walna Scar Shepherds Meet November.

The picturesque village of Torver is situated some three miles south-west of Coniston. Torver beck runs through the valley into Coniston Lake and thereby gives its name to the village.

Probably the earliest traceable reference to Torver (or Thorwerge) arises from a land dispute between the Abbot of Furness and William Fitzgilbert in

1163 in the reign of Henry 11 although prehistoric evidence in the form of stone circles and cairns scattered over High Common above the village indicates settlement of the area dating back 3,500 years to the time of the great forest clearances.

When the railway came to the village in 1859 life was made a lot easier for the residents as it was then able to carry the stone and slate from the extensive quarrying industry, as well as iron from the bloomeries and bobbins, together with swills and charcoal from the many woodland crafts. The railway continued through until 1958.

The original chapel of Torver came with the founding of the priory of Conishead sometime between 1154 and 1189. The dead of the parish would have had to be taken to Ulverston for burial...a journey in excess of 16 miles all over mountain track. The chapel was later consecrated as a church by 1884.

A farming tradition is kept alive here by the formation of the Walna Scar Shepherd's Meet. It is an organisation of local shepherd's for the exchange of stray sheep...an annual meeting being held in July, together with an annual show in November. Today it is a social occasion with a show of hill sheep, sheep dog trials, fell races and hound trails.

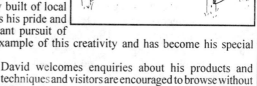

TROUTBECK.

Map ref. F.10.
Next nearest Town or Village "Windermere"
Location. 3 miles north of Windermere.

TOWNEND

The village of Troutbeck is close to the major tourist centres of Windermere and Grasmere, and surprisingly enough still remains relatively un-spoilt.

Troutbeck is first mentioned in 1282 and is be-lieved to be so named because the beck was (and still is) a spawning place for trout.

Troutbeck has some of the noblest views in Lakeland, and is a popular place of call for visitors who find much of interest in this long village stretching for over a mile, with houses built some 400 plus years ago, many with quaint gables and round chimneys showing finely among sycamore and apple trees. With streams in its old streets, the village has many water troughs in cool recesses, relics of the coaching days when horses had to be watered before beginning the hard climb over Kirkstone Pass to Patterdale.

A close inspection of the village will indicate that it is a small cluster of hamlets namely, Townend, The Cragg, Longmire Yeat, High Green, and Townhead...all stretching along the road...and originally forming around a series of small wells many of them dedicated to various saints...St John, St James, St. Margarets.. It is obviously a place of great antiquity even though few build-ings pre-date the mid 17th century. As many visitors will be aware..prior to 1650 the mainly timber framed buildings generally with walls of wattle and daub,clay, turf or roughly piled fieldstones ,would not have been permanent enough to survive until today.The prime concern of the houses in those days was to build them on one side of the valley ...the sunny side. They were built around springs, beneath the snow line in order to catch the winter sunshine.

Many of the old buildings of Troutbeck fortu-nately do still remain, although in some instances, as the 'The Mortal Man' the old core has been obscured by later building. The Inn in itself is interesting, it was originally called 'The White House' Inn when it was built in 1689. It was re-named so it is believed around the early part of the 18th century and now bears its unusual sign. The church built in 1736 has an unusual dedi-cation to Jesus. Rather lonely is this simple church, which has twice been rebuilt in the past 200 years, though it still keeps a fine roof with massive oak beams.In its noble little 18th cen-

JESUS CHURCH

Holbeck Ghyll
COUNTRY HOUSE HOTEL
Holbeck Lane, Windermere
Cumbria LA23 1LU
Tel: 05394 32375 Fax: 05394 34743
A.A. Red ★   Two Rosettes

Holbeck Ghyll is a hotel of outstanding character and charm, situated peacefully in its own landscaped gardens and many acres of natural woodland, with breathtaking views across Lake Windermere and the Langdale Fells.

Built in the early 19th century, the house was bought in 1888 by Lord Lonsdale for use as his hunting lodge. The "Yellow Earl" ,as he was known, was the first President of the Automobile Association, and bequeathed the famous Lonsdale belt to boxing. The Lord led a colourful life and made a lasting impression on the style and appearance of Holbeck Ghyll.

Public rooms are elegant and comfortable, some with log fires, and throughout there is an abundance of magnificent features in the style of Charles Rennie Mackintosh with a wealth of oak panelling and stained glass. Bedrooms are individually designed and refurbished to the highest of standards.

Dining is an integral part of ones stay at Holbeck Ghyll and provides for a memorable experience. The interesting and extensive menu features dishes which are classically prepared and artistically presented, much in the English style, yet with a French influence; exciting and unusual vegetarian items are included in every course.

HOLBECK GHYLL......*A true country house where quality and professionalism combine with a warm welcome and outstanding service*.

Resident Proprietors:
David and Patricia Nicholson M.H.C.I.M.A.

tury tower is a bell which was ringing long before the Civil War and its plain oak altar table which is 300 years old. Its chief treasure is the beautiful east window, one of the first designed by Sir Edward Burne-Jones.

The schoolhouse was built in 1637 though today it is active as a day nursery. Certainly a good deal of the houses date back to the 16th and 17th century, with many preserving their old spice and court cupboards.

One property 'Townend' formerly owned by the Browne family is now a National Trust property and is open to the public as an excellent example of a 'statesmans' house and contains much of the families carved oak furniture, as well as a fine library.

Troutbeck Park Farm was a property one time owned by Beatrix Potter...in fact some of her work was done in a little study there. On bequeathing the farm to the National Trust she stipulated that her flock of Herdwick Sheep should be preserved.

ULDALE.

Map ref. D.6.
Next nearest Town or Village "Ireby"
Location. 4 miles south-west of Caldbeck,
Gala days/festivals.Shepherds Meet. 1st Monday in December.
Uldale Village Show. 2nd Weekend in September.

Uldale is a small village one mile north of Overwater. The village sits at the foot of a steep hill which leads over the Uldale Common to Caldbeck. Uldale is the setting of David's House in Hugh Walpole's novel 'Rogue Herries'

Aughertree is a small hamlet where remains of Roman camps can still be seen, and in a field near Orthwaite are the vestiges of another Roman camp.

The first school to be built in Uldale was back in 1726 when a certain Matthew Caldbeck, a former Ruthwaite man ,gave £100, and persuaded over 40 other landowners in the region to give an equal amount. One wonders today how hard a task this would have been when one considers how far such an amount would have gone in those days close to 300 years ago..

The school was built on part of the village green and was in use until 1895 when a bigger school

Northern Fells Gallery and Tea Room

The Gallery & Tea Room are open

MARCH to OCTOBER
Daily 10.30am to 5.00pm

NOVEMBER, DECEMBER & FEBRUARY
Friday, Saturday & Sunday
10.30am to 5.00pm
**The Old School,
Orthwaite Road,
Uldale, Carlisle**
Tel. No. Low Ireby 06973 71778
Proprietors: Felicity & Peter Wiseman

**Free Parking : Free Admission :
Facilities for the Disabled.
Summer Demonstrations and
Exhibitions.**

Built in 1895 this magnificent building, a school up to 1990, is now open as a Gallery and Tea Room.

Run by a professional dressmaker, whose studio is on the premises, the gallery offers a superb selection of original works by local artists and craftsmen including watercolours, photographs, ceramics, stained glass, dolls, embroideries, knitwear and jewellery.

In addition to the gallery sales area a programme of art and craft demonstrations are staged throughout the year.

Morning coffee, light lunches and afternoon teas can be enjoyed in the pleasant Victorian Tea Room with its cosy wood burning stove for those colder days

was built on the Orthwaite Road out of the village. The school building closed as a school in 1990 and today is open as a gallery and tea rooms. Shepherd's Meets are still held here. Until some 20 years ago these meetings would have been held on the fells themselves, with the shepherds walking to the meeting point, gathering stray sheep as they went, whence the strays would be returned to their rightful owners. These valley meetings are still held on the first Monday in December...nowadays though utilising five different pubs in the same area. On the same day the Blencathra Fox hounds also meet.

OLD SCHOOL HOUSE

ULLSWATER.

Map ref. F.8.
Next nearest Town or Village "Pooley Bridge"
Location. Approx 5 miles south of Penrith.

Ullswater is the regions largest lake, a little less than eight miles long and with two distinct bends to it.

Some people consider the lake superior in beauty to Windermere, but there are distinct differences. Unlike Windermere, Ullswater has its head in the steep Borrowdale volcanic rocks, and its feeders pour off Helvellyn to the south west, and off a tangle of rough fells to the south east. You will notice from the centre that the landcape changes rapidly, as the lake penetrates the more friable Skiddaw Slates, and at the foot there are flatter plains of limestone and sandstone stretching towards Penrith.

The Ullswater Navigation Company runs a 'steamer' service in the season. The journey south from Pooley Bridge Pier offers, without doubt, the best view of the changing scene. Behind the pier is Dunmallot on top of which is the ruin of a ditch and

ULLSWATER

mound Romano-British fort. The ancient British road, High Street, high to the south-east was improved by the Romans.

The next pier south is at Howtown (no town incidentally, just a few houses and the delightful Sharrow bay Country House Hotel) The route then goes through the narrows with "Skelly Neb' to the north. In the old times a net was spread across the lake here, to catch the 'Schelly', a whitefish found only in this lake. Above to the south is Hallin Fell, which can be climbed easily from the minor road on its south side. Its views are among the best anywhere. 'Gowbarrow

THE RAVEN

Park' on the north side was once a deer park and it was here that Wordsworth saw his daffodils. To the west is Aira Force a spectacular waterfall on Aira Beck with viewing bridges in a wooded ravine. The lake then turns south, with the Helvellyn range seen to the south west and Place Fell closing in on the east. The south pier, incidentally is at Glenridding. The lake holds trout and perch as well as the aforementioned 'schelly' Powered boats are allowed on the lake but at a maximum speed of 10mph. Craft can be launched at Glenridding and also at Howtown.

One of the best walks in the Lake District is along terraced paths on the wooded east shore.

KNOTTS MILL COUNTRY LODGE

Originally a Saw Mill, Knotts Mill has been rebuilt and refurbished to become a comfortable, warm and friendly guest house. The lounge has beautiful views of the surrounding fells as do all of the rooms at Knotts Mill.

All nine bedrooms are en-suite. The rooms vary in size but all have colour television, tea making facilities and a hairdryer. The majority of rooms have a direct dial telephone, some have a bath as well as a shower. There are four ground floor rooms, two of which are family rooms and one has been fitted with disabled people in mind.

Dinner is a focal point of our day when a good selection of dishes are offered, together with an interesting wine list.

Morning coffee and Afternoon Tea is served to guests free of charge.

Further details - Jane & Chris Jones
Knotts Mill Country Lodge
Watermillock,
Ullswater, Penrth
Cumbria CA11 0JN
Telephone: (07684) 86472
Fax: (07684) 86699

Troutbeck Head Caravan Park
....For your Lakeland holiday

Troutbeck Head Caravan Park is a small secluded family park, owned and operated by your hosts Bob & Vera Scott. It is easily accessible from the M6 Junction 40 along 'A' class roads, midway between Penrith and Keswick and only 4 miles from tranquil Lake Ullswater. We are ideally situated for walking, painting and exploring Lakeland, historic Carlisle and the Scottish Borders.

We pride ourselves in having a quiet Park catering for genuine 'Lake District Lovers' The Park itself nestles in a sheltered valley between Great Mell Fell and Blencathra

Troutbeck Head Caravan Park is licensed for 75 Holiday Home Caravans all being fully serviced. There are 54 Touring pitches, all with mains electric 10 amp. Hook up points, on grass and hard standing.

ENJOY LAKELAND IN WINTER

Our Park is the pioneer in Winter opening for touring caravans in Lakeland, and is now open during the winter months, being closed only for six weeks (14th January to 1st March)

Troutbeck Head Caravan Park
Troutbeck, Penrith,
Cumbria CA11 0SS
Tel. 07684 83521

PARK FACILITIES INCLUDE:

General Store, Centrally heated toilet block with shaving points, hair dryers and free hot showers.Coin operated launderette with deep sinks, washing machine, tumble dryer and ironing facilities, Public payphone, Calor Gas and camping gaz stockist , TV and information room. Games room, Large childrens play areaAdjacent to pony trekking and farm activity centreWell behaved dogs are welcome, but must be kept on a short lead at all times, except on our 8 acre dog exercise area.

Netherdene Guest House

Troutbeck, Nr. Ullswater,
Penrith, Cumbria CA11 0SJ
Telephone. 07684 83475

Netherdene Guest House is set against the backdrop of the Northern fells. It is situated on the A5091 just 10 minutes drive from Junction 40 on the M6 motorway.

This traditional Lakeland Guest House is set in its own quiet grounds with extensive mountain views. To provide some of he modern day comforts Netherdene has recently been refurbished. All bedrooms are attractively furnished, some with en-suite facilities all with colour TV and tea and coffee making equipment, all centrally heated.

Cosy lounge with log fire, where books and maps are available for guests use. Pleasant dining room where freshly prepared Aga cooked food is served. Accommodation is on a Bed & Breakfast basis with option of Evening Dinner. Ample parking for cars, Regrettably pets are nor permitted. Open all year Except Christmas Day.

Netherdene has been awarded the English Tourist Board 2 Crowns and Commended Status for its quality and standard of accommodation. An ideal base from which to explore the Lake District, Fellwalking, Pony Trekking, Boating, and golf are all nearby

ULVERSTON.

Map ref. E.13.
Next nearest Town or Village "Baycliffe"
Bus service. Post Bus + Cumberland Buses Route 6. 6A. 6B, 9, 513, 18, 10 11, 12 510, 512, 514, 509, 511, 513, 518, 530, 531, 535, 730, 735
Trains. Railway Station.
Tourist Information Centre. Coronation Hall.
Location. North-east of Barrow on A590 road.
Early closing. Wednesday.
Market day. Thursday and Saturday.
Gala days/festivals. North Lonsdale Agricultural Show. Last Wednesday July.

Ulverston is north east of Barrow-in-Furness on the A590 trunk road. It is now a small market town (charter 1280 by Edward 1)with some local industry.
Until the rise of Barrow, Ulverston was the principal town of that part of Lancashire lying cut off from the main county by Morecambe Bay. It was a quiet town until the late 18th century, when several economic developments led to population increases...not only being a market and labour hiring centre, but by the 1820's with a number of flax and cotton mills, a considerable trade in iron tools, hats, linen and iron making itself.
It has had an extraordinary history.Its market expanded, according to tradition when Dalton the nearest neighbour was stricken by plague in 1631.Following its own personal 'industrial revolution' it enjoyed the status of a port when the engineer John Rennie caused a canal to be made one mile to the sea, with the port eventually clearing 600 vessels each year. It was the coming of the railway in 1856 which killed the port and subsequently gave Barrow the superiority.
The parish church of St Mary was founded in 1111 and has a few interesting items worth inspecting.
In earlier times Leather Lane and Soutergate here were well known sites for the footwear trade.The word 'Souter' means shoemaker. The local cobblers shod the rich and poor for many generations until the introduction of mass produced footwear.
More important however was the Wesleyan Methodists who had a very early chapel. Also associations with the Quakers were strong as George Fox (a Leicestershire man)came under

Cumbrian (or Lancashire as it was then) influence nearby at Swarthmoor.

He found much help from the Fell family of Swarthmoor Hall, and married the widow Fell after her husband...the well known Judge ,died. The old Hall today is a magnificent survivor of the 17th century.

One of Ulverston's famous son's was Sir John Barrow (1764-1848) He was a distinguished voyager and author.His monument in the shape of a reduced scale model of Eddystone Lighthouse,Plymouth, is on nearby Hoad Hill, and being so obvious to all visitors to the region is always the first thing they always ask about..His adventurous spirit led him to the Greenland Whaling grounds at one time, later returning home to Ulverston with a magnificent pair of whale jawbones which stood outside his cottage for many years.

Later Barrow was appointed tutor to a young boy named Tom Staunton who could speak Mandarin Chinese.Not missing an opportunity Barrow rapidly learned this language and it enabled him to land a job in China. After writing about his travels some prominent members of the British Government decided they would like to make use of Barrow's knowledge and appointed him Second Secretary of the Admiralty. Another northerner Sir James Graham was appointed First Sea Lord. Between them these two able men revolutionised the navy's operations, thus ensuring the defeat of Napoleon at Trafalgar.

In May 1850 virtually all Ulverston turned out to watch the laying of the foundation stone of the tower to which all manner of people from Royalty to peers and Admirals had subscribed.Church bells rang, the local brass band played, the Yeomanry marched, and the school children sang anthems. Even in the workhouse the day ended with a great feast for the incumbents.

Another locally born man. but at the other end of the spectrum..was Stanley Laurel of the famed Laurel & Hardy. He was born on the 16th June as Stanley Jefferson at 3, Argyle Street, Ulverston. A plaque commemorates his living at that house, and there is a delightful Laurel and Hardy Museum in the town centre.

In Mill Street there is a nice restoration of a 17th century corn mill, now open as a craft shop and gallery and today known as Ulverston Point.

Ulverston has managed to produce three heroes over recent years. .Harry Christian won a V.C. at Givenchy in 1915, Frank Jefferson of the Lancashire Fusiliers won his V.C in Italy in 1944, and finally Basil Weston won a V.C. at Meiktila (Burma) in 1945.

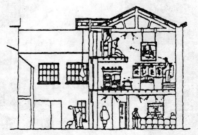

UNDERBARROW.

Map ref. F.11.
Next nearest Town or Village "Crosthwaite"
Location. 3 miles west of Kendal.

Three miles west of Kendal, at one time the village of Underbarrow was the largest village in what was originally known as Westmorland, and an important coaching stop on the woollen route from Kendal to Ulverston.

The turnpike road from Kendal climbs westward over the windswept limestone escarpment of Scout Scar, with its far reaching views of the Lakeland hills and the Kent estuary, dropping steeply past Toll Bar Cottage to the green and fertile parish of Underbarrow.

In the second half of the 17th century the village was strongly in favour of the new Quaker religion (The Society of Friends) and in fact the locals talk of a Quaker burial ground in the vicinity, though to date this has never been found,

Though today, little more than a hamlet, the village can boast of famous individuals associ-

TOLL HOUSE

ated with it. Their most famous visitor would undoubtedly have been Henry V111 who visited his (to become) sixth wife Katherine Parr at nearby Cunswick Hall in 1542.Lesser but nevertheless a character in his own right was William Pearson who was one of the survivors of the "Charge of the Light Brigade' in the Crimean War back in 1854. Though seriously injured he was nursed back to health by Florence Nightingale.

The ancient packhorse road from Kendal, preceding the turnpike and probably known to the Romans, came over haunted Cunswick Scar and past the oldest house in the parish.. Cunswick Hall, ...once a pele tower, now a farmhouse. Helpot, another farm was traditionally an Inn to serve travellers and packmen alike on their journeys to Ulverston or Kendal.

The area these days is more noted for its show of spectacular plants, not just the fields of daffodils and Lily of the Valley that grow wild, but the lesser known but no less spectacular crimson-purple of the Bloody Cranesbull, together with the brilliant yellow of the horseshoe vetch.

BEECHWOOD COTTAGE

The Punch Bowl

Underbarrow, Kendal.
Telephone: 05395 68234

Settling very comfortably into this olde worlde atmosphere of this delightful village is the 350 year old Punch Bowl Inn, located in the centre of Underbarrow village.

It has had a long and chequered history starting life as a corn mill, then farm-house and smithy, finally becoming an ale-house...all of which will become apparent upon entering. Reclaimed ships timbers from the structure form the building and it abounds with history through its oak beams, antique furniture, open wood fire and brasses.

The Punch Bowl is a 16th century coaching Inn and serves as the 'local' for this rural village. It is located in the picturesque Lyth Valley approximately five miles from Kendal and south-east of Windermere, off the A5074, and within easy reach of Junction 36 off the M6.

Very much under the careful management of the owner David Howarth, very little is being allowed to change since its early days as an ale-house. Visitors will soon be advised where the Priests Hide can be found.

David is keen to move the pub away from its image of being solely a local pub, believing that his inn has much to offer the tourist. Consideration was initially given to his stock of wines, spirits and beers, to such a degree that in 1992 Alan Bennett the well known journalist for the Daily Telegraph stated in his newspaper that he considered the Punchbowl at Underbarrow offered the best pint of draught bass in the north-west...Honour indeed.

Bar meals are distinctly interesting. David, who does all the cooking himself believes only in fresh meat and vegetables for his diners, he cooks his own hams and visits the market daily for fresh fish. 'Specials' of the day are clearly announced on the blackboard.

Adjacent to the inn is a beautifully laid out beer garden, and also a small caravan park where he is siting new Pemberton holiday caravans for sale and rental.

Town Yeat
Underbarrow
endale LA8 8DN
Telephone:05395 68383

Lyth Gallery

A new and virant gallery situated at the head of the Lythe Valley, the Lyth Gallery prides itself in presenting the quality work of leading artists and new talent of one of the most beautiful and relaxed settings in the Lake district.

The Lyth Gallery offers

Original works in a unique setting.

Oils, watercolours, pastels and many other media represented.

All work on one level with easy access for all.

Easy and ample parking. Admission FREE

All work is ORIGINAL and the ongoing exhibition ombines contemporty and traditional work in the realms of fine art and sculpture.

UNDERSKIDDAW.

Map ref. D.7.
Next nearest Town or Village "Portinscale"
Location. 3 miles south of Bassenthwaite.

Underskiddaw lies at the foot of Skiddaw, along with its associated peaks. It is a parish comprising the villages of Millbeck, Applethwaite, Ormathwaite, Brundholme and Thrushwood.

It was in 1880 that the woollen mills at Applethwaite and Millbeck provided employment. It was Applethwaite that produced blankets, whilst Millbeck once a corn mill...later turning to wool....sending blankets, caps and bonnets to all parts of the world. In 1903 the Millbeck mill was converted into Millbeck towers and is now owned by the National Trust. Applethwaite Mill is now a private house.

URSWICK.

Map ref. D.13.
Next nearest Town or Village "Lindal-in-Furness
Bus service. Cumberland Buses Route 10, 12
Location. 2 miles south of Ulverston.
Gala days/festivals. Urswick Rushbearing Approx 29th Sept.

Great & Little Urswick are one community. Urswick is in a valley and to the east above the village is Birkrigg Common and over which the road leads to the sea. Traditionally persons born and brought up in the village are known as 'Ossick Coots'

The church of St Mary and St Michael dates from the early 12th century. A traditional stone still give entry to the churchyard.

The village school will be found in Little Urswick. It was built in 1585 by order of Queen Elizabeth 1. with a charter which still exists today. When first built it was for the education of boys alone ...now it is a primary school for all. In the old days the schoolroom on the ground floor would probably have been a large, heavily beamed, dimly lit area, with a fire-place at one end. Spartan by todays standards, with only hard wooden forms set around the perimeter of the room for the scholars and a chair of throne-like proportions at the centre for the Master of the day.

Writing lessons often depended upon itinerant masters, who moved from school to school spending about six weeks at a time in each. Equipment was limited, sand boxes or quills and paper were used for writing, the ink being kept in ink horns complete with stopper, while reading equipment consisted of 'horn'books and soft backed printed volumes which quickly wore out. Discipline , as shown in many pictures of sixteenth and seventeenth century schoolmasters was maintained with a birch rod. The school day was a long one, in summer beginning as early as 6.0 am and continuing until 5.00pm with a two hour break at midday, in winter running from 7.00 am until 4.00pm, with a one and a half hour break.

In front of the school is the village green, on a rise.It is on record that cock-fighting took place here. Many of the older houses here still have cock lofts.

WABERTHWAITE.

Map ref. B.11.
Next nearest Town or Village "Ravenglass"
Location. 4 miles south-east of Ravenglass.

Waberthwaite is a hamlet some one and a half miles north east of Eskmeals on the Esk.

The name Waberthwaite is of Norse origin and is believed to mean 'Wyburgh's Clearing'

Its a lonely little place near the coast. Here the River Esk flows around the finely wooded hill of Muncaster Castle, with its beacon tower 250 feet up, and here on the edge of a sandy creek, crouches one of the counties ancient white-walled churches. Low and simple, it has only five windows to light it, some of them 16th century.The east window is enriched with a picture of the Good Shepherd.The 300 year old pulpit has carved panels and borders, and hidden in one of the old box-pews is a Norman font two feet hight, looking rather like the base of a pillar.The bell turret was rebuilt in Queen Anne's reign.In the graveyard will be found a 9th century cross shaft which at one time stood on a well used route for travellers heading north from the village. At the start of the century, quarrying was the name of the game for this village. It had started at Broad Oak with granite sets of different sizes being sent to many Lancashire towns. For years the quarry offered work to around 50 men until 1946 when it was closed. The quarry site is now a site of Special Scientific Interest.

The village shop here was opened by a Mrs Hannah Woodall in 1828. Its still there today, under the same family ownership, though today it now proudly displays a Royal Warrant for traditional Cumberland sausage...and is better known for its ham,bacon, and sausage nationwide labelled 'Woodalls of Waberthwaite'

WAITBY.

Map ref. I.9.
Next nearest Town or Village "Kirkby Stephen"
Location. Just over 1 miles south-west of Kirkby Stephen.

Is a small village just one and a half miles south-west of Kirkby Stephen. It is believed to have been a market town complete with castle, chapel, and cemetery...though no trace can be found today. The name Waitby originates from the Wate family who originally lived at Wateby Manor.

The free school for Waitby and Smardale was situated on Waitby Fell and was erected in 1680 following an endowment of £400 by a Mr James Highmore, a native of Waitby.

WALTON.

Map ref. G.3.
Next nearest Town or Village "Lanercost"
Location. 4 miles north of Brampton.

Walton, or Walton on the Roman Wall, as it is otherwise known..

...is still a beautiful and unspoilt part of England, with its streams of Irthing, King, and Cambeck, flowing through the village. It is located some four miles north of Brampton.

Its a very small village but very attractive, and has a fine view of the Irthing Valley. A few white cottages round a three cornered green, and a little sandstone church looking on. Down at the bottom of the hill below the village a small section of the Wall overlooks King Water. The church is modern, and boasts one of the heaviest bells for miles around, it has also an unusual reredos in the form of a big mosaic panel with vines and acanthus leaves on a background of blue.

The 'Big House' as it is commonly known today is still occupied by the Johnson family...whose family actually built the property at the latter end of the 18th century. Roman House is the beautifully preserved cruck cottage. Along at the Corn Mill the fourth generation of the Wilkinson family still reside, though the mill has now ceased to operate. Castlesteads is a great house almost on the site of a Roman camp. The three acres of the camp have become its beautiful garden, a much loved place where Roman figures and altars have been dug up and set among flowers and trees.

WARCOP.

Map ref. I.8.
Next nearest Town or Village "Brough"
Location. 5 miles south east of Appleby.
Gala days/festivals.Rushbearing Ceremony.
29th June.

Warcop is undoubtedly a pleasant little village, with the River Eden acting as its boundary. Warcop parish is situated just off the A66, some five miles south east of Appleby, and close to the Yorkshire borders. It includes the hamlets of Sandford and Bleatarn.

On the fellside a thousand feet above sea level near Howgill Fold, ancient man has left entrenchments and circles of stone much older than the Roman road close by. Higher still are the spoil heaps of old mines where men worked for lead and barytes.

There was once a castle at Kirksteads where Haber and Lowgill becks join to flow through the village, but little remains of the fortified tower and manor house, replaced now by an 18th century farmhouse which stands on the site above the river. Here a narrow mediaeval bridge spans the river on three massive arches. The bridge is believed to be the oldest in use over the river Eden, and is only eleven feet wide, with recesses for pedestrians.

In the centre of the village is an old smithy now noted for wrought iron work and nearby a tall maypole with a pheasant wind-vane stands by the roadside on the site of the old village cross.

The church dedicated to St Colomba and built of warm red sandstone stands away from the village along a road shaded by lofty beeches. Ancient yews stand in the churchyard. Part of the church is very old and at one time was a Rectory in the gift of the Cliffords of Appleby Castle who in the 14th century gave it to the Abbot, the Convent of Shap. Traditions live long in this village. The Reading Room Society founded some 130 years ago is still very active and Warcop is one of the few places where the ancient rushbearing ceremony is still observed each year..The children parade through the village with banners and music, the girls carry gay crowns of fresh flowers and the boys hold rushes made into small crosses.

Telephone:
Robert and Jane
Ellwood
07683 41524

Welcomes you and your family...............

Meet "Bess & Bella" (our Vietnamese pot bellied pigs), and all their farmyard friends...Turkeys,hens, goats, donkey, Berkshire pigs, ducks, rabbits, guinea pigs, together with breeds of calves and sheep.

Come and see the cows being milked....

TASTE OF CUMBRIA

Why not take home something for family and friends? Here, at 'Taste of Cumbria' we stock food products, all made in Cumbria, be it the Cumberland Mustards from Alston, or the tasty home-made cheese from Wigton. Try one of the many traditional pickled foods or preserves from Longtown, or maybe even the delicious cakes and biscuits from Melmerby.

The rum truffles from Kendal, make an ideal present, in their attractive tins, and if you haven't far to travel, then why not take home some of the locally made ice-cream with natural flavours.

Relax over coffee and snacks in our indoor picnic area, whilst the children play in safety. Swings and sandpits available

OPENS: Good Friday thro to end of October
Tuesday - Sunday 10.30 - 5.00 pm
Find us just 300 yards out of Warcop on the
road to Kirkby Stephen.

Can't Drag Yourself Away!

Then our modern 3 bedroom (6 Berth) caravan in a small paddock close by could be the solution. It has outstanding views of the Pennines and is within easy reach of the Lake District and Yorkshire Dales. The Caravan has all modern conveniences.

For availability Tel: 07683 41524
Eden Farm Friends,
Warcop, Nr. Appleby

 # MADE IN CUMBRIA

It's by no accident that the logo of the Made In Cumbria organisation, which comprises some 300 crafts people living and working within the country, depicts the beauty of the hills and lakes of Cumbria. Often the combination of spectacular mountains, rugged fells, green valleys and numerous lakes and watercourses has been the inspiration for their products.

Made in Cumbria was established in 1989 by Cumbria County Council to promote the craft and giftware producers of the county, who are to be found in towns, villages and hamlets throughout the region. The wide range of products reflect the countryside from which they emanate. Textiles and tweeds are manufactured in the area sing local wools and yarns, or in traditional styles. Pottery and ceramics are fashioned from local clay and glazes mixed with indigenous minerals.

A wide range of fine products can be found by the visitor in many locations: at country fairs and festivals, in craft workshops and studios and in Made in Cumbria retail outlets specialising in Made in Cumbria goods.

During your visit to the area make sure that you take back something to remind you of the essence of any visit to Cumbria. This could be a print illustrating your favourite Lakeland scene, a walking stick or useful item made from the horn of the native Herdwick sheep, delightful crystal which will mirror the sunlight on a mountain stream or warm outdoor clothing for those bracing walks to the fell tops.

Wherever you travel in the County make sure that your mementos are genuine and bear the Made in Cumbria logo for proof of origin.

PROMOTING CUMBRIAN CRAFT AND GIFTWARE

WARWICK.

Map ref. G.4.
Location. 5 miles east of Carlisle.

The village of Warwick is located directly on the A69 Carlisle to Brampton road, some five miles east of Carlisle.

The bridge which gives the village its name is three arched, and links Warwick with Corby Hill and Little Corby, which together make up the village community.

Certainly one of the most interesting old buildings in Warwick has to be the still operational corn mill. Though the present building dates from 1839 it does however stand on the site of a much older mill..a Manorial one belonging to Corby Castle. The water wheel incidentally is sixteen feet in diameter and is powered by a mill-race from the cairn beck. Almost unbelievably the traditional lubricant is suet.

Until 1970 the cairn beck also fed another mill-race.. the Waddell Otterburn Mill, and it is where most of the village people would have worked at one time or another. Local wool was processed here, and the goods then sold worldwide. Their best customer was the Royal Family who used their famous cot blankets. These days the area is better known as a racing stables.

Along a shady winding lane, which branches off the busy main road to Carlisle, yet so hidden away as to be easily missed, is a remarkable little church with the work of Norman builders who may have come over with the Conqueror.It is just a nave and a chancel much restored, but it treasures still a striking Norman apse and a splendid Norman arch.

Warwick has a busy village neighbour Warwick Bridge, where as well as a factory for tweeds, there is a big white inn and a long white house built in 1711, thatched until recently. Howard Cottage..Mass was celebrated here until the church was built. Look for the attractive stone plaque let into the gable end. There is a pleasing little Roman Catholic church, and much more prominent an impressive nunnery among the beeches.It was built last century in Tudor style, with many gables, embattled turrets, and a great array of tall chimneys in groups, it was known as Holme Eden Hall. From the lodge gate the spire of the 19th century church of St Paul rises above the trees almost on the river bank.

At Warwick Knowe there are green mounds of ancient earthworks.

WATERMILLOCK.

Map ref. F.8.
Next nearest Town or Village "Pooley Bridge"
Location. 7 miles south-west of Penrith.

Watermillock is situated on the north side of Ullswater some seven miles south-west of Penrith, and a mile or so from Pooley Bridge.

Just out of site is an impressive new church of dark slate, built to give the appearance of dry-stone walling, and is the work of local craftsmen. One attractive window shows the scene of Paul's conversion and in another he is preaching at Athens. The font keeps in remembrance five small children from this neighbourhood.

In 1891 the community as it was then was able to boast various trades operating in the parish along with two schools, a post office, two pubs and 46 farms. The last 100 years have seen so many changes throughout the country, and nothing like this amount of activity exists today.

In the early years a great deal of the higher land was forest and deer park,no doubt popular with visiting royalty. Substantial stone walls...the 'fell' or'moor'dyke, often as high as 5 feet high generally marked the boundary between farmland and waste. The tenants until quite recently had certain privileges...for example, 'green hue' and ;fern bound' cutting brushwood as winter feed for cattle, and bracken for bedding or thatching. The forest was actualy enclosed in 1816 with some two thirds being converted to farmland, and the remainder left for the wild red deer. These days roe deer,badgers, foxes, buzzards, hawks, and herons roam free making it a naturalists paradise.

Near the lakeside road stands Watermillock House, built in the late 17th century, with interesting mullioned windows and across the water one sees the long ridge of High Street.

WELTON.

Map ref. E.5.
Next nearest Town or Village " Caldbeck"
Location. Just over 8 miles from Carlisle south.

Welton village is situated some eight and a half miles from Carlisle on the B.5299 road to Caldbeck. The name derives from the existence in the old days of many wells...17 of them at one time...with the water ,it is said, being pure and sweet.

The school here..Stoney Cross...is just along the Sebergham road, and dates back to 1745. Close by the church of St James was opened in 1873 having been built of local stone...a lot of it from the now defunct Sebergham Hall.

Welton is undoubtedly famous as being the home of the Cumberland Farmers Foxhounds who are kennelled along the Borrans Hill road. The opening meet is usually held on the first Saturday in November..at which time one can expect to see a crowded village all watching the Master and two huntsmen in hunting pink, plus many other riders around the green, and drinking the stirrup cup in front of the 18th century Royal Oak Pub.

Rylands Farm Restaurant

Farmhouse bed and breakfast, Welton, Carlisle CA5 7HJ

At Rylands Farm we offer bed and breakfast together with delicious meals in our small restaurant. The twenty acre farm is set high above the village of

Caldbeck and has wonderful views of High Pike and the northern fells. Set a third of a mile from the road, the farm is beautiful and very interesting for the children...who are incidentally, most welcome. We keep rare breeds of sheep and pigs and use our own eggs, vegetables and fruit which we grow using no artificial fertilisers or pesticides.

The restaurant seats eighteen and serves a variety of excellent meals using our own or locally grown produce whenever possible. We are licensed and our wine list features a good variety of reasonably priced organic wines and beers. The farmhouse has central heating and a wood burning stove in the residents sitting room. There are two double and one twin bedded room each with shower, w.c. and washbasin. Rylands Farm offers the ideal place to stay if you want to visit the lakes but return to tranquility in the evenings. Equally it is convenient for walkers undertaking the Cumbrian Way as a stopover for those travelling north to Scotland. For horse owners we offer grazing and miles of riding in the delightful northern fells. The restaurant has access and a w.c. for wheelchair users.

Tel: (06974) 78396

Please note: Restaurant Closed Mondays.

WESTNEWTON.

Map ref. C.5.
Next nearest Town or Village "Aspatria"
Location.8 miles west of Wigton.

Westnewton is a small rural village three and a half miles from the Solway coast at Allonby and eight miles west of the market town of Wigton. Recent excavations have shown that at one time the village was occupied by the Romans. Certainly a Roman road went through the village, and there are the remains of a Roman fort.

In more recent years the village has had its own castle (or Manor House) but little remains of it today and historical evidence is regretfully non-existent. Most of the houses around are inclined to be 19th century and onwards, though the beautifully restored Yew Tree Farm is dated 1672.

A native of the village John Todd having made his money as a Manchester merchant, invested a great deal of his time and money in the village in the mid 1800's. He provided the where withal for the building of St Matthew's church, along with the school, school house, vicarage and four alms houses. Westnewton was Cumbria's best kept small village in 1990, 1991,and 1993 and also the winner of the small village section of the Britain in Bloom competition in 1991.

WESTWARD.

Map ref. C.5.
Next nearest Town or Village "Abbey Town"
Location. Close to Abbey Town.

Somewhat of a scattered village, close to Abbey Town near to the west coast of Cumbria. It stands where the land begins to rise from the Solway Plain to the high fells of Lakeland, its farms are scattered on the hills or hiding in trees with the church and the school in a deep valley of the Wiza beck. From the road above the village we have the majestic mass of Criffell towering beyond Solway Firth, and a sight of Carlisle and Dumfries.

At Church Hill stands the church of St Hilda...which is the mother church of the parishes of Westward, Rosley and Welton. Visitors should look for the 1648 brass memorial tablet to one Gentleman Richard Barwise...late of Islekirk though thought to be a corruption of Hilda's Kirk.

Nicknamed Giant Barwise, early records show that he was a man of great strength...and it is said that he could walk around his courtyard carrying at arms length his wife on the one hand, and an enormous stone of great weight on the other.

St Hilda's it is recorded was preceded by a chapel near the River Waver thought to have been near Islekirk Hall, and which had been built by the monks from Holm Cultram Abbey nearby at Abbeytown. In the ravine just below St Hilda's church is a rebuilt house once a farmhouse and Inn still known today as Church Hill Farm, and dating back to the early 19th century. During these days of the Resurrectionists the churchyard readily lent itself to these ghoulish marauders (or grave robbers to give them another name)

The Innkeeper, together with local residents were forced to form a guard around a recent burial site and keep watch nightly for at least 9-10 nights after a funeral. At one time when many believed in ghosts and the supernatural, it wouldn't have been the most pleasant of tasks.

Most famous residents of the village were undoubtedly Sir William Henry Bragg (1862-1942) who was born at Stoneraise Place, and his son Sir Lawrence Bragg, who jointly shared the Nobel Prize for physics.

WETHERAL.

Map ref. F.4.
Next nearest Town or Village "Cumwhinton
Location. 5 miles south-east of carlisle.

The village of Wetheral is situated five miles south-east of Carlisle just above the wooded bank of the river Eden.

Proud of its reputation as one of the prettiest villages in Cumbria,, many of its dignified houses are grouped around a triangular green with its very old cross.In one of the garden walls are five great millstones.

In 1088 Benedictine monks from York built a priory here after realizing that the Eden was one of the finest rivers in the country.Today only the gatehouse remains .Built in three storeys of red sandstone, with embattled walls and a vaulted archway, it is a reminder of the Priory founded here by Ranulph de Meschines who was also the first builder incidentally of Appleby Castle.

Today you can still see their salmon traps, and cut into the sandstone cliffs...St Constantine's Cells. Tradition says that these man-made caves nick named 'The Wetheral Safeguards' were used by St Constantine the Hermit..Later they made a safe hiding place for the treasures of the local priory when the Scots came raiding, and for those seeking refuge from religious persecution.

St Constantine, so legend informs us was a Scottish king who relinquished his throne in the 6th century to follow St Columba and later came to live here by the Eden.

The church of the Holy Trinity, St Mary and St Constantine celebrated its 900 th anniversary in 1988.It is the only church in England dedicated to this latter saint. The anniversary coincided with the restoration of the Howard chapel...one time Roman Catholic...owned by the Howards of Corby Castle, and annexed to this Anglican building.

Look for Joseph Nolleken's sculpture 'Faith' which is to be found in the chapel.

WHITEHAVEN

Map ref. A.8.
Next nearest Town or Village ""St. Bees"
Bus service. Cumberland Buses Route 01, 02, 03,
09, 05, 07, 12, 08, 17 22, 20, 27, 30, 35, 36 300
(Clipper)
Trains. Railway Station.
Tourist Information Centre. Civic Hall,Lowther
Street.
Location 8 miles South of Workington
Early closing. Wednesday.
Market Day. Thursday and Saturday.
Gala days/festivals. Copeland Carnival 3rd Week
June

FISHING FLEET

Whitehaven is to many ideally situated on the West Cumbrian coast...just a few short miles from the Lake District National Park.

'Georgian' Whitehaven was in fact one of the first post-renaissance planned towns in the country, and is one of the forty-two 'Gem Towns' of England.

Almost unbelievable today. Whitehaven in the mid 18th century was a larger port than Liverpool .Indeed in business terms it was second only to London and Bristol.Its prosperity was built on coal and the enterprise of the Lowther family who owned the mines, and built the first quay here in 1634. It was actually Sir John Lowther who built the present town on a grid system...even specifying the type of buildings.His new town of Whitehaven he had laid out to plans inspired by Christopher Wren's designs for rebuilding London after the Great Fire of 1666. He even went to the extent of having factory chimneys designed in the shape of his favourite silver candlesticks.

Only one coal mine in the area is still working today, but several pit structures have been preserved in the south beach recreation area as monuments of industrial archaelogy.

Here too in 1718 Carlisle Spedding invented one of the earliest steam engines...designed to pump water from the pits, as well as experimenting with coal gas...going so far as to lighting his own office with it.

Besides coal, much of Whitehaven's early prosperity was built on the import of tobacco from America and rum from the West Indies. Cumberland Rum Butter today is still very much a local delicacy.

The towns connection with the 'New World' goes much beyond trade. George Washington's grandmother...Mildred Warner Gale, lived in Whitehaven, and is buried in St Nicholas Gardens. Additionally John Paul Jones, said to be the father of the American Navy (and later Admiral in the Russian Navy) made a raid on the town in 1778 during the American War of Independence. Historians of this era will note that two cannons used during the attack can still be seen near the old fort. Interestingly enough this sortie was the last ocassion upon which the English mainland was invaded from the sea. Patriotic Scots regarded John Paul Jones as a traitor. He had physical courage, true..but he was considered despicable particularly as he was in the slave trade for many years.

There was another, different attack in 1915 when Whitehaven sustained some damage as the result of shelling by a German U.Boat.

The port today, though still busy is more geared to the activity of its fishing fleet, and as always, its many small pleasure boats...rather than the large ships of old. An indication of its famous past is shown in the following figures....In 1676 the town had 32 ships, In 1682- 40 ships, and in 1706...77.

WHITEHAVEN

Because of its unspoilt state, the entire harbour has been declared a conservation area. Here can be seen monuments to mining history...the candlestick chimney...the mine bogeys, and the winding wheel.

Whitehaven Castle incidentally, which was built by the 1st Earl of Lonsdale in 1769 is now a hospital.

Many of Whitehaven's elegant Georgian buildings have been preserved, particularly in the Lowther Street area. The magnificent Georgian interior of St James Church is reputed to be the finest in the country.

WHITEHAVEN HARBOUR

WIGTON.

Map ref. D.5.
Next nearest Town or Village "Thursby"
Bus service. Cumberland Buses 38, 38A, 39,
300 (Clipper) 600
Trains. Railway Station,.
Location. 11 miles south of Carlisle.
Early closing. Wednesday
Market day. Tuesday.

Wigton is a small market town some eleven miles south west of Carlisle, and possibly one of the most pleasant'est towns in Cumbria.

For centuries this bustling little town has been the centre of business and social life on the Cumbrian Plain. It has had a Royal Market Charter since 1262, and the market is still held on Tuesday too, though now its a tame affair compared to the days when pigs and poultry were sold live in the High Street, and there was bull-baiting by the Market cross (now the site of the fountain). All commodities brought to the market were assigned a special part of the town. See the letters O.B.W....oats, barley, and wheat..marked out in white cobblestones in front of the church.

At that time the town was only four adjacent hamlets. The two main throughfares, King Street and High Street, were built in the latter half of the 1700's when the town was entering a period of prosperity mainly owing to the manufacture of cotton and linen, also dyeing, printing, tanning, and other things using water from the stream which flows round the east side of the town. The weaving was a home industry and weavers cottages can be seen at Tenters in what used to be the working part of Wigton.

One name that is strongly linked to the town is George Moore...(Samuel Smiles wrote a biography about him).He apparently made a fortune in London..after a childhood in Wigton.... Part of his Whitehall mansion remains at Mealsgate.

He died in the 1870's after being hit by a cart in Carlisle. His fortune gave a lot of help to the poor of the district in their education, together with many other good causes. The fountain at the junc-tion of the two main roads in town is actualy in memory of the wife he fell in love with when he was a poor ambitious apprentice of nineteen, newly come to London from Wigton, seeking his fortune, and she Eliza Flint Ray, his master's daughter, was a child of ten. This fountain is possibly the most attractive item in town with its gilded floriate panels against crimson Shap granite, and with a golden cross surmounting the whole.

The church is a plain building refashioned in the 18th century, but it stands on a more ancient site.

MEMORIAL FOUNTAIN

There are streets all round but the churchyard has been made into a pleasant garden. The spacious carpeted interior has galleries on three sides supported on columns and an unusual colour scheme in grey relieved here and there by gold including even the pews. The high ceiling painted Arabian blue has decorative roundels with an oval centre in white and gold.

In 1653 George Fox,the founder of Quakerism visited the town. Other visitors were John Wesley, who preached on Market Hill in 1759 and Charles Dickens who stayed at the Kings Arms Hotel when he and Wilkie Collins were on their 'Lazy Tour of two Idle Apprentices'

LAKE DISTRICT
NATIONAL PARK AUTHORITY

14 millon people visit the Lake District every year...which is more than the population of London!!...And why do they visit? Whether for serious walking or rock climbing on the numerous magnificent fells or for a quiet water based pursuits on one of the sixteen lakes or simply for a scenic drive and a visit to the local shops and attractions...the Lake District has something to offer everyone.

Within the Lake District sits the Lake District National Park Authority. You may notice a boundary sign telling you this on your way into the Park. Established in 1951 to preserve and enhance the beauty of the area and to promote quiet public enjoyment and understanding, the National Park Authority is the local govenment body established for these reasons. The NPA tries to ensure development in the Park is appropriate to the needs of the landscape and the local community through plans, the control of development and the work specialists who provide advice on land management, ecology, landscape design, the built environment and recreational planning.

Offering information about the area, the NPA runs a network of tourist information centres at..Coniston, Hawkshead, Pooley Bridge, Glenridding, Keswick, Bowness Bay, Seatoller Barn, Ambleside and Grasmere..in addition to the National Park Visitor Centre on the shores of Windermere at Brockhole, on the A591 halfway between Windermere and Ambleside. All National Park Tourist Information Centres can be easily distinguished by their familiar green colour marked with the circular NPA logo showing Wast Water and Great Gable.

In the quieter regions of the National Park where the happy wanderer may seek information, the NPA has established ten local information points at Far Sawrey, High Lorton, Ennerdale Bridge, Ulpha, St Bees, Gosforth, Forest Spinners-Rusland, Barn Door Shop - Wasdale, Maple Tree Corner Shop - Elterwater and Bampton Grange.

In partnership with the NPA these village shops and post offices are open during normal trading hours offering a range of saleable items, together with friendly advise and free information.

Maintaining and improving the landscape of the Lake District is not a easy task for the NPA who help to look after the designated 885 square miles. The NPA do not own much land within the Park. Much of it is owned by private landowners with whom the National Park Rangers work closely to ensure that the 1800 miles of footpath are accessible to both residents and visitors.

The remaining lands fall under the ownership of the National Trust, who own over a third of the area inside the National Park boundary, and who also seek to preserve and permanently protect the landscape. The National Trust was empowered by an Act of Parliament in 1907 to declare its property inalienable and subsequent legislation gave it the right to appeal to parliament against a compulsory purchase order on its inalienable land. The NPA and National Trust work closely together to protect the Lake District's landscape which is now under serious threat from visitor pressure. Millions of feet on the fells annually and the thousands of motorcars blocking the roads at peak periods highlights the importance for effective management of the area.

WINDERMERE.

Map ref. F.10.
Bus service. Cumberland Buses Route 108, 518, 555, 556
Trains. Railway station.
Tourist Information centre. Victoria Street. Windermere.
and...Lake District National Park HQ..Brockhole.
Location. 10 ,miles north west of Kendal.
Early closing. Thursday.
Gala days/festivals.Lake Windermere Festival. One week early June.
Lake Windermere Festival Week - July
Windermere Power Boat record attempts - 3rd week October

FROM ORREST HEAD

Most English towns have begun life after receiving a market charter...Windermere chose to be different.It began life with a railway station, which originally opened in 1848 at the hamlet of Birthwaite',the result was the sudden appearance of a settlement on the rising land above the old centre of Bowness.

The town was originally in the chapelry and township of Applethwaite, but a new parish was created with St Mary's as its church...a church which has a clock which doesn't chime between the hours of 11pm and 6.a.m. so as not to disturb the visitors.

Windermere was a small close knit community with plenty of shops to service the village,but as its popularity grew so the shops changed to suit the tourist trade.

As to be expected some of the earlier landmarks

CONT

have disappeared. For example the Leyland drinking fountain which had been located near the old railway station for years, is now to be found at the Brewery Arts Centre In Kendal. The drinking trough for the horses still survives and today can be seen in the wall on the main Windermere to Ambleside road. The Baddeley Town Clock is still there too...a memorial incidentally to M.J.B.Baddeley the famous guide book writer. He died in 1906 and his grave in Bowness Cemetery has a headstone made from rock brought from the summit of Scafell Pike...Also to be seen still is Jordan's granary in the centre of town.The parish church of St Martin's is actually in Bowness, and stands close to the lake.Three striking features in the large white interior are the decorated walls and pillars and its two great possessions...a magnificent east window, and an old wood carving of the patron saint,

It is the east window that catches the eye, glowing with crimson and blue.Most of it has been here two generations, but some of it was in the old church, some was new when the church was made new in the 15th century,and some was brought from Cartmel Priory. It is crowded with figures and full of colour.

The figure of St Martin is one of the rare carvings of a saint in wood, it is believed to be the work of a local craftsman and to be over 300 years old.It shows the saint sitting on a horse, wearing a queer hat and dividing his cloak and sharing it with a beggar standing by with a stick. The sculpture is about six feet high and is interesting because it is one of a very small group of equestrian statues in our English churches...in fact there are only four in England, two of which are in bronze,one in marble,

and the Windermere one, of course, in wood. It was lost sight of for nearly half a century, though it was known to have been in the church before its restoration in 1870.In 1915 the saint on horseback turned up again and was presented to the church by one of its friends.

Holehird, built by the Dunlop's last century ,has some beautiful gardens which are open under the auspices of the local horticultural society. Also Elleray, at one time the 19th century home of John Wilson, the well known writer..is now part of St Anne's School. Rayrigg was a home for the Flemings in the 17th and 18th centuries.

England's largest lake...Lake Windermere has to be the area's main attraction. The rivers Rothay and Brathay pour into the lake. It is ten and a half miles long and just one mile wide (at its maximum point). I suppose it could be said that amongst its most important visitors was a youthful William Clinton who proposed to Hilary here.

The largest island is Belle Isle...once called Longholme. From 1250 it was the seat of the Lord of the manor, though when the Phillipson's owned the island there was a siege of eight months during the Civil War when it was a Royalist stronghold. A Mr English built the present circular house in 1777, with the Curwen family becoming owners a few years later.It was then that the name 'Bel Isle' came into being...being an abbreviation of Isabel Curwen.

There has been a ferry here since 1575. The then Lords of Graythwaite Manor received six shillings and eight pence per year (approximately .33 new pence) for the right to ferry people across the middle of Windermere.

THE OAKTHORPE HOTEL

and LAMPLIGHTER BAR
High Street, Windermere,
Cumbria, LA23 1AF.
Telephone: Windermere (05394) 43547

16 Beautiful bedrooms, superby home cooked food in either bar or restaurant.
National Camra Guide.

On the eastern side of Windermere, close to the Lowood Inn, one will find inscriptions engraved on the rocks. The letters vary in size from six to twenty-four inches in height. On one large stone, roughly about ten feet square is inscribed 1833..Money, Liberty, Wealth.

Another large rock is covered with names..Sun, Bulver, Dryden, Davy, Burns,Scott, Burdett, Garrick, Kemble, Gray, Kean, Milton, Henry Brougham, James Watt, Professor Wilson, Dr Jenner...then the phase 'The Liberty of the Press'. On another rock one can read the unusual message 'National Debt £800,000,000 'O Save my Country Heaven, George and William Pitt', together with many other names and words.The man responsible places his name on one stone John Longmire..Engraver. It is said that he spent some six years chiselling away in all weathers.

Close by on the Windermere/Ambleside road is the National Park Visitor Centre, which is open every day, and on Rayrigg Road is the ever popular Windermere Steamboat Museum.

Brockhole incidentally was built in the late 1800's by a Henry Gaddum, a wealthy Manchester merchant. Following his death in 1945, the house was a convalescent home for a while. It was in 1966 that the house was bought by the Lake District Planning Board and subsequently opened to the public for the first time as a Visitor Centre in 1969. Today there are displays, special events and course's, along with regular programmes of lectures on geology, natural history, literary associations and farming. The 30 acres of attractive grounds extend to the shore with plenty of room for picnics as well as a large car park, a nature trail

ORREST HEAD HOUSE Windermere, Cumbria

Orrest Head House is a charming country house dating back to 1671. Set in 3 acres of garden andwoodland with distant views to the lake and mountains beyond, this house offers en-suite B & B accommodation.

There are 5 comfortable bedrooms...two twins and 3 doubles, all with their own bathrooms, T.V.'s, Tea and Coffee making facilities.

A comfortable guests sitting room, seperate dining room. Private parking.

Walkers will soon discover thatwe are pleasantly located with many local walks...in fact we are only 20 minutes to Cumbria's famous viewpoint of "Orrest Head". Just 1 1/2 miles away is Lake Windermere with all that it has to offer visitors.

Phone Brenda Butterworth 05394 44315

Lake District National Park

BROCKHOLE VISITOR CENTRE

Idyllically situated on the shores of Windermere lake amid 30 acres of formal gardens and parkland.

☆ **Cruise from our jetty on Windermere**
☆ **Gaddum's Restaurant & Tea Rooms with Terrace Seating**
☆ **Exciting Adventure Playground**
☆ **Visual Art Exhibitions**
☆ **Audio Visual Presentations**
☆ **Putting & Croquet**
☆ **Dry-stone Walling**
☆ **Gift and Bookshop**

PLUS... *Special Weeks of Events and Activities*
☆ **For details pick up your free copy of the Events booklet at any Lake District Information Centre, or from Brockhole.**

FREE ADMISSION *
* Please note: an admission charge may be applied for Special Events

Daily parking charge, season tickets available on request, booked coaches/minibuses free of charge
Open Daily 10.00 am- 5.00 pm Easter - November
(Special out of season arrangements can be made for groups)

Brockhole is situated on the A591 midway between Windermere and Ambleside
Tel: *(05394)* 46601

Water Margin

Gallery & Craft Studio

Situated on the A.591 between Ambleside & Windermere

Erika Lindsday-Murray of invites you to browse around her unique gallery. A large selection of original paintings can be seen by several well known artists in watercolour and oils along with limited edition prints. Exclusive sculptures including art deco are on view in bronze, stone, ceramic and wood. Commissions are undertaken by all artists, we specialise in portraits of adults, children and animals.

The craft studio boasts a wealth of local handmade crafts at prices to suit all pockets. Crystal, slate work, wood turning, paperweights, pressed flower pictures, wrought iron candle holders, hand knitted woollen sweaters, scarfs and hats, rugs and shawls, toys, jewellry, candles, dried flower baskets, preserves, designer waitscoats, silk and patchwork cushions. The Studio houses some of the finest ceramics in Lakeland

We specialise in presentation pieces and business gifts.

Low Wood Hotel,
Windermere, Cumbria.
Tel: 05394 31472

Opening Hours:
9.a.m. - 6. p.m. Summer Season:
FREE ADMISSION
Out of season: By appointment.

A warm welcome awaits you

ST. ANNE'S SCHOOL
WINDERMERE

A SCHOOL WITH A VIEW TO THE FUTURE. . .

International Independent Boarding and Day School for Girls
(350 pupils, age 4 to 18)

★ Situated in the heart of the English Lake District, overlooking Lake Windermere, St. Anne's provides an outstanding environment for personal, academic and social development.

★ Pupils are taught in small classes and entered for GCSE, A-level and Oxbridge Entrance, as well as for the Royal College of Music and RSA Computing and Word Processing examinations.

★ A wide, balanced, extra-curricular programme and superb facilities - Specialist centres for Science, IT, Languages, Art, Music, Drama, Dance and Sport.

★ Intensive courses for girls from any country in the world who wish to enter the British system of education are offered by The International College - a new department of St. Anne's.

.★ Excellent boarding accommodation, including a specially designed sixth form house where students are prepared for an independent and purposeful life.

★ Up to 18 Scholarships and Awards available each year to pupils of academic, musical or artistic ability.

○ A member of the Round Square Group of Schools in Association with centres of excellence worldwide, giving opportunities for multi-cultural education
Round
Square and exchange programmes.

For further information and a copy of the school prospectus, please contact the
Headmaster's Secretary, St. Anne's School, Windermere, Cumbria, LA23 1NW
Tel: (05394) 46164 of Fax: (05394) 88414

Lake Road, Windermere,
Cumbria LA23 2EQ
Tel: (05394) 42272

Ideally situated midway between Windermere and Bowness villages, Fir Trees offers luxurious bed and breakfast in a Victorian guest house of considerable charm and character. Antiques and beautiful prints abound in the public areas, while the bedrooms, all having en-suite facilities, are immaculate and furnished and decorated to a very high standard. The resident proprietors, Ira and Allene Fishman, have achieved an enviable reputation for their hearty breakfasts, while extending warm and friendly hospitality to their guests from the moment they arrive. Fir Trees is enthusiastically recommended by many leading guides such as Ashley Courtenay's Highly Recommended Hotels and The Best Bed & Breakfast Guide. Last but certainly worthy of mention, one gets excellent value for money when choosing to stay with Mr. & Mrs. Fishman.

Highly Commended Award by
English & Cumbria Tourist Boards.

NEWSTEAD

NEW ROAD, WINDERMERE, CUMBRIA LA23 2EE
Telephone:(05394) 44485
E.T.B. 2 Crown Commended R.A.C. Highly Acclaimed

Elegant detached Victorian house, conveniently situated between Windermere and the Lake in large grounds with secure private parking. Newstead has been totally refurbished and offers superb en-suite facilities of the highest quality - spacious rooms, beautifully decorated but retaining original woodwork and Victorian fireplaces and features. All bedrooms have colour T.V. and tea/coffee making trays.

In all - a house that is sure to delight the most discerning guest.

We serve full English breakfast / Vegetarian / Special Diets - All freshly prepared and cooked...
We are happy to provide all the information / maps / guide books etc you need to plan your day, whether your preference is for walking, boating on the Lake, sightseeing by car or just relaxing in the beautiful Lake District.
Personal attention of the owners Sue & Bill Jackson assures every satifaction.
We offer Special Spring and Autumn Breaks and hope we may be able to welcome you to Newstead in the near future.   Non-smoking household

𝔙ILLAGE 𝔕ESTAURANT

VICTORIA STREET, WINDERMERE, CUMBRIA.

Situated about 150 yards down from the station building on the left hand side travelling into the village, lies this impressive Lakeland stone buding. Owned by Chef David Courtman and his wife Trish, this restaurant offers you good home cooked food, at affordable prices, served in

warm, friendly surroundings. The decor of dusky pink/honeysuckle curtains compliments the antique tables, linen napkins and masses of dried flower arrangements...all made by Trish. The menu is varied and includes two course fixed price dishes. David is renowned for his delicious soups, pate and main dishes, including steaks, pizza's, lasagnes and pork, lamb and chicken in luscious sauces, plus fresh local and sea fish. The range of desserts include the popular "Sticky Toffee Pudding" and mouthwatering fresh Strawberry Pavlova, and there is a good selection of wines.

Childen are catered for, as are vegetarians. Access and Barclaycard are accepted. (No smoking)
Opening Hours from 6.00 p.m. Closed Thursday. (except Bank Holidays & Mid Nov - Mid Feb.)

"THE BIRDS AND WILDLIFE OF BRITAIN"

By

BRIAN WINSTANLEY.

*Original watercolours * Paintings by commission*
Prints supplied framed/unframed. Both trade & Retail

5, Ghyll Close, Windermere, Cumbria. Tel: 05394 46807

JOHN KERSHAW POTTERY

40 MAIN ROAD, WINDERMERE, CUMBRIA.

Tel: Windermere (05394) 44844

The workshop and showrooms are right in the centre of Windermere Village, down a ginnel. I make a wide range of functional and decorative stoneware and Raku. I work on the large scale, linking simple strong shapes and strong textured surfaces. Besides a range of breadcrocks and storage jars, I make many containers for plants and flowers. as well as lampbases and other purely decorative pieces.

Pottery Workshop
College Road
Windermere

DEMONSTRATIONS TUITION
Leading, and Amateur Potters work on view, and for sale
Open Daily from 10.00 am. onwards
Car Parking
Rita Murphy Telephone 05394 47457

WINSTER.

Map ref. F.11.
Next nearest Town or Village "Bowness on Windermere"
Location. 2 miles from Bowness.

Winster is a very attractive little village on the A.5074 Bowness to Levens road, just two miles from the active village of Bowness.

A winding lane amongst grand old chestnuts and beeches brings us to a spot too easily missed by travellers today. On the Lancashire border, it is just a group of quaint houses with an inn, a tiny school, and a small church among the trees. In springtime it is lost in a glory of apple and damson blossom, in summer it is a rare corner of wild flowers and here about the gateposts are slabs of stone pierced by five holes with bars through...though nobody seems to know why..

The village is named after the river that flows through the centre. At one time the river formed the Westmorland/Lancashire county boundary.

One of Winsters most notable characters would have been Jonas Barber, the famous clockmaker. During the period 1682-1720 he worked from Brime House. and was later succeeded by his son and subsequent grandsons in the work. Jonas Barber (the third) died in 1802 leaving all his clock making materials to Henry Phillipson who moved to Ulverston. As you can imagine, every house of importance had at least one of his 'grandfather'clocks.

At the same house in later years too lived William Pearson, a poet and naturalist who was never happier than when he was showing Wordsworth the loveliness of this lonely valley.

Winster's history spans many centuries and first records of it go back to 1170. The first church here was built in the late 16th century but since then has been replaced by the current Holy Trinity Church, consecrated in 1875.

Winster is without fear of argument an unspoilt village of scattered white-washed stone cottages, the focal point being the 'The Brown Horse' pub...itself dating back to the early 1800's.

WINTON.

Map ref. J.9.
Next nearest Town or Village "Kirkby Stephen"
Location. 1 mile north of Kirkby Stephen.

Winton is a tiny village one mile north of Kirkby Stephen, just off the A685 Kirkby Stephen to Brough road.

Winton was at one time famous for its schools, and education, back in the early 1800's when fees were around twenty two guineas a year. Charles Dickens is reputed to have based his character Nicholas Nickleby on a pupil from the school here . As the boys were treated like prisoners and were not allowed to return home until the end of their education in case they told of their life at school...its easy to accept that!

The school was run in conjunction with Winton Hall, an old building dated 1665, though its mediaeval appearance suggests it is older, with its stone buttresses and mullioned windows with iron bars.

Winton Hall was for many years the home of the Scaife family who with other local inhabitants founded the village school in 1659.

Winton is also famous for being the birthplace of Dr John Langhorne, the translator of Plutarch..the Greek philospher, and also Richard Burn, the builder of Orton Hall, and author of many books.

Nearby at Winton fell are the nine standards, a popular spot for walkers. The nine standards are a rough row of slender beacons which have stood there for centuries for no apparent reason. Also popular here with walkers is the 'Wheels are turning' walk...a very picturesque stroll taking in Kirkby Stephen, Hartley and Winton.

Look for the old waterwheel on the beck which in the past has provided power for the corn mill and generator, but now turns no more.

An unusual site for this area (or any area for that matter) is seeing low flying parrots, macaw's and cockatoo's from Eden Place nearby.

The Bay Horse
Winton, Kirkby Stephen, Cumbria
Recommended by the English Tourist Board.

The name Winton means 'pasture farmland', and like many Cumbrian villages dating back to medieval times once followed the two field system of agriculture. In fact you can still find evidence of this in the long thin field to the north of the village. These in medieval days would have been individual strips, which were later enclosed in the 17th and 18th century. Winton Hall the oldest building hereabouts, with its particularly fine medieval crook-beams. The front part of the house incidentally dates back to the 17th century

The centre point of the village is indisputably The Bay Horse Pub. This close to 350 year old stone floored pub...complete with oak-timbered ceilings and wood burning fire...almost seems incomplete without serving wenches in their long flowing gowns. No doubt though they were some two hundred years ago when it started life as an ale-house and coach-stop

Hosts of this very popular pub are Sheila and Derek Parvin, and although their pub is much in demand for its real ale, they now feel their Inn has become known to a wider range of customer due to 'Feature Nights'...which take the form (for example) 'curry nights'...'Mediterranean Nights'...and 'steak nights'. Cooking incidentally is prepared roughly 90% by Sheila and 10% by Derek, and the menu even on ordinary nights is enormous, with all the food of the home-cooked variety utilising locally purchased fresh produce.

Three en-suite rooms are available, for visitors who can't drag themselves away, and weekend bargain breaks too are available.

Telephone: 07683 71451

WITHERSLACK.

Map ref F.12.
Next nearest Town or Village "High Newton"
Location. 5 miles north-east of Grange over Sands.

Witherslack is a tranquil rural village situated between Whitbarrow and the east bank of the river Winster, five miles north-east of Grange over Sands.

Witherslack Hall one time seat of the Earl of Derby is now a school. One must assume that the locals of Witherslack must be proud of their noble ancestors .The first Earl's name appears here in 1487 when all the lands hereabouts were made over to him by Henry V11. In much later years the 14th Earl was three times Prime Minister. His son Lord Stanley of Preston was Governor-General of Canada from 1888, together with Lord Mayor of Liverpool, Chancellor of Liverpool University, and Chancellor of Oxford.

St Mary's Chapel stood near Witherslack Hall, but was in such a ruinous state in 1664, that Dean Barwick, who died in 1664 (and is buried in St Paul's Cathedral) bequeathed monies for repairs to the chapel, together with money for a new burial ground, for until then the dead had had to be carried across the sands to the mother church of Beetham for burial.

WITHERSLACK HALL

WITHERSLACK / WOODEND / WOODLAND

St Pauls Church was built on ground donated by the Earl of Derby...which was later consecrated by the Bishop of Chester in 1671. It has a fine canopied pulpit, once a three decker, and a charming marble figure of a baby boy asleep. Like the small school, the church was a gift of John Barwick, a Royalist who became Dean of St Paul's. His shield will be seen in one of the windows, and has the red and gold rose given him by Charles 11 for his loyalty.

Peter Barwick was the King's physician, and a friend of William Harvey.He was one of the few doctors who did not run away from the plague in 1665.Every day he attended old St Paul's to minister to miserable sufferers, and when the great Fire of London destroyed his home he lived very simply at Westminsiter, He was blind for the last eleven years of his life, but even then advised poor people free of charge.

Peter Barwick, the executor of Dean Barwick's will, further endowed funds to provide an income for a school, apprenticeships dowry for the local maids, together with fuel for the aged and infirm.

An outlaw who lies somewhere among the wooded hills is Sir Thomas Broughton, who joined Lambert Simnel's rebellion against Henry V11 and had to flee for his life. It is said that for months he was hiding in a cave hereabouts, and that his tenants took him food. He died in hiding, and was buried in the forest.

WOODEND.

Map ref. A.9.
Next nearest Town or Village "Egremont"
Location. Approx 5 miles south of Whitehaven.

Woodend is a quiet dormitory hamlet literally tucked away between the A595 Whitehaven to Egremont road, and the A5086 Cleator to Egremont road, close to the banks of the River Ehen.

At one time it was a busy iron-ore mining area, and the village was, no doubt, an important junction between the mines and the railway shunting yard at close by Moor Row. A row of railway cottages is built here, with Woodend railway station being a popular freight link. The railway as such, doesn't unfortunately stop here anymore, but the old station masters house is still here and still occupied (though not by the station-master), and the adjoining waiting rooms are now converted into an attractive bungalow.

Hidden behind the trees is Clintz Quarry, a protected conservation site, where rare species of wild flowers may be seen.Close by too is Woodend Mill, one time corn mill, and the Longlands Lake and Country Park...once an iron ore pit and flooded over in 1938.

WOODLAND.

Map ref. D.11.
Next nearest Town or Village "Broughton-in-Furness
Location. 1 mile north of Broughton-in-Furness.

Woodland is neither a town, village, hamlet or chapelry. Its just a rather pleasant, broad valley of scattered homes, hemmed in by the north-south ridge of the Woodland fells to the east and the outlying ridge of Broughton Moor to the west.

As many visitors will be aware, it is one of the Lakelands richest area for prehistoric remains. Various Bronze Age field systems and a mediaeval homestead have been discovered. The 'Giants Grave' reputed to be the last resting place of one of a family of huge men...though in truth its much more likely to be a Bronze Age barrow.

Just below is the simple church built in 1865, though it is believed to stand on the foundations of a much earlier one. Close to the church is Monks Walk, a bridle way which leads to Torver.In the past it would have been used, as the name implies, by the monks of Furness Abbey in the Middle Ages, and in addition corpses were brought this way for burial...in fact between Bridgend and Hawes is a ruin known as Nether Bolton, said to have been an inn where the funeral parties would have rested, and refreshed themselves.

In the 17th century there was a forge here, and a bloomery...remains of which can still be seen.

WORKINGTON.

Map ref. A.7.
Next nearest Town or Village "Harrington"
Bus service. Cumberland Buses Routes 30, 35, 36, 46, 47, 48, 49, 50, 51, 52, 55, 300 (Clipper)
Trains. Railway Station.
Tourist Information Centre. Central Car Park.
Location. 10 miles south of Maryport.
Early closing.Thursday
Market days. Wednesday and Saturdays
Gala days/festivals.West Cumbria Vintage Club Machinery Rally & Gymkhana. Ist Sunday July.
Curwen Fair. Spring Bank Holiday Monday.
Cumbria & North Lancs Dance Festival. Mid Feb;
Little Theatre Dance Festival. Wed to Sat following Easter Monday.
Workington Musical Festival. October.

Workington is a busy town and deep-water port. It began life as a fishing village, the estuary and the river Derwent which flows through the town was famed for its salmon.

Until mid-Victorian times, the town was long and narrow..not at all the creation which visitors will see today. In its development since Tudor times as port and market centre it was quite different to near neighbour and rival Whitehaven. A planned 17th and 18th century town of regular appearance.

The port was largely dependent on the coal and coastal trade, especially to Ireland, the Isle of Man, and Solway ports.

Prosperity really came with the exploitation of the coal fields in the area. When deeper mining became possible in the 18th century, there were at one time 14 mines in the area and the port had some 160 ships averaging 130 tons each, operating a thriving export trade. By the later 18th century in addition, there were two major blast furnaces, a number of smaller ones, and a thriving foundry. Even the production of cannons was a speciality here. The town received its charter as a municipal borough in 1888.

The contraction of the coal and the iron and steel industries in much later years brought problems to Workington. Signs of its early prosperity can be seen in a walk around Portland Square, where the 18th century buildings give a special charm.

The Helena Thompson Museum housed in .an 18th century house illustrates very clearly much

local history. The house was bequeathed to the people of Workington in 1940 by local philanthropist Miss Helena Thompson. There are displays here of pottery, silver, glass, furniture, women's and children's dresses from the 18th to early 20th century together with accessories and jewellery. It also has an interesting local history gallery.

Workington Hall, built around a 14th century pele tower. This striking ruin was at one time one of the finest manor houses in the region, owned by the Lords of the Manor. It was a refuge for Mary Queen of Scots during her last night of freedom in May 1568, and also home for the ;Ghost of Galloping Harry Curwen, who was murdered in 1623...Mary at this time was just 25 years of age, and in the heyday of her loveliness, mistress of modern languages, a poet and writer of prose. Into ten years had been crowded triumph and tragedy enough for many lives...married at 16, Queen of France at 17, and a widow in a year, at 23 she had married Darnley and two years afterwards was privy to his murder by Bothwell, whom to the horror of the world, she married within two months of the crime. The country had certainly risen against her, and shattered her forces, and here she came flying to throw herself on the mercies of Elizabeth 1.

Curwen Hall is the ruins of a 14th century castle built for the family of the same name. It has over the years been extensively altered and at one time by John Carr of York for John Christian Curwen, who as John Christian had married the Curwen heiress Isabella Curwen

A unique Workington football game played between the 'uppies' and the 'downies' (inhabitants of the upper town and lower town) over Easter still flourishes today.

The pitch covers about a mile of the grass flat near the harbour, the ball about the size of a small schoolboys football, only a good deal heavier. and the objective is to get the ball by any means from one end of the pitch to the other, throw it up three times and catch it. About a hundred players take part and a high degree of physical fitness is essential. St Michael's Church is a refashioned building with a massive tower and lofty arcades, but it has a list of rectors going back to 1150, and one or two things that the first rector on the list may have seen. There is a simple Norman arch in the tower, a Norman capital, and a Norman font bowl no longer used. There are fragments of ancient crosses with interlaced work, and several mediaeval coffin stones.

WREAY.

Map ref. F.5.
Next nearest Town or Village "Negill"
Location. 5 miles south of Carlisle.

Wreay is but a small village five miles south of Carlisle. The name is thought to be derived from a Norse word meaning a bend in the river...the river Petteril is just a half mile away.

Though records of the village date back to 1319 it doesn't have a great deal of historical interest. However they do have what is locally known as 'The Twelve Men'. This refers to meetings which have been held by a self-electing body of men responsible for the welfare of the villagers. Today the Twelve Men still meet once a year, at the Plough Inn, smoking their clay pipes and conducting what little business they still have to discuss. Minutes of their meetings go back 250 years, and no doubt the olden days would make interesting reading.

PLOUGH INN

The church here is of unusual design, and is the only one of its kind in Cumbria. It was consecrated in 1842 (though there had been a chapel here for 400 years before that) with funds provided by a Miss Sarah Losh of Woodside. Miss Losh actually

ST. MARYS CHURCH

In some of the windows of the nave are fragments of old glass picked up in the ruins of an Archbishop's palace in Paris, or collected as odds and ends from various places, and many of the small windows are unique in having thin alabaster instead of glass, the light coming through flowers and leaves cut out like fretwork. The chancel alone has thirteen of these, making a fine little gallery of fossil pictures showing some of the first forms of life.

Here also there is something which is older than any church standing on earth. It surely must be thrilling for the preacher here to remember that he is in a pulpit made from a tree that was growing before the world had heard of Bethlehem. The pulpit was fashioned from the hollow trunk of a single piece of bog oak, rescued from a submerged forest in such a fine condition that it was possible to transform it into this beautiful rostrum and to shape it after its natural form and decorate it with fossils. A small branch at one side is carved with leaves to make a candle holder.

Scaleseugh Hall of 1684 stands near by, it was enlarged early in this century and is now a home for spastics. Exotic and unusual trees from many countries flourish in the grounds close to the A6 highway.

sent a local stone-mason to Rome to gain first hand knowledge before building the church in an Italian style. Besides this church the good lady also built the school along with the schoolmasters house. She was truly a lover of art as will be seen by the birds, fir-cones, butterflies, water lillies, snakes and alligators incorporated into the interior decorations of the church.

Much ingenuity and loving labour was put into this remarkable church, as well as the fine craftmanship.

THE NATIONAL TRUST
for Places of Historic Interest or Natural Beauty

The National Trust is not a Government department, but a charity, dependent totally on the voluntary support of the public and its members, which protects land and buildings for the benefit of the nation as a whole. It is the largest private landowner and conservation society in Britain, and was originally founded in 1895 by three Victorian conservationists...Canon Hardwicke Rawnsley, Miss Octavia Hill, and Sir Robert Hunter. For close to 100 years it has worked for the preservation of places of historic interest and natural beauty in England, Wales and Northern Ireland.

The Trust administers its estates through sixteen Regional Offices and now protects over 460 miles of unspoilt coastline (more than a third of the finest that remains), over 140,000 acres of fell, dale, lake, and forest in the Lake District alone; prehistoric and Roman antiquities, downs and moorlands, fens, farmland, woods and islands; nature reserves, lengths of inland waterways and all or the greatest part of forty-four villages.

All are open to the public at all times, subject only to the needs of farming, forestry and the protection of wildlife.

Amongst properties owned in Cumbria and the Lake District, and which you shouldn't fail to visit.

Townend House, Troutbeck, Cartmel Priory Gatehouse, Sizergh Castle, Dalton Castle, Tower Bank Arms, Sawrey, steam Yacht 'Gondola', Wansfell Pike, Troutbeck, Hill Top, Near Sawrey.

Wordsworth House , Fell Foot Park, , Beatrix Potter Gallery, Hawkshead, and Acorn Bank Garden.

...In fact The National Trust in the Lake District conserves over one quarter of the Lake District National Park, most of the central fell area is owned or leased by the Trust, and they protect six of the main lakes.

Enquiries for membership are very welcome.

Five information centres are open in the Lake District...namely Bridge House, Ambleside, together with Grasmere, Hawkshead, Keswick and Fell Foot Park.

NORTH WEST REGION . THE HOLLENS . GRASMERE
AMBLESIDE . CUMBRIA LA22 9QZ
Telephone Grasmere (05394) 35599 Facsimile (05394) 35353

ADVERTISERS INDEX.
See Advertiser listed under relevant Town/Village

Letter.A.
Abbey Horn.Holme.
Abbot Hall.Kendal.
Allanajade. Kendal.
Ancient Recipes. Longtown.
Appleby Castle. Appleby.
Architectural Antique. Cartmel Fell.
A Room with a View. Hawkshead.
Arrowfield Country Hotel.Coniston.
Austin Friars School.Carlisle.

Letter B.
Bailey Mill Farm. Newcastleton.
Peter Bain-Smith.Cartmel.
Bank Court Cottage.Cartmel.
Bank Ground Farm.Coniston.
Barbon Inn. Barbon.
Barn Shop & Tea-Rooms. Sizergh.
Barn Studio. Hawkshead.
Barron Wood Restaurant.Armathwaite.
Bateman Car Museum.Coniston.
Bateman Motors.Grange-over-Sands.
Bay Horse Inn.Winton.
Beckmill Gallery .Cover
Beech House. Glenridding.
Beechmount.Near & Far Sawrey.
Beechwood Cottage.Underbarrow.
Beers in Particular. Kendal.
Birchleigh Guest House.Grange over Sands.
Birdoswald.Gilsland.
Birds & Wildlife of Britain.Windermere.
Birds of Prey Centre. Lowther.
Biskey Howe Villa. Bowness on Windermere.
Blake Hills Farm.Mungrisdale.
Blenheim Lodge. Bowness on Windermere.
Blue Bell Hotel.Heversham.
Boot & Shoe Inn. Greystoke.
Book Shop.Maryport.
Bradley Riding Centre. Ennerdale.
Brantwood. Coniston.
Brendan Chase.Windermere..
Britannia Inn.Elterwater.
Britannia Inn. Penny Bridge.
Brockhole Visitors Centre.Windermere.
Brockwood Hall.Millom.
Brookfield.Sedbergh.
Brooklyn House. Keswick.
Broomriggs.Hawkshead.
Broughton Craft Shop.Broughton in Furness.
Brownside Coach House. Alston.
Bruno's Restaurant.Whitehaven.
Buckle Yeat.Near & Far Sawrey.
The Bungalows.Threlkeld.
Burnside Hotel. Cover

Letter.C.
Calvert Trust Adventure Centre. Bassenthwaite.
Carlisle City Council. Carlisle.
Castle Hotel.Brough.
Character Country Cottages.Boot.
Jon Cheney. Ambleside.
Chequers Motel.Dalton in Furness.
Clare House.Grange over Sands.
Claremount House.Keswick.
Cliff House Farm.Kirklinton.
Cliff Inn.Kirklinton.
Clifford House Crafts. Brough.
Cobble Country Cottages. Sedbergh.
Cockermouth Antique Markets .Cockermouth.
Cockles.Flookburgh.
College House.Windermere.
Compston House Hotel.Ambleside.
Conishead Priory. Bardsea.
Coniston Ferry Service. Coniston.
Coniston Hall. Coniston.
Cookhouse Gallery.Ambleside.

Copper Kettle. Kirkby Lonsdale.
Country Furnishers. Witherslack.
Courtyard Gallery.Appleby.
Craiglands Hotel. Grange over Sands.
Creative Leisure.Sedbergh.
The Croft.Hawkshead.
Croft House. Warcop.
Croglin Toy Shop. Lazonby.
Croppers.Burneside.
Cross Keys Hotel.Milnthorpe.
Cross Keys Hotel.Tebay.
Crosthwaite House. Crosthwaite.
Cumberland Buses. Facing Map
Cumberland & Westmorland Antiquarian & Archaeological Society.Kendal.
Cumbria Rustic. Torver.
Cumbria Wild Life. Ambleside.

Letter D.
Dalegarth House. Portinscale.
Dalton Pottery. Dalton in Furness.
Danes House. Staveley.
Dent Aerated Water Co.Cleator.
Denton House.Caldbeck.
Derwent Cottage.Portinscale.
Derwentwater Hotel.Keswick.
Dovecote.Kirklinton.
Dove Cottage.Grasmere.
Drunken Duck.Hawkshead.
Dungeon Ghyll Hotel. Langdale.

Letter. E.
Eagle & Child. Staveley.
Eagles Head.Grizedale.
Eagle Quest. Keswick.
Eden Farm Friends. Warcop.
Edenhall Hotel. Edenhall.
Edenvale.Ambleside.
Ees Wyke Country House. Near & Far Sawrey.
Elleray Hotel.Windermere.
Eltermere Country House Hotel.Elterwater.
Engine Inn. Cark in Cartmel.
Eskdale Mill. Boot.
Esthwaite Howe Farm House. Near & Far Sawrey.

Letter. F.
Fagan's. Cockermouth.
Fairfield Clothing.Sedbergh.
Fairlight Guest House. Glenridding.
Fair Winds. Kendal.
Farrer's Coffee House. Kendal.
Fat Lamb. Ravenstonedale.
Fell House. Shap.
Fellside Lane End Cottage. Elterwater.
Fell View.Kendal.
Field & Stream. Keswick.
Fir Trees. Windermere.
Fisherbeck Hotel.Ambleside.
Fleece Inn. Kirkby Lonsdale.
Fold End Gallery. Boot.
Force Mill Farm.Grizedale.
Forest Enterprise. Grizedale.
Four Seasons Farm.Calthwaite.
Foxghyll. Ambleside.
Grace Fry Guest House. Whitehaven.
Friar Hall Farm. Caldbeck.
Furness Galleries. Ulverston.

Letter G.
Galava Gate. Ambleside.
Garth Country House. Near & Far Sawrey.
Gate Hotel. Appleby.
George Hotel. Orton.
Gighouse Gallery. Elterwater.
Gilsland Spa Hotel.Gilsland.
Glen Rothay Hotel.Rydal.
Glittercomb.Bowness on Windermere.
Golf Centre. Penrith.
Golf Club.Casterton.
Golf Club.Kirkby Lonsdale.

Gosforth Arts & Crafts. Gosforth.
Gosforth Hall Hotel. Gosforth.
Gosforth Pottery.Gosforth.
Gossipgate Gallery.Alston.
Gowbarrow Lodge. Watermillock.
Grammar Hotel. Cartmel.
Grasmere Gardens. Grasmere.
Grasmere & Wordsworth Museum. Grasmere.
Grass Roots. Bowness on Windermere.
Graythwaite Hall Estates.Graythwaite.
Greenbank Country House Hotel. Hawkshead.
Green Gables Guest House. Windermere. Greenhowe Caravan
Park. Langdale.
Greystones. Keswick.
Grizedale Lodge Hotel. Grizedale.
Grove House Gallery. Keswick.
Guide over Sands. Allithwaite.

Letter H.
Halecat Garden Nurseries. Witherslack.
Holbeck Ghyll. Troutbeck.
E.S.Hartley. Kirkby Lonsdale.
Harney Peak. Portinscale.
Hawkshead Country Wear. Hawkshead.
Hawksmoor.Windermere.
Hayes Garden Centre. Ambleside.
Hazlemere Cafe. Grange over Sands.
Heaton Cooper Studios. Grasmere.
Heaves Hotel. Levens.
Hellena & Pillars. Keswick.
Heredities.Kirkby Stephen.
Heritage Centre. Ulverston.
Heron Corn Mill. Beetham.
Hide & Horn. Ambleside.
High Adventure. Bowness on Windermere.
Highfield House. Hawkshead.
High Hall Rare Breeds. Dent.
Highland Laddie. Kirkbride.
Hillcrest. Keswick.
Hobby Ceramic. Milnthorpe.
Hollywood Guest House. Windermere.
Holmcroft. Sedbergh.
Horseshoe Hotel. Ambleside.
Howe Head Cottages. Coniston.
Howscales. Kirkoswald.
Hunday Manor. Workington.
Hundith Hill Hotel. Cockermouth.
Hutton in the Forest. ..Hutton in the Forest.
Hyning Cottage. Levens.

Letter J.
Jennings Bros. Cockermouth.
Jolly Anglers Inn. Burneside.

Letter K.
'K' Shoes. Kendal & Shap.
Keen Ground Farm. Hawkshead.
Kendal Museum Kendal.
Kentdale Ramblers.Kendal.
J.Kershaw Pottery. Windermere.
Keswick Bridge Time-Share. Keswick.
Keswick Launch. Keswick.
Kings Arms Hotel. Shap.
Kings Head Hotel. Keswick.
Kirkstone Galleries. Skelwith Bridge.
Malcolm D.Knight. Milnthorpe.
Knoll Hotel. Bowness on Windermere.
Knotts Mill Country Lodge. Ullswater.

Letter. L.
Lacet House Hotel. Ambleside.
Lairbeck Hotel. Keswick.
Lake District National Park HQ. Windermere.
Lake District Trail Riding Centre.Rydal.
Lakeland Equestrian. Windermere.
Lakeland Ford. Kendal.
Lakeland Hampers. Kendal.
Lakeland House. Coniston.
Lakeland Knitwear.Ambleside.

Lakeland Land Rover.Coniston.
Lakeland Skirts. Kendal.
Lakeland Time-Share. Ambleside.
Lakeland Wild Life Oasis. Milnthorpe.
Lakes Craft & Antiques. Grasmere.
Lakeside. Bassenthwaite.
Lakeside & Haverthwaite Railway. Newby Bridge.
Langdale Chase Hotel. Ambleside.
Langdale Craft Shop. Elterwater.
Langdale Time-Share. Elterwater.
Langley Hotel. Langwathby.
Laurel & Hardy Museum. Ulverston.
Laurel House. Bowness on Windermere.
Leisure Pool. Keswick.
Levens Hall. Levens.
Lightwater Farm House. Cartmel Fell.
Lingholm Gardens. Portinscale.
Lingmoor. Windermere.
Lloyds Motors. Carlisle.
Log House. Ambleside.
Longlands Caravan Park.Kirkby in Furness.
Low Hall Farm. Dent.
Low Plain Park Farm. Brigsteer.
Lowther Park. Lowther.
Low Wood Hotel. Ambleside.
Lyndhurst Hotel. Ambleside.
Lynehurst Hotel. Grange over Sands.
Lyth Gallery Underbarrow.

Letter. M.
Made in Lakeland. Bowness on Windermere.
Maia Lodge. Bowness on Solway.
Meadfoot. Windermere.
Meadow House Caravan Park. Allonby.
Meadow Ing Farm. Appleby.
Mere Mountain/Leisure in Pleasure. Windermere.
Millers Beck. Kendal.
M.Milton.Tourist Guide. Milnthorpe.
Minstrel Gallery. Hawkshead.
Mirehouse. Bassenthwaite.
Mountain Goat Holidays. Windermere.
Maurice Mullens. Caldbeck.
Muncaster Castle. Ravenglass.
Rita Murphy. Windermere.

Letter N.
Nab Cottage. Rydal.
National School of Falconry. Penrith.
Natland Millbeck Farm. Kendal.
Near Howe Hotel. Mungrisdale.
Netherdene Guest House. Ullswater.
Netherwood Hotel. Grange over Sands.
Newby Bridge Hotel. Newby Bridge.
Newlands Adventure Centre. Keswick.
Newlands Guest House. Kendal.
Newstead. Windermere.
New Village Tea Rooms. Orton.
Nichol End Marine. Keswick.
Northern Fells Gallery. Uldale.
Nunnery House Hotel. Kirkoswald.

Letter 0
Oak Bank Fisheries. Longtown.
Oak Bank Hotel. Bowness on Windermere.
Oak Head Caravan Park. Newby Bridge.
Oakhurst Garden Centre. Cockermouth.
Oaklands. Coniston.
Oakthorpe Hotel. Windermere.
Old Granary & New Mills Trout Farm. Brampton.
Old School House. Hawkshead.
Old Smithy. Caldbeck.
Old Vicarage Hotel. Witherslack.
Orrest Head Hotel. Windermere.
Orton Craft. Orton.

Letter P.
Past & Present. Bowness on Windermere,
Patchwork by Newberys. Barbon.
Pennine Hotel. Kirkby Stephen.

Pepper House. Grizedale.
Pheasant Inn. Bassenthwaite.
Pine & Design. Kirkby Stephen.
Pipercroft. Coniston.
Plough Inn.Selside.
Ponsonby Farm Park. Calderbridge.
Postillion Restaurant. Bowness on Windermere.
Priest Mill. Caldbeck.
Prospect Hill House. Kirkoswald.
Punch Bowl. Underbarrow.

Letter Q.
Queen's Arms. Barrow in Furness.
Quiggins & Sons. Kendal.

Letter R.
Raesbeck Guest House. Ambleside.
Ravenglass & Eskdale Railway.Ravenglass.
Ravenstone Lodge.Bassenthwaite.
Red Dragon. Kirkby Lonsdale.
Red House Hotel. Keswick.
Red Lion. Grasmere.
Red Lion. Sedbergh.
Rickerby Grange. Portinscale.
River Kwai. Barrow in Furness.
Riverside Craft Studio. Cockermouth.
Riverside Restaurant. Cockermouth.
Riverside Workshop. Keswick.
Fred.Robinson. Ulverston.
Rockside Guest House.Windermere.
Rookin House Farm. Ullswater.
Rosemount Private Hotel.Windermere.
Rothay Garth Hotel. Ambleside.
Rough Close Country Hotel. Hawkshead.
Royal Hotel. Kirkby Lonsdale.
Royal Oak Inn. Lindale in Cartmel.
Rydal Lodge. Rydal.
Rylands Farm House. Welton.

Letter. S.
Salutation Hotel. Ambleside.
Sandown. Bowness on Windermere.
Sawrey Hotel. Near & Far Sawrey.
Sawrey House Country Hotel.Near & Far Sawrey.
Sawrey Knotts. Near & Far Sawrey.
Scotgate. Braithwaite.
Sedbergh School. Sedbergh.
Sellet Hall Gardens. Kirkby Lonsdale.
Seymour House. Keswick.
Shap Wells Hotel. Shap.
Sharrow Bay Country Hotel. Pooley Bridge.
Shinglers. Ambleside.
Ship Inn. Coniston.
Snooty Fox. Kirkby Lonsdale.
Snooty Fox. Uldale.
Sockbridge Mill Trout Farm. Sockbridge.
Sophie's Wild Woollens. Dent.
Souterstead.Torver.
South Quay Restaurant. Maryport.
Spindle Craft. Drigg.
Spoon Hall. Coniston.
Spout House. Crosthwaite.
Spring Hag Kennels.Staveley.
Springlea Caravan Park. Allonby.
Squirrel Loft. Kendal.
St Annes School.Windermere.
St Bee's School. St Bee's.
Stepping Stones. Rydal.
Stewartson. Hawkshead.
Sticklebarn Tavern. Langdale.
Stott Park Bobbin Mill. Newby Bridge.
Sun Dial House. Kendal.
Sun Hotel. Coniston.
Sun Inn. Hawkshead.
Swarthmoor Hall. Ulverston.

Letter. T.
Tarragon Gift Ware. Cartmel.

Theatre in the Forest. Grizedale.
Thompson Ground Farm. Hawkshead.
Thornthwaite Hall. Thornthwaite.
Thornthwaite Galleries. Thornthwaite.
Thorneyfield Guest House. Ambleside.
Tossbeck Farm. Kirkby Lonsdale.
Touchstones. Penrith.
Towerbank Arms. Near & Far Sawrey.
Town End Farm. Troutbeck.
Townson Ground. Coniston.
Three Shires Inn Langdale.
Travellers Rest.Grasmere.
Troutbeck Head Caravan Park. Ullswater.
Tullie House. Carlisle.
Ann Tyson Cottage. Hawkshead.

Letter U.
Uplands Hotel. Cartmel.

Letter V.
Verdant Stores. Ambleside.
Village Bakery. Melmerby.
Village Restaurant. Windermere.
Virginia House. Ulverston.

Letter W.
Walpoles.Kendal.
Jenny Walter. Milnthorpe.
Wanslea Guest House. Ambleside.
Warren Guest House. Carlisle.
Watchgate Farm. Selside.
Waterhead Guest House. Coniston.
Water Margin Gallery. Windermere.
Watermill. Great & Little Salkeld.
Water Mill Inn. Ings.
Waterside House. Pooley Bridge.
Water Yeat. Ulverston.
Waverley Hotel. Windermere.
Webbs Garden Centre. Kendal.
West Coast Indoor Karting. Maryport.
Wetheriggs Country Pottery. Penrith.
Whicham Old Rectory. Silecroft.
Whins Pond Fishing.Edenhall.
Whitbarrow Hall. Greystoke.
White House.Clifton.
White Lodge Hotel. Barrow in Furness.
White Moss House. Grasmere.
Whitewater Hotel. Newby Bridge.
Willow Cottage. Bassenthwaite.
Willowfield Hotel. Arnside.
Winbrook House.Windermere.
Windermere Balloon.Co. Penny Bridge.
Windermere Iron Steamboat Museum. Cover
Winmaur Guest House. Kendal.
Woodleigh Guest House. Grange over Sands.
Wreaks End Cottage. Broughton in Furness.

Letter Y.
Yates Brewery.West Newton.
Yewfield.Hawkshead.
Yew Tree Tracking. Egremont.
Y.M.C.A. Newby bridge.

Letter Z.
Zefferelli's. Ambleside.

GENERALLY LOCATED
National trust.
Cumbria Tourist Guide.
Halifax Property. Services
Video Book/Studio 21.
Made In Cumbria.
Cumbrian Cottages.
Peter Rabbit & Friends Opposite Authors introduction
Solway Eden Byways.
W.C.F.
W.C.F.Country Collections
Herdwick Lamb.

INDEX. A.

A.A. Lowther,Nateby.
Abbot Hall,Kendal.
Abbot of Douai, Cleator.
Ackenthwaite. Hincaster.
Acorn Bank. Temple Sowerby.
Adam of Beaumont. Piel Island.
Addingham. Glassonby,Little Salkeld.
Dr Addison. Appleby,Bridekirk.
Queen Adelaide. Bowness on Windermere.
Agincourt. Moresby.
St.Agnes. Allithwaite.
Agricola. Dalton, Natland.
St.Aidan. Kirkoswald.
Aira Force. Patterdale.Ullswater.
Alauna. Kendal,Maryport.
Prince Albert. Dent.
Alcfrith Cross. Bewcastle.
Allen Tarn. Nibthwaite.
Allerby Hall. Cross Canonby.
Ambleside clag-em. Ambleside.
Ambleside Hall. Ambleside.
Anchorite Well. Kendal.
Ancient Mariner. Cockermouth.
St Andrew. Crosby Garrett,Dacre, Dent,Kirkandrews, Penrith.
St Anthony. Cartmel.
St Anthony's Tower. Milnthorpe.
Antonine Wall. Bewcastle.
Queen Anne. Waberthwaite.
St Anne's Hospital. Appleby.
Appleby Castle. Appleby, Warcop.
Appleby family. Kirklinton.
Appleby Gypsy Fair. Morland.
Appleby Horse Fair. Long Marton.
Applethwaite. Underskiddaw.
Little Appleby. Morland.
Arkleby. Plumbland
Armada. Morland.
Archie Armstrong. Longtown.
Armathwaite Hall.Bassenthwaite.
Arnison Store. Penrith.
Dr Arnold. Rydal,Ambleside.
Arnside Tower. Arnside.
King Arthur. Armathwaite,
Bassenthwaite,Beetham,Brougham,Kirkby
Stephen,Lazonby.Longtown,Mallerstang,
Pooley Bridge,Eamont Bridge,Ravenglass.
Arthuret. Longtown.
Asby Gill.Asby.
Asby Hall. Asby.Great Asby.
Little Asby.
Thomas Ashburner. Burneside.
Askerton Castle. Bewcastle.
Sir Hugh Askew. Boot.
Askham Hall. Lowther.
King Athelstan. Dacre.
Captain Robert Atkinson. Kaber.
Atkinson Family. Little SalkeldAughertree.Uldale.
Augustinian Canons. Carlisle,Cartmel,Cartmel Fell.

B.
Backbarrow Iron Furnace. Newby Bridge.
MJB Baddeley. Windermere.
Ballantyne Dykes. Dovenby.
Bampton Grange. Bampton.
Sir John Bankes. Keswick.
Bannockburn. Kirkoswald,Casterton.
Jonas Barber. Cartmel,Winster.

Barbon beck. Barbon.
Barbondale. Barbon.
Bardsea Hall. Bardsea.
Bardsea Country Park. Bardsea.
Baronwood. Lazonby.
Barton. Pooley Bridge.
Sir John Barrow. Ulverston.
Barrow Iron Shipbuilding Co. Barrow.
St.Bartholmew. Loweswater.
Bernard Barton. Ivegill.
Richard Barwise. Westward.
Dean Barwick Witherslack.
Peter Barwick. Witherslack.
Bassenfell Manor. Bassenthwaite.
Sir Adam de Bassenthwaite. Bassenthwaite.
James Bateman. Burnside.
Roger Bateman. Old Hutton.
Battle of Bayonne. Bassenthwaite.
Battle of Britain. Bowness on Windermere.
Battle of Langside. Moresby.
Battle of Stoke. Piel Island.
Lizzie Baty. Brampton.
Monsieur Beaumont. Levens.
Beckfoot. Bampton.
Thomas a Becket. Kings Meaburn, Kirkby Stephen.
Beck Mill Gallery. Langwathby.
Beckside. Old Hutton,Kirkby in Furness.
Beckside Boggle. Eskdale.
Sir Bedwere. Bassenthwaite.
St.Bees. Ennerdale Bridge.
Beetham Hall. Beetham.
Mrs Beeton. Thursby.
St.Bega. St Bees,Bassenthwaite.
Bekansgill..Barrow.
Sir James Bellingham. Levens.
Belle Isle. Bowness on Windermere,Windermere.
Belsfield.Bowness on Windermere.
Bents.Crosby Garrett.
Betsy Croft. Newbiggin on Lune.
Beuth. Bewcastle.
Beuth's Castle. Bewcastle.
Bewcastle Cross. Bewcastle.
Bewby Castle. Bolton.
Bicc di Loringe. Levens.
Biggar Village. Barrow.
Bigland Hall,Backbarrow, Newby Bridge.
Birdoswald. Gilsland,Bewcastle.
Birkbeck family. Orton.
Birker Force. Eskdale.
Anne Birketts Dame School. Penrith.
Birkrigg. Bardsea.
Bishops of Carlisle. Bolton.
Bishops Dyke. Dalston.
Bishop of Glasgow. Caldbeck.
Bishop Rock. Thornthwaite.
Bishops Well. Aspatria.
Black Combe. Barrow, Bottle, Corney, Grange- over-Sands, Millom, Silecroft.
Black Death. Kendal, Edenhall.
Black Dub. Crosby Ravensworth.
Black Fell Moss. Mallerstang.
Black Tom of the North. Camerton.
Susan Blamire. Dalston.
Thomas Bland. Crosby Ravensworth.
Blawith. Lowick.
Blea Tarn. Langdale, Warcop.
Bleaberry Tarn. Buttermere.
Blea Rees. Langdale.
Bleaze Hall. Old Hutton.
Blencathra.Threlkeld.
Blencathra Hunt. Braithwaite. Threlkeld.
Blencogo. Bromfield.

Blencow Hall. Blencow.
Great Blencow. Blencow.
Little Blencow. Blencow.
John Blennerhasset. Flimby.
Blindcrake Hall. Blindcrake.
Eric Bloodaxe. Stainmore.
Bloody Field. Kirkbride.
Anne Boleyn. Moresby.
Chris Bonnington. Caldbeck.
Borrans Field.Ambleside.
Borrowdale. Keswick.
Bothel Park Farm. Bothel.
Thomas Bouch. Thursby.
Bowfell. Grange over Sands.
Bowland Bridge Cartmel,Cartmel Fell.
Joe Bowman. Matterdale.
Old Bowness. Bowness on Windermere.
Bowscale. Mungrisdale.
de Boyvill Family. Kirklinton Egremont.
Colonel Thomas Braddyll.Bardsea.
Sir Lawrence Bragg. Westward.
Melvyn Bragg. Caldbeck,Buttermere.
Sir William Henry Bragg Westward.
Brandlehow. Keswick.
Branthwaite Boggle.Dean.
Branthwaite Hall. Dean.
Brantwood. Coniston.
Brathay Bridge Clappersgate,Ambleside.
Bravinacum.Kirkby Thore.
Brayton Hall. Aspatria.
Brewery Arts Centre. Kendal.
St Bride.Kirkbride.
Bridge House, Ambleside.
St.Bridget. Calderbridge,
Moresby,Beckermet,Bridekirk.
Colonel Brigg.Kendal.
Rev.Ralph Brocklebank. Bothel.
Bronte House. Casterton.
Charlotte Bronte.Casterton,Dent.
Bronte Sisters.Casterton.
Emily Bronte.Dent.
Broomrigg Plantation. Ainstable.
Brough Castle. Stainmore. Brough
Lord Brougham. Witherslack.Brougham.Clifton.
Brougham Castle. Brougham.
Brougham Hall. Brougham.
Udard de Brougham. Brougham.
Sir Thomas Broughton. Witherslack.
Broughton Mill. Broughton.
Broughton Tower. Broughton.
Brovacum.Broughton.
Giles Brownrigg.Ireleth.
Edward Bruce. Dalston.
Robert Bruce. Lanercost, Beaumont.
Brundholme. Underskiddaw.
Sir James Brunlees. Bowness on Solway.
Bryce Institute. Burneside.
Duke of Buccleuch. Piel Island.
Buckbarrow. Piel Island.
Bulgill. Cross Canonby.
Burbank House. Blencow.
Burblethwaite. Cartmel Fell.
Burgh Marsh. Burgh by Sands.
Burn. Orton.
Richard Burn. Winton.
De.Burneshead Burneside.
Burne-Jones. Brampton, Staveley, Troutbeck.
Burneside Hall. Burneside.
Robert Burns. Carlisle.
Bushfield. Nicholforest.
Dame Clara Butt. Beetham.
Buttermere Fells. Buttermere.

Buttermere Lake. Buttermere,Loweswater.
Butterwick. Bampton.
Butts Hill Night. Milburn.
Butts Hill Night. Milburn.

C.
Caernarvon Castle. Beckermet.
Caesars Tower. Appleby.
Ewen Caesario. Armathwaite. Penrith.
Caldbeck Fells. Ivegill.
Calder Abbey. Beckermet,Calderbridge.
W.S.Calverley Aspatria.
Raisley Calvert.Mungrisdale.
Camerton Hall. Camerton.
Donald Campbell.Coniston.
Canons of Conishead. Beetham.
Capon Tree. Brampton.
Cardew.Cumdivock.
Cardowleas.Cumdivock.
Cardew Hall.Dalston.
Cardunneth Pike. Castle Carrock.
Cark Hall. Cark in Cartmel.
Carkettle.Pennington.
Will Carling. Sedbergh.
Carlisle & Annan Navigation Co.Ltd.Port Carlisle.
Carlisle Canal. Beaumont.
Carlisle Castle. Carlisle.
Carlisle Cathedral. Brougham, Carlisle, Cumdivock.
Carlisle Priory.Cross Canonby,Finsthwaite.
Carlisle to Settle Railway. Armathwaite,Burgh-by-
Sands,Langwathby.
Carlyle. Bassenthwaite.
Charlotte Carpenter. Gilsland.
John Carr. Kendal.
Castle Dairy. Kendal.
Castlerigg Stone Circle. Keswick, Lazonby.
Castle Hall. Pennington.
Thomas Castley Keld.
Cartmel Fell. Crosthwaite.
Cartmel Priory.Ayside,Backbarrow,Bowness on
Windermere,Caldbeck,Cartmel,
Lindale in Cartmel,Newby Bridge,Grange-over-
Sands,Windermere.
Cartmel Races.Cartmel.
Carus-Wilson.Casterton.
Carwhinley.Longtown.
Casterton Fell.Casterton.
Castle Brewery.Lorton.
Castle Cottage.Near & Far Sawrey.
Castlehaw.Sedbergh.
Castle Head.Lindale in Cartmel.
Lord Castlereugh Gt Corby.
Castlesteads. Plumpton.
Catbells. Keswick.
St.Catherine. Crook.
Catlowdy.Nicholforest.
Causey Pike.Braithwaite.
Cavendish House. Carlisle.
Lord Cavendish. Cark in Cartmel.
Cawdle Moor. Patterdale.
Chambers Family. Abbey Town,Heversham.
Chapel Butts,Newbiggin-on-Lune.
Chapels.Kirkby in Furness.
Chapel Stile. Langdale.
William Chapman.Port Carlisle.
Charles 1. Brougham,Longtown.
Charles 11. Burton-in-Kendal, Colton, Crosby Ravensworth,
Kaber, Millom, Flookburgh, Greystoke Witherslack.
Bonnie Prince Charlie. Brampton, Carlisle, Longtown,
Finsthwaite, Irthington, Sedbergh, Shap,
Clifton,Orton.
Colonel Charteris. Burton-in-Kendal.

Childrens Society.Natland.
Fletcher Christian. Cockermouth.
Civil War. Beetham, Cockermouth, Dalton, Kendal, Kirklinton.
Claife Heights.Bowness on Windermere.
Thomas Clarkson.Matterdale,Pooley Bridge.
Clawthorpe Fell. Holme.
Cleator Grotto. Cleator.
Admiral Cleburne. Cliburn.
Clergy Daughters School.Casterton.
Cliburn Hall.Cliburn.
Robert de Cliburn. Cliburn.
Lord Clifford. Appleby,Brough.
The Cliffords. Beetham,Crosby Ravensworth,Warcop.
Lady Anne Clifford. Appleby, Brough, Brougham, Dalston, Mallerstang,Stainmore.
Lady Margaret Clifford. Appleby.
Robert de Clifford. Shap.
Clifton. Keld.
Clifton Hall.Clifton.
Clifton Moor. Clifton,Milburn.
William Clinton. Windermere.
St.Cuthbert. Cliburn.
Clydesdale Horses. Camerton,Kirkbride.
Cobblers Hallow. Bassenthwaite.
Cockermouth Castle. Papcastle, Plumbland, Gt & Little Broughton.
Coel Hen.Carlisle.
Coledaw Horseshoe.Braithwaite.
Hartley Coleridge. Keswick,Rydal,Sedbergh.
S.T. Coleridge. Caldbeck, Clappersgate.
Cockermouth. Grasmere.
Wilkie Collins.Wigton.
W.G.Collinwood.ConistonColton Old Hall. Colton.
Conishead Priory. Bardsea,Nibthwaite.
Coniston Hall. Coniston.
Coniston Lake.Coniston,Nibthwaite.
Coniston Old Man.Lowick.
Coniston Water. Blawith.
Constable.Clappersgate.Levens.
King Constantine of Scotland.Dacre.
St.Constantine's Cells.Wetheral.
Conyger Hurst. Pennington.
Roger of Conyer.Hayeswater.
William & Ann Cookson.Penrith.
Coop Carnal Hotel.Kirkby Stephen.
Corby Castle. Great Corby.
Cote How.Rydal.
Cotman.Levens.
Cowan Bridge. Casterton.
Cowmire.Cartmel Fell.
Crab Fair.Egremont.
Crake Trees. Crosby Ravensworth.
Crake Valley. Blawith.
Crecy. Castle Carrock.
Croglin Water. Armathwaite.
Cromwell. Allonby,Appleby,Burton-in-Kendal,Corney, Crosby Ravensworth,Great & Little Broughton,Greystoke.
Crookdale. Bromfield.
Crooklands. Preston Patrick.
Crook Mill. Crook.
James Cropper plc. Burneside.
Bing Crosby. Cockermouth.
Crosby. Cross Canonby.
Crosby Fell. Crosby Ravensworth.
Crosby Hall.Crosby Ravensworth.
Crosby Ravensworth.Orton.
Cross-a-moor. Pennington,Swarthmoor.
Cross House. Newby.
Crummock. Loweswater.
Culloden. Brampton,Orton.

Earl of Cumberland. Brougham,Clifton,Milburn.
Cumberland & Westmorland Yeomanry Museum. Dacre.
Cumbrian Coast Express. Arnside.
Cunswick Hall. Underbarrow.
Cunswick Scar.Underbarrow.
J.C.Curwen. Bowness on Windermere.
Curwen family. Camerton,Windermere.
Curwen Hall. Camerton.
Harry Curwen. Workington.
St.Cuthbert. Braithwaite, Carlisle, Cartmel, Clifton, Dufton, Kentmere, Keswick, Kirklinton, Lorton,Milburn, Plumbland.

D.
Dacre Bears. Dacre.
Lord Dacre. Brampton.
Dacre Castle. Dacre.
Dacre Family. Dacre,Kirklinton,Greystoke.
Dacre School. Dacre.
Joseph Dacre. Kirklinton.
Lord Humphrey Dacre. Lanercost.
Dalegarth Force. Eskdale.
Dallam Tower. Milnthorpe,Heversham.
Dalston Hall. Dalston.
John Dalston. Dalston.
Thomas Dalston. Flimby.
John & Lucy Dalston. Temple Sowerby.
Dalton Castle. Dalton.
Dalton Hall.Burton-in-Kendal.
John Dalton. Cockermouth.
Dalton-in-Furness.Kendal.
Charles Darwin. Dent.
King David.Lanercost.
Humphrey Davy. Thirlmere.
Debatable Land. Longtown.
Deerdale. Patterdale.
Dentdale. Dent.
John Denton. Dalston.
Denton Hall. Denton.
Denton Upper. Gilsland.
8th Earl of Derby. Bassenthwaite.
Derventio. Papcastle.
Derwent Island. Keswick.
Derwentwater. Keswick,Portinscale,Braithwaite.
Devil's Bridge. Kirkby Lonsdale.
Devoke Water. Eskdale.
Charles Dickens.Bowness on Windermere.Wigton,Winton.
Richard Dickenson. Castle Carrock.
Dillicar. Grayrigg.
Dixon's Chimney.Carlisle.
Dixon Ground. Nibthwaite.
Tommy Dobson. Eskdale.
Docker. Grayrigg.
Dock Museum. Barrow.
Dockray.Matterdale.
William Dodding.Skelsmergh.
Domesday Book. Barbon,Beetham,Broughton,Burton-in-Kendal,Casterton,Kirkby Lonsdale, Middleton,Pennington,Preston Patrick.
Dora's Field. Rydal.
Dove Cottage. Grasmere.
Dovedale Red Screes. Patterdale.
Dovenby Hall. Dovenby.
Dovenby School.Dovenby.
Dowcraggs.Lowick.
Drakes Bowls. Levens.
Drawdykes Castle. Linstock.
Druids Circle.Casterton.
Drumburgh. Bowness on Solway.
Duchy of Lancaster. Cartmel fell.

Duddon Estuary.Kirkby-in-Furness.
Duddon Gorge. Broughton.
Duddon Sands. Patterdale.
Dufton Hall. Dufton.
Mary Dugdale. Ambleside.
Duke of Cumberland. Nibthwaite,Orton,Kendal.
Duke of Gloucester.Penrith.Dungeon Ghyll.
Langdale.
Dunmail.Grange over Sands.
Dunmail Raise. Thirlmere.
Dunmallet. Pooley Bridge.
Thomas Dykes.

E.
Eamont Bridge. Brougham,Pooley Bridge.
Eamont Valley. Dacre.
Earls of Northumbria. Barrow.
Eddystone Lighthouse. Alston.
Eden Gorge. Armathwaite, Brough, Castle
Carrock,Cliburn ,Culgarth, Kirrkby Stephen,
Musgrave,Nateby.
Luck of Edenhall. Edenhall.
Edmund. Grange over Sands.
Edward.1. Abbey Town, Beaumont, Bewcastle,
Keswick, Kirkby Stephen, Linstock,Orton,
Flookburgh, Skelton, Ulverston.
Edward II. Burgh by Sands, Dacre.
Edward III. Beaumont,Bootle,Brough,Dalton.
Edward IV. Burton in Kendal.
Edward VI. Bootle.
Edward VII. Brougham.
Egremont family. Cockermouth.
Elizabeth 1. Appleby, Bootle, Dovenby, Levens,
Old Hutton, Eamont Bridge, Ivegill, Threlkeld,
Urswick,Workington.
Elleray. Windermere.
Ellergil. Tebay.
Ellengrove. Cross Canonby.
Ellerhow Tower. Lindale in Cartmel.
Elterwater. Langdale. Nibthwaite.
Eleanor Engayne. Clifton.
Endmoor. Preston Patrick.
Ennerdale. Cleator.
Esk. Grange over Sands.
Eskdale & Ennerdale Pack. Eskdale.
Eskdale Mill. Boot.
Eskdale Valley. Boot.
Eskmeals. Bootle.
Esperance. Bowness on Windermere.
Esthwaite. Near & Far Sawrey.
Eusemere. Pooley Bridge.
King Eveling. Ravenglass.
Ewe Close. Crosby Ravensworth,Orton.
Jane Eyre. Casterton,Dent

F.
Faerie Queen. Cartmel.
Fairy Steps. Beetham.
Farleton Knott. Hutton Roof.
Fauld Mill. Longtown.
Fawcett Forest. Orton.
Fearon Fallows.Cockermouth.
Judge Fell. Swarthmoor.
Margaret Fell. Bardsea, Rampside, Swarthmoor.
Fell Family. Ulverston.
Kathleen Ferrier. Silloth.
Fetherstonhaugh's Family. Kirkoswald.
Earl of Fife. Kendal.
Fleetwood. Arnside.
Lady Fleming. Burneside.
Fleming Family. Coniston.
Sir Michael le Fleming. Gleaston,Rydal.

Abraham Fletcher.Great & Little Broughton.
Henry Fletcher. Cockermouth.
Fletcher Family. Moresby,Hutton in the Forest.
Florence Mine. Egremont.
W.E.Forster. Ambleside,Nicholforest.
George Fox. Cark in Cartmel, Dean,Lindale in Cartmel,
Lorton, Orton, Grayrigg, Rampside,
Sedbergh, Swarthmoor, Ulverston, Wigton.
Fox How. Rydal.
Benjamin Franklin. Ings.
Friars Crag. Keswick.
Furness Abbey. Barrow,Bowness on Windermere,
Calderbridge, Dalton, Lanercost, Lindale in Furness, Piel
Island, Eskdale, Grange over Sands, Grasmere,
Hawkshead,Rusland, Woodland.
Furness Fells. Bouth.
Furness Museum. Barrow.

G.
Gaisgill. Tebay.
Galava. Ambleside.
Mildred Warner Gale. Whitehaven.
Daniel Gardner. Kendal.
Anthony Garnett. Kendal.
Garrigdill & Nenthead Mines. Alston.
Garsdale. Dent.
Mrs Gaskell. Lindale in Cartmel.
Gatebeck. Preston Patrick.
Elizabeth Gaunt. Ravenstonedale.
Sir Gawain. Hutton in the Forest.
Gelts Wood. Brampton.
St George. Aspatria.
George III. Broughton,Kirkby Lonsdale.
Giant of Tarn Wadlyn. Armathwaite.
Giants Grave. Bampton.
The Gill. Cumdivock.
Gillallee Beacon. Bewcastle.
Gilpin Dale. Crosthwaite.
Gilpin Gamily.Gimmer Crag. Langdale.
Gladstone. Barrow.
Glassonby.Little Salkeld.
Gleaston Castle. Gleaston.
Glencoin.Patterdale.
Glenderameckin Beck. Mungrisdale.
Glennaventa. Ravenglass.
Glenridding. Patterdale, Ullswater.
Goat Scar. Longsleddale.
Godman Hall. Burneside.
Goldilocks & Three Bears. Keswick.
William de Goldington. Appleby.
Gondola. Coniston.
Dr Norma Goodrich.Longtown.
Rev Harvey Goodwin. Dalton.
Goose Green.Preston Patrick.
Gosforth Cross.Aspatria.
Gosforth. Irton.
Gosforth Hall. Gosforth.
Thomas Gospatric. Shap.
Charles Gough.Patterdale,Tirril & Sockbridge.
Gough memorial. Glenridding.
Gowbarrow Park. Matterdale, Ullswater.
Sir James Graham. Ulverston.
George Graham. Kirklinton.
Robert Graham. Longtown.
Grasmere Gingerbread. Grasmere.
James Woodcock Graves. Caldbeck.
John Graves. Portinscale.
Graythwaite.Finsthwaite.
Great Dockray. Penrith.
Great Gable. Ennerdale Bridge.
Great Musgrave. Musgrave.
The Green. Thwaites.

Greenodd. Nibthwaite,Spark bridge.
Greta Hall. Keswick.
Greystoke. Carlisle.
Greystoke family. Greystoke.
Grey Yauds.Cumwhitton.
Archbishop Grindal. St.Bees.
Grisdale. Braithwaite,Patterdale, Greystoke,
Grisdale Tarn. Thirlmere.
Grisdale Pike.Keswick.
Grizedale Forest.Rusland.

H.
Haaf Fishing. Anthorn.
Hackthorpe. Lowther.
Hadrian's Wall.Beaumont,Bewcastle,Bowness on
Solway, Brampton, Burgh-by-Sands, Carlisle,
Cumdivock, Denton, Kirkandrews-upon-Eden,
Kirkbride, Lanercost, Linstock,
Longtown,Plumpton,Gilsland.
Hallin Fell,Ullswater.
Hall Santon. Irton.
Hallthwaites. Thwaites.
Hampsfell Hospice. Grange over Sands.
Hampton Court. Levens.
Hardrigg Hall. Skelton.
Theodore Bayley Hardy. Hutton Roof.
Hard Knott. Beckermet,Boot, Eskdale.
Hard Knott Castle. Boot.
Haresceugh Castle. Renwick.
Harlock. Pennington.
Harrington's. Allithwaite,Burton in Kendal.
Harter Fell. Longsleddale.
William Hartley. Penny Bridge.
Hartside Pass. Melmerby.
Mary Harrison. Caldbeck.
Harrison Stickle. Langdale.
Hartsop. Patterdale.
Hassall Family. Dacre.
Battle of Hastings. Beetham.
Warren Hastings. Blencow.
John Hatfield. Caldbeck.
Haverigg. Millom.
Haverthwaite. Backbarrow.
Haweswater Lake, Bampton,Mardale,Shap.
Hawkshead Grammar School. Hawkshead.
Haycock. Ennerdale Bridge.
Hayton Castle.
Hazelslack Tower. Arnside.W.Heaton Cooper.
Ambleside.
William Heelis. Nr & Far Sawrey.
St Helen's Well. Asby,Newbiggin-on-Lune.
Helm Wind. Dufton,Melmerby,Natland.
Helvellyn. Keswick,Glenridding,Thirlmere,Ullswater.
Felicia Hemans. Ambleside.
Henry 1. Bothel,Carlisle,
Henry 11. Kings Meaburn,Pennington, Torver.
Henry 111. Beaumont,Melmerby.
Henry 1V. Dovenby,Kendal, Piel Island.Flookburgh.
Henry. V1. Burton in Kendal,Cumwhitton,Irton.
Henry V11. Penrith,Piel Island. Witherslack.
Henry V111. Armathwaite,Kendal,Kirkby
Stephen,Kirkby Thore, Kirkoswald, Moresby,
Nateby,Flimby, Rusland, St.Bee's, Underbarrow.
Sir Herbert's Isle. Keswick.
Herdwick Sheep.Drigg.
St. Herbert. Braithwaite.
Heron Corn Mill,Beetham.
Herriot Country. Kirkby Stephen.
Hesket in the Forest. Calthwaite.
Heversham Hall. Heversham.
Battle of Hexham. Cumwhitton.
High Beckfoot,Barbon.

High Casterton. Casterton.
High Crag. Buttermere.
High Newton. Ayside.
High Sea. Mallerstang.
High Seat.Nateby.
High Style. Buttermere,Braithwaite.
Miss Octavia Hill,Keswick.
Hilltop. Nr & Far Sawrey.
Hilton Family. Ormside.
Thomas Hobson. Bowness on Windermere.
Hodbarrow, Millom.
Hodge Hill. Cartmel.
William Hodgson. Low Row.
Holebiggerah. Pennington.
Holehird. Windermere.
Holker Hall. Cark in Cartmel.
Hollins Hall. Crook.
Holm Cultram Abbey. Abbey Town, Flimby,
Holme St Cuthbert,Newton Arlosh, Silloth
Westward.
Hugh Holme. Mardale,
Holme Eden Hall. Warwick.
Holmescale Farm,Old Hutton.
Colonel Honeywood. Milburn.
Honister. Buttermere.
Robin Hood. Camerton.
Horace. Pennington.
Hornby Castle. Burton in Kendal.
Howards. Greystoke,Wetheral.
Mary Howard.Levens.
Lord William Howard. Brampton, Gt Corby.
Howgills. Orton,Grayrigg,Sedbergh.
Howgill Castle. Milburn.
Howgill Fells. Newbiggin on Lune. Grayrigg,
Howgill Fold. Warcop.
Howtown. Ullswater. Glenridding.
Joseph Huddart. Allonby.
Hudlestone Family. Millom.
Hugill Hall. Ings.
Cardinal Basil Hume. Cleator.
Humphrey Head. Allithwaite.
Hunsonby. Little Salkeld.
Mary Hutchinson. Penrith,Grasmere.
Hutton in the Forest. Calthwaite. Skelton.

I.
Ibbeth Petril Cave. Dent.
Ill Bell. Kentmere.
Indigo Jones. Camerton.
Industrial Revolution. Backbarrow,Newby Bridge.
Douglas Ing. Hoff.
Inglewood Forest.
Armathwaite,Caldbeck,Calthwaite,Plumpton,Hutton
in the Forest,Skelton..
Lord Inglewood. Calthwaite,Hutton in the
Forest.Skelton.
Ireby. Bassenthwaite.
John de Ireby. Ireby.
Jack Ironteeth. Alston.
River Irt. Drigg.
Irthing Valley. Lanercost,Gilsland.
Bishop Irton. Linstock.
Irton Hall. Irton.
Thomas Irwin. Calderbridge.
Thomas Henry Ismay. Maryport

J.
Jackdaw Scar. Kings Meaburn.
William Jackson. Keswick.
James 1. Brougham,Kendal,Moresby.
James 11. Levens.

St James. Burton in Kendal,Buttermere,Long Marton,Ormside..
Jedbergh Convent. Longtown.
Jenkin Crag. Ambleside.
Jennings Brewery. Cockermouth,Lorton.
King. John. Lanercost,Piel Island,Irthington,Newton Arlosh, Old Hutton.
St John. Clifton, Corney, Cross Canonby,Melmerby.
St.Johns. Beckermet. ...Beckermet.
John Paul Jones. Whitehaven.

K.
Kaber Rigg plot. Kaber.
The Kaiser. Bowness on Windermere.
Kendal. Dent.
Kendal Bowman. Kendal.
Kendal Castle. Kendal.
Kendal Green. Kendal.
Kendal Mint Cake. Kendal.
Lord Kenlis. Kirkby Lonsdale.
River Kent. Arnside. Kendal,Longsleddale.
Kentmere Hall,Kendal.
Kent Valley. Burneside.
St.Kentigern. Aspatria, Bromfield, Caldbeck, Keswick ,Longtown.
Kepple Cove. Patterdale.Glenridding.
Mark Kerrs. Clifton.
Kershopefoot.Nicholforest.
Keswick Mountain Rescue Team. Thornthwaite.
Keswick School. Keswick.
King of Patterdale. Patterdale.
Kings Own Royal Border Regiment. Carlisle.
Kipling Groove. Langdale.
Kirkandrews Tower. Longtown.
Kirkbeck. Bewcastle.
De Kirkby Family. Kirkby in Furness.
Kirkby. Cross Canonby.
Kirkby Hall. Kirkby in Furness.
Kirkby-Irleth.. Kirkby in Furness.
Kirkby Thore Hall..Kirkby Thore
Kirk Fell. Ennerdale bridge.
Kirklinton Hall.Kirklinton.
Kirkoswald Castle. Kirkoswald.
Kirkstone Pass. Ambleside. Patterdale.
Knights Hospitallers. Temple Sowerby.
Knights Templar. Temple Sowerby.
Knipe. Bampton,Cartmel Fell, Rampside.
The Knott. Arnside.

L.
Colonel Lacy. Little Salkeld.
Lacy's caves. Little Salkeld.
Ladyhall. Thwaites.
Laings. Sebergham.
Lakeside. Bowness on Windermere.
Lakeside & Haverthwaite Railway. Newby Bridge.
The Lambs. Caldbeck.
Lammerside Castle. Nateby.
Lamplugh Hall.Lamplugh.
Lamplugh's family.Dovenby,Lamplugh.
Lanbrigg.Grayrigg.
Lancashire Ultramarine Co. Backbarrow,Newby Bridge.
Lancaster-Kendal Canal. Burton -in-Kendal.,Natland.
Lanercost Priory. Brampton, Lanercost, Lazonby, Irthington,.
Dr John Langhorne. Winton.
Great langdale. Langdale.
Little Langdale. Langdale.
Langdale Pikes. Langdale.Grange over Sands.
Langdale. Nibthwaite,Ambleside.
Langdale Fell. Tebay.

Lanty Slee. Langdale.
Stanley Laurel. Ulverston.
Laversdale. Irthington.
Edward Law. Blencow,Cartmel.
Sir Thomas Lawrence. Kendal.
St Lawrence. Cross Canonby,Crosby Ravensworth,Morland.
Sir Wilfred Lawson. Aspatria,Bassenthwaite.
John Leake. Ainstable.
Dr Thomas Legh. Calderbridge.
Leighton Moss. Arnside.
River Leitch. Cliburn.
Miss Cecil Leitch.Silloth.
St Leonard. Asby,Bootle.
River Leven. Newby Bridge.
Leybourne family. Skelsmergh.
Dr.Lickbarrow. Longsleddale.
Earl of Lincoln. Piel Island.
Lindisfarne Priory. Clifton,Kirklinton. Carlisle.
Henry Lindow. Penny Bridge.
Lingholme. Portinscale.
Lingmoor fell. Langdale.
Linstock Castle. Linstock.
William Linton. Coniston.
St.Lioba.Beetham.
Little Musgrave. Musgrave,
Little Salkeld. Glassonby.
Charles Lloyd. Clappersgate..
Lodge Garde. Ornside.
London Lead Co.Alston.
Long Meg & her Daughters. Kirkoswald,Little Salkeld,Glassonby.
Lords Isle. Keswick.
Lord Lonsdale. Bowness on Windermere, Casterton, Causewayhead..
Thomas Longmire.Bowness on Windermere.
Lonsdale Belt. Lowther.
Loppergarth. Pennington,Swarthmoor.
Lords Seat. Whinlatter Pass.
Lord Warden.Penrith.
Lorton Hall. Lorton.
Loughrigg Fell. Ambleside,Clappersgate,Rydal.
Low Barrow Bridge. Tebay.
Low Casterton. Casterton.
Lowes Court.Egremont.
Lowick Bridge. Lowick.
Vale of Lowick. Lowick.
Low Park. Preston Patrick.
Lowther Valley. Bampton.
Sir James Lowther.Cockermouth,Flimby.
Lowthers. Crosby Ravensworth,Lowther,Whitehaven.
Lowther Newtown.Lowther.
Lowther Hall.Lowther.
Lowther Leisure Park. Lowther,Orton.
de Lucy Family. Egremont.
Luguvaluim.Carlisle.
St Luke. Lowick.
Lune Valley. Barbon,Orton.
River Lune. Kirkby Lonsdale, Middleton.
Roger Lupton. Howgill.
Skeffington-Lutwidge.Irton.
Lyth Valley.Crosthwaite,Levens.
Lyulph's Tower.Matterdale,Patterdale.
River Lyvennet. Crosby Ravensworth,Kings Meaburn.

M.
Mallerstang. Brough.
Joseph Mann. Abbey Town.
Mardale. Bampton, Clifton,Shap.
Mardale fells. Shap.
Mardale Shepherd's Meet. Mardale.
King of Mardale. Mardale.

Mardale Valley. Keld.
St.Margaret's. Long Marton.
St.Mark. Natland.
St Marks Boys Home for Waifs & Strays. Natland.
River Marron. Dean,Lamplugh.
William Marshall. Cartmel.
Marshall Family. Keswick,Patterdale.
Marshside. Kirkby in Furness.
Marston Moor. Plumbland.
Harriet Martineau. Ambleside.
Marton Hall.Long Marton.
St.Mary. Cleator, Crosthwaite, Cumwhitton,
Longsleddale, Mallerstang, St.Mary's, Hutton Roof.
Mary Queen of Scots. Anthorn, Carlisle, Cockermouth
,Matterdale, Moresby, Eamont Bridge,Workington.
Mary's Pillar. Keld.
Mary's Tower. Anthorn.
Mayburgh.Brougham,Eamont Bridge.
John McAdam.Penrith.
Cyrus McCormick..Abbey Town.
Meaburn Hall. Crosby Ravensworth.
Melbreak Foxhounds.Loweswater.
Melkinthorpe.Lowther.
Melmerby Hall. Melmerby.
Merlin. Kirkby Stephen.Longtown.
Ranulf de Meschines.
Calderbridge,Cockermouth,Wetheral.
William de Meschines.Egremont.
Mewbray. Holme St.Cuthbert.
St.Michael. Dalston,Kirkby
Thore,Lamplugh,Longtown,Burgh by Sands.
St.Michael's Well.Little Salkeld.
Mickledon. Langdale.
Middleton Fell. Middleton.
Middleton Hall. Middleton.
Middleton Family. Middleton.
Middleton in Teesdale. Brough.
Sir George Middleton. Burton in Kendal.
Millness. Preston Patrick.
Millom Castle. Millom.
Millrigg. Culgarth.
Milton. Preston Patrick.
Mirehouse. Bassenthwaite.
George Moore. Wigton.
Morecambe Bay. Allithwaite,Arnside,Bardsea,Barrow.
Moresby family.Moresby.
Moresby Hall. Moresby.
Morrcambe Bay. Anthorn.
Morland. Temple Sowerby.
Mortham's Tomb. Stainmoor.
Hugh deMorville. Kings Meaburn,Kirkby
Stephen,Lazonby.
Mosedale.Mungrisdale.
John Mounsey. Patterdale.
Cavalier Randal Mulcaster. Irthington.
Mumps Hall. Denton.
Muncaster Castle. Ravenglass,Waberthwaite.
St.Mungo. Brisco,Bromfield.
Mungo's Well. Caldbeck.
Musgrave Family. Asby,Kirkby
Stephen,Penrith,Edenhall,Hayton.
Musgrave Hall.Penrith.
Mutiny on the Bounty.Cockermouth.

N.
Nab Cottage. Rydal.
Nanking. Appleby.
Napoleon. Burneside,Corney,Levens,
NATO. Anthorn.
National Park Visitor Centre. Bowness on Windermere,
National Sporting Club. Lowther.
Naworth Castle. Brampton,Kirkoswald,Lanercost.
Horatio Nelson. Irton.

Nent Force. Alston.
Nenthead & Tynedale Lead & Zinc Co. Alston.
Netherby.Longtown.
Nether Denton. Low Row.
Netherhall.Maryport.
Nether Harescough.Kirkoswald.
Neuk Cottage. Dean.
Anne Neville. Penrith.
Newbiggin.Hutton Roof,
Newbiggin Fell. Hutton Roof.
Newby Hall. Morland, Newby.
Newby. Irthington.
Newby family. Ivegill.
Newison family. Morland.
Newlands Pass. Buttermere,Portinscale.
Newton Fell. Lindale in Cartmel.
Newtown. Irthington.
Nibthwaite Grange. Nibthwaite.
St.Nicholas. Lazonby.
Nichol End. Portinscale.
Norman Nicholson. Millom, Gosforth.
Florence Nightingale. Underbarrow.
St.Ninian. Brisco,Brougham,Newton Arlosh.
John Noble. Corney.
Nook.Preston Patrick.
Norman Conquest. Appleby,Barrow,Bewcastle.
Christopher North. Keswick.
North Pennines Heritage Trust. Alston.
North Scale. Barrow.
Ivor Novello. Beetham.
Nunnery Walks. Armathwaite.Kirkoswald.
Nunwick Hall. Gt Salkeld.

O.
Odenndale. Crosby Ravensworth.
Old King Cole. Carlisle.
Old laundry Visitor centre. Bowness on Winder-
mere.
Old Wall. Irthington.
Ormathwaite. Underskiddaw.
Ormside Cup. Ormside.
Ormside Hall. Ormside.
Orton Moor. Hoff.
Orton Scar. Orton.
St.Oswald. Dean,Kirkoswald.
Outhgill.Mallerstang.
Overburrow. Casterton.

P
Pardshaw. Dean.
Pardshaw Craggs. Dean.
Pardshaw Hall School. Cockermouth.
Joseph Parkin. Camerton.
Katherine Parr. Brigsteer,Kendal, Lanercost,
Underbarrow..
Thomas Parr. Kendal.
Parsonby. Plumbland.
Pate Hole. Asby.
St.Patrick. Kirkbride,Patterdale, Preston Patrick.
Patterdale Hall. Patterdale.
Patton.Grayrigg.
Lancelot Patty. Patterdale.
St.Paul. Causewayhead.
William Pearson. Hawkshead,Winster.
John Peel.Caldbeck,Keswick,Ireby.
Joseph Peel. Maryport.
Pele-o-Hill. Bewcastle.
Pelham House. Calderbridge.
Earl of Pembroke. Brougham.
Pendragon Castle. Kirkby Stephen,Mallerstang.
Prince Uther Pendragon. Kirkby Stephen,
Mallerstang.
Pennington family.Pennington,Ravenglass.

Pennine Way. Slaggyford.
William Penny. Penny Bridge.
Penrith Grammar School. Blencow.
Penrith.Beacon. Penrith.
Penrith Castle.Penrith.
Penrith Museum. Penrith.
Penton. Nicholforest.
Henry Percy. Cockermouth,Levens.
Bishop Hugh Percy. Dalston.
Percy House. Cockermouth.
St Peter. Camerton,Kirkbampton,Lindale in
Furness,Nr & Far Sawrey.
River Petteril. Blencow.
Philipson family. Crook.
Major Philipson. Kendal.
Thomas Pickering.Cark in Cartmel.
King of Piel. Piel Island.
Piel Castle. Barrow, Piel Island.
Pike o'Stickle.. Langdale.
Pilgrimage of Grace. Kirkby Stephen.
Battle of Pinkie. Bootle.
Gilbert Pipard. Papcastle.
William Pitt. Burneside.
Plaice Fell. Ullswater.
Plymouth Hoe. Levens.
Joseph Pocklington. Keswick.
Poet Laureate. Keswick.
Poltross Burn. Gilsland.
Ponsonby Hall. Calderbridge.
Pool Bank. Crosthwaite.
Popping Stone. Gilsland.
Willy Porter. Eskdale.
Beatrix Potter. Ambleside,Bowness on Windermere,
Near & Far Sawrey,Eskdale, Hawkshead,
Herdwick Sheep,Troutbeck.
Potters Fell. Burneside.
Pow Maughan Beck. Cumwhinton.
George Preston. Cartmel.
Prior of Carlisle. Caldbeck.
Q.
Quakers. Alston, Bardsea, Blencow, Dean, Dufton,
Kirklinton, Morland, Newby, Orton, Preston Patrick,
Grayrigg .Ivegill, Scotby, Swarthmoor, Underbarrow.
Queen Elizabeth School. Kirkby Lonsdale
de Quertons. Nateby.
Thomas de Quincey.
Caldbeck,Keswick,Patterdale,Rydal.

R.
Bishop Rainbow. Dalston.
Raiset Pike. Crosby Garrett,Kirkby Stephen.
Rampside. Barrow, Piel Island.
Rampside Hall. Barrow.
Sir James Ramsden. Barrow.
Randal Holme. Alston.
Arthur Ransome. Bowness on
Windermere,Coniston,Nibthwaite,Piel Island Rusland.
William Rathbone.Bassenthwaite.
Rathmoss.Pennington.
Ravenglass & Eskdale Railway. Boot, Eskdale,
Ravenglass.
Ravens Barrow. Cartmel Fell,Lindale in Cartmel.
Rawlinson Family. Rusland.
Hardwicke Drummond Rawnsley. Keswick.
Rayrigg. Windermere.
Reay family. Bromfield,Scales.
Reckitt & Colman.Backbarrow,Newby Bridge.
Redgill.Tebay.
de'Redman. Levens.
Red Pike.Buttermere.
John Rennie. Sedgwick Ulverston.
Ray Cross.Stainmore.

Rheged. Carlisle.
Richard 11. Hoff.
Richard 111. Penrith.
Gordon Richards. Greystoke.
Joseph Richardson. Keswick.
Roa Island. Piel Island.Rampside.
Roanhead. Barrow.
Robert the Bruce. Abbey Town.
Robin Hoods Bay. Orton, St.Bees.
Robinson Crusoe. Maryport.
Cedric Robinson. Allithwaite.
Mary Robinson. Buttermere.
Tom Robinson. Coniston.
Robinson family.
Robinson School. Penrith.
'Rocket'. Hallbankgate.
Roman Vallum. Linstock.
William de Romilly.Egremont.
George Romney. Dalton,Kendal,Rusland Sizergh.
Rosalind.Countess of Carlisle. Hallbankgate.
Rose Castle. Cumdivock, Dalston, Penrith,
Raughtonhead
Rosgill with Hegdale. Keld.
Rossall School. Kirklinton.
Rothay. Ambleside.
Rothschilds. Bowness on Windermere.
Round House. Bowness on Windermere.
Rounthwaite. Tebay.
RSPB. Millom.Rubens. Levens.
William Rufus. Ainstable, Bothel,
Brough,Carlisle,Kendal.
Rugby School. Ambleside.
Ruleholme. Irthington.
John Ruskin.Coniston.Keswick,Elterwater.
Ruskin Museum.Coniston.
Ruskin's View.Kirkby Lonsdale.
Ruthwaite. Ireby.
Rydal Hall. Burneside.Rydal.
Rydal Mount. Ambleside Rydal.

S.
Saddleback. Keswick. Mungrisdale.
Salkeld family. Keld.
Salkeld Hall. Little Salkeld.
Saltcoates. Arnside.
Samlesbury Hall. Bardsea.
Sampsons Cave. Armathwaite.
Sandford. Warcop.
Sandside. Kirkby in Furness.
Sandy's family. Colton.Hawkshead.
Santon. Irton.
Santon Bridge. Irton.
Sarkfoot. Longtown.
John Saul.Kirklinton.
Abbot of Savigny.Barrow. Piel Island.
Scafell Pike. Beckermet, Buttermere, Eskdale,
Glenridding, Keswick, Grange over Sands,
Seascale,Windermere.
Scales. Bromfield,Buttermere,Mungrisdale.
Scandal Beck. Ravenstonedale.
Scalescuegh Hall. Wrey.
Henry William Schneider. Bowness in Windermere.
Mary Scott. Clifton.
Peter Scott. Arnside.
Sir Walter Scott. Carlisle, Keswick,Kirkby Lonsdale,
Longtown, Patterdale, Gilsland, Glenridding.Thirlmere.
Scout Scar. Levens,Underbarrow.
Scuggate.Nicholforest.
Seaton Nunnery. Bootle.
Sebergham Hall.Welton.
Sedbergh School. Dent,Howgill,Sedbergh.
Adam Sedgwick.Dent.

Seldom Seen.Thornthwaite.
Sella Park. Calderbridge.
Alexander Selkirk. Maryport.
Sempringham Monks. Newbiggin on Lune.
Humphrey Senhouse. Maryport.Gosforth.
Settle & Carlisle Railway Line. Appleby,Crosby
Garrett,Cumwhinton,Dent.
Ann Sewell. Embleton.
River Severn. Backbarrow.
Shaddon Cotton Mill. Carlisle.
Shap Abbey. Camerton,Keld, Kirkby
Thore,Mardale,Preston Patrick,Shap.
Shap Fells. Orton.
Sharrow bay. Ullswater.
Shawkfoot.Cumdivock.
Sheep Island. Rampside.
Shelley.Keswick.
Thomas Shepherd. Kendal,Burneside.
Sheriff of Westmorland. Cockermouth.
Silver Hill. Keswick.
Lambert Simnel. Piel Island.
Sizergh Castle. Brigsteer. Sizergh.
John Skelton. Armathwaite.
Richard Skelton. Armathwaite.
Skelwith Force. Skelwith Bridge.
Skiddaw. Bassenthwaite, Caldbeck, Keswick,
Underskiddaw.
Skiddaw Hermit. Keswick.
Skinburness. Newton Arlosh.
Slackhead. Beetham.
Adam Slee. Blindcrake.
Sir Hans Sloane. Ings.
Smardale Gill. Smardale.
John Smeaton. Alston.
Sir Robert Smirke. Lowther.
Smithfield. Kirklinton.
General Thomas Sneyd. Finsthwaite.
Solway Firth. Burgh by Sands.
Solway House. Port Carlisle..
Solway Moss.Longtown.
Solway Viaduct. Bowness on Solway.
'Protector'Somerset.Bootle.
Sour Milk Gill. Buttermere.
Soutergate.Kirkby in Furness.
Southey. Bassenthwaite,Clappersgate,Keswick.
Edith Southey. Grasmere.
South Tyne Railway Preservation Society. Alston.
Spanish Armada. Levens.
Spark Bridge. Bouth.
Speddings. Bassenthwaite,Whitehaven.
Spout Force. Whinlatter Pass.
River Sprint. Burneside,Longsleddale.
Stainmore. Appleby.
Stamphouse. Ambleside.
Stanleys. Beetham, Calderbridge,Eskdale.Witherslack.
William Stanley. Bardsea.
Stanley Ghyll. Eskdale.
Stars & Stripes. Windermere.
St.Bees. Orton.
Steamtown Museum. Arnside.
Edward Steele. Kendal.
Steeple. Ennerdale Bridge.
King Stephen. Barrow,Cartmel Fell,Piel Island
St.Stephen. Kirkby Stephen.
George Stephenson. Hallbankgate.
Stock Gill. Ambleside.
Stoneygarthside Hall. Nicholforest.
Stoneygate.Nicholforest.
Strathclyde.Burneside.
Stricklands. Penrith,Hincaster,Sizergh.
Bishops Strickland. Bolton.Dalston.
Thomas Strickland. Brigsteer.

Striding Edge. Patterdale.
Stybarrow Crag. Patterdale.
Swarthmoor Hall. Pennington, Rampside,
Swarthmoor, Ulverston.
Swindale Beck. Keld.

T.
Ive de Taillebois. Kendal.
Talkin Tarn. Brampton.
Talkin Tarn Country Park.Talkin.
Tan Hill. Brough.
Tarn Crag. Patterdale.
Samuel Taylor. Keswick.
Tarn Crag. Patterdale.
John Teasdale.Lowther.
Margaret Teasdale.Denton.
Alfred Tennyson.Bassenthwaite,Coniston,Keswick.
Tent Lodge. Coniston.
Thackmoor. Renwick.
Theatre in the Forest.Grizedale.
St.Theobald. Musgrave.
St.Thomas.Milnthorpe.
Helena Thompson Museum.Workington.
William Thompson. Kirkby Lonsdale.
Thornthwaite Forest. Whinlatter Pass.
Thornthwaite Hall. Keld.
Thorphinsty.Cartmel Fell.
Thorphinsty Hall. Cartmel
Sir Lancelot Threlkeld. Crosby
Ravensworth,Threlkeld.
Thrushwood.Underskiddaw.
Thurland castle. Kirkby Lonsdale.
Thwartterden Hall. Crook.
Sir William de Thweng..Staveley.
Thomas Tickell. Bridekirk.
Tillman. Alston.
Tinkler Library. Bampton
Titanic. Maryport.
Todd family. Crosby Ravensworth.
Tolson Hall. Burneside.
Tom Tompion.Kirklinton.
Torfin.Middleton.
Torpenhow. Bothel.
Torsin.Burton in Kendal.
Torver fells. Lowick.
Tottlebank. Colton.
Townend. Troutbeck.
Townend farmhouse. Clifton.
Treasonfield. Barbon.
G.M.Trevelyan.Elterwater.
Trinkeld. Pennington,Swarthmoor.
Sir Tristram. Pooley Bridge.
Tristamont. Pooley Bridge.
Anthony Trollope. Penrith.
Edward Troughton. Corney.
Troutbeck family. Dacre.
Chancellor Tullie.Carlisle.
Tullie House. Bewcastle. Carlisle.
Sir Brian Tunstall. Kirkby Lonsdale.
Turner. Coniston,Keswick.
Ann Tyson. Hawkshead.
. U.
Ullock Dean Ullswater, Matterdale, Patterdale,
Pooley Bridge.
Ullswater Navigation Co.Ullswater.
Underwood House. Milburn.

V.
Vale of Eden. Appleby.
Waler Vane. Bassenthwaite.
Robert de Vaux. Irthington.
Sir Roland de Vaux. Lanercost.

Venerable Bede. Dacre.
Maud de Veteripont.Kings Meaburn.
Vickers Shipbuilding (VSEL) Barrow.
Queen Victoria. Dent.
Vikings. Bassenthwaite,Bowness on Windermere.
Vinegar Bible. Cartmel.
Robert de Vipont. Brough.
Voreda Fort. Lazonby.Plumpton.

W.
Waberthwaite. Corney.
Tarn Wadling. Lazonby.
Alfred Wainwright. Orton,Embleton,Sedbergh,St.Bees.
Mary Wakefield Music Festival. Sedgwick.
Roger Wakefield. Burneside.
Dr.Walker. Matterdale.
Wallend. Kirkby in Furness.
Walls Castle. Ravenglass.
Walmgate head. Mardale.
Walney Island. Barrow.
Sir Hugh Walpole. Keswick,Uldale.
Waltheof. Cockermouth,
Walthwaite. Pennington.
Wannop family. Linstock.
Wansfell Pike. Ambleside.
Wardhall. Plumbland.
Warmell Hall. Sebergham.
War of the Roses. Brough,Crosby
Ravensworth,Millom,Irton.
Warwicksland.Nicholforest.
Earl of Warwick. Piel Island.
Warwick the Kingmaker. Brough,Penrith.
George Washington. Bowness on Windermere,Brigsteer.
John Washington. Bowness on Windermere.
Augustine Washington. Appleby.
Lawrence Washington.. Appleby.
Wastwater. Irton.
Warchgate. Selside.
Watercrook. Natland.
Waterhead. Bowness on Windermere.Gilsland.
Waterloo. Levens.
Wath Bridge. Cleator.
Duke of Wellington. Levens.
John Wesley. Lorton,Nenthead,Old
Hutton,Gamblesby,Seaton,Wigton.
de.Wessington.Brigsteer.
Earl of Westmorland. Penrith.
Wetheriggs Pottery. Clifton.
Wetherham. Lowick.
Whale. Lowther.
Lord Wharton. Kirkby Stephen. Shap.
Wharton Hall. Kirkby Stephen,Nateby.
Wharton Park. Ravenstonedale.
Whernside Manor. Dent.
Whinfell Forest/ Cliburn,Grayrigg.
Whinlatter Pass. Braithwaite,Thornthwaite.
Whitbarrow Scar. Cartmel fell.Crosthwaite.
Whitby Abbey. Crosby Ravensworth.
George Whitehead. Blencow,Ormside,Orton.
Viscount Whitelaw.Blencow.
White Moss House. Rydal.
White Star Line.Maryport.
Whitestock Hall. Rusland.
Dick Whittington. Gt.Salkeld.
Wicked Jimmy. Lowther.
Wild Boar Fell. Mallerstang, Nateby,Ravenstonedale.
St.Wilfred's. Brougham.
'Watery'Wilfred. Aspatria.
John Wilkinson. Backbarrow, Lindale in Cartmel,Newby
Bridge.
Thomas Wilkinson. Tirril & Sockbridge.
William the Conqueror. Burton in Kendal. Musgrave.

William the Lionheart. Appleby, Bromfield,
Plumbland, Lanercost, Scales.
William of Orange. Kirkby Stephen.
William of Thweng. Brigsteer.
Sir Joseph Williamshop.Bridekirk.
Christopher Wilson. Burneside.
Edward Wilson. Heversham.
Elizabeth Wilson. Casterton.
George Wilson. Kendal.
John Wilson. Windermere.
Wilson family. Heversham.
Windermere Steamboat Museum. Bowness on
Windermere,Windermere.
River Winster. Lindale in Cartmel.
Peter de Wint. Kendal.
Winton Hall. Winton.Witherslack. Cartmel Fell.
Witherslack Hall. Witherslack.
Cardinal Wolsey.Armathwaite.
Wolsty Castle. Holme St.Cuthbert.
Wood Hall. Bridekirk.
Woodalls Cumberland Sausage. Eskdale.
Woodrow Wilson. Carlisle,Port Carlisle.
Dorothy Wordsworth.
Bassenthwaite,Caldbeck,Matterdale,Pooley
bridge,Grasmere,Rydal.
John Wordsworth.Cockermouth,Patterdale,
Mary Wordsworth. Grasmere.
Richard Wordsworth.Tirril & Sockbridge.
William Wordsworth. Ambleside, Bassenthwaite,
Bootle, Caldbeck, Clappersgate, Cockermouth,
Keswick, Langdale, Lorton, Matterdale,
Mungrisdale, Nr & Far Sawrey, Patterdale, Penrith,
Egremont, Ennerdale Bridge, Glenridding,
Grasmere, Hawkshead, Ings, Rydal, Sedbergh,
Thirlmere,Tirril & Sockbridge, Winster.
Wray Castle. Ambleside.
Wraysholme Tower. Allithwaite.
Wuthering Heights. Dent.
Wyberghs. Clifton.
Wythop.Embleton.
Wythop Mill. Embleton.

Y.
Yanwath Hall. Eamont Bridge.
Yellow Earl. Lowther.
Yewbarrow Hall.Longsleddale.
Yewdale Farm.Coniston.
Yew Tree Farm. Westnewton.
Yew Tree Hall. Lorton.
Yorkshire Dales National Park Dent,Kirkby
Stephen,Sedbergh.

BUS INFORMATION
☎ 0946 63222

Cumbria Wide

Open 7 am 'til 7 pm (Monday to Saturday) and
9 am 'til 5 pm (Sundays)

✦ SERVING CUMBRIA, NORTH LANCASHIRE AND THE
SCOTTISH BORDERS WITH A NETWORK OF BUS SERVICES

✦ COACH & MINIBUS CHARTER AT COMPETITIVE PRICES

✦ CONTRACT CHARTER FOR WORKS AND OFFICES

FOR FURTHER INFORMATION ON THIS OR OUR OTHER
SERVICES, OF FOR A FREE QUOTATION, SEE US IN YELLOW
PAGES

HEAD OFFICE, TANGIER STREET, WHITEHAVEN

Cumberland

PART OF THE STAGECOACH GROUP